Protecting C KV-155-525
Promoting Their Rights

Protecting Children
Promoting Their Rights

Edited by
Norma Baldwin

Whiting & Birch Ltd
MM

Published by Whiting & Birch Ltd,
PO Box 872, London SE23 3HL, England.
N. America: Independent Publishers Group,
814 N. Franklin St, Chicago, IL 60610.

British Library Cataloguing in Publication Data.
A CIP catalogue record is available from
the British Library

ISBN 1 86177 012 X (cased)
ISBN 1 86177 013 8 (limp)

Printed in England by Intype

Contents

Acknowledgements viii

Introduction
Norma Baldwin ix

1 Protecting children: Promoting their rights?
Norma Baldwin 1

2 The legal framework for child centred practice
in England and Wales
Judith Masson 20

3 Children's rights and children's welfare in Scotland
Brian Kearney 37

4 Links between social deprivation and harm to children
Vic Tuck 51

5 Work partnerships with Black communities:
Issues and principles for social work education,
training and service delivery
Alexandra Scale and Michaela Mkandla 68

6 Issues in education
Tricia David 84

7 The abuse of disabled children
Margaret Kennedy 94

8 Myriad Voices:
Feminist and poststructuralist understandings
of childhood sexual abuse
Sara Tibbs 101

9 Sexual harassment in everyday life:
Protection in the context of power relations
Jacqui Halson 112

10 What do children need by way of child protection?
Who is to decide?
Mary MacLeod 130

11 Young men, power and sexuality:
Challenge and change
Christine Harrison 144

12 Strategic planning to prevent harm to children
    Norma Baldwin and Nick Spencer 159

13 Towards user friendly assessment
    Chris McCarrick, Adrian Over, Pam Wood 172

14 A framework for assessment in child protection
    Chris Mccarrick, Adrian Over and Pam Wood 186

15 The Search for clarity in complex assessments
    Jan Rushton 222

16 Assessing family strengths
    Vivienne Barnes 237

17 A partnership approach in working with a family
    Chris McCarrick 253

18 'Unfit and blamed':
    Lessons from mothers whose children have been sexually abused
    Annie Mullins 263

19 From victim to survivor :
    The groupwork support of sexually abused boys
    Andrew Durham 281

20 Private fostering of Nigerian children:
    A community based approach to child protection and welfare
    Alban Unsworth 298

21 Promoting effective family support and child
    protection for Asian children
    Sandeep Atkar, Norma Baldwin, Rajinder Ghataora, Vyomesh Thanki 312

22 Family support strategies: The Henley Project
    Norma Baldwin and Lyn Carruthers 337

    Biographical Notes 353

Acknowledgements

Our thanks to the children and families whose experience has been drawn on in the Reader.

Many thanks to Gillian Sharp for her patience and persistence in grappling with text in every conceivable format; to Judy Ahola for detective work with some references and with the more obscure software packages; to Rhona Goodall for help with word processing of some chapters. Brigid Daniel, Elaine Ennis, Julie Taylor made many helpful suggestions to help sharpen and clarify sections of the text.

The views expressed are those of individual authors and do not necessarily represent those of their organisations.

Introduction

Norma Baldwin

This Reader is concerned with understanding and finding constructive ways of responding to children and families who have complex and diverse needs: a subject which enjoys an enormous literature, covering many disciplines.

What can we hope to add to such a rich and varied stream? This collection of papers on issues, perspectives and theory, with some detailed accounts of how workers in a range of settings have tried to put theory into practice, aims to share thinking and practice which may encourage a sense of optimism. It should be of value to practitioners, planners and managers in social work and related fields. It may be of particular interest to the increasing numbers of students working to gain post qualifying awards, whose competence and effectiveness in theory and practice are being assessed.

Motivation for the book

The motivation for the book came from continuing discussions between a group of academics, practitioners and post qualifying social work students about the need for detailed examples of effective practice in child care and protection.

The Department of Applied Social Studies at Warwick University had set up Master's and Advanced Award level courses in Child Protection and in Methods of Research and Evaluation, to meet the requirements of the post qualifying framework of the Central Council for Education and Training in Social Work.

These courses were supported by academic staff who had substantial commitments to practice development and applied research, and by practitioners and managers from local authorities and the voluntary sector. Some of the development work for the courses, as well as the provision of a small child care and protection resource centre, was supported by funding from Barrow Cadbury Trust, Home Office Safer Cities and HEFC funding for Continuing Professional Development (CPD).

There was an unprecedented surge of literature on what was involved in good childcare practice. Those involved with the courses were surrounded by checklists, inquiry reports, theories, analysis, principles, guidance on how assessments and interventions should be undertaken (DoH 1988 & 1989; Family Rights Group 1989 & 1991; REU/NISW 1989\90; Home Office et al 1991; Pietroni 1991; CCETSW 1993; Audit Commission 1994). However, there were very few accounts which students could turn to in the literature as *examples of practice which had been helpful to children and families* (Harris 1987; Sainsbury (ed) 1988; Gardner 1992). We felt surrounded by information about disasters in the child protection system and analysis of its failings.

Theories and accounts of why and how children continued to be harmed and their families to be left unsupported were plentiful. Inadequate resources, systems which were not sufficiently flexible or sensitive, and practice which workers felt to be hurried, procedurally driven, sometimes unskilled, sometimes discriminatory, provided the background to many discussions.

It seemed that at a time of escalating problems in the economy and in social conditions, of ever increasing concern with problems of child protection, of frequently changing organisational structures, and a time of uncertainty and demoralisation amongst workers in the child protection system, much of the literature increased professionals' sense of pressure.

Students identified the need for positive examples of practice - to encourage and reinforce their belief that good practice was possible, and that it was happening down the road! Many practitioners were confident that they and colleagues were engaged in constructive child centred practice, managing to tread the tightrope between rights and protection.

As staff, students and practitioners compared experiences - of planning and trying to write about work which would reflect the human and theoretical complexities of all work with families and children, work which could recognise commonalities of experience whilst valuing uniqueness - the idea for a Reader was developed.

Students, practitioners, course tutors, regular and occasional presenters on the courses, as well as others who were associated with the resource centre, agreed to write up their work. It represents a wide range of issues, perspectives, theory and practice examples which may help and encourage all those who struggle with difficult situations in child care and protection, working to improve conditions and opportunities for families. We believe that many will recognise common dilemmas and attempts to resolve them. We offer reflections on our work - with all its imperfections, gaps, room for improvement - to encourage a wider sharing and confidence amongst students, practitioners, researchers and teachers.

Current priorities

Since this work was done, there has been increasing emphasis on the urgency for social work practice to be based on the most up to date evidence of what works. (Gough 1993; Macdonald & Roberts 1995; Macdonald 1997; Oakley et al 1998; Macdonald 1999). Single case studies and one off accounts of complex neighbourhood development work, or of consultation with and support for minority groups, cannot make more than a modest contribution in this movement towards systematic evaluation. However, the willingness to set out in detail the objectives and processes of work, reflecting critically on what, why and how, is an important step in fostering rigorous enquiry.

The complexity of the situations social workers have to deal with, involving multiple interactions of personal, social, environmental and economic factors, means that evidence will continue to be hard won, contested in interpretation and application. It will not always be obvious which factors or combination of factors in a package of interventions lead to intended changes.

The role of theory is crucial here. A clear understanding - based on up to date insights into theory and practice - is needed, to inform attempts to move policy and practice in the right direction. Equally important are the principles and values on which work in personal social services are based.

Theory and practice

Contributions to the Reader have been made with full acknowledgement of continuing debates and controversies, recognising that in complex human situations matters of fine judgement are involved. There can be no certainties, only commitment to endless critical reflection and continuing development of understanding and skills. It is however possible to work systematically, drawing on theory, knowledge, research and experience *to explain why* decisions were made to work in a particular way. We wanted to take account of the broad theoretical debates, the principles and contradictions associated with any approach which tries to keep the needs, rights and interests of the child at the centre. The Reader is a contribution to the continuing debate about how far it is possible to protect children from harm and to promote their rights - to health and social well being - to express their views and have them taken seriously and to achieve their potential.

The first part concentrates on theoretical issues and debates which are common in child care and protection work. There is not one single cohesive theoretical framework, rather a coming together of an inter connected, developing range of perspectives and material relevant to the changing complexity of the subject. An ecological approach is broadly relevant to all the accounts.

The examples of practice were all from England, but have a wider currency. By the time I was editing the material I had moved to Scotland and it seemed important to supplement Judith Masson's analysis of the legal framework in England and Wales with an account of the Scottish framework. Sheriff Brian Kearney kindly agreed to write this, to demonstrate how common themes relate to the different legal contexts.

The second part focuses on examples of practice which people associated with the resource centre and the courses were engaged in, trying to draw on theory, principles and values outlined in the first part. Accounts of direct work range from the development of user focused assessment tools, through assessment and interventions with individuals and families, group work with mothers and with boys, to action research and community development approaches in family and neighbourhood support. The individuals and groups whose experience is referred to had given permission for their experience to be written about. Nevertheless some changes have been made to details reported, to ensure that no one could be identified. Names of course have been changed.

The examples share common values of working towards openness and partnership. They attempt to resist the narrowing and at times abusive consequences of crisis driven, fragmented approaches which have been depressingly common in social work, (Audit Commission 1994; DOH 1995; Parton 1997).

Throughout the Reader there is a strong emphasis on the context within which needs and problems arise, on keeping the child at the centre but recognising the child's connections with family, friends, neighbourhood and culture. The best ways of doing this are continually debated, contested. Competing and conflicting explanations of children's needs and of causes of harm can lead to very different interventions. As children grow and develop towards autonomy, the meaning of promoting their rights will change. It will change for the practitioners charged with protecting their interests and their safety. It will change according to the situations, risks, competence of the individual children. It will be different for every child. Equally there can be no hard and fast view of what will be the best way of protecting an individual child, or the best ways of protecting all children. The complex situations and issues which are discussed in this Reader have been difficult and sometimes painful for the practitioners and researchers. Yet this does not compare with the pain and difficulties experienced by many children in the child care and protection systems.

We hope that out attempts to reflect critically on current theory and practice, to explain how we have grappled with theory in concrete situations, will be of value to others working with children and families. By trying to make connections between wide societal processes and the everyday life of children and families, by trying to take a holistic, child centred approach, we can come nearer to providing services which will promote the wellbeing of all children.

References

Audit Commission (1994) *Seen But Not Heard: Coordinating Community Child Health and Social Services for Children in Need.* London: HMSO.

CCETSW (1993) *Northern Curriculum Development Project: Improving Practice with Children and Families.* Leeds: CCETSW.

DoH (1988) *Protecting Children: A Guide for Social Workers undertaking a Comprehensive Assessment.* London: HMSO.

DoH (1989) *The Care of Children: Principles and Practice in Regulations and Guidance.* London: HMSO.

DoH (1991) *Patterns and Outcomes in Child Placement: Messages from Current Research and their Implications.* London: HMSO.

DoH (1995) *Child Protection: Messages from Research.* London: HMSO.

Family Rights Group (1989) *Child Protection Procedures: A Guide for Families.* London: FRG.

Family Rights Group (1991) *The Children Act 1989; Working in Partnership with Families. Trainers Pack.* London: FRG/HMSO.

Gardner, R. (1992) *Supporting Families: Preventive Social Work in Action.* London: National Children's Bureau.

Gough, D. (1993) *Child Abuse Intervention: A Review of the Research Literature.* London: HMSO.

Harris, R. (ed) (1987) *Practising Social Work.* University of Leicester.

HMSO (1988) *Report of Inquiry into Child Abuse in Cleveland 1987.* London: HMSO.

Home Office, Dept. of Health, Dept. of Education and Science, Welsh Office (1991) *Working Together Under the Children Act 1989: A Guide to Agreements for Inter-Agency Cooperation for the Protection of Children from Abuse.* London: Home Office.

Macdonald, G. & Roberts, H. (1995) *What Works in the Early Years: Effective Interventions for Children and Families in Health, Social Welfare, Education and Child Protection*. Ilford: Barnardo's.

Macdonald, G.M., (1997) ' Social work research: the state we're in'. *Journal of Interprofessional Care*. 11.1. 57-65.

Macdonald, G. with Winkley, A. (1999) *What Works in Child Protection?* Ilford: Barnardo's.

Oakley, A., Roberts, H. (eds) (1996) *Evaluating Social Interventions: A Report of Two Workshops*. Ilford: Barnardo's.

Oakley, A., Rajan, L. & Turwen, H. (1998) 'Evaluating parent support initiatives: lessons from two case studies' in *Health and Social Care in the Community* Vol. 6 (5) 318-330.

Parton, N. (1997) *Child Protection and Family Support: Tensions, Contradictions and Possibilities*. London: Routledge.

Pietroni, M. (ed) (1991) *Right or Privilege? Post-Qualifying Training with Special Reference to Child Care*. London: CCETSW.

REU/NISW (1989/90) *Race in Child Protection: A Code of Practice*. Black and White Alliance. London: REU/NISW.

Sainsbury, E. (ed) (1988) *Working with Children in Need*. London: Jessica Kingsley.

1
Protecting children: Promoting their rights?

Norma Baldwin

Introduction

Issues of rights and protection for children are immensely complicated and unlikely to be definitively resolved. An understanding of the links between the situations of individual children and wider social influences is a necessary starting point for planning how best to protect children and promote their rights. Theories and experience which are drawn on in attempts to maintain children as the central focus of services need to be made explicit (Baldwin 1990; The Violence against Children Study Group 1999). Equally, the unfinished and contested nature of knowledge needs to be recognised and the importance of working with uncertainties stressed.

This chapter attempts to set the context for the chapters which follow. The chapter draws on an ecological approach to illustrate connections between policy, economic and social factors, the range and style of organisational responses and the quality of life for children. It focuses particularly on aspects of disadvantage and issues of gender and race which have implications for policy makers, planners and individual workers concerned with rights and protection. These are important at both ends of the spectrum of services - for those concerned with individuals' needs and for those aiming to provide population wide support and prevention of harm. Later chapters develop some of these themes.

This chapter emphasises the importance of taking account of the knowledge, experience and views of children and young people themselves. Some of the tensions inherent in trying to reconcile children's rights with their need for protection are discussed. Children vary in stages of development towards autonomy and independence according to age, ability, social, cultural and economic opportunities. Unlike adults, they cannot claim full civil rights. Whilst capacities to claim and exercise rights are developing, they are dependent on the judgement and definitions of more powerful adults, about their competence and about their needs (Harding 1999). The tension between rights and protection is vividly demonstrated when a child is seriously harmed by a parent yet begs to be allowed to remain with that parent in circumstances which others judge to pose continuing and substantial risks. Principles and values, policy, legislation and available resources all affect how knowledge, theory and skills will be used to reconcile the tensions in both general and particular circumstances.

Theoretical frameworks

Hallett (1995, p. 531) suggests the need, 'in a post-modern context', for 'the abandonment of the search for grand causes in favour of more modest and specific endeavours'. Many of the chapters in this Reader would fit the priority of 'modest and specific endeavours'. However I would want to defend still the 'search for grand causes'. The connection between specific, particular situations and problems, and wider economic and social influences is strong. Unless a theoretical overview linking the interpersonal and the societal informs policy, organisational structures and day to day practice there is risk of perpetuating a series of 'patch up' services, or of pouring resources into short term and fragmented initiatives which do little to tackle underlying causes of problems. Theories will be influential, whether explicit or implicit.

Without a critical theoretical perspective, planners may develop strategies of family support which rely on the commitment of mothers, unintentionally maintaining women in their roles as custodians of care and safety for all children. Practitioners may give priority to work with mothers, perpetuating the invisibility of fathers (O'Hagan & Dillenburger 1995; Farmer 1997; Featherstone 1999; Humphreys 2000). Such strategies take insufficient account of the part male behaviour plays in creating safety or danger in family and neighbourhood environments, and the importance of gender issues in the planning process.

Organisational arrangements may be developed to respond to allegations of child abuse, which lead to difficulties for individual workers in maintaining commitments to child welfare (Parton 1997), and a focus on the child's needs and interests.

At all levels, focus on an incident of abuse or on the minutiae of family dynamics may mask the importance of financial and social circumstances.

An ecological approach (Bronfenbrenner 1979; Garbarino & Sherman 1980; Melton & Barry 1994; Acheson 1998) which tries to take account of the web of interacting factors influencing individuals, groups, communities, can inform planned interventions at different levels, whilst recognising their interconnections and supporting 'radical and creative responses' to 'developing preventative, supportive and helping child welfare services' (Parton 1997, p.19).

Reality for every child is experienced in a social context: for each one it is different. Theory from many disciplines can help in understanding common features of context and social environment. An overarching, interdisciplinary, ecological perspective can help ensure that the child will not move from the centre of our focus, can avoid observations and assessments becoming fragmented or depersonalising. Alongside an attempt to understand the material and social realities in which children grow up, sensitivity is needed to the feelings, thoughts, lived experience of individual children.

Tunstill (1997, p.46) draws attention to the importance which underlying perspectives have in influencing policy and practice. Academic analysis may be manipulated to serve differing ideologies.

Focused attention on limited aspects of problems affecting children may obscure a multiplicity of factors which are also relevant. Fox Harding's (1991) discussion of tendencies towards 'ideal type' explanations of underlying causes of problems and preferred ranges of solutions is helpful: a reminder of the limiting and potentially dangerous consequences of one dimensional approaches in theory, policy and practice.

The web of interacting factors influencing individual situations

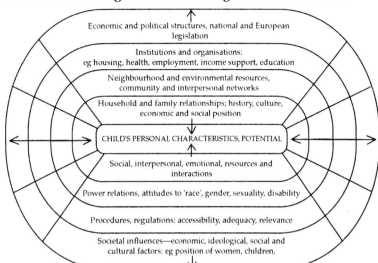

Where a multiplicity of factors, which are hard to disentangle and difficult to measure accurately, converge, the temptation is strong to focus narrowly on one segment of the situation. For example generalisations may be made about the crucial importance of parenting behaviours on children's development, without taking account of the wider context (Taylor et al 2000). An additional problem comes from disputed definitions of what constitutes child abuse (Starr 1982; Browne 1988; Baldwin & Spencer 1993) and of difficulties for local authorities in deciding precisely what it means to be a child in need (Tunstill 1995 & 1997).

The processes associated with individual harm and also with apparent 'cycles' of abuse and harm are complex. Inter generational continuities of disadvantage may be at least as important as personal characteristics, behaviours and experience (Brown & Madge 1982; Brown 1983; Egeland 1989; Pelton 1994; Taylor et al 2000). We need to avoid simplistic or one dimensional explanations, such as victims of abuse being likely to become abusers. Far more women than men have been victims of sexual abuse yet rarely go on to become abusers: the factors which may influence these differences need to be taken into account.

Common attitudes to power, sexuality and violence both reflect and reinforce behaviours. A unique blend of social and economic factors, attitudes, organisational responses, stresses, personal characteristics and situations influence behaviour (Rutter and Smith 1995).

These issues have major consequences for policy and for the organisation of services, as well as for individual workers grappling with the minutiae of a child's needs and rights.

Increasingly there is an attempt to identify from research findings the approaches and interventions most likely to be effective (Macdonald 1999). Little (1997) stresses the importance of bringing together conceptual frameworks, research and principles in trying to grasp the multi-dimensional picture.

A holistic overview of individuals in society, what promotes and what harms their well-being, is a crucial starting point for those planning services, so that differing messages from research and differing strands of evidence can be used appropriately. Within an ecological perspective it is possible to focus on different levels (Hardiker et al 1996, Hardiker 1999), whilst trying to remain conscious of the connections between them. Assessments - population wide as well as individually or family focused - are key to effective service planning. The Acheson Report (1998) after reviewing the impact of inequalities in health, argues for 'upstream' and 'downstream' initiatives. This perspective informs the 'Framework for the Assessment of Children in Need and their Families' (DoH et al. 2000). Although the Framework is clearly focused at the individual end of the spectrum, it emphasises that 'problems facing families are often interlinked' and that it is the 'purpose of Children's Services Planning to identify the broad range and level of need in an area and to develop corporate, inter-agency, community based plans of action' (p.1).

A range of assessment tools is needed to inform policy, planning and service delivery. To take account of the linkages, tensions, complexities, all need to encompass:

- an overview of economic and social conditions in which healthy survival and development of children is likely, where parents and care givers have the resources to exercise their responsibilities effectively.
- an understanding of social attitudes which promote and those which impair healthy development.
- recognition that child care systems and legal and bureaucratic processes may work against the rights and interests of children.
- recognition that children's rights and needs are bound up with those of other family members, or people significant to them, yet may at times be in conflict with them.
- commitment to promote the needs and rights of children at all stages of policy development and service delivery and in all stages of the process of investigation, assessment and interventions with children and their families.

Principles underlying policy and legislation

The UN Convention on the Rights of the Child, the Children Acts of 1989 and 1995 for England and Wales and for Scotland, all emphasise that:

- the best interests of children are paramount
- their welfare should be safeguarded and promoted
- their views should be heard
- the rights and responsibilities of their parents and other legally responsible adults should be respected.

There is an assumption underlying policy and legislation that children have rights to all that they need for nurturance, health, physical security and protection from harm.

At this level of generality there can be no clear-cut separation between needs and rights. The legislation assumes that the needs of children are connected with, but not identical to, the needs of their families.

> *States parties shall ensure to the maximum extent possible the survival and development of the child.* (UN Convention (Article 4))

The association between social and political conditions and the possibilities for children to develop, to have opportunities to exercise rights, appears to be accepted. There is the opportunity for child care and protection services to move from a defensive position of limiting harm to a positive, promotional approach. Yet we are far from a situation where all children in the UK can assume that even their basic needs will be met.

Policy contexts

In discussing developments in children's rights, Fox Harding (1996) argues that in the 80s and 90s when legislation was pushing towards greater autonomy for children and towards a right not to be physically assaulted, government policies were exacerbating child poverty, thus impeding progress on rights relating to health and welfare. The dependence of rights on economic conditions is also stressed by Franklin and Parton (1996). They draw attention to the adverse effect of government policies on young people, particularly the 1996 Housing Act on those leaving care. The exclusion of 16 and 17 year olds from income support from 1988 (Fox Harding 1996) has been a further bar to young people's rights and a major source of pressure on family relationships. A small study of young people living away from home showed that two thirds of the 16 and 17 year olds involved had been thrown out by their families (NCH 1992). In such circumstances young people are particularly at risk of physical harm and sexual exploitation. Their opportunities to find employment and suitable accommodation are severely limited. Possibilities for them to exercise their rights and to be protected from harm are poor. Should they in turn have children whilst young and in materially deprived circumstances they will be faced with immense problems and stresses in bringing them up.

Service developments have been fuelled by an ideological cocktail of views about society, its moral priorities, about ideals of family life and child rearing practices, political and media views about social work and social workers (Parton 1997; Violence Against Children Study group 1999; Taylor et al 2000). Extreme cases, where children have died, where gross abuse and neglect have not been recognised early enough, or responses have been inadequate, have led to a child protection system which has been procedurally and legalistically driven (Parton 1997; p.13 Sharland 1999).

The Audit Commission (1994) drew attention to the need for a broader based, public health promotion and community development strategy to protect children and promote their well being (Parton 1997; Baldwin and Carruthers 1998). Family and community support services need to run alongside services to safeguard children in individual cases of risk, abuse and harm.

Messages from Research (DoH 1995) reinforced this - emphasising the large numbers of child protection investigations which ended without registration or court action. It showed the harmful effects for families of being subjected to investigations, the lack of support for them in dealing with these, or with other difficulties they might be experiencing.

The tone of the summary and some of the subsequent discussions appeared to suggest that the main changes needed were in the *behaviour of social workers*, as though *individuals* had the professional autonomy, as well as access to resources, needed to work in supportive ways with families and prevent harm and abuse. Little attention was paid to the way in which social workers' responses were constrained by government regulations and procedures. Little exploration was made of ways in which the dynamics of groups and inter-agency tensions may drive the agenda (Kelly and Milner 1996). This mirrored the impossible position social workers were placed in following media attention to cases where children had died or the process of investigation had gone badly wrong: they were pilloried for failing to protect children at the same time as being hounded for being over-zealous in investigating potential harm.

Messages from Research (DoH 1995) emphasised the harmful effects of environments which are low in warmth, high in criticism, yet did not highlight the material and social conditions needed to encourage and sustain more positive loving, nurturing environments. This did little to take forward the Audit Commission (1994) emphasis on the development of neighbourhood and community networks of support and to bring the known links between disadvantage and a range of harm to children on to centre stage alongside skilled investigations and interpersonal work (NSPCC 1996; Childhood Matters 1996).

The planning process

If preventive and supportive services are to be developed without simply withdrawing resources from systematic investigations and assessments and from intensive work with the small but significant number of cases where harm is substantial and long term, the resources available through social inclusion initiatives will need to play a major role. The strategic planning mechanisms across social work, education, health and other agencies will need to ensure that this extra funding is used to strengthen groups and communities in the long term, in parallel with improvements to the intensive investigative, rehabilitative and therapeutic work which are still needed.

To achieve this, plans need to take realistic account of the real pressures different groups experience. Analysis of population wide needs must be joined up with the individual assessments of cases where harm is apparent. The multiple stresses, the obstacles to children's healthy development in disadvantaged communities and families, will need continuing attention, through initiatives which support but do not stigmatise (Tuck ch. 4; Seale & Mkandla ch. 5; David ch. 6; Kennedy ch. 7; Baldwin & Spencer ch. 12).

Bridges are needed for vulnerable children and their families between the intensive services and the more supportive, preventive, readily accessible and therefore less stigmatising, services, based on assessments of population wide need.

Social experience

Disadvantage

The current government has accepted the link between poverty and disadvantage and a range of harm to children's health, education, social and personal wellbeing (Acheson Report 1998, HM Treasury 1999, Cooper 2000). They have acknowledged that there is an immense distance to travel before all families will be able to rely on an income adequate to provide for the basic needs of children. Substantial changes have been made to support family incomes since a Labour Government came to power in 1997, yet the Chancellor's target for eradicating child poverty *within 20 years* demonstrates how far away we are from meeting the obligation to ensure 'the survival and development of the child'.

In a study of what a realistic income would be to sustain a 'modest but adequate' lifestyle, a group of experts came to the view that a mother living with 2 children on income support in 1997 would have only 33% of the income needed (NCH 1998). A couple with 2 children on income support would have 46% of what was needed to support a 'modest but adequate' lifestyle. A survey of 120 young people on low income showed that none had eaten the recommended daily nutrients in the previous 24 hours (ibid). Meanwhile the major inequalities in childhood mortality, health and educational opportunities between the affluent and those in poverty continue (Acheson 1998). Reading (1997) shows that in 1993 infant mortality in England and Wales was 4.3 per thousand in the most affluent class but 18.3 per thousand in the poorest class. Such inequalities are particularly marked in countries where there are wide differences of income such as UK and USA (Wilkinson 1996). They are also associated with problems of social cohesion.

Black families and families of children with disabilities are the most financially disadvantaged of all. Children from these groups may be particularly vulnerable to entering the public care system (Cook and Watt 1992; Booth and Booth 1994; Twigg and Atkin 1994; Oppenheim and Harker 1996; Barn et al 1997; Bowes and Sims 1997; Beresford et al 1999). Kennedy in chapter 7 and Atkar et al in chapter 21 draw attention to the daily stress and social difficulties associated with prejudice and discrimination.

Tuck in chapter 4 emphasises that some families living in poverty may lack the resources to keep their children safe and healthy, being pushed into a downward spiral of difficulties in coping and caring. Some families however find ways of protecting their children from the worst consequences of deprivation. We need to study what factors may be protective, within and outside families. For example, some areas of multiple deprivation with high concentrations of Asian families have few child protection referrals from within the Asian communities. The Hifazat Surukhia Projects (ch. 21) are exploring with Asian groups their views and definitions of abuse, their child rearing and family support patterns, discussing whether these provide protection and whether changing social conditions and increasing isolation may increase risks, as they appear to do from other studies (Egeland 1989, Garbarino 1992, 1994, 1995).

Children of African Caribbean origin have been over-represented amongst children in the care of local authorities (Cheetham 1982; ABSWAP 1983; Ahmed et al 1986; Ahmad 1990; Barn 1990; Barn et al 1999). This is not simply a reflection of their economic situation, but is associated with lack of understanding of black family patterns and with institutionalised racism in social work agencies. Bebbington and Miles (1989) show that the vulnerability of children of mixed parentage to coming into care is even higher. We need to try to understand the reasons for under and over-representation of some groups - whether it relates to the protection provided by certain child rearing attitudes and patterns, or to unwillingness to use racist services, to stereotyping and over-surveillance and to stresses associated with discrimination, in varying combinations.

Questions arise about how far high referral rates for abuse and neglect may reflect higher surveillance of deprived neighbourhoods by police and social workers; how far high accident rates reflect lack of safety features in substandard housing, unsafe play space, greater volumes of traffic and other characteristics of poor neighbourhoods (Roberts et al. 1995). There are questions about whether some incidents labelled abuse or neglect in a deprived family would be labelled differently in a more affluent home. Are children from middle class homes more likely to be taken to their own GP following an injury whilst poorer children are more likely to be taken to the casualty department, with consequent increased likelihood of being referred to social services departments? The definitions of what is considered abuse are elastic, and imprecise (Starr 1982; Dingwall 1989; Baldwin & Spencer 1993; Taylor et al 2000).

This is the context in which those responsible for child care and protection services have to look for the most effective strategies.

Disadvantage is a constant burden. High income is the single most protective factor for children as they grow up (Sedlak 1993; Spencer 1996; Reading 1997; Acheson 1998; Taylor et al 2000). Yet other realities, reflected in attitudes to children and the cultures and images which surround them, also have a major impact.

Gender and culture

Whether boys and girls have different innate characteristics and whether they are or should be treated the same in their early socialisation is a debate as old as time, yet one which has shown disappointingly little influence on social planning. The increasing gap between boys' and girls' achievements in school has led to a recent upsurge in discussion of problems of 'laddish culture'. Yet there is little evidence that the severity of problems associated with male behaviours is fully acknowledged.

The extensive reports of violence associated with Euro 2000 football matches contained little debate about issues of gender. In announcing major spending increases for the police and criminal justice system, Jack Straw, Secretary of State for the Home Department (2000a) emphasised that the 'Government's strategy for fighting crime is comprehensive and long term' and includes attempts to prevent criminal behaviour. Yet no mention is made of the major problems of male behaviour. Nor is it highlighted in his press release on crime reduction (2000b). The debate on increasing rates of violent crime is largely conducted in gender neutral language, as though *people in general* rather than *males in particular* are responsible for these crimes. In the main points summarised from Recorded Crime Statistics up to March 2000, the only reference to gender is a brief comment about the victims of sexual offences (Povey et al 2000).

Whilst there are useful government initiatives on domestic violence, on bullying and on working with young sex offenders, the links between these problems and wider social influences are not sufficiently acknowledged.

Boys and young men are much more likely to be involved in antisocial behaviour and crime than girls. They are surrounded by images and expectations of rowdiness, pushiness, aggression, ideas such as 'you fight your corner', 'act first, think later'. Some common expectations are passed on in what might be termed 'street culture', both reflected and reinforced in the media.

Aggressive and antisocial behaviour, racial and sexual bullying is common in schools. Exclusion from schools is three or four times more likely for boys than girls, yet in a study of 176 schools (Lloyd 1998) only two head teachers perceived gender as an issue.

Excitement is associated with violence. Hostility between schools, areas, football teams, religions, is seen as normal. Young people from two rival areas of Dundee interviewed on a Channel 4 programme (Wired Up 7.12.97) about the hatred between their areas and the regular fights between some groups of boys, saw this as a natural part of living in these areas. Yet some young men were working with youth leaders to try to counteract these destructive reactions.

In Northern Ireland work with children and young people on the Cost of the Troubles (Smyth 1998) recognises the consequences of male cultures:

The longstanding 'uncoolness' of articulation of emotional vulnerability or any emotional expression for males (except perhaps anger), is particularly marked in a militarised culture and in situations where violence and danger to life are commonplace. (p.76)

Emotional expressions of grief are often forbidden to boys and young men. Yet the expressions of violent feelings in group situations is not:

See, when the riots come up, everybody gets a mad head on. And they go, 'Aye, I'd love to kill one of them cunts!' Protestants, you know. (p.71)
You've got boys, even on the other side of the divide, were fired up by Paisley's speeches, who joined up, ended up killing a Catholic and doing twenty years. And all they were doing, they were young boys, pumped up, full of fear, full of hatred. (p.73)

In a study of riots and violent disturbances in England, it was shown that most took place in areas with unusual levels of law breaking (Power and Tunstall 1998). Young males, particularly in areas of high unemployment, with high concentrations of young people, are far more likely to be involved than young women.

Young women may be able to take different routes, in part gaining satisfaction through relationships, and status through parenthood, yet these present only limited and traditional opportunities. In Northern Ireland there are problems with an increasing number of births to mothers between 14 and 16 and even younger:

a number of young women and girls left with the burden of childcare at increasingly younger ages, and young men are isolated outside the structure of family and personal life, consigned to the world of unemployment and depersonalised violence. (Smyth p.77)

These issues are not confined to troubled Northern Ireland. They are echoed in many disadvantaged environments across the world (Wolfe et al. 1997). Cultures of male violence are common - most young males will experience physical assaults from other males. Most will not think them worth reporting.

The problem of violence affects many areas of life, for many groups: where women go at night, whether some women and children will feel safe to go home, or fear violence there. Recent studies of young people's attitudes to domestic violence found a high proportion of young people - males and females - who showed a tolerance or acceptance of domestic violence. Older boys - 15 to 16 years old - were the most likely to excuse perpetrators (Zero Tolerance Charitable Trust 1998; Scottish Women's Aid 1999, Mullender et al 2000).

The threat of violence and the abuse of power connect with young people's experience of bullying. Many children experience bullying and intimidation on the streets, in schools, but black children describe bullying and racial abuse as common experiences (Hamilton et al 1992). Black families are often afraid to let their children play outside: in chapter 21 Atkar et al show that among the most common worries of parents are racism, racial abuse and bullying (Atkar et al. chapter 21).

These social and cultural experiences need to be taken fully into account in planning work which will protect individual children and services which can improve the safety of all children and foster positive attitudes towards them.

Sexual attitudes and social relationships in which abuse thrives

Some bullying - of males and females - has elements of sexual harassment, degradation and abuse. When offenders are challenged, a defence is often 'Can't you take a joke'.

Images of girls and women as commodities, sexual objects, are common throughout the media. It is not only the 'top shelf' magazines where images of girls and women are problematic. Daily Sport newspapers are available throughout the country in family newsagents alongside other broadsheets, yet advertise women's sexual services alongside explicitly sexual pictures. In one edition, headlines of 'Low, low, prices', accompanied pictures of open legs and genitals. In the same edition pictures of young women dressed - or partly dressed - in school uniform were set alongside a report of rape and sexual assault of a schoolgirl (30.4.1994).

An article in the Guardian (24.9.94) titled 'Kinder whoring' described a sinister nexus between sexuality, 'faux innocence' and death, illustrating it with reference to lyrics and behaviour of popular music stars. A picture of Courtney Love dressed in baby clothes, with teddy bear, sucking her thumb, accompanied it, as well as pictures of models in stereotypical little girl poses. Wolfe (1997) emphasises the distortion of gender roles in music videos: increasingly violent and sexist. Alongside these images, girls of four and five years old are involved in beauty pageants where glamourous seductive clothes and overtly sexualised behaviour are the norm. The BBC2 programme 'Under the Sun' (2.2.1998) showed the mother of a five year old expressing delight that she had bred 'the perfect Barbie doll' and the male presenter crooning to a small girl, glamorously dressed and made up, 'I can't help falling in love with you'. Another young girl shrugged off her chiffon wrap in strip tease manner as part of her presentation.

Such images and double messages provide a confusing environment, for both boys and girls, in which to develop a sexual identity which values respect and equality.

The chapters by Tibbs (8) Halson (9), Harrison (11) and Durham (19) explore the spectrum of attitudes, behaviour and consequent harm. They link problems to common social attitudes, exploring links between power, sexuality, gender, masculinity, as the backdrop to the sexual abuse of children.

Issues of 'race'

Particularly difficult is the position of black women and girls. There is an added burden where there is an allegation against a black man. There is a racist mythology of black women as 'loose' and racist stereotyping of black men, as feared and desired sexual predators. Both aspects of the stereotyping tie in with the complex power relations between black and white, men and women, adults and children (hooks 1989 & 1991; Wilson 1993).

In 'Taking on the taboo' Darcus Howe (1998) acknowledges the problems of opening up such issues but, more aggressively than hooks or Wilson, asserts 'Broadcast and be damned'. He claims:

> *Race is at the heart of public discussion ... At the core of this fast and furious debate is the position of the young black male in British Society. His social group is synonymous with crimes of violence up to murder and thieving.*

Seale and Mkandla (chapter 5) reflect on the implications of such issues for social work and education, emphasising the complexity of drawing together understandings of race, gender, social and economic factors.

Linking individual situations and wider social and organisational factors

Problems arise if a focus on any single aspect of a problem outweighs attention to the total picture. Equally, concern with 'grand causes' (Hallett 1995) which does not also concentrate on the dynamics and characteristics of families where harm has been experienced can do little to provide protection or promote the rights of individual children.

The linkages of micro and macro systems have implications for children's rights and needs in individual cases as well as in planning population wide protective and supportive services.

A precise picture of the daily lives of children and families needs to be built up, taking account of these wider aspects, if rights and protection are to be given adequate attention. McCarrick, Over and Wood (Chapters 13 & 14) describe how they developed a framework for assessing the material realities of children and families, in partnership with them, taking account of risk and need. This approach at least has the possibility of asking critical questions about the range of influences on particular situations, without assuming that the problems reside only in the individuals most closely involved (Rushton ch. 15; Barnes ch. 16; Mullins ch. 17; Unsworth ch. 20).

The views of children and young people

In this complex picture, the rights of children and young people to have their views and experience taken seriously remains a priority.

Young people have insights which are crucial. Yet their views and experience will not necessarily simplify the complex tasks involved in maintaining their interests at the centre of services. Attempts to promote their rights still need to acknowledge their need for (and right to) protection from exploitation, harm, abuse. Their right to have their views heard is paralleled by a right to expect protection. Those with power to decide their futures have the responsibility to strive for balance.

MacLeod's chapter (10) on 'What do children need by way of protection: who is to decide' vividly illustrates this complexity. It shows the pain children and young people experience, as do those by Tibbs (8), Halson (9) and Durham (19). Mullins in chapter 18 draws attention to the dilemmas and sufferings of mothers in these situations. In the face of children's pain and suffering a tendency to rush to protective action is understandable. Yet the emotional, intense and contradictory responses to the Cleveland (Butler-Sloss 1988) and Orkney (Clyde 1992) inquiries demonstrated the difficulties. Different groups have their interests to defend: professionals, pro-family lobbyists, women's rights groups, those who argue men's rights and responsibilities in childcare, advocates for young people and groups of young people themselves. Fears, prejudice, ignorance, even when underpinned by child centred values can lead to confusion or polarisation. The stakes are very high for children in this process. They are as much at risk from hasty, ill thought out reactions to suspicions of abuse as they have been in the past from a collective failure to acknowledge the extent of abuse, to listen to, hear and take seriously children's own accounts as well as their needs and wishes (Kent 1997; Utting 1997).

Distressing investigations may be started in haste. Young people who attempt to speak in confidence about abuse or other worries may find rigidity in responses:

Sometimes we were discouraged from talking by being told: 'You realise that if you tell me I'll have to do something'.
What the victim needs and wants isn't the same as what the person investigating is looking for. You're scared and unsure but the adults just get on with organising. (Scotland's Children Speaking Out 1994)

Where young people feel that they have lost control of their situations or fear the consequences of speaking out, they may withdraw allegations, continuing in their risky situations.

Their right to safeguards throughout all systems of health, education, leisure and social care has been very difficult to achieve. This partly relates to the sheer complexity of the systems, to the difficulty of designing sensitive, humane and child-centred systems in large inter-related organisations, to a lack of time, training or sensitivity on the part of staff involved and partly to the continuing risk posed by the skilled manipulations of those who would exploit and harm. In order to make the systems work for them, children and young people who lack power, experience, skills, will need the help of skilled adults who will engage fully with them, share their attempts to develop and to have their needs met (Butler & Williamson 1994). The paradox remains: this dependency on adults means that protection is invariably accompanied by risk.

Children's rights in child protection

It has not always been possible for social workers who are co-operating with the police in an investigation to give equal weight to the welfare of the child and the exigencies of the investigation. Nor can it be assumed that parents will always act in the best interests of their children. Nevertheless they and their children are entitled to full explanations of what is happening and of their legal rights.

The Cleveland (Butler-Sloss 1989) & Clyde (1992) Reports gave accounts of children who were puzzled about what was happening, kept from contact with parents against their will. There are questions still about whether independent people need to be available to work with individual children in more situations and at earlier stages of proceedings than currently. Investigations, assessments and other interventions have major consequences for the civil liberties of children and parents, and for their well-being.

The Children's Legal Centre recommends that children who cannot express their views because of extreme youth or disability should have an independent person involved with them with the specific defined role of assessing and representing their interests - comparable to the role of the Guardian ad litem in the Courts. This would provide an important safeguard, acknowledging that children's rights and interests may be at risk from the beginning of an investigation.

If there are concerns about the ability of the parents to support the child through an investigation, efforts must be made to find out from the child who is a suitable trusted person to support her or him and to check credentials. For children with disabilities or special needs this is a major issue reflecting problems about the suitability generally of procedures and services (Kennedy 1995 and in chapter 7 of this volume; Cigno & Gore 1999).

An approach committed to full co-operation with parents can be criticised as naive, potentially risking complicity with an abuser in covering tracks, frightening an abused child into continued silence. Yet any other approach fails to respect due process, and risks infringements of the civil liberties of parents and of children. An adversarial or legalistic investigative approach can set up dynamics where the concerned, natural attempts by parents to protect their children from distressing experiences can be interpreted as attempts to impede the inquiry, defend themselves or prevent the investigators from getting at the truth. It can put parents in a position where they are prevented from exercising their responsibilities. A commitment to respect rights need not mean that the danger of parents or other care-givers attempting to put pressure on the child to maintain secrecy about abuse is ignored. This possibility can be evaluated and risks assessed on the basis of what is known during the pre-investigation planning. The child's view of potential supporters in the situation can be given priority.

Policy and legislation is based on the principle that nothing should take priority over the welfare of the child. Durham's chapter (19) highlights some of the difficulties of keeping hold of this when the legal process takes over, such as huge delays in being able to offer therapy, but shows what commitment, knowledge, experience and skill can achieve even in a flawed system. Masson (ch. 2) and Kearney (ch. 3) show how essential is an understanding of the way the law can be used for the benefit of the child, of its possibilities and constraints.

Issues of power and resources

The realities of power have to be acknowledged: the power of the different parties in situations where children are at risk cannot be equal. Many local authorities have been sufficiently concerned about this as a problem to move to independent chairing of case conferences and reviews of children on their child protection registers, and to find ways of supporting and preparing children, parents and other significant adults to be involved in discussions about future plans. Open records can help to ensure that conflicting judgments and opinions will be acknowledged, the basis on which they have been made given and the reasons why one judgment is preferred over another, spelled out (Shemmings & Shemmings 1996).

Such an approach depends on workers who have the training, skills, support and supervision, time and resources to implement it. Workers must have the time available to work intensively with children, to build up enough rapport with the child to gain the child's trust, to involve other significant people with whom the child already has a trusting relationship (Butler & Williamson 1994). Time is needed to explain fully to all involved what is happening, possible outcomes, their rights in the situation; time to help the child digest and understand what is being said, to reassure about the next steps, take seriously the child's views, wishes and needs. The child's behaviour needs to be observed in detail with parents and other significant people, in safe and appropriate surroundings. If there may be a risk for the child at home, the family and friendship networks need to be explored to see if the child can be looked after safely for a period in familiar secure surroundings, and avoid the trauma of removal from home to stay with strangers.

Children should have the right to expect that at a time of crisis significant people in their lives will be treated with respect, helped to maintain their caring roles, to remain in contact in protected situations with them. This has major implications for the provision of a range of caring and protective environments, with suitable accommodation and domiciliary care arrangements for children, mothers or other close relatives. An abrupt break in a relationship even with an abusing adult may be extremely damaging, because the child's unmet needs and hopes of care and love, as well as inappropriate feelings of guilt, may be very pressing. There is no question of leaving a child in demonstrably high risk situations, but the different risks need to be weighed against each other, in judging the best way to protect the child and ensure her or his well-being and security. The multiple risks, where removal from one may precipitate another, need to be acknowledged. Rights and protection cannot be assured without ready access to a wide range of appropriate resources, planned and integrated for the long term.

Social workers and agencies have extremely onerous responsibilities in child care and protection. It is an area of work which demands specialist skills, fine judgments, yet one where training, knowledge and expertise still need major development. Management, training and support structures, planning mechanisms and reviews which can facilitate child centred work need parallel development. The success of individually focused as well as population wide services depends on the ability of policy makers and those with the power to plan and implement services to understand the complexity of children's needs, the multiplicity of influences involved in protecting and promoting their rights and needs.

Taking seriously the views of children and young people

Responses to human problems - including abuse - rely on judgments which are inevitably formed on partial knowledge, information and understanding. The practical implication of a commitment to children and to their families is to make this, and potential conflicts of interest, explicit at every stage. Children and young people - and their families - can play a major part in developing the safeguards and services needed. Involvement of parents and of children in the development of services is a necessary part of social inclusion (Baldwin & Carruthers ch. 22) and necessary for an understanding of what works most effectively. The energy, commitment and wisdom of young people can provide the future resources.

Young people value qualities of openness, involvement, partnership, in their relationships with teachers, social workers, health professionals. They want to have control of what happens to them. They do not want to be seen as someone's 'professional case' (Sinclair et al. 1997).

> *Everyone's concentrating on the incidents, but we're not just abuse victims. We've got a past and that should be respected.* (Scotland's Children Speaking Out 1994)

Young people in the Scottish Who Cares organisation discussing some of these issues with me stressed how they want their lives and situations to be understood in the round. They identified education as a key factor, wanting social workers and teachers to talk together more, to recognise that school can be a place of refuge as well as of education. They stressed that when they were experiencing difficulties there was not enough easily accessible support in their neighbourhoods, nor enough intensive help for them or their parents when things went wrong. Some felt they had not been able to rely on the long-term engagement of one or two key people in their lives. Two young people described how pre-occupation with paperwork could lead young people and social workers into playing games, knowing the expectations of organisations and meeting them in the letter but not the spirit. One of them described what a difference it had made to her and to her friends that some workers did manage to stay alongside them, against the odds, making a real difference to how they felt about themselves.

Young people had strong and clear views about the connections between their rights, their personal situations and wider social influences. They stressed the need to:

'Catch 'em early.'
'Work locally.'
'Involve young people.'

They were conscious of the wide range of influences on them and of their reciprocal responsibilities. They wanted people to help them in ways which would enable them to give something back to the community.

Within an ecological perspective it is possible to develop policy, organisational structures and practice which take seriously the rights, protection and views of young people. The complexity and tensions involved can be acknowledged even if they cannot be fully resolved.

References

Audit Commission (1994) *Seen But Not Heard: Coordinating Community Child Health and Social Services for Children in Need.* London: HMSO.

Acheson, Sir D. (Chair) (1998) *Independent Inquiry into Inequalities in Health Report.* London: TSO.

Ahmed, S., Cheetham, J., Small, J. (eds). (1986) *Social Work with Black Children and their Families.* BAAF: /Batsford.

Ahmed, S. (1990) *Black Perspectives in Social Work.* Birmingham: Ventura Press.

Baldwin, N. (1990) *The Power to Care in Children's Homes.* Aldershot: Avebury.

Baldwin, N., Spencer, N. (1993) 'Deprivation and child abuse: implications for strategic planning', *Children and Society*, 7: 4: 357-375.

Baldwin, N., Carruthers, D. (1998) *Developing Neighbourhood Support and Child Protection Strategies: The Henley Safe Children Project.* Aldershot: Ashgate.

Barn, R., Sinclair, R., Ferdinand, D. (1997) *Acting on Principle: An examination of race and ethnicity in social services provision for children and families.* London: BAAF.

Beresford. P., Green, D., Lister, R., Woodard, K. (1999) *Poverty First Hand: Poor People Speak for Themselves.* London: CPAG.

Booth, R., Booth, W. (1994) *Parenting under Pressure: Mothers and Fathers with Learning Difficulties,* Milton Keynes: Open University Press.

Bowes, A., Sims, D. (1997) *Perspectives on Welfare: the experience of minority ethnic groups in Scotland.* Aldershot: Ashgate.

Bronfenbrenner, U. (1979) *The Ecology of Human Development: Experiments by Nature and Design.* Cambridge Mass: Harvard University Press.

Brown M., Madge N. (1982) *Despite the Welfare State.* London: Heinemann Ed.

Brown M (1983) *The Structure of Disadvantage* SSRC/DHSS Studies in Deprivation and Disadvantage. London, Heinmann.

Browne, K. (1988) 'The nature of child abuse and neglect: an overview' in Browne, K., Davies, C., Stratton, P., (eds) *Early Prediction and Prevention of Child Abuse.* Chichester: Wiley.

Butler, I., Williamson, H. (1994) *Children Speak: Children, Trauma & Social Work.* Harlow: Longman.

Butler-Sloss (1988) *Report of the Inquiry into Child Abuse in Cleveland in 1987.* London: HMSO.

Cheetham, J. (1982) *Social Work & Ethnicity.* Allen & Unwin.

Childhood Matters: Report of the National Commission of Inquiry into the Prevention of Child Abuse. London: TSO.

Cigno, K., Gore, J. (1999) 'A seamless service: meeting the needs of children with disabilities' in *Child & Family Social Work* Vol. 4 No. 4 pp. 325-336.

Clyde, J.J. (1992) *The report of the Inquiry into the Removal of children from Orkney in February, 1991. HMSO.*

Cook, J., Watt, S. (1992) 'Racism, Women and Poverty' in Glendinning, C. and Millar, J. (eds), *Women and Poverty in Britain.* Hemel Hempstead: Harvester/Wheatsheaf.

Cooper, Y. Minister for Public Health (2000). Foreword in Bynner, J., Joshi, H., Tsatsas, M, *Obstacles and Opportunities on the Road to Adulthood.* London: The Smith Institute.

DoH (1995) *Child Protection: Messages from Research.* London: HMSO.

DoH, DfEE, HO (2000) *Framework for the Assessment of Children in Need and their Families.* London: TSO.

Egeland, B. (1989) 'Breaking the cycle of abuse: Implications for prediction and intervention' in Browne, K., Davies, C., Stratton, P.,(eds) *Early Prediction and Prevention of Child Abuse.* Chichester: Wiley.

Featherstone, B. (1999) 'Mothering in the Child Protection System' in The Violence against Children Study Group, *Children, Child Abuse and Child Protection: Placing Children Centrally.* Chichester: Wiley.

Fox Harding, L. (1991) 'The Children Act 1989 in context: from perspectives in child care law and policy' 1 & 2, in *Journal of Social Welfare and Family Law*, 3 & 4, pp 179-193 and 285-302

Fox Harding, L.M. (1996) 'Recent developments in 'children's rights': liberation for whom?' in *Child and Family Social Work.* 13: 141-150.

Franklin, B., Parton. N., (1996) 'Suffer Little Children', *Community Care* 2.10.96.

Garbarino, J., Sherman, D. (1980) High risk neighbourhoods and high risk families: the human ecology of child maltreatment'. *Child Development*, 51, 188-198.

Hallett, C. (1995) 'Taking stock: past developments and future directions' in Wilson K. & James, A. (eds) *The Child Protection Handbook.* London: Bailliere Tindall.

Hamilton, J., Gosling, S., Donald, P. (1992) *'No Problem Here'* Research Report. University of Stirling and Central Region.

Hardiker, P., Exton, K., Barker, M. (1996) 'The prevention of child abuse: a framework for analysing services', in *Childhood Matters: Report of the National Commission of Inquiry into the Prevention of Child Abuse Vol. 2.* London.: HMSO.

Hardiker, P. (1999) 'Children still in need indeed: prevention across five decades' in Stevenson, O. (ed) *Child Welfare in the UK..* Oxford: Blackwell.

Harding, L. (1999) 'Children's Rights' in Stevenson, O. (ed) *Child Welfare in the UK.* Oxford: Blackwell Science.

H.M. Treasury (1999) *Tackling Poverty and Extending Opportunity.* No. 4 The Modernisation of Britain's Tax and Benefit System. London

hooks, b. (1989) *Ain't I a Woman: Black Women and Feminism.* London: Pluto.

hooks, b. (1991) *Yearning: Race, Gender and cultural Politics.* London: Turnaround.

Kelly, N., Milner, J. (1996) ' Child protection decision making' in *Child Abuse Review*, 5, 91-

102.

Kennedy, M. (1995). 'Perceptions of Abused Disabled Children' in Wilson, K., James, A (eds) *The Child Protection Handbook*. London: Bailliere Tindall.

Kent, R. (1997) *Children's Safeguards Review*. London: TSO.

Little, M. (1997) 'The refocusing of children's services: the contribution of research' in Parton N. (ed) *Child Protection & Family Support: Tensions, Contradictions & Possibilities*. London: Routledge.

Macdonald, G., Winkley. A. (1999) *What Works in Child Protection?* Ilford: Barnardo's.

Melton, G.B., Barry, F.D. (1994) *Protecting Children from Abuse and Neglect*. New York: The Guilford Press.

Mullender, A., Kelly, L., Hague, G., Malos, E., Imam, U. (2000) 'Children's needs, coping strategies and understanding of woman abuse'. Research report ESRC.

NCH Factfile (1992) 'Children in Britain 1992'. London: NCH.

NCH Factfile (1998) London: NCH.

NSPCC (1996) *Messages from the NSPCC: a Contribution to the Refocusing Debate*. London: NSPCC.

O'Hagan, K., Dillenburger, K. (1995) *The Abuse of Women in Childcare Work*. Buckingham, OUP.

Oppenheim, C., Harker, L. (1996) *Poverty: the Facts*. 3rd edition CPAG.

Parton, N. (1997) 'Child protection and family support: current debates and future prospects.' in Parton, N. (ed) *Child Protection and Family Support*. .London: Routledge.

Pelton, (1994) 'The role of material factors in child abuse and neglect' in Melton, G.B., Barry, F.D. *Protecting Children from Abuse and Neglect*. New York: Guilford.

Povey, D., Cotton, J., Sisson, S. (2000) 'Recorded Crime Statistics: England & Wales April 1999 to March 2000' . London: Home Office.

Power, A., Tunstall, R. (1998) *Riots and violent disturbances in thirteen areas of Britain*. York: Rowntree Foundation.

Reading, R. (1997) 'Poverty and the health of children and adolescents' in *Archives of Disease in Childhood*. 76, 463-467.

Roberts, H., Smith, S.J., Bryce, C. (1995). *Children at Risk: Safety as a social value*. Buckingham: OUP.

Rutter, M., Smith, D. J. (eds) (1995) *Psychosocial Disorders in Young People: Time Trends and their Causes*. Chichester: Wiley.

Scottish Women's Aid (1999) *Young people speak out about domestic violence*. Edinburgh.

Sedlak, A. (1993) *Risk Factors for Child Abuse & Neglect in the US*. Paper presented at the 4th European Conference on Child Abuse & Neglect: Acting upon European Strategies for Child Protection. ISPCAN. Padua: Italy.

Shemmings, D., Shemmings, Y. (1996) 'Building trust with families when making enquiries, in Platt, D & Shemmings, D. (eds) *Making Enquiries into Alleged Child Abuse and Neglect: Partnership with Families*. Brighton: Pennant/Pavilion.

Smyth, M. (1998) *Half the Battle: Understanding the effects of 'The Troubles' on children and young people in Ireland*. Londonderry: INCORE (University of Ulster and the United Nations University).

Spencer, N. (1996). *Poverty and Child Health*. Oxford: Radcliffe Medical Press.

Starr, R. (1982) (ed) *Child Abuse Prediction*. Cambridge Mass.: Ballinger.

Straw, J., Secretary of State for the Home Office Department (2000) 'Police & criminal justice spending review' 19.7.2000 London: Hansard..

Straw, J., (2000) 26.07.2000 'Jack Straw calls time on crime' Press Release, London: Home Office.

Taylor, J., Spencer. N., Baldwin, N. (2000) 'The social economic and political context of parenting' in *Archives of Disease in Childhood*, 82: 113-120.

The Violence against Children Study Group (1999) *Children, Child Abuse and Child Protection*. Chichester: Wiley.

Tunstill, J. (1995) 'The concept of children in need: the answer or the problem for family support?' *Children and Youth Services Review*, 17, 5/6: 651-664.

Tunstill, J. (1997) 'Implementing the family support clauses of the 1989 Children Act: legislative, professional and organisational obstacles' in Parton, N. (ed) *Child Protection and Family Support*. London: Routledge.

Twigg, J., Atkin, K. (1994) *Carers Perceived*. Buckingham: Open University Press.

Utting, Sir W. (1997) *People Like Us: The Report of the Review of the Safeguards for Children Living away from Home*. London: TSO.

Wilkinson, R.G. (1996) *Unhealthy Societies: the Afflictions of Inequality*. London: Routledge.

Wilson, M. (1993) *Crossing the boundary: black women survive incest*. London: Virago.

Wolfe, D.A., Wekerle, C., Scott, K. (1997) *Alternatives to Violence: Empowering Youth to Develop Healthy Relationships*. Thousand Oaks, Canada: Sage.

Zero Tolerance Charitable Trust (1998) *Young People's Attitudes Towards Violence, Sex and Relationships*. Edinburgh.

2
The legal framework for child centred practice in England and Wales

Judith Masson

Introduction

The United Nations Convention on the Rights of the Child provides a set of agreed principles to be incorporated into law and practice in each country for the benefit of children. The Convention has been ratified by over 190 countries, including the United Kingdom, which ratified in December 1991. The Convention endorsed both the best interests standard for decisions about children by courts and social services agencies (Art.3.1) and the view that children's welfare is best promoted by recognising that children should have rights both as members of families and as individuals. Amongst the obligations in the Convention are the requirements that States assure the right of competent children to express their views in all matters which affect them and that they assure that these views are given due weight. Children must have an opportunity to be heard directly or indirectly in any judicial or administrative proceeding which might affect them (Art.12). States must undertake all appropriate measures to implement rights recognised in the Convention and with regard to economic, social and cultural rights undertake such measures to the maximum of their available resources (Art.4). Under United Kingdom law the Convention is not directly effective so individual children cannot rely on it in the courts but it should influence the content of new legislation and guidance.

The legal framework for child protection practice is now largely provided by the Children Act 1989 and the court rules and regulations made under it. The Children Act 1989 '[a]ccords very closely with the principles in the Convention' (UK 1994, 5), and was influenced by the European Convention on Human Rights. The Human Rights Act 1998 will strengthen the influence of the Convention generally. Child centred practice can be taken forward within the existing framework if it is recognised that the law sets minimum standards which can be developed through professional practice. Detailed guidance has been provided by the Department of Health on issues of practice and local Area Child Protection Committees have developed procedures which seek to ensure professional practice and active interagency cooperation in individual cases. Increased emphasis on prosecuting those who abuse children has led to greater involvement of the police in investigations and focused investigation on obtaining evidence for court proceedings. Child centred practice thus depends on the extent to which this collection of rules either promotes this approach or leaves space for individual professionals to develop it.

The Children Act 1989 does not simply provide the grounds for state intervention to protect children, it also imposes duties on local authorities to provide services to safeguard and promote the welfare of children in need and to promote their upbringing within their families (s.17(1)). These provisions were intended to re-emphasise both the role of the state in providing support and the value to children of remaining with their family. They would redress the balance between the family and the state by asserting the importance of prevention and of partnerships between local authorities and families, and by clarifying the voluntary nature of arrangements which are not backed by court orders. In this way it was hoped that the need for compulsory intervention and court orders could be reduced. This approach is emphasised again in the Department of Health report, Child protection: messages from research (DOH, 1995).

The responsibility of the local authority has not extended to owing children or their families an enforceable duty of care. In *X v. Bedfordshire* C.C. (1995), the House of Lords held that local authorities should be immune from liability in negligence and thus from paying compensation to children harmed by the negligent operation of the child protection system. Similarly, children who are harmed because their need for protection has not been properly considered or because they have been placed in an abusive foster home without proper checks (*H.v. Norfolk C.C.* 1997) have obtained no redress from the local authority. In contrast, social workers who suffer from ill health because they are subjected to too much stress in their work may do so (*Walker* v. *Northumberland C.C.* 1995). However, following decisions of the European Court of Human Rights, public authorities can no longer claim immunity for their actions. Some children at least will be able to get compensation if they are harmed by local authority of police negligence (*Osman v U.K. 1998*).

The Children Act 1989 is not primarily about the rights of children. In emphasising the value of the family the Act could be seen as recognising children's right to be brought up in their own families but it can also be interpreted as strengthening the rights of parents and, in consequence, putting both children's rights and welfare at risk. The Children Act 1989 is both about children and for them. It is not, however, by them, although the National Association of Young People in Care, the Voice for the Child in Care and the Children's Legal Centre lobbied actively during its passage through Parliament. The contents of the Children Act and of the law relating to children generally have been determined largely by disputes between adults where issues of adults' rights (both substantive and procedural) have been crucial.

Children's rights

In civil law all those under the age of eighteen are defined as children. As such they are not full citizens, but are regarded, in law, as having limited capacity to make decisions about their own lives and are subject to control in their families through the principle of parental responsibility. The term 'parental responsibility' was introduced in the Children Act 1989 because it reflected better the purpose of parental power - that is rights which enabled parents to carry out their duties to care for their children and bring them up. But the Act did not define parental responsibility, a point of criticism in the recent report on safeguards for children living away from home (Utting 1997, para. 6.2). In 1985, the House of Lords in *Gillick v W. Norfolk and Wisbech AHA* accepted that parental responsibility did not give absolute power to determine how children spent their life, rather it enabled parents to take action where their child lacked maturity to make decisions. The law recognises that children who have sufficient understanding to grasp the relevant information and to comprehend the wider implications of a decision for themselves and others, have the capacity to make that decision without parental consent, unless a specific age limit is imposed by statute.

The 'Gillick competence' test is subject specific - an individual child may have sufficient understanding to consent to medical procedures surrounding vaccination but not a major operation. It applies to a wide range of situations relevant to child protection including the refusal of consent to an assessment ordered by the court (Children Act 1989, s.38(6), 43(8), 44(7), Sched. 3 paras 4(4), 5(5)), and the instruction of a solicitor in legal proceedings (Family Proceedings Rules 1991, r.4 12(1)(a)). The child's legal competence empowers her. If protective action is planned, it becomes crucial for all professionals to obtain her cooperation - working with her rather than merely for her. However, a finding of competence depends on each professional's assessment that the child has sufficient understanding. Those who are unwilling to work with children in ways which are consultative and to encourage them to evaluate for themselves the different potential outcomes may seek to deny the maturity of a maltreated child on the basis that she is too damaged to cope with all the necessary information or to understand the issues. This is most likely to occur if her wishes conflict with the professional's view of how she should be protected (*Re H. (a minor) 1993*), particularly where a medical assessment is considered necessary to provide evidence for care proceedings and the child's non-cooperation may undermine the protection plan. There is a danger in such cases that pressure is put on the child to cooperate or that the child's refusal is re-interpreted as a sign of immaturity.

Legal competence is not however sufficient to ensure that only action which the child supports is taken. Under its inherent jurisdiction, the High Court has claimed powers which are greater than parental responsibility and which continue until a child reaches the age of 18. These may be used where the court accepts that it is in the interests of the child to override her refusal of medical treatment; for example, to require a 16 year old with anorexia nervosa to accept treatment at a particular hospital (*Re W (a minor) 1993*), or to place a difficult 15 year old in a therapeutic unit despite her objections (*South Glamorgan C.C. v W. & B. 1993*).

Welfare and rights

'When a court determines any question with respect to ... the upbringing of a child ... the child's welfare shall be the court's paramount consideration' (Children Act 1989, s.1). Similarly the local authority is under a duty to 'safeguard and promote the welfare' of any child it is looking after (s.22(3)(a)). This approach should facilitate the resolution of disputes by focusing on the interests of the child at the centre of the dispute rather than the claims of any of the parties. The child's wishes and feelings and the child's needs are only aspects of her welfare and neither has automatic priority; in any individual case these or other aspects of welfare, such as risk of harm or parental capacity to care, may be given greater weight.

The general power to make welfare-based decisions is restricted in English law to decisions about children. Adults, even those with severe learning difficulties or mental illness, are recognised as having rights which can be overridden only in limited circumstances and not merely for their general good. For example, in *Re C.* (1994), a man with schizophrenia was able to obtain an injunction to prevent the therapeutic amputation of his leg. This contrast between the position of adults and children highlights the potential conflict between rights and welfare. One way of concealing this conflict is to claim that children have the right to have decisions made which further their welfare and that this right takes priority over any right to self-determination. Thus a course of action may be justified on the basis that it is the child's right even where it is opposed by the child. Although the child may subsequently be content that her wishes were over-ridden, denying children any right to make decisions contrary to their welfare would seem to prevent them having opportunities to learn from experience. It also suggests that adult wisdom necessarily produces better outcomes, a position which the history of child care (institutionalisation, forced emigration and the cutting of family ties) makes hard to justify. An alternative way of minimizing conflict between rights and welfare necessitates ensuring that each decision about the welfare of a child involves a consideration of what that child might or does want in the particular circumstances and seeking to reach a conclusion which incorporates this rather than relying on adult view points (Eekelaar, 1992, p.230).

Focusing on the child's welfare rather than her rights may avoid burdening her with very difficult decisions and free her from the pressure others might put on her if she were seen to have greater influence on the decision. Requiring decision-makers to consider wishes and feelings may be seen as enabling them to respond realistically to older children. This is not always the case in practice. For example, children who reject welfare-based decisions by running away from care are not always viewed as expressing clear objections to the way their wishes have been given insufficient attention but are labelled absconders and often returned to restrictive, secure placements although this is contrary to Department of Health guidance (DOH, 1991c, para.8.5).

Despite the checklist in the Children Act 1989, s.1(3), the meaning of welfare is generally unclear. Understandings about what is in children's best interests have changed over time. Decisions have been justified as in children's best interests which have subsequently been considered to be quite inappropriate; for example, placing siblings separately, concealing information about the child's adoption or background, not allowing children in foster placement visits from parents until they had settled in, using (or not using) residential care.

Notions of child welfare are influenced by beliefs in the community about children's place in society. Despite the UN Convention on the Rights of the Child children are widely regarded as needing control and constraint rather than respect and recognition. Some changes in welfare based decision-making have occurred as research into child care or child development has increased understanding about the impact of decisions on children but, until recently, research about children routinely excluded children's own views about their situation (Singleton, 1995). Child welfare science (King & Piper, 1990, p.126) can provide only some of the answers. Lack of clarity about the meaning of welfare may encourage the parties to negotiate a settlement to their dispute. There is a danger, particularly if the child is not represented, that such bargaining will produce results which conflict with both the child's needs and her wishes. The emphasis in the Children Act 1989 on avoiding court proceedings may encourage this (Bainham 1990, 220).

Current approaches to welfare decision-making in the courts particularly emphasise the specialist nature of child welfare knowledge. Considerable resources are expended in obtaining expert assessments from professionals who frequently have only limited contact with the child and family (Brophy and Bates, 1998). This empowers professionals at the expense of parents or relatives who may have a much better understanding of the child as a person. It may also lead to repeated assessments of children as the parties seek evidence to strengthen their case. The consequence for the child may be a better decision but this is likely to have taken far longer to reach and also to involve being subjected to these assessments. In the case of assessments more does not always mean better; the passage of time and the assessment process may damage a child and close options rather than identify the best way forward. Even where experts identify a way forward, there is no guarantee that the necessary services will be provided for the child.

Working in partnership with children and parents

Child victims of abuse need to be safe from harm, but their compulsory removal from home should be the last option, used only when there is no alternative. The Children Act 1989 intends that only extreme cases will require adjudication by the courts (DOH, 1995, 32) which is necessary if action is to be taken without the parents' agreement. Unfortunately, in a small proportion of cases, about 5,000 per year, the local authority considers that it has no other way forward. However, recent research suggests that a wider range of services and more emphasis on work to involve family members when children are at risk may increase cooperation from parents and improve children's welfare without compulsory action. (DOH, 1995).

Prior to the implementation of the Children Act 1989 children could be provided with voluntary care (accommodation) at their request, if they were Gillick competent. This provided a means whereby abused teenagers, particularly victims of sexual abuse, could be helped to leave their families without the need for detailed investigations of their claims, collection of evidence or the uncertainty of court proceedings. This avenue is no longer open; parental consent is now required for accommodation of any child under the age of 16 (Children Act 1989, s.20(7), (11)). Refuges for child runaways provide only limited assistance because they are not allowed to accommodate children for more than 14 days (or 21 days in any three months) and only a few refuges exist (Children Act 1989, s.51; Refuges etc. Regulations 1991, reg. 3(9)). Although parents may agree to their child entering accommodation temporarily, they are unlikely to do so if this can be interpreted as an admission that she was abused.

Provision of accommodation may therefore only avoid the use of an emergency protection order pending the first hearing of a care application. Where the child is looked after by the local authority, parents who are not on Income Support or Family Credit can be required to contribute towards this (Children Act 1989, Sched. 2, para. 21(1)(5)). Contributions are usually less than Child Support payments but may be substantial.

The Children Act 1989 empowered local authorities to provide accommodation so that alleged perpetrators could leave the family home (Sched. 2, para. 5) but not all have done so. Local authorities cannot currently take proceedings to have a parent excluded from their home (*Nottingham C.C. v. P.* (No. 2) 1993) but may obtain orders to have other perpetrators kept away (*Devon C.C. v. S.* 1994). Also, the Family Law Act 1996 now enables the court to make orders excluding a perpetrator from the child's home when it makes an emergency protection order or an interim care order (Children Act 1989, ss. 38B, 44B). The use of such a strategy depends on there being someone to care for the child at home, belief that the parent with care will not collude with, or succumb to pressure from, the perpetrator, and an acceptance that the authority rather that the parent should bring the proceedings. The opportunity to work to support the parent may be rejected if she is viewed as at fault in failing to protect her children.

Where local authorities cannot work with parents to agree a plan for the child's protection they may have to invoke the powers of the court to remove the child. Even where alternative arrangements for the child's care are available the local authority may be able to obtain a care order, thus the power in the negotiations lies with the local authority (*Re M.* 1994). This is because the significant harm test does not have to be satisfied at the date of the hearing but only in relation to the earlier crisis when the local authority commenced protective action. Although proceedings may have some advantages for children who will be represented by a guardian ad litem and a solicitor, the outcomes for children who have been involved in proceedings may be worse than in comparable cases dealt with by negotiation (Packman et al., 1986; DOH, 1991a; DOH, 1995).

Children who know someone who is willing to care for them may, if they are Gillick competent, seek leave to apply for a residence order which gives that person parental responsibility for them (Children Act 1989, ss. 8, 10(8)). Alternatively, the adult concerned may apply for the order. The decision whether or not to grant a residence order is subject to the same welfare test whoever makes the application. The current rules make it easier for children rather than adults to obtain Legal Aid to bring the proceedings, but the courts are uneasy about allowing children to take the initiative in bringing proceedings (Thorpe 1994, p.20; Masson, 1996). Cases have to be heard in the High Court (*Re CT.* 1993; Practice Direction 1993); the court may appoint the Official Solicitor as amicus curiae to ensure it has an independent view of the child's welfare (*Re S.* 1993). In at least one case the court has refused an order because it thought that formalizing the situation might exacerbate disputes within the family (*Re C. (a minor) (leave to seek s.8 orders)* 1994). Local authorities are empowered to support children who are cared for by people other than a parent or step-parent under residence orders (Children Act 1989, Sched. 1, para. 15; SSI 1995). However, unless the child was previously looked after by the authority it is much more likely that the child will be dependent on her parents' resources, those of her carer or the State, through Income

Support. If the parents and the carers do not reach a private arrangement or the carer claims Income Support, maintenance for the child will be calculated using the Child Support formula (Child Support Acts 1991-5). The high rate of payment required from 'absent parents' in employment is likely to mean that few can be expected to be willing to support their children living elsewhere.

The current system of limited children's rights and broad parental financial obligations operates to lock children within their families unless parents are willing to release them, local authorities decide to exercise their powers to obtain a court order to remove them, or they are able to find someone willing to care for them and they obtain their parents' or the court's sanction for this arrangement. Self rescue, apart from short term and potentially dangerous running away, is not an option for young people under sixteen because the law is designed to contain them within families who must take responsibility for them. For over sixteens the picture is scarcely any better with almost no recourse to state benefits, only limited rights to obtain financial support from parents (Masson, 1994, p.2) and the local authority's duty to provide accommodation restricted to cases where their welfare would be 'seriously prejudiced' (s.20(3)).

Where a local authority looks after (or proposes to look after) a child, it is required to consult the parents, the child and any other appropriate people and to give due consideration to their views and feelings in relation to any decision it makes about the child (Children Act 1989, s.22(4)(5)). These provisions, together with the parents' retention of parental responsibility even where their child is subject to a care order and the written agreement about the arrangements for the child, provide the legal basis for the working partnership between social workers, children and their parents. The balance of power between the local authority and the parents or children is redressed to a limited extent by giving parents and children a right to make representations or complaints (s.26). However, the Children Act 1989 does not require the authority to take action where a complaint is well founded. There is no right to redress or even an apology although the Court of Appeal has suggested that a local authority which completely ignored the recommendations of a complaints board could find its decision overturned by the court (*R. v. Brent L.B. ex parte S.* 1994). Other aspects of the partnership - treating the parties with respect, sharing information with them and explaining the reasons that their wishes are not followed etc. - are not matters dealt with by the Act but are left to statements of good practice (DOH, 1989, p.8) or other guidance (DOH, 1991, p.4).

The extent to which working in partnership is a new approach to social work practice in child care is contentious. However it is clear that much of child protection practice in the 1980s occurred with only limited attempts to involve parents (DOH, 1995). Parents were not expected to be invited to case conferences (DHSS, 1988, p.29); before 1986, they were not parties to care proceedings. Partnership with parents now has to occur within a context where this has not been the universal approach. Similarly partnership has to be developed with children within a legal and social framework which does not empower them but emphasises both the parents' and the professionals' roles. It should not be surprising, therefore, if children feel unable to put forward their views or to make their objections known. Even where they do try to voice their wishes these are not always heard, nor followed.

Investigation and assessment

The investigation of a child protection case is no longer only a matter of professional judgment and interagency practice. The Children Act 1989, s.47 requires the local authority to make enquiries where they have reasonable cause to suspect that a child in their area is suffering or is likely to suffer significant harm. These enquiries must be geared to enabling the authority to decide whether it should bring court proceedings or provide services and involve seeing the child unless it already has sufficient information. This provision gives the authority no right of access to the child. If parents refuse to cooperate local authorities are required to apply for an emergency protection order, child assessment order, care order or supervision order unless they are satisfied the child's welfare can be satisfactorily protected without an order. In most cases concerns about child protection do not lead directly to proceedings; but in cases which reach a sufficient threshold of concern there is an interagency planning meeting and a case conference. This may lead to the development of a child protection plan which may or may not involve proceedings. Half of all investigations are not followed by further action despite clear evidence of need for services (DOH, 1995, p.28).

Where a child needs to be protected immediately, recourse may be had to the powers of the police to take her into police protection for up to 72 hours (Children Act 1989, s.46). In some areas police protection is being used instead of court proceedings for emergency action out of office hours (Masson et al 2001). The local authority must be informed and the child placed in local authority accommodation (or a refuge) as soon as possible (s.46(3)). All action must be explained to any child who appears capable of understanding and the wishes and feelings of all children should be ascertained (s.46(3)(c)(c)). Children who have run away, perhaps to escape abuse, should not be returned home but should be kept in safety while the matter is investigated. Parents have no right to know the child's whereabouts but must be allowed reasonable contact with her if this is in her best interests (s.46(4),(10)). But determining what is in the best interests of an individual child is always difficult and takes time; in times of crisis workers may not be able to give priority to direct work but need to focus on complying with the requirements of procedural manuals such as making contacts with other agencies.

Child protection investigations are frequently initiated because the child has indicated to someone, perhaps a teacher or a school nurse, that she has been abused. The duties on that person to operate within the interagency framework and the expectation that information will be shared mean that this person cannot offer confidentiality to the child (DOH, 1999, para 7.27-7.33). Nevertheless the child needs to know what action will be taken as a result of her statement. Only if she is fully informed can she establish that she has the capacity and thus the right to continue to participate actively in her own protection. If she is Gillick-competent she may consent to further investigations but these will necessarily involve her parents because no child aged under 16 may enter local authority accommodation if a person with parental responsibility who is able and willing to care for her objects (s.20(7)).

Working Together (DOH, 1999) recommends that whenever children have sufficient understanding and are able to express their wishes and feelings and to participate in the process they should be allowed to attend their case conference (para 5.57). It recognises that there may be conflicts between the interests of parents and children and states that in such cases children's interests should take priority. The courts have accepted that parents only have a right to have their views put forward, not to attend case conferences (*R v L.B. Harrow ex parte D.* 1990). Where children do not attend the case conference or any review, the authority has a duty to establish the child's views and feelings and to communicate them to the conference so that due consideration may be given to them (DOH, 1999, para 5.57). In practice, children's attendance at case conferences is still quite rare. One recent study found that the majority of children who attended were very young; they were present with their parents not to participate but because alternative arrangements for their care had not been made (Farmer and Owen, 1995, p.108).

Representation in proceedings

If the authority starts proceedings for an emergency protection order, child assessment order, care order or supervision order, the child is a party to those proceedings and a guardian ad litem must be appointed unless this is not necessary to safeguard her interests (Children Act 1989, s.41(1)(6)). The guardian ad litem is an independent child care expert, usually a social worker, whose duties include investigating the case, advising the court about the child's wishes and providing a report for the court on the child's interests (Family Proceedings Rules 1991, r.4.11). The guardian also has a role in managing the case before the courts. The purpose of this 'is not to ease the passage of the case through the courts' as an end in itself but to secure the welfare of the child by so doing (DOH 1992, 9, 102). The guardian ad litem is required to appoint a solicitor for the child (Family Proceedings Rules 1991, r.4.11(2)). The child's solicitor will usually be a member of the Law Society's Children Panel. He or she will therefore be a specialist in child law, have taken additional training to gain information about child development and social work practice, have agreed to give personal attention to the case and be able to communicate directly with children of all ages (Law Society 1991). The guardian ad litem instructs the solicitor for the child unless the child has the capacity to do so and wishes to give conflicting instructions (FPR 1991, r.4.12(1)(a)).

Where a child is capable of understanding the issues before the court and giving coherent and consistent instructions to her solicitor she has the right to separate representation from the solicitor even though her wishes are thought by other parties to conflict with her welfare (*Re H.* 1993).

Where the child is not giving separate instructions to the solicitor, the solicitor must represent the child's best interests (r.4.12(1)(c)). The guardian ad litem and solicitor should together form a view of what is in her best interests and ensure that this position is fully advocated throughout the proceedings. They should also ensure that the child is aware of what is being proposed and that her views about any plans are communicated to the court (r.4.11(4)(b)). The availability of alternative orders, for example a residence order in favour of a relative, and the need to satisfy the court that the child's welfare demands the making of the order (Children Act 1989, s.1(5)) mean that the courts now expect far more information about the local authority's plans and scrutinize them more thoroughly than they previously did (*Re J.* 1994; DOH 1991, para 2.62.LAC 99 (29)).

Where the child instructs the solicitor, the Court Rules provide that she has most of the rights which adult clients have to put her case before the court and is also safeguarded by the presentation of an independent welfare view. Younger and less mature children have few rights and must rely on the guardian and solicitor communicating their wishes whilst advocating for their welfare.

Although children are formally parties to these civil proceedings taken for their protection they generally play no direct part in them. Rules allowing the admission of hearsay evidence mean that someone who has heard what the child has said may give these statements in evidence (Children (Admissibility of hearsay evidence) Order 1993). The court's power over the child's attendance (s. 95) and the attitudes of the judiciary mean that children are generally excluded from their court hearings, a sharp contrast with the pre Children Act requirement for all children over the age of 5 years to attend care proceedings in the magistrates' court. The Act spares some children considerable anxiety but also excludes others who want to see and hear what is said. It has been suggested that this exclusion of older children from their proceedings may be a factor in their disengagement from the process (Masson and Winn Oakley, 1999).

Children's attendance at the hearing has been constructed as a welfare issue not a right. If the child is represented by either a guardian ad litem or a solicitor the proceedings may take place in her absence, even where she is competent to give instructions to her solicitor (FPR 1991, r.4.16(2)). The High Court has commented adversely about the presence in court of a 13 year old girl considering that it would not be in her welfare to hear what was said, noting that the duration and complexity of proceedings made them unsuitable for children to attend (*Re C. (a minor)(Care: child's wishes) 1993*). In contrast, the guardian ad litem considered that being at the hearing benefited the child because she knew that nothing had been said or done behind her back. However, the guardian also reflected that the girl had been 'wholly unaware of the issues debated' other than whether she could return home, a comment which suggests that insufficient attention may have been given to preparing the girl for the proceedings and explaining them to her. The Children Act Advisory Committee has endorsed the judicial view that children's attendance at court should be regarded as exceptional (CAAC, 1997, 36).

Current practice relating to the child's participation in the proceedings cannot be regarded as child-centred, rather it is narrowly paternalistic. A direction that the child 'need not attend' coupled with explanations to the child about the process and facilities so that she can leave if she finds the proceedings too upsetting would provide a way of accommodating a child who wishes to attend but this would necessitate a change in approach from the courts. However, such a limited change would not address a major barrier to children's participation in care proceedings, the domination of the process by adult language and procedures.

The current system of representation of both wishes and welfare may assist the court to reach a decision which is both just and in the child's best interests but care proceedings cannot be regarded uncritically (Masson and Winn Oakley, 1999). The role of the guardian ad litem and the child's solicitor are both limited to the conduct of the proceedings. The child may place trust in these people over a protracted period, on average 9 months in county court cases (CAAC, 1994, p. 77) but cannot turn to them for ongoing support. Decisions made by the courts are constrained by the fact that neither the child's representatives nor the court itself can ensure that services which the child needs are provided for her. The court has no ongoing supervisory role but is restricted to refusing an order on the basis that the case for it has not been made or that it would be better to make no order (s.1(5)). Considerable emphasis is placed by guardians ad litem on their independence from the social services department but most of them obtained their child care training and experience with local authorities and this may still determine their approach to child welfare. The notion that the local authority's plan should be supported by the court remains strong, for example in attitudes to contact between children in care and their parents (*Re B* 1993; Masson 1990, 97). The courts can be expected to refuse a parent's application for contact if a local authority which has planned to secure the child's welfare through an adoptive placement opposes it.

In practice, the tandem system for representation of children in care proceedings promises more than it delivers. A recent in depth study of children aged 9 years and over, represented by guardians from 2 Midlands panels and by specialist solicitors, indicated that children's agendas were frequently not taken up by their representatives. Rather than facilitating children's participation in the court process representatives shielded them from it. They responded to children's questions but sometimes relied on children to take the initiative by asking and, according to the children, few gave them adequate opportunities to read reports presented to the court about them (Masson and Winn Oakley, 1999).

Confidentiality

Children who are able to give instructions to their solicitor have a right to confidentiality for all their communications with the solicitor because of legal professional privilege. The solicitor, unlike other professionals concerned with the child's protection, is bound not to reveal the child's confidences unless these involve seeking advice about the commission of future crimes or there are exceptional circumstances which justify a breach of confidentiality. Abuse of the child client is not an exceptional circumstance but the Law Society advises that it is permissible to attempt to persuade the child to reveal details of the abuse (Law Society, 1991a, para B(i)(c)). This rule may place considerable stress on the solicitor but enables discussions between the solicitor and the child to be more open because the solicitor has no conflicting responsibilities to other professionals. Where the solicitor knows or strongly suspects that younger siblings are being abused or the child is at risk of serious injury, the solicitor has a discretion to breach the child's confidence (Law Society, 1991a, para B(ii)(d)). Although legal professional privilege has been limited in cases concerning child welfare to ensure that the courts have the fullest information about any case these limitations do not remove the child client's right to a confidential relationship with her solicitor (*Oxfordshire v M* 1994; *Re L.* 1996).

Child protection and the criminal law

During the 1980s there was increasing concern about the inadequacy of the criminal justice system to deal with crimes against children, particularly child sexual abuse. English law regarded children as unreliable witnesses, 'prone to lie and fantasize' (Heydon, 1984, p.84). It rejected their evidence unless they could understand the nature of the oath, required children's evidence to be corroborated and gave child witnesses no special protection within the proceedings (Spencer & Flin, 1993). The pressure placed on children by the accused and his lawyers in cross-examination frequently prevented them from completing their evidence. Prosecutions were dropped or never started because child witnesses were unable to satisfy the rigours of the law or the courts.

Pressure from lawyers, academics and child care organisations led to reforms introduced in the Criminal Justice Acts 1988 and 1991, and the Criminal Justice and Public Order Act 1994. These removed the need for children's evidence to be corroborated (Criminal Justice Act 1988, s.34), the requirement that the judge should warn of the dangers of convicting for sexual offences without corroboration (Criminal Justice and Public Order Act 1994, ss. 32, 33), and provided for children to give evidence unsworn (CJA 1991, s.52; CJA 1988, s.33A). Perpetrators were precluded from cross-examining children directly (CJA 1991 s.55(7); CJA 1988, s.34A). Child witnesses and victims of sexual offences aged under 17 years of age (and those of violent offences under 14 years of age) could be permitted by the judge to give their evidence in chief through a pre-recorded video tape and be cross-examined at the trial without entering the courtroom, using an interactive video system (CJA 1991, s.54; CJA 1988, ss. 32, 32A). Guidance has been issued about video recording evidence and the storage of tapes (HO/DOH 1992). The protection of all vulnerable witnesses is codified in the Youth Justice and Criminal Evidence Act 1999.

These provisions have changed markedly the process of investigating allegations of child abuse; very large numbers of video recordings have been made but few have been used in criminal proceedings; there has apparently been little effect on the prosecution and conviction rates (Butler, 1993, p.14) which remain unacceptably low (Utting, 1997, p.189). In response to these changes and the expectations of the civil courts, in sexual abuse investigations, social workers and the police now place emphasis on making the child's video, a process which must occur early in the investigation if it is not to be rejected as having been influenced by those seeking to help the child. In some cases the video will be made before the child has made any allegation but the interviewers must not suggest to the child that she has been abused. This is not to say that the interviews are not skilled but that the the current demands of the criminal justice system have produced a process for both civil and criminal cases which is unhelpful to children and which consequently does not protect them. In some areas it has been recognised that the practice of making many videos is wasteful, unproductive and potentially abusive to children and efforts are being made to restrict video-recording to cases where evidence is likely to be obtained.

Although the process of recording an interview with the child could be undertaken in a way which focused on the needs and interests of the child neither the law nor the Memorandum of Good Practice on Video Recorded Evidence promotes this. The focus is on the provision of a statement which can be used as evidence. The criminal law seeks to counter any pressure that the alleged offender might use to prevent a witness giving evidence. Children who have made a statement and are competent to give evidence are compellable witnesses and therefore their consent to participate is not required. A child may refuse to make a video but not to give evidence (para. 2.29). The Memorandum discourages the provision of a supporter for the child during the interview (para. 2.27). It emphasises the importance of proceeding at the child's pace (para. 2.18) but also expects that the interview should last less than an hour (para. 2.17) and that sufficient information should be obtained in a single interview. Although the reason for making the video should be explained (para. 3.7), the interviewer cannot say what use will be made of it, for example that it will avoid the child giving evidence, because a decision about its admissibility can only be made by the judge.

The Memorandum of Good Practice states that children should be encouraged to speak freely and spontaneously but the formal nature of the communication which is being recorded and the rules of evidence which are applied to it do not help the child to do this. Prompts, in the form of leading questions - questions which include information which has not come from the child - should not be used (para. 3.25). Whereas the processes of being interviewed to tell their story, preparing a witness statement and giving evidence are separated for adults, children are expected to be able to give a single account in the form of evidence for the court. If they do not the perpetrator cannot be brought to justice. Children may see this as their failure but in reality the system has failed them.

Children who are unable or unwilling to give a formal account of their abuse when the police and social workers try to record an interview may not be given further opportunities. Pressure of work, particularly the additional burden of undertaking memorandum interviews, forces workers to close cases if evidence is not obtained; without evidence the possibility of proceedings under the Children Act 1989 is also reduced.

Children who succeed in providing a recording which is accepted as evidence must still attend court and be cross-examined if the alleged offender does not plead guilty. Court proceedings are frequently delayed or adjourned putting more stress on the child (Davies and Noon, 1991, p.140; CPS, 1998; Durham - later chapter in this volume). The trial may be as much as a year after the offences were first disclosed. During this period the child may be provided with little information about the reasons for the delay or help to cope with the abuse. Although considerable progress has been made in preparing and supporting child witnesses, their needs are secondary to criminal proceedings. Cross-examination is the most stressful part of giving evidence; defence barristers frequently seek to undermine witnesses' evidence by accusing them of lying. Such questioning may upset or confuse a child so much that she is unable to finish giving her evidence. Judges have powers to curtail counsel's questions but are reluctant to use them in case this undermines the fairness of the trial. Browbeating witnesses including children has long been accepted as a way of getting at the truth although psychological research suggests that the contrary is true (Spencer & Flin 1993, p.272).

Many of these problems are inherent in a system which seeks to protect the accused through a fair trial, demands that this should be based on an oral adversarial process, and has traditionally paid little attention to the needs of victims. Proposals have been made (Pigot, 1989) which, if implemented, would enable child witnesses to be examined in a separate process with questions put to them by specially trained questioners who would not be permitted to adopt the tactics which are used now. Criminal procedures in this form have been developed in a number of jurisdictions for example Israel (Spencer, 1990). However, the Conservative Government rejected these proposals and implemented the current system. Although the reforms may make it somewhat easier to obtain a conviction using the evidence of a child this advantage is outweighed by the adverse effects of subjecting very many children to a system which neither helps them to speak about their problems nor assists professionals to protect them. Resources which might have been used to develop new services under the Children Act 1989 are being spent on child protection investigations which do not help the children concerned. This has been recognised by the Department of Health but it remains to be seen whether the child protection juggernaut can be redirected to support children and their families. One possibility is to stop prosecuting abusers and encourage them and their families to seek help as occurs in some continental jurisdictions (Marneffe, 1992; Masson, 1997). Although this may further children's welfare it will not necessarily reflect their wish to see justice in the form of punishment of those who have abused them.

Conclusion

The Children Act has provided a clearer legal framework for decisions about children than existed previously. However, the law relating to children remains complex; parents' and children's rights derive largely from the common law rather than a statutory code which does not make it easy for either parents or children to know what their rights are. This lack of clarity does not assist children to take control of decision making in their lives. When parents and children are in dispute the onus is generally on the child to seek a prohibited steps order to overrule the parent's decision. Only mature children can seek such an order and there is no guarantee that the court will support their point of view.

Welfare rather than rights remains the guiding principle when disputes about the care or upbringing of children are brought before the court (Children Act 1989, s.1) or local authorities become involved in providing supportive services or child protection (ss.17,22). Understandings of welfare have developed to give a greater emphasis to children's views and wishes but the desire of adults for control and paternalism continue to have very strong influence on those with the power to make decisions about children. The law has not checked professional power, nor has it imposed on professionals standards which exclude paternalism. It has supported professionals by enabling them to refer matters to the courts for welfare based decisions which override even mature children's wishes.

Children's concerns, for example to maintain contact with brothers and sisters placed separately in care, to remain with particular foster carers or to continue to attend a particular school are not adequately reflected in child care law. The Children Act places power and responsibility in the hands of the local authority so that it can manage the child care system. It does not provide a robust system for making local authorities or social workers accountable to children. Rather than providing redress for children who are harmed through the operation of the care system the courts have sought to exempt local authorities from any liability to them in negligence.

Although the Children Act 1989 sought to place more emphasis on the role of the local authority to support children in need and their families rather than to intervene in family life through court proceedings, child care practice has continued to be dominated by child protection. The law in the form of powers to control families has cast a long shadow over creative social work based on negotiating solutions to problems defined by children and families. Outside court proceedings, children's rights in child protection are obscured by procedures and obtaining evidence, particularly if the investigation is undertaken following the Memorandum of Good Practice.

The development of the guardian ad litem service and its extension to a wider variety of cases provided representation for children in proceedings involving local authorities. However this has not developed to facilitate children's participation, rather it has shielded them from the process. Guardians ad litem can promote children's concerns but are required to safeguard the child's interests rather than advocate their wishes. Children who are able to give instructions can have their wishes advocated by their solicitor but the court will always determine the case according to its view of the child's welfare.

Where the dispute does not involve the local authority, children are disempowered. Children face many barriers in having their concerns heard. They are not usually parties to cases about their residence or about contact, and can only initiate proceedings if they have sufficient maturity and are granted leave. Cases brought by children must start in the High Court, not in the local family proceedings court.

Although some changes have been made which enable children to be witnesses in criminal proceedings and which take account of their vulnerable position, the concerns of the criminal justice system remain almost exclusively on the accused.

The complexity of the proceedings and their formality means that children are heavily dependent on adults once they become involved in legal proceedings. High quality representation provides only a limited solution to the problem of proceedings and processes which are simply too complex. Complexity is disempowering both because of the confusion it causes and its effect on the court's willingness to find that children have sufficient understanding to initiate proceedings or to instruct a solicitor without a guardian ad litem. At present, the United Nations Convention on the Rights of the Child, and the U.K. government's attitude to it provide little hope for reform.

References

Aldridge, J. and Freshwater, K. (1993) 'The preparation of child witnesses' 5 J *of Child Law* 25-27

Bainham, A. (1990) 'The Privatisation of the Public Interest in Children' 53, M.L.R. 206-221

Brophy, J and Bates, P. (1998) 'The position of parents using experts in care proceedings: a failure of "partnership"' 20, 1 *J. Soc. Welfare and Fam Law* 23-48

Butler, T. (1993) 'Spare the Child' *Police Review*, December 10, 1993 14-15

CAAC (1994) *Children Act Advisory Committee report 1993/94* Lord Chancellor's Department

CAAC (1997) *Final Report of the Children Act Advisory Committee* Lord Chancellor's Department

CPS (1998) *The Inspectorate's report on cases involving child witnesses* Crown Prosecution Service

DOH (1989) *The Care of Children Principles and Practice in Regulations* and Guidance HMSO

DOH (1991) *The Children Act 1989: Guidance and Regulations Volume 3 Family placements* HMSO

DOH (1991a) *Patterns and Outcomes in child placement* HMSO

DOH (1991c) *The Children Act 1989: Guidance and Regulations Volume 4 Residential Care* HMSO

DOH (1992) *Manual of Practice Guidance for Guardians ad litem and Reporting Officers*

DOH (1994) *Children Act Report 1993* cm. 2584

DOH (1995) *Child protection : messages from research* HMSO

DOH et al. (1999) *Working Together to Safeguard Children.* TSO

D.H.S.S. (1988) *Working Together* HMSO

Davies, G. and Noon, E. (1991) *An Evaluation of the line link for child witnesses*, Home Office

Davies, G. Wilson, C. et al. (1995) *Videotaping children's evidence: An evaluation*, Home Office

Eekelaar, J. (1992) 'The importance of thinking that children have rights' in Alston, P., Parker, S. and Seymour, J. (ed) *Children, Rights and the Law* O.U.P. 221-235

Farmer, E. and Owen, M. (1995) *Child protection practice: private risks and public remedies* HMSO

HO/DOH (1992) *Memorandum of Good Practice* HMSO

Heydon, J. (1984) *Evidence Cases and Materials* (2nd ed) Butterworths

King, M. and Piper, C., (1990) *How the Law thinks about Children* Gower

Law Commission (1992) *Domestic Violence and the Occupation of the Family Home*

Law Com No.207 (1992 H.C. 1)

Law Society (1991) *The Law Society's Family Law Committee's guidance for solicitors working with guardians ad litem*

Law Society (1991a) 'Confidentiality and privilege - child abuse and abduction' *Professional Standards Bulletin No.5*

Marneffe, C. (1992) 'The confidential doctor centre- a new approach to child protection work' 16 No. 4 *Adoption and Fostering* 23

Masson, J. (1990) 'Contract between parents and children in the long term care of others: the unresolved dispute' 4 *Int J Law & Fam* 97-122

Masson, J. (1992) 'The official solicitor as the child's guardian ad litem under the Children Act 1989' 4 *J of Child Law* 58-62

Masson, J. (1994) 'The Children Act 1989 and young people: dependence and rights to independence' in Lockton, D. (ed) *Children and the Law*, Cavendish 1-11

Masson, J. (1996) 'Representations of children' in Freeman, M.D.A. (ed.) *Current Legal Problems* 1996 O.U.P. 245-265

Masson, J. (1997) 'Non-punitive approaches to child protection: legal issues' in Parton, N. (ed) *Child protection and Family Support* Routledge 92-109

Masson, J. and Winn Oakley, M. (1999) *Out of Hearing* Wiley

Masson, J. et al (2001) *Working in the Dark.* Warwick University

Packman J. et al. (1986) *Who needs care?* Blackwell

Pigot, T. (1989) *Report of the Advisory Group on Video evidence* Home Office
Singleton, R. (1995) Address given at Barnardo's Conference *Listening to children*, June 28, 1995
SSI (1995) *Residence orders study* Social Services Inspectorate DOH
Spencer, J. & Flin, R. (1993) *The Evidence of Children* (2nd ed) Blackstone Press
Spencer, J. et al (1990) *Children's evidence in legal proceedings* Cambridge
Thorpe, M. (1994) 'Independent representation for minors' *24 Fam Law 20-22*
U.K. (1994) *The U.K.'s First Report to the U.N. Committee on the Rights of the Child* HMSO
Utting, W. (1997) *People like us* T.S.O

Case list

Re B. (minors)(care: contact: local authority's plans) [1993] 1 FLR 543
Re C. (a minor)(Care: child's wishes) [1993] 1 FLR 832
Re C. (refusal of medical treatment) [1994] 1 FLR 31
Re C. (a minor) (leave to seek s.8 orders) [1994] 1 FLR 26
Re CT. (a minor) (wardship: representation) [1993] 2 FLR 278
Devon C.C. v. S. [1994] Fam. 169
Gillick v W. Norfolk and Wisbech AHA [1986] A.C.112
Re H. (a minor) (care proceedings: child's wishes) [1993] 1 FLR 440
H. v. Norfolk C.C. [1997] 1 FLR 384
Re J. (minors) (care: care plan) [1994] 1 FLR 253
Re L. (police investigation: privilege) [1996] 1 FLR 731 H.L.
Re M. (a minor)(care order: significant harm) [1994] 2 FLR 577 H.L.
Nottingham C.C. v. P. (No. 2) [1993] 2 FLR 134
Oxfordshire v. M. [1994] 1 FLR 175
Osman v. U.K. [1998] 5 BHRC 293 ECEHR
Practice Direction [1993] 1 FLR 668
R. v. Brent L.B. ex parte S. [1994] 1 FLR 203
R. v. L.B. Harrow ex parte D. [1990] 1 FLR 79
Re S. (a minor)(representation) [1993] 2 FLR 437
South Glamorgan C.C. v W. & B. [1993] 1 FLR 574
Re W. (a minor) (consent to medical treatment) [1993] 1 FLR 1
Walker v. Northumberland C.C. [1995] 1 All E.R. 737
X v. Bedfordshire C.C. [1995] 2 FLR 276 H.L.

3
Children's rights and children's welfare in Scotland

Brian Kearney

Introduction

Judith Masson has set out the legal framework of child care practice in England and Wales. The legal system in Scotland has always been separate from the system south of the border. I will try here to give a brief summary of the set-up in Scotland, highlighting some of the similarities and points of difference. I believe that in this field each system has much to learn from the other and hope that this short piece may go some way to promoting cross-fertilisation.

Scots law and courts structure

Scots law is rooted in the Roman-Dutch tradition. Our supreme institutional writer, Lord Stair, spent some years in Holland before publishing in 1693 the enlarged edition of his *Institutions of the Law of Scotland* which derived the principles of our law from its sources in Roman, canon and feudal law and is still referred to in our courts. The Act of Union of 1707 preserved to Scotland her independent legal system. The independence of our legal system is preserved and reinforced by the Scotland Act 1998. Our courts system is distinct. The local professional judge is the Sheriff, who is an advocate (a member of the Faculty of Advocates - the Scottish equivalent of a barrister) or solicitor of at least ten years' standing. The Sheriff is the approximate equivalent of a Circuit Judge of England and Wales. Our lay judges, the justices of the District Court, have a very limited criminal jurisdiction and, in contrast with the magistracy of England and Wales, no civil jurisdiction whatever. Until the Divorce (Scotland) Act 1976 jurisdiction in divorce was reserved to our Supreme Court, the Court of Session in Edinburgh. Nowadays the Sheriff exercises concurrent jurisdiction with the Outer House of the Court of Session as a court of first instance in divorce as well as in relation to almost all civil claims without limitation as to financial amount. Almost all family actions are now raised in the Sheriff Court. In civil matters there is generally a right of appeal from the Sheriff to the Sheriff Principal of the Sheriffdom and a right of appeal from the Sheriff and from the Sheriff Principal to the Inner House of the Court of Session with a final appeal on point of law to the House of Lords. In criminal matters the Sheriff has jurisdiction to try any crime except treason murder and rape which are reserved to the High Court of Justiciary. When sitting with jury of fifteen the Sheriff may impose up to three years' imprisonment or remit to the High Court for sentence. The Sheriff in criminal jurisdiction may be appealed to the High Court of Justiciary in its appellate capacity There is no appeal to the House of Lords in criminal matters.

While many of the statutes of the United Kingdom have to a very large extent equated our law with that of England and Wales in such fields as company law, taxation and road traffic, our law of persons, including the law of parent and child, has remained distinct and distinctive. The enactment of the Social Work (Scotland) Act 1968, brought into being, with effect from 1971, the Children's Hearings system. This now deals with almost all the cases of offending children and children in need of care and protection and is very different from the systems of dealing with children's cases in England and Wales and in Northern Ireland.[1] The 'common law' (using the term in its broad sense, meaning the basic corpus of law - Scotland does not share the 'common law' of England) of Scotland is expounded by our great institutional writers such as Stair, Erskine and Bell in relation to civil law and, in relation to criminal law, by Hume and Alison. The great Scottish criminal jurist of this century is Sheriff Gerald H Gordon QC whose writings cannot be accorded institutional status while he remains, happily, still with us. As in England and Wales case law is an important source of law.[2]

The old law

The link between the powers of the parents and their responsibilities has long been recognised. Stair,[3] in 1693, put the matter thus:

> That there are natural obligations betwixt parents and children, not proceeding from the consent of either party, or from the constitution of any human law, but from the obedience man oweth to his Maker, who hath written this law in the hearts of parents and children, as to their interests and duties, with capital letters, is evident by the common consent of all the nations of the world, how barbarous soever.

Erskine,[4] writing in the mid-eighteenth century, stated:

> Parents lie under the strongest obligations, from nature itself, to take care of their issue during their imperfect age, in consequence of which they are vested with all the powers over them which are necessary for the proper discharge of their duty.

The concept of the importance, if not the paramountcy, of the interests of the child and the right of the mature child to express a view have also been long recognised as principles which the courts would uphold, at least for those who could afford to go to law. The facts of *Harvey v Harvey*[5] were admittedly extreme: a father who had been divorced on ground of incest with his wife's sister applied to the court for 'custody' (the term used until 1995) of his son, aged 15 and his daughter, aged 14, after he had been absent abroad for 12 years - but they enabled our most eminent nineteenth century judge, Lord Justice-Clerk (as he then was) Inglis, to declare:

1.   *That the control to which a minor pubes is subjected, does not proceed on any notion of his incapacity to exercise rational judgement or choice, but rather arises, on the one hand, from a consideration of the reverence and obedience to parents which both the law of nature and the Divine law enjoin, and, on the other hand, from a regard to the inexperience and immaturity of judgement on the part of the child, which require friendly and affectionate counsel and aid.*

2.   *That the power of a father, at this age, is conferred not as a right of dominion, or even as a privilege for the father's own benefit or pleasure, but merely, or at least mainly, for the benefit, guidance, and comfort of the child.*

3.   *That, therefore, the father's authority and right of control may at this age of the child be easily lost, either by the apparent intention to abandon it and leave the child to his own guidance, or by circumstances or conduct showing the father's inability or unwillingness to discharge rightly the parental duty towards his child.*

4.   *That in all questions as to the loss of parental control during puberty from any of these causes, the wishes and feelings of the child himself are entitled to a degree of weight corresponding to the amount of intelligence and right feeling which he may exhibit.*

The law up to 1995

As will be seen the law always recognised the responsibilities of 'parents', but, in the Roman tradition of *patria potestas*,[6] placed greater emphasis on the role of the father. As time went by the role of the mother was increasingly recognised and formal parity was accorded by the Guardianship Act 1973 which was a UK statute having application to Scotland. The principle that the welfare of the child was to be the 'first and paramount' consideration in determining matters affecting the upbringing and custody of children was enacted for Scotland in another UK statute, the Guardianship of Infants Act, 1925.

In 1985 the famous case of *Gillick v West Norfolk and Wisbech Area Health Authority*,[7] was decided. This case, although an English appeal, would be regarded as highly persuasive in Scotland. In it the Scottish Law Lord, Lord Fraser of Tullybelton, observed that parental rights 'exist for the benefit of the child and exist only so long as they are needed for the protection of the child'. The Law Reform (Parent and Child) (Scotland) Act 1986 enacted that each parent had equal 'rights' in relation to the upbringing of the child. Although the language of rights was used in the 1986 Act it was made clear in s 3(2) of that Act that in any parental rights proceedings 'the court shall regard the welfare of the child involved as the paramount consideration and shall not make any order relating to parental rights unless it is satisfied that to do so will be in the interests of the child'.

The Children (Scotland) Act 1995

The language of the Children (Scotland) Act 1995 ('the Act' or 'the 1995 Act') reflects the intention of the legislature to make explicit the child-centred nature of this field of law. Section 1(1) of the Act leads with the provision that a parent has 'the responsibility' to safeguard the child's welfare and s 1(4) makes it clear that the provisions of the Act in this regard are to replace the existing common law. Section 2(1) of the Act sets out 'rights' of the parent but provides explicitly that these are conferred 'in order to enable [the parent] to fulfil his parental responsibilities in relation to the child'. The parental rights listed are: to have the child live with the parent and otherwise to regulate his/her residence; to control and guide the child appropriately; to act as the child's legal representative; and, where the child is not living with the parent, to maintain contact.

In section 2 and elsewhere the ancient nomenclature referring to 'custody' of and 'access' to children is swept away. Section 11 of the Act defines the powers of the courts to intervene in family life including the consideration of disputes as to whom the child should stay with and how much the non-residential parent should have to do with the up-bringing of the child. The courts are empowered inter alia to grant 'residence' and 'contact' orders and also 'specific issue' orders when there is not agreement as to how parental responsibilities are to be carried out. Section 11 also defines the principles which are to govern such decisions by providing that in considering such matters the court:

a.   *shall regard the welfare of the child concerned as its paramount consideration and shall not make any such order unless it considers that it would be better for the child that the order be made than that none should be made at all; and*

b.   *taking account of the child's age and maturity, shall so far as practicable*
   (i) *give him an opportunity to indicate whether he wishes to express his views;*
   (ii) *if he does so wish, give him an opportunity to express them; and*
   (iii) *have regard to such views as he may express.*

The foregoing principles may be referred to as the paramountcy principle, the no non-beneficial order principle (not the 'minimum intervention principle'[8]) and the consulting the child principle. The enactment of these provisions was in large part a consequence of the ratification by the United Kingdom of the United Nations Convention on the Rights of the Child, but it is interesting to note that the Act, like its English counterpart,[9] goes further than Article 3 of the Convention by making the interests of the child the paramount, and not merely 'a primary', consideration.

Implementing the Act: The role of the local authority

Since 1994 Scotland has comprised 32 'unitary' local authorities.[10] Each must have a Chief Social Work Officer who may or may not be a Director of Social Work in charge of an independent Social Work Department. Scottish Office has an overviewing and supporting function in the shape of Social Work Services Group which is headed by a civil servant at what used to be known as Under Secretary level. There is an inspectorate of Social Work comprising 16 inspectors headed by the Chief Social Work Inspector.

Following long established practice dating back to and even before the Poor Law statutes, the 1995 Act confers upon local government pivotal responsibilities in relation to the comprehensive role of the state as *parens patriae*.[11] A novel requirement is the obligation under s 19 to prepare and publish a plan for the provision of services of children in their area, subject to the right of the Secretary of State for Scotland to issue directions to local authorities. In preparing the plan the local authority must consult with a number of other agencies including Health, relevant voluntary organisations, housing associations and also the Principal Reporter and the chair of the children's panel for the area concerned. It would not appear however that these provisions give to parents or children a right which would be enforceable in the courts. There is no Scottish case analogous to *X v Bedfordshire CC*[12] but it is thought that the reasoning which commended itself to the House of Lords in that case would be adopted by the Scottish courts.[13]

The local authority has the responsibility of complying with the statutory requirements in respect of any child who by operation of any of the statutory procedures becomes a 'looked after' child,[14] including a child who has been made the subject of supervision requirements made by children's hearings.[15] The obligations on the local authority in this regard are set out in The Arrangements to Look After Children (Scotland) Regulations 1996,[16] which, inter alia, provide[17] that the local authority 'shall, so far as is reasonably practicable, make a care plan to address the immediate and longer-term needs of the child with a view to safeguarding and promoting his welfare'. The Scottish Office has issued four volumes of guidance for the implementation of the various statutory requirements.[18] In relation to the preparation of this care plan this guidance includes the following:[19]

> *The gathering of information is the first step in assessing the need for a child to be looked after and is the foundation for future action. Assessment aims to identify the needs and problems which face the child and other members of the family and their potential for relief, reduction or change. It should highlight ways in which problems can be addressed, needs can be met and strengths can be built upon.*

The local authority also has the responsibility of providing information to the children's reporter (see below) and of preparing reports for children's hearings.[20]

The role of the courts

The introduction of residence and contact orders under s 11 of the 1995 Act was complemented by appropriate rules of court. Parties may still pursue such actions by employing the procedures appropriate to other forms of civil cause, with full written pleadings a 'Closed Record' (the Scottish term for written pleadings in their final form) and a Proof - the Scottish term for the trial of a civil cause. The new rules[21] introduced a new procedure known as a Child Welfare Hearing which may and in certain cases must be held when parties put in issue questions as to residence and contact with children. The Sheriff may fix such a hearing at any time - parallel provisions exist for proceedings in the Court of Session, but as the great majority of such cases are raised in the Sheriff Court only the Sheriff Court procedures are referred to here. The Sheriff is enjoined to 'seek the expeditious resolution of disputes in relation to the child by ascertaining from the parties the matters in dispute and information relevant to that dispute' and is given wide powers as to the steps which s/he may order to be taken to achieve this end. It has been held by a Sheriff Principal that the Child Welfare Hearing procedure may be used to decide the issue of residence finally[22] and, in an appropriate case, on the basis of affidavits and other information without the necessity of sworn oral testimony.[23]

The inquiry by Lord Clyde into the Orkney affair arose out of concerns regarding the possibility that children had been removed from home on the allegation of having been sexually abused by or with the connivance of their parents without the evidence having been adequately scrutinised. Social workers had employed the existing legal machinery, viz. a 'Place of Safety Order' (granted by the local Sheriff) under s. 37 of the Social Work (Scotland) Act 1968. Lord Clyde's report[24] recommended the introduction of a more sophisticated device to be known as a Child Protection Order (hereinafter 'CPO') which could only be granted where there was 'clear and cogent evidence to support the order'[25] and in relation to which the 'whole of the evidence which the applicant believes supports the contention that circumstances exist which give rise to the likelihood of the child suffering significant harm' should be presented to the person, ideally the Sheriff, but where unavoidable a Justice of the Peace. Lord Clyde also recommended that 'serious consideration be given to the introduction of a power to have a suspected abuser excluded from contact with the child, obtainable on application to the Sheriff on the presentation of sufficient evidence perhaps by affidavit to support a probable cause'.[26]

Following these recommendations the 1995 Act introduced the CPO and the Exclusion Order (hereinafter 'EO') whereby a suspected abuser may be removed from the family home. Both of these orders may be granted by the Sheriff - if in an emergency situation a justice of the Peace may grant an order permitting the child to be held pending the obtaining of a CPO within 24 hours. Both may be granted in the first instance by statements from one side only and without intimation to the other side. Both are subject to recall or review by the Sheriff within three working days of an application to recall or review. The Act also introduced the Child Assessment Order (CAO) also grantable by a Sheriff, which may empower a local authority to have the child removed and held for up to a maximum of seven days. The CAO is, oddly, not subject to any expedited appeal process. It may be that in theory a CAO could be appealed under the ordinary appeal procedures[27] but the short duration of the CAO would appear to rule this out as a practical proposition.

A CPO and CAO may contain inter alia directions as to contact with parents etc and directions for the child to be medically or otherwise examined and, if necessary as a result of such examination, treated. Section 2(4) of the Age of Legal Capacity (Scotland) Act 1991 ('the 1991 Act') provides that a child judged to have sufficient maturity may consent to a medical procedure. Section 90 of the 1995 Act provides that none of the foregoing provisions are to be read as prejudicing the rights conferred upon the child by s. 2(4) and expressly provides that in certain specified situations, for example where a child is held under a warrant granted by a children's hearing,[28] the mature child may refuse treatment. Nowhere does the Act provide expressly that a child of appropriate maturity may refuse to comply with a direction under a CPO or a CAO. It has been said: 'Capacity to consent to medical treatment necessarily includes capacity to refuse consent.'[29] This is not self-evident. The matter has yet to be determined by the Scottish courts. Wilkinson & Norrie,[30] writing in 1993, suggest that 'the express rejection of the welfare principle by the drafters of the 1991 Act encourages the view that in an application to the court to resolve a dispute between the parent and the child, the welfare principle in section 3(2) of the 1986 Act [quoted above] is not determinative.' Section 3(2) has been repealed by the 1995 Act[31] but the provisions of s. 11(7) of the 1995 Act, referred to above, are in substantially the same terms. In *Re W (a minor) (medical treatment)*[32] the Master of the Rolls, Lord Donaldson, regarded the parallel provisions of s 8 of the Family Law Reform Act 1969 as not giving the mature child a veto on medical treatment but rather as providing 'the legal 'flak jacket' which protects the doctor from claims by the litigious whether he acquires it from his patient, who may be a minor over the age of 16 or a 'Gillick competent' child under that age, or from another person having parental responsibilities which include a right to consent to treatment of the minor'. Wilkinson & Norrie[33] describe Lord Donaldson's approach as having 'a certain cogency' and it might well find support in the Scottish courts.

Intimation of the proceedings before the Sheriff in relation to CPOs, CAOs and EOs must be made to the children's reporter who will consider whether or not the child should be introduced into the children's hearings system.

The children's hearings system

Since 1971 children thought to be in need of compulsory care or protection and the great majority of allegedly offending children have been dealt with by the children's hearings system, originally enacted by the Social Work (Scotland) Act 1968 and now re-enacted with some significant but not fundamental changes by the 1995 Act. Each local authority area must identify persons, not specially qualified but having an interest in and facility for understanding and serving, the needs of children. After training under the auspices of the Scottish universities and interview by the Children's Panel Advisory Committee the successful aspirants are appointed to the Children's Panel of the local authority area concerned. From the persons on this Panel are drawn the individuals who are to make up the tribunal of three persons, in which each sex must be represented, known as a children's hearing. Panel members are appointed for a specified period, generally five years. They may be removed from office by the Secretary of State but only with the consent of the Lord President of the Court of Session.[34]

Children may be referred to a children's hearing only at the instance of the children's reporter. The reporters operate under the centrally administered Scottish Children's Reporter Administration whose chief executive is the Principal Reporter. A reporter who has practised for at least a year may, even if not a solicitor or advocate, appear before the Sheriff in procedures under the Act. The Secretary of State for Scotland has the statutory power, not so far exercised, to prescribe qualifications for the children's reporter. More than half the reporters have legal qualifications. Some have social work qualifications. Some have administrative qualifications and experience. Some have more than one or all of the foregoing characteristics.

Local authorities and others may refer a child to the children's reporter who must decide (a) whether on the evidence one or more of the 12 conditions of referral set out in s. 52(2) of the Act exists in relation to the child and, if so, (b) whether or not it is in the interests of the child to be brought to a hearing with a view to the imposition of compulsory measures of supervision. The 12 conditions of referral include the familiar concepts of 'beyond control', unnecessary suffering caused by lack of parental care, sexual and other abuse of a child, truanting, and offence by a child. Where grounds of referral have been stated then there are provisions enabling a hearing to detain a child for periods not exceeding 66 days, with a reserve power in the Sheriff to extend this period. The hearing and the Sheriff must be satisfied that such detention is in the interests of the welfare of the child. The hearing's decision to grant warrant for such detention is subject to expedited appeal to the Sheriff.

When a hearing takes place the *chairman* (even the 1995 Act retains this term!) of the hearing must explain the grounds of referral to the child and parents. If the child is able to understand the explanation and accepts that the ground of referral applies to him/her *and* if the parent(s) or guardian(s) accept the grounds of referral then the hearing is entitled to proceed to consider the child's case by examining the information provided to it by the local authority and discussing the case with the child, the child's representative and/or safeguarder (see below) if any, parents, social worker and reporter. If the hearing members think it necessary the hearing may be continued for further reports. At the end of their deliberations the hearing may (unless they think no action is required, in which event they will discharge the referral) if they consider that compulsory measures of supervision are required, impose a supervision requirement subject to such conditions, residential or otherwise, as they consider appropriate. Conditions may include conditions as to medical examination and treatment but the Act specifically provides that where a child has the capacity to consent under s. 2(4) of the Age of Legal Capacity (Scotland) Act 1991 then such examination and treatment shall only be carried out if the child consents.[35] There are provisions for review of the hearing's decision as to how to deal with the case after specified periods of time. Such reviews may be called for by the local authority and by or on behalf of the child and/or parents. The hearing itself may fix a review hearing. The hearing must give reasons in writing for the decision and their decision is subject to appeal to the Sheriff at the instance of the child and/or the parents. The hearing's determination of the case is subject to appeal to the Sheriff at the instance of the child, the safeguarder, and the parent(s) but not at the instance of the children's reporter.

The right of a hearing to deal with a child's case is dependent on the grounds of referral being admitted by the child and parents or, if not so agreed, by a decision of the Sheriff. If there is no agreement, or if the child does not understand the explanation of the grounds, the hearing, unless minded to discharge the referral, must direct the children's reporter to make application to the Sheriff for a determination as to whether or not the grounds are established. Within 28 days of an application being made to the Sheriff there must commence a hearing before the Sheriff at which the reporter is entitled to lead evidence - such a hearing may be adjourned to a later date if parties require more time to prepare.

At this hearing - referred to as a 'proof' - before the Sheriff, the reporter leads evidence in support of the grounds of referral. Evidence in rebuttal may be led by or on behalf of the child and parent(s). Witnesses are subject to cross-examination. The proceedings are in chambers and the Sheriff does not wear wig and gown. It has been said of the hearings procedures generally that they are non-adversarial and in a leading case[36] Lord President Emslie said: 'To such proceedings accordingly, although the basic rules of evidence must be observed in the application before the Sheriff the ordinary codes of civil and criminal procedure do not apply.' Nevertheless at the stage of the proof the principles of due process must be observed and the children's reporter must ensure that all the necessary evidence is laid before the Sheriff to prove the existence of the condition of referral concerned.[37]

In any ground of referral other than a ground based upon an offence by the child the Sheriff has to be satisfied on the balance of probabilities - even where a serious offence against a named person is alleged.[38] In a case based upon an offence by a child the criminal standard of proof - proof beyond reasonable doubt - must be applied. It is the practice of some Sheriffs to state to the child and parents in ordinary language that the purpose of the proof is to ensure that the law is observed and that although the proceedings are comparatively informal the child's rights will be observed as scrupulously as would the rights of an adult in an adult court. It is open to child and parent when appearing before the Sheriff to change their position from that adopted at the hearing in relation to admitting or not the grounds of referral. If child and parents agree the grounds of referral before the Sheriff then the Sheriff has a discretion to dispense with the hearing of evidence and to hold the grounds of referral established on the basis of the admission(s).

After hearing the evidence the Sheriff must hear from parties or their representatives and decide whether or not the grounds of referral have been proved to the appropriate standard. If the Sheriff decides that the grounds have been so proved, or if the Sheriff, on admission of grounds, exercises his/her discretion to hold grounds established without evidence, then the Sheriff directs the reporter to take the case back to a hearing for disposal. If the Sheriff is not satisfied to the appropriate standard that the grounds of referral have been proved then the s/he dismisses the application and discharges the referral, thus removing the child from the system and cancelling any order which may have been made for the interim detention of the child.

The decision of the Sheriff after proof is appealable on point of law by the child, safeguarder (see below) on behalf of the child, the parent(s) and by the children's reporter. The appeal may be, in the choice of the appellant, to the Sheriff Principal or to the Court of Session. The decision of the Sheriff Principal may, provided that she grants leave, be appealed to the Court of Session. A decision of a Sheriff against his/her decision in an appeal against a decision of a hearing as to how to deal with a child is also subject to appeal on point of law to the Sheriff Principal and the Court of Session in like manner. There is no appeal to the House of Lords.

Representation of children: Listening to the child

In cases before the ordinary Sheriff Court parties may be represented by counsel or by a solicitor. In the Court of Session parties may be represented by an advocate or by a solicitor-advocate, that is a solicitor who has acquired right of audience in the Court of Session. A child may be, but infrequently is, a party to such an action. Where the child is a party, free Legal Aid is generally available.

In making decisions affecting children the courts are generally bound to ascertain so far as practicable if the child, allowing for age and maturity, wishes to express a view and, if so, to give him/her the opportunity to express that view and to take account of it.[39] A child of 12 and over is presumed to be able to express a view.[40] Where an action involving a child is brought before the court for the first time the Sheriff must consider whether it appears from the pleadings that the child should have the action intimated to him/her. The Sheriff may dispense with intimation and will generally so dispense if the child is under 10.

Where intimation is served on the child a Form (which tells the child in as simple language as the statutory draftsman has been able to manage) is sent to the child. It asks him/her if s/he wishes to express a view and indicates the ways whereby such a view may be expressed. It tells the child that s/he may wish to get help from the Scottish Child Law Centre, the name and address and phone number of which are supplied.

A child's views may be expressed in one or more of various modes: by the child stating his/her views on the Form or in a separate letter, by the child getting a friend to come to court, by the child coming to court and speaking directly to the Sheriff or by the court appointing a curator ad litem - generally a local solicitor who is known by the court to have expertise in children's law - who may make a verbal or, more frequently a written, report.

In the proceedings before the Sheriff in relation to children's hearings cases, children are generally represented by solicitors or counsel and free Legal Aid is almost always available.

The views of the child must be taken account of by the hearing in so far as the child's age and maturity, in the opinion of the hearing, allows. In hearings cases the hearing must at the outset consider appointing a safeguarder. Safeguarders are persons drawn from a list of persons appointed under statutory authority by the local authority to safeguard the interests of children in hearings proceedings before the hearings and before the Sheriff. There is at present no prescribed qualification to be a safeguarder but in practice they are persons with legal, academic, social work or administrative experience in the field of children's welfare. In most applications to the Sheriff, including applications to recall or vary a CPO, applications to hear evidence in a disputed referral, and in appeals to the Sheriff, the Sheriff must consider appointing a safeguarder under the 1995 Act. The Sheriff may also use his/her powers at common law to appoint a curator ad litem. I consider that the curator ad litem is often an ideal medium for delivering to the court the views of the child. Moreover the intervention of the curator, who is seen by the family as independent of 'the system' will often have the result of 'settling' the case with consequent avoidance of unnecessary acrimony for the parties and trauma for the child, not to mention saving of expense.

The views of the child will not often be relevant for the Sheriff at the stage of considering evidence in respect of a disputed referral but they will often be relevant where the Sheriff is considering whether or not to recall or review a CPO or in an appeal by the child or parent against the disposal by a hearing. The Sheriff, but not the hearing, has the power to obtain 'confidential' views from the child which the Sheriff may order not to be disclosed to parties. The following paragraphs set this out in more detail.

'Confidential' views of the child to the Sheriff

The Sheriff in family proceedings and the Sheriff (but not the children's hearing) in children's referral proceedings[41] has the discretion, where the child has expressed a view, to direct that the written record of such views should:

- be sealed in an envelope marked 'Views of the child - confidential';
- be kept in the court process without being recorded in the inventory of process;
- be available to a Sheriff only;
- not be opened by any person other than a Sheriff; and
- not form a borrowable part of the process.

The concept of 'confidential' information is alien to a judge who is habituated to letting all sides know all the relevant information. In England and Wales reports and proceedings under the Children Act of 1989 are, I understand, freely disclosed to parties and legal representatives.[42] In *B v B (Minors) (Interviews and Listing Arrangements)*[43] Wall J, delivering the judgment of the Court of Appeal, stated:

> I entirely accept that it is impossible to give an unconditional promise to a child that everything the child says will be treated as confidential to the child and the judge. The reason why such a promise should not be given is self-evident: it is because it cannot be kept without the risk being run that the overall judicial inquiry would be vitiated.

However in the field of adoption law, the rules provide that any report made to the court by a guardian ad litem shall be confidential,[44] and in *In re D (Adoption Reports: Confidentiality)*[45] the House of Lords, while holding that there was a strong presumption in favour of disclosure, recognised that

> non-disclosure should be the exception and not the rule. The court should be rigorous in its examination of the risk and gravity of the feared harm to the child, and should order non-disclosure only when the case for doing so is compelling.[46]

The confidentiality provisions, involving as they do the possibility of keeping the child's views from parties, may however lead to difficulties in the European Court of Human Rights where the principle of 'equality of arms' is respected: in *McMichael v United Kingdom 1995 (20) EHRR 205* that Court held that failure to make all reports in a children's hearings case available to parties contravened Article 6 of the European Convention. As a consequence of the McMichael case the Hearings rules were changed so as to require that all parties receive the reports which hearings have before them.

On the other hand, Article 12 of the UN Convention on the Rights of the Child provides:

1. *States Parties shall assure to the child who is capable of forming his or her own view the right to express those views freely [emphasis supplied] in all matters affecting the child, the views of the child being given due weight in accordance with the age and maturity of the child.*
2. *For this purpose, the child shall in particular be provided the opportunity to be heard in any judicial and administrative proceedings affecting the child, either directly, or through a representative or an appropriate body, in a manner consistent with the procedural rules of national law.*

How, it may be asked, can a child express his or her views *freely* if s/he knows these views will in ten minutes be passed on to an abusing carer?

There are obvious practical limitations to the concept of the views of the child being kept secret: little difficulty may arise if these views are consistent with other evidence, but where these views are in conflict with most of the other information but regarded as pivotal by the Sheriff it will not be too difficult for the adult whose views the child has not favoured to draw his/her own conclusions. Nevertheless the 'confidentiality' provisions are there and it is my view that it is appropriate for the Sheriff who sees a child in order to obtain his or her views to advise the child of this provision and also to mention the practical limitation alluded to. There may be difficulties which have to be resolved having regard to the concept of equality of arms and the principles of natural justice. In Scotland a very robust view has been taken to upholding the interests of the child. In two cases[47] Lord Justice-Clerk Ross and Lord President Hope respectively approved the proposition that in child care cases: 'The principles of natural justice must yield to the best interests of the child'. Given that the rules, made under statutory authority, expressly provide for the possible non-disclosure of the child's views, it may be that Scottish courts, differing in emphasis from the approach of the House of Lords in *In re D*, would countenance non-disclosure not only 'when the case for doing so is compelling' but also in situations where, on the balance of probabilities, disclosure would present significant danger to the child.

Notes

1. For a comprehensive survey of the substantive and procedural laws of Scotland see *The Stair Memorial Encyclopaedia of the Laws of Scotland* (1987-1997), Butterworths/Law Society of
Scotland, Edinburgh. For a comprehensive study of Scots family law see the continuously up-dated
Scottish Family Law Service (1995-1998), Butterworths, Edinburgh. For family law generally see J M Thomson, *Family Law in Scotland* (3rd ed, 1996), Butterworths, Edinburgh. The standard modern textbook is A B Wilkinson and K McK Norrie, *The Law Relating to Parent and Child in Scotland* (1993), W Green/Sweet & Maxwell, Edinburgh. For the law and practice affecting Children's Hearings see B Kearney, *Children's Hearings and the Sheriff Court* (1987), Butterworths/The Law Society of Scotland, Edinburgh, K McK Norrie, *Children (Scotland) Act 1995* (1995), W Green/Sweet & Maxwell, Edinburgh, and K McK Norrie *Children's Hearings in Scotland* (1997), W Green/Sweet & Maxwell, Edinburgh. For a survey including contributions from a wide range of disciplines see A Lockyer and F H Stone, *Juvenile Justice in Scotland: Twenty-five years of the welfare approach* (1998), T & T Clark, Edinburgh.
2. The reports of the Court of Session were formerly cited by reference to the year of reporting and the initial of the reporter, e.g. 'D' for 'Dunlop'; nowadays they are contained in the 'Session Cases' (SC). The other principal contemporary reports are the *Scots Law Times* (SLT), the *Scottish Civil Law Reports* (SCLR) and the *Scottish Criminal Case Reports* (SCCR). The practice rules governing the courts in Scotland are promulgated under the authority of the Lord President of the Court of Session as 'Acts of Sederunt'.

3. *Institutions* I, v, 1.

4. *The Institutes of the Law of Scotland*, I, vi, 53.

5. (1860) 22 D 1198.

6. *Patria potestas*: the name given to that power which, under Roman Law, a father had over all the members of his family.

7. [1986] AC 112. 1985 3 All ER 402, [1986] 1 FLR 224, HL.

8. The writer does not favour the description of this principle as 'the minimum intervention principle' because the statute merely enacts that the order proposed should be preferable to no order at all: this does not entail that the proposed order should be 'minimal' compared with any other order. The writer respectfully disagrees with the discussion by Professor Norrie in *Norrie* (1995) p 35, commentary on Act s 11(7).

9. Children Act 1989 s 1.

10. Local Government etc (Scotland) Act 1994.

11. In *Re W (a minor) (medical treatment)* [1992] 4 All ER 627, the Master of the Rolls, Lord Donaldson, observes at 637f: 'There is ample authority for the proposition that the inherent powers of the court under its *parens patriae* jurisdiction are theoretically limitless and that they extend beyond the powers of a natural parent'.

12. [1995] 2 FLR 276 HL.

13. Cf Lilian Edwards *Suing Local Authorities for Failure in Statutory Duty: Orkney reconsidered after X v Bedfordshire* (1996) 1 Edinburgh Law Review 115.

14. Act s 17.

15. Acts 71.

16. S.I. 1996 No 3262 (S.252).

17. Ibid reg 3(1).

18. *Scotland's Children - The Children (Scotland) Act 1995 Regulations and Guidance* (1997), The Stationery Office, Edinburgh. (ISBN: 0 7840 5821 4; 0 7480 5822 2; 0 7480 5823 0; and 0 7480 5845 1.)

19. Op cit vol 2 p 2.

20. Act s 53; Children's Hearings (Scotland) Rules 1996 ('Hearings Rules') r 24.

21. Ordinary Cause Rules r 33.22A (introduced by the Act of Sederunt (Family Proceedings in the Sheriff Court) 1996 (S.I. 1996/2167).

22. *Hartnett v Hartnett* 1997 SCLR 525

23. *Morgan v Morgan* 1998 SCLR 681.

24. *The Report of the Inquiry into the Removal of Children from Orkney in February 1991*, HMSO,

Edinburgh 27 October 1992.

25. op cit para 16.16.

26. Ibid para 15.51.

27. Act s 51.

28. Act s 66(4)(a).

29. Norrie (1995) 187, cf Norrie (1997) 167.

30 Wilkinson & Norrie (1993) p 186

31. Children (Scotland) Act 1995 Sched 5.

32. [1992] 4 All ER 627 at 635c.

33. Wilkinson & Norrie (1993) p 185.

34. Tribunals and Inquiries Act 1992 s 7(1)(e) and Sched 1 para 61(a).

35. Act s 90.
36. McGregor v D 1977 SLT 182 at 185.
37. Cf *Ferguson* v F 1992 SCLR 866 where the reporter's failure to establish that a child normally lived in household with a parent was held by the Court of Session to be fatal to the reporter's case based on membership of the same household as a person who had been convicted of child abuse.
38. *Harris v F* 1991 SCLR 124.
39. Act s 16(2), echoing Act s 11(7)(b).
40. Act s 16(2).
41. Act of Sederunt (Child Care and Maintenance Rules) 1997, S.I. 1997 No. 291 (S.19) rule 3.5(4).
42. Family Proceedings Rules 1991 (S.I. 1991 No. 1247 (L.20)) r 4.23(1).
43. [1994] 2 FLR 489 at 496A
44. Adoption Rules 1984 rr 6(11) and 18(7)
45. [1996] AC 593.
46. Per Lord Mustill at 615H.
47. *Kennedy v A* 986 SLT 358 and *O v Rae* SCLR 218, 1993 SLT 570.

4
Links between social deprivation and harm to children

Vic Tuck

What is the nature of links which may exist between social deprivation and harm to children? While there seems to be broad acceptance that poverty and social disadvantage are likely to influence the prevalence of child abuse, in particular physical injury and neglect, relatively little has been written about what the links might look like and how they may operate. In this chapter I shall consider some of the existing evidence of links between social deprivation and harm to children, and then explore the nature of the links. I shall consider the implications for the ways in which we define 'child abuse' and for the services provided for children and families.

Assessing the evidence

The view that child abuse is a classless phenomenon, unrelated to the socioeconomic status of families (Steele, 1975) was challenged by Pelton (1981). In exposing the 'myth of classlessness', he does not argue that poor people in general abuse and neglect their children, the evidence is that relatively few do. Nor does he contend that children are not harmed in more affluent homes. However, he criticises the notion that abuse and neglect are 'classless' in the sense that they are not identifiable with low socioeconomic groups:

> *The lower socioeconomic classes are disproportionately represented among all child abuse and neglect cases known to public agencies to the extent that an overwhelming percentage - indeed the vast majority of the families in the cases live in poverty or near-poverty circumstances.* Pelton, 1981, p.26)

More recent evidence in the U.K., based on large scale studies of families who experience child protection investigations, indicates that 57 per cent of these families lack a wage earner. 54 per cent are in receipt of Income support (Department of Health, 1995). Earlier statistics compiled by the NSPCC paint a similar picture. Figures relating to the periods 1983-87 and 1988-90 indicate that 56 per cent of the families of children appearing on child protection registers were in receipt of supplementary benefit (now Income Support). This figure rises to 77 per cent (1983-87) and 74 per cent (1988-1990) for families where the children were registered by reason of neglect (Creighton and Noyes, 1989; Creighton, 1992). In a discussion of these figures Baldwin and

Spencer (1993), point out that 40 per cent of fathers were found to be unemployed, rising to 48 per cent for neglect cases. This compared with a national unemployment figure for fathers in 1989 of 5 per cent. 64 per cent of mothers were unemployed, again rising sharply in cases of neglect to 74 per cent. Over the period 1983-1990 for which the NSPCC compiled figures, unemployment among fathers with children on registers always remained ahead of the national rate. Where parents were in paid employment these were mainly semi-skilled and unskilled occupations with low pay (Creighton, 1992). Baldwin and Spencer (1993) draw attention to the fact that there were so few parents in social classes I and II over the period 1988-90, that the data for them was amalgamated with social class III(N) to provide a non-manual occupational category.

Other studies have identified 'clustering' of children on child protection registers in deprived areas of cities. In Coventry 25 per cent of the children on the local register lived in one of the most deprived electoral wards. Yet only 12.4 per cent of the children in the city lived in the ward (Baldwin and Carruthers, 1993 & 1998). In Strathclyde 60 per cent of the children on the regional child protection register lived in Glasgow, which has the highest concentration of poverty but only 27 per cent of the region's population. Within the city: 'the three areas of highest poverty accounted for four times as many registered children as the other areas of the city' (Baldwin and Spencer, 1993, p.6). Gillham et al (1998) document connections between male unemployment and high rates of child protection registration. These studies reflect the findings of Garbarino (1981) in the USA and are confirmed by my own research in one metropolitan borough in the Midlands (Tuck, 1995).

The evidence pointing to links between social deprivation and harm to children is strong. However, some caution is needed in its interpretation. This evidence is based upon the application of official definitions of child abuse to individual incidents. But there are problems in the use of these definitions to record incidents of actual or likely harm to children. The 'Working Together' document (Department of Health, 1991) presents child abuse as though it comprises diagnostic categories which are self-evident. Yet as Gelles (1975) has argued, in reality there 'is no objective phenomenon that can be defined as child abuse'. Officially recognised cases are really the products of social labelling and social processes by which the behaviour of the caretaker is labelled as abusive or their children are recognised as being abused. The process used to assign the label of child abuse may mean that certain children and families are 'tagged' as abused and abusers while others may be 'insulated' from the label even if they are engaged in the same behaviour. In a UK study of health professionals diagnosing possible child abuse in hospital accident departments, Dingwall, Eekelaar and Murray (1983), observed that official definitions of abuse and neglect are:

the product of complex processes of identification, confirmation and disposal rather than inherent in a child's presenting condition, and at least in some sense, self-evident. (Dingwall et al, 1983, p.21)

Parton has widened the debate:

Child abuse is not a naturalistic category, nothing is 'naturally' child abuse. It is only child abuse if it has been proscribed in a given society and if the control agencies act in such a way as to enforce the proscription. (Parton, 1985, P.148)

Moreover:

> *It is a product of a particular culture and context and not an absolute unchanging phenomenon.*
> (Corby, 1993, p.39)

Dingwall (1989) has referred to the 'diagnostic inflation' of child abuse whereby definitions of harm have been expanded to embrace physical injury, neglect, emotional abuse and sexual abuse. 'Organised abuse' can be seen as a further example of this diagnostic inflation. So child abuse is a social construction and for Gelles (1979) it is not so much a diagnostic category as a political description designed to call attention to the issue. And what of those forms of harm which may be excluded from these categories - the effect on many children of living in poverty in the UK, for example, which has serious consequences for their health, safety and development? Corby (1993) has argued that we should always seek to understand who is doing the defining and what their aims and intentions are.

The question of whether and why the poor are disproportionately represented in official statistics has to be addressed. Dingwall et al (1983) argue that there is a strong social class component in the processes by which some children and families may be 'tagged' as abused and abusers while others are 'insulated' from the label. They conclude from their study of health professionals that the processes by which decisions are made to intervene are based on political judgements about the social condition and moral character of the parents and children under suspicion, and these processes tend to subject poorer people to compulsory intervention while filtering out those from the more 'respectable' strata of society:

> *This effect is achieved by tests which are not class-biased in any simple or overt sense but which different social groups are differentially able to meet. (Dingwall et al., 1983, p.101-2)*

Differential rates of identification and referral between professionals may have some bearing upon the tendency of cases to 'cluster' in particular neighbourhoods. Extending the arguments of Dingwall et al., those professionals operating in more affluent local areas might encounter a higher level of resistance to agency interventions and more sophisticated defences to allegations of abuse from articulate parents. There might therefore be more reluctance to identify and report possible abuse. By contrast, professionals who are more used to following up concerns about children and who as a consequence are more practised in the skills of identification and investigation are likely to see their work result in higher numbers of referrals and registrations: a catch 22 situation in areas where there is a high level of surveillance.

It may be argued that the effect of these processes is bias in the social class distribution of reported cases and does not reflect the real distribution of the problem, since poor families are disproportionately represented among cases known to social agencies. The implication is that there are proportionately more *unreported* cases among the more affluent classes than among the poorer social classes. Some would argue that the problem is more or less proportionately distributed among all classes.

Garbarino and Crouter (1978) and Pelton (1981) have contested these arguments. Pelton accepts that the lives of poor people are more open to inspection by social agencies and that 'middle' and 'upper' class people are less likely to turn to these agencies when help is needed. However, while an increased level of public awareness has led to a rise in the number of reported cases of abuse and neglect in all social groups, the proportions from the different social classes have altered very little. The NSPCC statistics bear this out. While there was a marked increase in the overall levels of registrations in all categories between 1975 and 1990, the social class distribution of referrals remained stable (Creighton, 1992).

Secondly, the public scrutiny argument does not explain why child abuse and neglect are related to degrees of poverty even within the lower social classes, so that the highest incidence of the problem occurs within families experiencing the most extreme poverty: 'the abusing and neglecting families are the poorest of the poor' (Pelton, 1981, p. 28).

Thirdly, even among the reported cases the most severe injuries have occurred in the poorest families. In his survey Gil (1970) reported that injuries were more likely to be fatal or serious amongst the poorest families.

This still has to be weighed against the possibility that the poorer the family the greater the degree of surveillance.

Garbarino and Crouter (1978) have set out strong empirical evidence which refutes the argument that greater surveillance of the poor has a distorting effect on child abuse statistics. In studies of the reporting patterns of abuse and other indicators of quality of life, they demonstrate that the *source* of the reports on child abuse varies with other ecological characteristics in the locality. Areas experiencing economic stress are areas where 'distant sources' - hospitals, schools, social agencies and law enforcement groups - are more likely to report child abuse. Conversely, in higher income areas reporting is more likely to be carried out by 'close sources' such as family members, neighbours and friends.

Their studies revealed a strong positive correlation between indicators of low income, stress on mothers and overall child abuse with the percentage of cases reported by distant sources. They found a strong positive relationship existed between higher income and the likelihood of child abuse being reported by close sources.

Garbarino and Crouter argue that if reporting by distant sources is biased along socioeconomic lines then it presumably discriminates against less affluent groups and areas. However, their studies revealed that workers in law enforcement offices and child protection services held a widespread belief that people in low income areas were less likely to report on their neighbours and families (close sources). They accounted for this as follows:

> ... it appears that community standards used in defining inadequate and unacceptable child care are lower in the most socio-economically distressed areas. Put more directly (and bluntly), in the informed opinion of fieldworkers, patterns that would be judged abusive or neglectful in more affluent areas are likely to be accepted (with resignation perhaps) in less affluent areas. (Garbarino and Crouter, 1978, p.611)

It may also be that a perception that children living in poor families and poor communities are more likely to be taken into public care if concerns are expressed about them, acts as a deterrent to reporting by close sources in such areas.

Garbarino and Crouter observed that if there is over reporting by institutional sources in low income areas, there is likely to be under reporting by non-institutional sources: 'The net effect, we hypothesised, was that the overall validity of the report data was good' (ibid.). There are therefore strong arguments to support the view that the social class distribution of reported cases may reflect the real distribution of the problem.

Child sexual abuse

A further issue needs to be considered when assessing possible links between harm to children and social deprivation. This concerns the forms of child abuse which are being described. There seems to be some acceptance that links may exist between physical abuse and neglect and social deprivation. However this relationship is more contentious and more difficult to accept with regard to child sexual abuse.

There are arguments that sexual abuse is more appropriately seen as the result of the use and abuse of male power over women and children (Driver and Droisen, 1989). The roots of the problem lie within male sexuality, and the offending behaviour of male perpetrators of sexual abuse follows patterns and processes which are not easily attributable to the effects of poverty and deprivation. Moreover, to argue this might allow the perpetrator to shift responsibility for his behaviour away from himself and confirm him in his offending cycles.

While this is a powerful and credible analysis, it needs to be acknowledged that the NSPCC statistics for the period 1983-87 showed strong similarities in the socioeconomic circumstances of children who were physically abused and those who were sexually abused. 51 per cent of families registered by reason of child sexual abuse were in receipt of supplementary benefits, and 46 per cent in the period 1988-90 received income support. For cases involving both physical and sexual abuse this rises to 63 per cent. Sedlak (1993) found the same correlations between poverty and sexual abuse as poverty and physical abuse. In my own study, which set out primarily to investigate links between physical harm and neglect to children and social deprivation, I found similar correlations between all forms of abuse (Tuck, 1995). Cases involving combinations of physical and sexual abuse, all of which were characterised by particularly violent and disturbing domestic circumstances, were to be found only in the most severely socially disadvantaged areas in the metropolitan borough in which the study was conducted: neighbourhoods with the poorest housing, the highest rates of unemployment, the highest concentrations of low income families and the poorest social amenities. One possible example of linkage could be the tendency of male sex offenders to target vulnerable women in order to secure access to children. Socially deprived neighbourhoods are characterised by relatively large numbers of lone parents, usually mothers, living on low incomes and coping with a range of material adversities. Some may be socially isolated. The likelihood that only certain types of cases - where there are major injuries or overtly inappropriate behaviours on the part of the child, associated with sexual abuse - will come to light in childhood also needs exploration.

The brutalising effects of poverty and social deprivation on human behaviour and their role in reinforcing typical male attitudes to power and sexuality may therefore need to be given far grater attention in trying to understand child sexual abuse. The complex interrelationship between commonly accepted 'norms' of male behaviour, male sexuality, often defined in popular culture in violent, aggressive and exploitative terms; the personal characteristics of offenders, their targeting of vulnerable families; local levels of sexual and violent assault; all need further scrutiny. Links between social deprivation and all forms of harm need exploration.

This discussion does not challenge the fact that accounts of survivors of child sexual abuse show that it is present in all socioeconomic groups. In the same way, although the evidence points to its concentration in socially disadvantaged families, physical abuse is by no means unknown in more affluent families. What may make the situation even more complex with regard to child sexual abuse is a greater capacity to 'mask' the problem through the silencing of children by perpetrators, than may be possible in cases of physical injury and neglect.

Links between deprivation and other child care problems

There is also evidence that poverty is linked to more general manifestations of child care problems,. As part of a controlled study of family support in local areas, Gibbons (1990) reports significant differences in the material circumstances of families referred to the social services for child care problems when compared with a community sample. A highly significant difference was noted between families referred to social services and the community sample families when measured against a 'disadvantage index' based on the percentage of families with large numbers of children, overcrowding, temporary housing, lack of basic amenities and consumer goods, and without a wage earner.

Bebbington & Miles (1989) show how children from the most deprived circumstances have a far greater chance of coming into public care than those from more advantaged homes. As well as the disadvantage associated with individual circumstances, they claim that living in a poor neighbourhood has an independent effect on the probability of entry into care. Children from poorer families are also more likely to experience accidents (Roberts et al, 1995). The Black Report claimed: 'Households in occupational classes IV and V simply lack the means to provide their children with as high a level of protection as that which is found in the average middle class home.' (Townsend and Davidson, 1982, P. 127-128).

Assessing the evidence

There is strong evidence to suggest that a link does exist between social deprivation, harm to children and more general child care problems. However there are many factors to consider. Wolfe (1993) identifies the relationship between the parent's abilities and resources and the child's emerging behavioural and emotional characteristics as key factors in child maltreatment. Parents' own experiences of abuse, low educational attainment, criminality of male partners, single parenting and other variables are also claimed as significant : an array which makes it difficult to discern causative pathways (Baldwin & Spencer, 1993).

Child abuse, as Parton (1985) argues, is best understood as arising from the operation of 'multiple interacting factors'. Yet as he and Sedlak (1993) contend, individual factors are likely to be strongly and consistently correlated with material deprivation. It is the nature and impact of this correlation which needs to be subjected to greater scrutiny.

Social deprivation blocks the fulfilment of the basic needs of children

In a study of the causes and effects of transmitted deprivation Madge (1983) poses the question: 'What are the needs of children which if not met, mean that families are at risk?' Referring to Piachaud (1981) she defines the physical needs of children. They require food, clothing, footwear, household provisions, heating, lighting, toys and presents, pocket money, expenses connected with schooling, entertainment and holidays. To meet these needs families need adequate levels of income. The physical well-being of children also depends upon good quality housing: crowded and insanitary housing can affect sleep, health and school performance (Brown and Madge 1982, Blackburn, 1991, Graham, 1993).

Children have emotional needs which must be fulfilled to promote their well-being and development. Emotional security and good relationships within the family are likely to be related to material as well as emotional factors. Adler & Wozniak (1981) demonstrate a link between poverty, debt and separation. It has already been shown that poor children are most likely to enter public care.

Children have social and intellectual needs and require stimulation and opportunities to develop linguistic skills. They need to be able to check out and expand their knowledge at home and at school. Yet low family income is associated with the risk of under achievement at school (Mortimer & Blackstone, 1982).

In a review of models of the processes and causes of deficits in child health, Blaxter (1993) emphasises that studies undertaken in the programme of research into transmitted deprivation in the 1970s, show that the inadequacy of income maintenance systems, poor housing and restricted opportunities and life choices have major implications for families.

Recent analysis of the material from the National Child Development Study confirms the importance of the social context of family life as a determinant of well-being (Buchanan & Ten Brinke, 1997).

A survey commissioned by the National Children's Bureau (Kumar, 1993) reveals that the number of children living in families with incomes below 50 per cent of the average increased from 1.4 million to 3.9 million between 1979 and 1991. This is a rise from 10 per cent to over 30 per cent of the child population, with another 10 per cent living on the margins of poverty. The gap between rich and poor families with children has grown. The average income of the bottom 20 per cent of married couples with children fell by 14 per cent in the same period while that of the top 20 per cent increased by 40 per cent. As Bradshaw in a foreword to the NCB survey observes: 'Britain has become a sharply more unequal society and the most common victims of this trend have been children' (Kumar, 1993, p.xxi).

These trends are associated with the growth of unemployment, particularly long term unemployment, low pay, demographic changes and government policies which increased indirect taxation, which has a disproportionate impact on poorer families. The level of benefits and services for children fell.

Newell (1991) claims that the UK is in breach of the UN Convention on the Rights of the Child. He shows how during this period homelessness has increased, with 79 per cent of homeless households in priority need in 1988 having dependent children or being pregnant women. Studies of families receiving benefits have found gross deficiencies in diet; unemployed parents and single parent households have been shown to be unable to maintain minimum necessary stocks of clothing (Bradshaw & Morgan, 1987, NCH Factfile 1998).

In contemporary Britain a third of the child population is by Madge's definition 'at risk' because their families are being denied the resources to practice effective child-rearing. The cluster of adversities identified by Wedge and Essen (1982) is confirmed in Blaxter's review (1993). These children live in households facing housing, familial and income difficulties. Their parents are more likely to be off work through sickness, unemployed or working in unskilled and poorly paid jobs or experiencing chronic ill health.

Yet even this does not fully convey the seriousness of the situation. Blaxter (1993) describes how studies of deprivation based upon longitudinal cohorts show that families continually fall in and out of different categories of disadvantage. The consequence of this is that children identified as disadvantaged at any one age represent only a small proportion of all the children who experience multiple disadvantage at some stage in childhood (Wedge and Essen, 1982). Much larger numbers of children are therefore likely to have experienced disadvantage at a significant period of development than is first evident.

Multiple disadvantage at any age may have long-term damaging consequences for the life chances of children. There appears to be continuing developmental delay in many young people even when they are no longer disadvantaged. However, for many, the adversities may be of a long-lasting duration as families find it impossible to escape the web of deprivation in which they are enmeshed (Coffield, 1980).

The research of Elizabeth Elmer (1977a, 1977b, 1981) provides further evidence of the harm to children caused by poverty and deprivation. The original intention of her research was to compare the development of matched age groups of abused and non-abused children rather than to describe the lives of poor children. However, Elmer discovered that:

> *Contrary to expectation, almost no differences were found between the groups; the entire sample...showed developmental and social problems and appeared depressed, anxious, and fearful. Since the one characteristic common to most of the children was membership in the lower social classes..., conditions associated with poverty appeared to be as powerful an influence on these children's development as child abuse. (Elmer, 1981, p.188).*

She admits to finding this an unsettling idea because the conventional wisdom has it that parental abuse is the most disastrous event possible in a child's life. However, she observes that whereas child abuse tends to be episodic, punctuated even by periods of relative calm and affection, the conditions associated with 'living poor' are monotonously repetitive and frequent, with a cumulatively more destructive impact. Elmer makes clear that she does not question the malignant effect of child abuse and neglect: 'What is questioned is the singular intense focus on abuse without regard for the matrix in which it flourishes' (Elmer, 1981, p.212).

Social deprivation can force parents into harmful patterns of parenting

To be 'living poor ' is an experience of 'doing without' - ' that touches every part of life and family health care.' (Blackburn, 1991, p.12). Studies of parenting in poverty agree that this experience affects the personality, attitudes and behaviour of those involved. Poverty can generate demoralisation, apathy, depression and a sense of powerlessness and helplessness: 'the psychological consequences of chronic anxiety and despair are hardly conducive to happy child-rearing.' (Brown and Madge, 1982, P. 16).

In a study of parents and children living in the inner city, Wilson and Herbert (1978) demonstrate how poverty forces parents into styles of parenting with which they themselves are not happy, and how they adapt to failure by lowering their expectations. Parton (1985) emphasises a self-perpetuating relationship between poor social environment and personal attributes which reinforce each other.

In accounting for why parents might care for children in ways with which they themselves are dissatisfied, Wilson and Herbert postulate an 'adaptational model' of society similar to that proposed by Gans (1968). This explains the effect of deprivation and chronic stress partly in terms of adaptations of behaviour and norms. Hence the behaviour and lifestyle of socially disadvantaged families is viewed as an adaptation to particular situations of deprivation. The impact of this process of 'adaptive retrenchment' on patterns of parenting and subsequent child development can be severe. Wedge and Essen (1982) argue that the constraints of parenting in poverty can have long term consequences for children; behaviours learnt in order to cope with adversity become very hard to change.

In her review of the research on caring for children's health in poverty, Blackburn (1991) develops these perspectives. She argues that many studies are based on the assumption that health and welfare work with families is about persuading parents to take responsibility for their children's health and welfare, and giving them the skills and knowledge to do so. The basis of such work rests on a further assumption that parents do not necessarily know how to be good parents and need to be taught appropriate parenting skills. The emphasis of health and welfare work is therefore problem oriented and based on interventions that seek to identify deficits in the child care skills and attitudes of parents.

In contrast to this approach, Blackburn cites Mayall's observation (1986, 1990) that it is valuable to distinguish between parents' child care approaches and their child care practices. Studies that look at child care practices will inevitably find differences between social groups. However, Mayall's study of child health care, by focusing on parents' child care approaches and what they wish to achieve found more similarities than differences in *attitudes* to child health care. Mayall suggests that differences in child care practices are more likely to reflect the environments in which parents carry out their child care rather than their attitudes or goals.

Parton sums up the implications of parenting in poverty:

> *Thus the social and economic stress, which is directly related to the structure of inequality, has direct consequences for the well-being of children in poor families. People feel their poverty more when it affects their children and they are invariably more humiliated by their failures when they affect their dependants. Such problems are reinforced by the fact that society has articulated expectations of family life, and poor performance in child care is closely monitored. Poor parents are very aware of this.* (Parton 1985, p.172)

Social deprivation contributes to stress in families

Chamberlin (1988) argues that for children and families, the ability to provide a healthy environment is strongly related to their ability to cope. This in turn relates to the balance between stress and support. It is the accumulation of stresses that tips the balance towards a negative outcome. Current situational strains are likely to be at least as influential as those in the past lives of 'neglectful' parents (Giovannoni and Billingsley, 1970). Taking up these themes, (Schorr, 1988) argues that it requires more than a single risk factor to produce a damaging outcome for children: 'Lasting damage occurs when the elements of a child's environment multiply each other's destructive effects' (Schorr, 1988, P. 280).

As has already been demonstrated, the experience of deprivation is characterised by the presence of multiple disadvantages and clusters of adversity which have a continuing destructive impact over time. The impact of multiple risk factors has been demonstrated empirically by Rutter (1979) and Quinton and Rutter (1976). In studies of children facing chronic adversities they found that psychiatric risk went up sharply when several adversities coexisted. Adverse effects do not just summate but potentiate each other so that their combined effects are greater than the sum of those considered separately. (Rutter, 1981).

Relating this analysis to her observations about families living in poverty, Schorr argues that: 'as family stress, regardless of source, increases, the capacity for nurturing decreases, and the likelihood of abuse and neglect increases' (Schorr, 1988, P. 150).

Rutter provides pointers as to how this process operates. He argues that throughout life it is normal to meet challenges and overcome difficulties. Coping successfully with stress situations can be strengthening:

> *The promotion of resilience does not lie in the avoidance of stress, but rather in encountering stress at a time and in a way that allows self-confidence and social competence to increase through mastery and appropriate responsibility' (Rutter, 1985, p.608).*

However, resistance to stress is relative rather than absolute and the base of resistance is both environmental and constitutional. The degree of resistance will vary over time and according to circumstance. It can therefore be argued that as families move into and remain in deprivation and experience the clusters of adversities associated with this, then the vulnerability of children and parents is increased, as protective factors such as the parent's sense of self-esteem and self-efficacy, are undermined by chronic stress.

Schorr argues that the informal supports from family, friends, institutions and services that could 'buffer' the effects of clusters of risk factors are less likely to be available for the poorest families. Yet all families, particularly those beset by multiple stress, need this support to mobilise coping strategies and adaptive behaviours.

Those parents who injure or neglect their children can, in these terms, be seen to have tipped the wrong way in managing the balance of stress, coping and support. However, in reality the mix of interrelated variables that come into play over time (psychological resources of the parent, contextual stress, developmental outcomes, characteristics of the child) makes it difficult to predict who will 'tip over' and who will not (Chamberlin, 1988).

Such an analysis stands in contrast to the more simplistic use of checklists of the alleged characteristics and personality traits of child abusers and abused children which have been used to try and predict 'high risk' families (cf. Greenland 1987. See Parton 1991, Baldwin & Spencer 1993 for critiques of this checklist approach).

The arguments presented here open up the prospect of a more sophisticated analysis of child abuse and neglect and a more rounded approach to assessment of need and risk. Causal relationships need to be examined in the form of chains and of linked sequences involving several different short and long term effects (Wedge & Essen, 1982; Rutter, 1988). The numerous chains of events at work are likely to be linked in different ways and in different orders in each individual or family (Blaxter, 1993). These chains, sequences and relationships need to be interpreted in relation to the socioeconomic context in which they occur. This analysis has major implications for policy and practice.

Towards a new understanding of links between social deprivation and harm to children

I have attempted to summarise evidence of links between social deprivation and harm to children and have addressed some of the difficulties in interpreting these links. I now want to summarise a framework which may be helpful in developing our understanding of these links.

It may be useful to conceive of social deprivation as representing both a *primary* and a *secondary* source of harm to children. By a primary source of harm I mean that by imposing severe material constraints and environmental hazards on families, social deprivation contributes to the *general prevalence* of harm to children. This is likely to be characterised by two main strands. Firstly, socially disadvantaged families are likely to live in socially and economically impoverished neighbourhoods where they are likely to find it difficult to provide a safe and healthy environment for their children.

Secondly, by creating material, social, interpersonal and intrapersonal stresses and barriers in families, social deprivation can prevent parents from achieving the standards of parenting to which they might aspire and which society expects of them.

In my study of parenting in social disadvantage (Tuck, 1995), I explored the perceptions and experiences of a group of mothers striving to raise their children in a neighbourhood characterised by high scores on indices of social deprivation and high levels of child protection registrations. In looking at issues related to housing, income, access to services and amenities for families, health and education, social support networks, it became apparent that the women encountered a range of hindrances and adversities that have a severe impact on the possibilities open to them as they endeavour to raise their children safely and in good health. Meeting the basic needs of their children is generally achieved in the face of enormous odds. They need to make, on a daily basis, a series of difficult and painful choices about which of their children's needs will and will not be met. It is likely to mean that the needs of the mothers themselves will often go unmet. On top of this, the mothers saw themselves as living in a harsh and unsafe social environment, abandoned and isolated by the wider society which, in the women's eyes, sees them as unfit and inadequate parents. The experiences of these mothers and the scale of the material and social deprivation they face was thrown into even more stark relief when I compared the neighbourhood in which they lived with more affluent parts of the borough in which the study was conducted. On every social and economic indicator, including housing, rates of unemployment, car ownership and take-up of free school meals (these last two are often taken as surrogates for family income) the social inequalities revealed were massive. Families living in different parts of the borough might only be living a few miles apart, but in terms of their day to day experiences and quality of life they might as well be living on different planets. These findings simply reflect in microcosm what more general data tells us about the growth of child and family poverty in the UK, and the widening of inequality over recent 16 years (cf. Kumar, 1993).

The experience of these women also highlighted how deprivation can be a secondary source of harm. By secondary source of harm I mean acts of violence, abuse or neglect, punitive or belittling behaviour, perpetrated by some severely stressed parents against their children. In interaction with many other factors, social deprivation can contribute to high levels of psychosocial stress within families that may lead some parents to physically injure or neglect their children.

It is crucial to stress that while it is possible to differentiate between social deprivation as a primary and secondary source of harm, the latter is inextricably *connected* to the former. The *cumulative* adverse impact on parents and children of having to cope with the many adversities and hindrances associated with social deprivation - living in an impoverished neighbourhood and feeling prevented from providing good standards of child care - can be severely damaging. Adversities and problems may potentiate each other.

As a consequence, some socially disadvantaged parents may experience a downward spiral of stress, inability to cope, helplessness and despair, the psychologically and physically debilitating effects of which could in some situations contribute to harmful behaviours and to the low warmth, high criticism child rearing environments emphasised as harmful in recent research (DOH 1995).

Thus recognition of the interplay of the three strands - primary, secondary and interactional - associated with harm to children opens up the prospect of developing multi-layered, multi-dimensional models which can help account for child abuse and neglect in terms of deficits in material resources and complex, interacting psychosocial stress factors. These models are able to take account of the importance of the personal characteristics and backgrounds of parents, in particular their ability to cope with stress, and how they have reacted to life experiences. They can take on board the 'meanings' which individuals attribute to these experiences and the actions they take, and the influence these attributions may exert over their behaviour towards their children. By blending insights derived from theories of psychosocial development (Rutter, 1981, 1985, 1988), 'learned helplessness syndrome' (Barbar, 1986), social labelling theory with other perspectives which have sought to explain the nature and experience of 'stress' and in particular how this is influenced by social deprivation, it becomes possible to develop the 'integrative' models of harm to children which (Corby, 1993) has discussed as a useful way of understanding the problem. We can then move to more constructive ways of responding.

New models for understanding harm to children: The implications

One important implication of these models is the challenge they present to official definitions of child abuse as described in the 'Working Together' document (DOH 1991). The definitions of physical injury, neglect, sexual abuse and emotional abuse set out in this document focus attention narrowly upon incidents and behaviours within families and do not encourage a focus upon family experiences in context. Moreover, the limited and individualised nature of these official definitions imply a tolerance of levels and forms of harm to children which may be equally detrimental to the health and development of many more children.

However, an interactional perspective on harm to children which recognises the interconnections of social, interpersonal, situational and material factors, demands that much greater attention is paid to the socioeconomics contexts in which child care takes place. This means greater emphasis should be attached by professionals to 'holistic' assessments of family circumstances and the risks posed by the wider child care environment, as opposed to a narrow focus on the abusive episode alone, as the more recent Assessment Framework emphasises (DoH, 2000).

It means expanding our definitions of child abuse to encompass the day to day realities of life for children and families. David Gil (1975, 1980) has proposed such a definition. He has defined harm to children as arising from:

inflicted gaps or deficits between circumstances of living which would facilitate the optimum development of children, to which they should be entitled, and their actual circumstances, irrespective of the sources or agents of the deficit. (Gil, 1975)

As a consequence:

Any act of commission or omission by individuals, institutions of the whole society, together with the resultant conditions which deprive children of equal rights and liberties, and/or interfere with their optimal development, constitutes by definition, abuse or neglectful acts or conditions. (Gil, 1980)

I would argue that such a definition is consistent with the United Nations Convention on the Rights of the Child to which the UK is signatory. Article 27(1) states: 'States Parties recognise the right of every child to a standard of living adequate for the child's physical, mental, spiritual, moral and social development.'

Gil's definition is also in tune with the description 'harm to children' which I have used throughout this chapter in preference to the more conventional term, child abuse. It reflects a broader concern with the welfare of children.

Acknowledging the links between social deprivation and harm to children, and a subsequent redrawing of definitional boundaries, has implications for the services provided for children and families. It implies a broader set of strategies for the protection of children than those associated with the investigation of individual allegations of abuse, though these must undoubtedly remain in place as part of the armoury of child protection. My study confirms that if families are to raise their children safely and in good health, particularly those living in socially disadvantaged neighbourhoods, then it is necessary for there to be in place comprehensive primary preventive services which provide a range of practical and emotional support. Families also need to have access to good quality housing, adequate incomes and decent amenities. These resources are likely to be most effective in keeping families out of the child protection system, a priority emerging from the findings of studies of this system commissioned by the government (Department of Health, 1995) and more recent policy emphases on tackling social exclusion. Such strategies are characterised by a population-based approach rather than focusing exclusively on individual families. However, what is likely to be crucial to their implementation is the presence of the necessary professional, corporate and political will. In this chapter I have sought to provide a theoretical and evidential base which can underpin such strategies.

References

Adler, M. & Wozniak, E. (1981) *The Origins and Consequences of Default*. Edinburgh University, Dept. of Social Administration.

Baldwin, N. & Curruthers, L. (1993) *Henley Safe Children Project Interim Report*. Coventry: NSPCC/University of Warwick.

Baldwin, N. & Curruthers, L. (1998) *Developing Neighbourhood Support and Child Protection Strategies*. Aldershot: Ashgate.

Baldwin, N. & Spencer, N. (1993) 'Deprivation and child abuse - implications for strategic planning in children's services', *Children and Society*. 7, 4, 277 - 296.

Barbar, J.C. (1986) 'The promise and the pitfalls of learned helplessness theory for social work practice. *British Journal of Social Work*, 16, 570-577.

Bebbington, A & Miles, J (1989) 'The background of children who enter local authority care'. *The British Journal of Social Work*, 19,5, 349-368.

Blackburn, C. (1991) *Poverty and Health: Working with Families.* Buckingham: Open University Press.

Blaxter, M.C. (1990) *Health and Lifestyles.* London. Routledge.

Blaxter, M.C. (1993) 'Continuities of Disadvantage' in Waterstone, T. (ed) *Perspectives in Social Disadvantage and Child Health.* Andover: Intercept Ltd.

Bradshaw, J. & Morgan, J. (1987) *Budgeting on Benefit.* Family Policy Studies Centre.

Brown, M. & Madge, N. (1982) *Despite the Welfare State,* London: Heinemann Educational.

Buchanan, A; Ten Brinke, J.A. (1997) *What Happened When They Were Grown Up? outcomes from parenting experience.* York: Rowntree Foundation.

Chamberlin, R.W. (ed) (1988) *Beyond Individual Risk Assessment: Community Wide Approaches to Promoting the Health and Development of Families and Children.* The Edited and Expanded Version of the Proceedings of a Conference held in Hanover, New Hampshire, Nov 1987. The Maternal and Child Health Clearing House, Washington D.C., USA.

Coffield, F (1980) *A Cycle of Deprivation? A Case Study of Four Families.* London: Heinemann Educational Books.

Corby, B. (1993) *Child Abuse: Towards a Knowledge Base.* Buckingham: Open University Press.

Creighton, S. & Noyes, P. (1989) *Child Abuse Trends in England and Wales, 1983-1987.* London: NSPCC

Creighton, S. (1992). *Child Abuse Trends in England and Wales, 1988-1990: and an overview from 1973-1970.* London: NSPCC.

Department of Health, Home Office, Department of Education and Science and Welsh Office (1991) *Working together Under the Children Act 1989:   A guide to arrangements for interagency co-operation for the protection of children from abuse.* London: HMSO.

DoH (1995) *Child Protection: messages from research.* London: HMSO.

DoH (2000) *Framework for the Assessment of Children in Need and their Families.* London: TSO

Dingwall, R., Eekalaar, J. & Murray, T. (1983) *The Protection of Children: State intervention and family life.* Oxford: Blackwell.

Dingwall, R. (1989). 'Some problems about predicting child abuse and neglect' In Stevenson, O. (ed) *Child Abuse: Public Policy and Professional Practice.* Hemel Hempstead: Harvester Wheatsheaf.

Driver, E. & Droisen, E. (eds). (1989) *Child Sexual Abuse: Feminist Perspectives.* London: Macmillan Education.

Elmer, E. (1977a) *Fragile Families, Troubled Children.* University of Pittsburgh Press.

Elmer, E (1977b) 'A Follow-up Study of Traumatised Children'. *Paediatrics,* 359, 273-279.

Elmer, E. (1981) 'Traumatised children, chronic illness and poverty' in Pelton, L. (ed) *The Social Context of Child Abuse and Neglect,* Human Sciences Press.

Gans, H.J. (1968) 'Culture and class in the study of poverty: an approach to anti-poverty research'. In Moynihan, D. (ed) *On Understanding Poverty.* New York: Basic Books.

Garbarino, J. and Crouter, A. (1978) 'Defining the community context for parent child relations. The correlates of child maltreatment' *Child Development,* 49, 604-616.

Garbarino, J. (1981) 'An ecological approach to child maltreatment' In Pelton, L. (ed). *The Social Context of Child Abuse and Neglect.* Human Sciences Press.

Gelles, R.J. (1975) 'The social construction of child abuse', *American Journal of Orthopsychiatry* 363-371.

Gelles, R.J.K. (1979) *Family Violence.* Sage.

Gibbons, J., Thorpe, S. & Wilkinson, P. (1990) *Family Support and Prevention: studies in local areas.* London: HMSO

Gil, D.G. (1970) *Violence Against Children.* Harvard University Press.

Gil, D.G. (1975) 'Unravelling child abuse'. *American Journal of Orthopsychiatry*, 453, 346-356.

Gil, D.G. (1980) Foreword to Volpe, R., Breton, M. & Mitton, J. (eds). *The maltreatment of the school-aged child.* Lexington books.

Gillham, B., Tanner, G., Cheyne, B., Freeman, I., Rooney, M. & Lambie, A. (1998) 'Unemployment rates, single parent density and indices of child poverty; their relationship to different categories of child abuse and neglect', *Child Abuse & Neglect*, 22 (2), 79-90.

Giovannoni, J. & Billingsley, A. (1970). 'Child neglect among the poor: a study of parental inadequacy in three ethnic groups'. *Child Welfare*, 49, 196-204.

Graham, H. (1993). *Hardship and Health in Women's Lives.* Hemel Hempstead: Harvester Wheatsheaf.

Greenland, G. (1987). *Preventing Child Abuse and Neglect Deaths: an international study of deaths due to child abuse and neglect.* London: Tavistock.

Kumar, V. (1993) *Poverty and Inequality in the UK: The Effects on Children.* London National Children's Bureau.

Madge, N (ed) (1983) *Families at Risk.* London: Heinemann Educational Books.

Mayall, B. (1986). *Keeping Children Healthy.* London: Allen & Unwin.

Mayall, B & Foster, M.C. (1990) *Child Health Care: Living with Children, Working for Childen.* Oxford: Heinemann Nursing.

Mortimer, J. & Blackstone, T. (1982) *Studies in Deprivation and Disadvantage - 4.* London: Heinemann Educational.

NCH Action for Children: (1998) *NCH Factfile.* London.

Newell, P. (1991). *The U.N. Convention and Children's Rights in the U.K.* London: National Children's Bureau.

Parton, N. (1985) *The Politics of Child Abuse.* London: Macmillan Education.

Pelton, L. (1981) 'The myth of classlessness' In Pelton, L. (ed.) *The Social Context of Child Abuse and Neglect.* Human Sciences Press.

Piachaud, D. (1981). 'Peter Townsend and the Holy Grail' *New Society*, 10.9.81.

Quinton, D. and Rutter, M. (1976). 'Early hospital admissions and later disturbance of behaviour: an attempted replication of Douglas' findings'. *Developmental Medicine Child Neurology*, 18, 447-459.

Roberts, H., Smith, S.J., Bryce, C. (1995). *Children at Risk: safety as a social value*, Buckingham : OUP.

Rutter, M. (1981) 'Stress, coping and development: some issues and some perspectives. *Journal of Child Psychology and Psychiatry*, 22, 322-356.

Rutter, M. (1985) 'Resilience in the face of adversity: protective factors and resistance to psychiatric disorder.' *British Journal of Psychiatry*, 147, 598-611.

Rutter, M. (1988) *Studies of Psycho-social Risk: The Power of Longitudinal Data.* Cambridge University Press.

Rutter, M. (1979). 'Protective factors in children's responses to stress and disadvantage'. In Kent, M.W. and Tolfe, J.E. (eds). *Primary Prevention of Psychopathology*, Vol. 3: Social Conference on Children. Hanover, N.H: University Press of New England.

Schorr, L.B. (1988). *Within Our Reach: Breaking the Cycle of Disadvantage.* New York: Doubleday.

Sedlak, A. (1993) 'Risk factors for child abuse and neglect in the US'. *Paper presented at the 4th European Conference on Child Abuse and Neglect: Acting upon European Strategies for Child Protection, Padua, Italy, March 1993.*

Steele, B. (1975) 'Working with abusive parents: a psychiatrist's view', *Children Today,* 43.

Townsend, P. & Davidson, N. (1982) *Inequalities in Health.* Harmondswoth: Penguin.

Tuck, V. (1995) *Links between Social Deprivation and Harm to Children: A Study of Parenting in Social Disadvantage.* Unpublished Ph.D. Thesis. The Open University.

Wedge, P & Essen J. (1982). *Continuities in Childhood Disadvantage.* London: Heinemann Educational Books.

Wilson, H. with Herbert, G.W. (1988). *Parents and Children in the Inner City.* London: Routledge and Kegan Paul.

Wolfe, D.A. (1993) 'Child Abuse Prevention: blending research and practice'. *Child Abuse ,* 2, 153-165.

5
Work partnerships with Black communities: Issues and principles for social work education, training and service delivery

Alexandra Seale & Michaela Mkandla

The changing social and economic structures in all societies inevitably influence social work education, training and practice. Educational institutions and agencies are charged with responsibility for drawing out the implications of these changes for policies and practices which will help to meet the needs of children and adults alike. In Britain, a number of statutes exist to ensure that those who are in need of state intervention receive services which are relevant and appropriate to their needs. A number of principles inform the behaviour of organisations. These include working in partnership with parents and the need to safeguard and promote the welfare of children within the context of their own families. More specifically, state organisations are required to take into consideration the child's religious persuasion, racial origin and cultural and linguistic background. (Children Act 1989 supported by the UN Convention on the Rights of the Child, 1989.)

This chapter will explore how these principles and requirements can be incorporated into:

• agency policy and procedures
• agency organisation and behaviour in service delivery and in determining appropriate modes of intervention
• a culture and practice of partnership between workers and families which could alleviate dysfunctional aspects of social work intervention in child protection cases.
• the curriculum of social work programmes at qualifying, post qualifying and advanced levels.

We will draw on experience of working on a Code of Practice on Race in Child Protection (REU: Seale et al 1990), the work of the Northern Region Curriculum Development Group (CCETSW, 1993) and our work in promoting child centred protective services and educational practice.

The questions we have faced are:

• How far the principles related to partnership, promoting the welfare of children, taking account of religion, racial origin, cultural and linguistic background, apply to Black families?

- How active are social work education programmes and their partnerships in addressing the implications for social work practice and learning in child protection?

Nature brings the child into the world but society creates the child into a social being and a corporate person. It is the community which must protect the child, feed it, bring it up and educate it. Children are the buds of society and every birth is the arrival of spring when life shoots out and the community thrives. The birth of a child is, therefore, the concern of not only the parents but of the whole community. (FSU 1992)

This must be a shared philosophy amongst world communities. The International Convention on the Rights of the child proposed by the Government of Poland in 1979 was adopted by the United Nations General Assembly in 1989 and has been ratified by about 120 countries to date. The Convention recognises that the protection of children requires a framework and standard agreed by the world community. Article 19 of the Convention deals with the rights of the child to protection from all forms of abuse, whilst articles 3 and 6 recognise the rights and responsibilities of the state and community towards the protection of the child.

The UN Convention is concerned with all children. Each country has developed legislation which forms the basis for policies designed to translate the principles of the Convention into procedures which should ensure the protection of its children. In Britain a number of statutes have been changed and updated to reflect constant changes in economic, social and political organisation. The Children Act 1989 and its supporting guidance tries to incorporate the spirit of the convention by recognising the strength in 'working together' for the protection of children. It also, perhaps for the first time, acknowledges the different needs children might have based on 'racial origin' and cultural and linguistic background. It encourages local authorities to take these into account when exercising their duty to children in their constituencies. In this chapter we will attempt to assess the issues for Black children and their families under this framework in relation to child protection and child abuse. The issues raised apply to social work intervention with Black communities more generally. All assumptions about Black people and other minority groups need to be examined. We discuss them in the context of partnerships and protection of Black children.

Partnership- policy implications

Partnership in child protection assumes working in partnership with parents and other significant people connected with the child and family and working together with other agencies - police, education, health, social services, probation and voluntary agencies. We want to argue that at all levels the issues of 'race', culture and religion are yet to be addressed effectively.

Procedures of individual agencies and of Area Child Protection Committees in the United Kingdom do not always reflect consideration of the Black child's needs, based on 'race', culture and religion. To understand this point it is important for the reader to interrogate their own agency policies and procedures on working with families to establish whether or not the issues have been taken into consideration. Does the agency provide relevant information in the language and format that is helpful to Black people? Are there written policies to take into account 'race', culture and religion? Are there supports in place - readily accessible - to help and empower people in investigations, assessments, and in making effective use of available services? Just as important - are Black people represented in the work force and on advisory and consultation groups? If not, then agencies will continue to fail the Black child.

There can be no excuse for this omission, given that there is now a range of literature produced by Black and white academics and practitioners which puts forward helpful suggestions for policy development and practice for example: 'Towards Black Perspectives in Child Protection' (Dutt, 1989) and 'Race in Child Protection; A Code of Practice' (REU, 1990) and the Curriculum Development publication on Children and Families (CCETSW, 1993). The Code of Practice (pp.6-8) includes the following guidelines for agencies in developing anti- discriminatory child protection services.

Policy Statement - should address:
- The organisational objectives and how the policy will impact on the consumer and the practitioner.
- What the target group is: children, families and their social networks.
- What is expected from the individual practitioner.

Policy Objectives - could include:
- Investigations and assessments should be ethnically aware and should be undertaken in the language of the child and family.
- Children and families should have easy access to an independent complaints procedure, supported by advocacy in the language of the child and family.

Strategic Implications include:
- As much attention is required to demonstrate how strategies may be achieved as to what the changes should be. Barriers to change must be identified and work done to re-educate, restructure, in ways which engender commitment to identified values and policies.
- Continuous updating of demographic information, with the involvement of different ethnic and community groups.

The following questions might be helpful in evaluating area child protection committee procedures. Do the procedures give guidance which assumes certain 'norms' for all children and their families? Do they give guidance about cultural or religious matters? What assumptions are made about issues such as female circumcision or infibulation? Do they give adequate guidance about what a social worker or manager should do, or how they should advise others in these circumstances? Are child abuse referrals monitored by ethnic origin? Just as important, are Black people represented in your Area Child Protection Committee?

We want to argue that there is a further policy issue at this level which it is essential to address if the Black child is to be protected. Partnership with parents involves both recognising that families have expertise and recognising their rights as citizens. For the partnership to work, families need to be provided with information presented in a language and format they understand, one that is free from jargon.

Families also need to be involved and to participate in the whole process. For this to happen sophisticated and readily accessible translating and interpreting services need to be available throughout the process. Families need to be assured that their views will be taken into account and that their needs will be met through the provision of appropriate services.

Agencies will only be able to provide appropriate child protection services for Black children and their families when they have extensive dialogue with the communities about the subject. Monitoring of child protection referrals is necessary in order to establish the nature and extent of child abuse in all communities and to provide the resources necessary to establish whether or not Black communities are referring children who may be experiencing abuse. In our experience this is not happening. Whereas a sizeable number of anonymous referrals are received from white people referring white and sometimes Black children, very few are received from Black people referring children of any ethnic origin.

Practice in social work agencies

To illustrate our arguments further, we want to consider the issues at the level of practice in Social Services Departments. Gender, disability, age, sexual orientation and race are all concepts that indicate or imply difference, e.g. gender: between men and women; race: generally between Black and white; age: young and old. If these concepts are unpacked in this way, it becomes obvious that any relationship between young / old / men / women, white/ Black have an imbalanced power base. These relationships are double edged. They can be a source of support but also of contention and conflict. Social work practice is a political activity and the politics of practice should be at the forefront of all practitioners' minds.

In a paper presented to a conference on 'Working with child abuse in Black families' in 1990 at the University of Bradford, Kum Kum Bavnani argued that 'racial' difference, like others, is a political concept, based on a notion of 'race' which has less to do with biological make up and more to do with ideology and economics in a given place and time in history. For example, South African Boers strongly believe that the Black person is inferior to themselves and they quote the scriptures to support this claim. That view may well change over the years given the political changes.

Within the United Kingdom and Europe Black people may still experience the consequences of that ideology, in spite of the existence of legislation on 'race' and a partial recognition and regard for what they have to offer. During times of recession, they are often seen as scroungers. At such times Black people feel that the project of the state in relation to them is the exercise of its machinery of control and surveillance. This includes immigration laws, law and order policies and social and fiscal policy. Social work and health care practitioners, the police and housing provision systems are significant players in this activity. Whether we want to believe it or not, the reactive rather than the preventive nature of our intervention controls more than it enables all families. We argue that this tendency to control is more prevalent when working with Black families (Roys, 1988; Barn et al, 1997).

We want to acknowledge efforts made by some agencies and individual social workers to democratise their processes and provision for Black children and their families. However, it is our experience and that of many researchers (Ahmad 1990; Barn 1993) that children are not well served by current arrangements and can be let down by white practitioners. This is often compounded by unthought through practices in deploying Black practitioners without the relevant and appropriate level of training and competence. An assumption is made that to be Black is to have a definitive understanding of all Black people.

White liberal practitioners and managers of practice may argue that they and their agencies take issues of race and culture seriously because they have access to consultants on cultural matters and adjust their practice accordingly. Sometimes, however, agencies offer an unhealthy, and unquestioning 'respect' for culture which ignores the differences among Black communities and Black peoples based on age, religion, gender, disability, sexual orientation and life experiences. As Ahmad states,

> Cultural understanding and knowledge of language have great benefits, however, these skills alone do not make a practitioner. It is the ability to apply the skills through an effective approach that makes social work credible. (Ahmad 1990 page 13).

Yet what we often see is an over-sensitivity to culture based on stereotypical assumptions about Black people. From the inquiry into the death of Tyra Henry it appears that workers assumed that her grandmother would cope because Black Caribbean women are used to coping with child rearing.(Channer & Parton, 1990).

Reluctance to challenge some aspects of 'cultural' practices is sometimes based on the fear that the practitioner may be seen as racist. It is generally agreed that cultures are neither static nor monolithic: what may have been culturally acceptable two generations or so back may not always be acceptable currently to certain groups or individuals. Some so called cultural or religious practices may not be widely supported by some groups and individuals. A good example of this is the practice of female circumcision and infibulation which Black women around the world have brought to attention. To fail to discuss such practices with a wide range of different groups in differing roles and relationships of power and subordination is to ignore the differences amongst Black people, between men and women and between adults and children. Imbalanced power relationships need attention. The politics of social work practice in child protection must be about challenging all those who are in powerful positions in relation to children.

On the other hand, there is a danger in assuming Black young people will be more progressive than their parents. Young people may be seen as needing protection from their parents who are 'locked up' in their cultural norms. This view leads to a punitive approach by the social worker which disadvantages the Black child further. Ahmad (1990) argues that Black clients are often associated with 'problems' and the practitioner fails to focus on the failure of their own profession. For example, where child abuse is alleged, the practitioner may act on the assumption that the Black community colludes and decide to intervene with a heavy-handed approach to break this perceived wall of secrecy.

For a more specific example, it may be believed that physical chastisement of children is culturally acceptable to most Black Caribbean parents and that it is very hard to change the attitude of the parents towards such punishment. This is sometimes combined with the criminalisation of Black people, including the child. To illustrate our point, consider this situation.

A child protection case conference was held on an 8 year old boy who had been physically chastised by his father for being involved in substance misuse. His behaviour was described by his teachers as being very disruptive in class and unmanageable at home; he was said to be stealing from children and adults alike and not receiving much education because of very poor school attendance. The head of the year felt that the school could work with him and his parents to try and improve his attendance and a programme was suggested. His class teacher however believed that he should be sent to a secure unit to correct his delinquent behaviour and protect him from his father, who may never change his attitude about using physical punishment.

This particular teacher was either not aware of or chose to ignore the guidance of the Criminal Justice Act about not locking children up or the Children Act that promotes looking after. With this suggestion, he was over reacting to both the child's and his father's behaviour. In so doing, he failed to recognise the needs of this child who did not wish to be separated from his parents. In fact, the measure of intervention suggested would have created a new problem of abuse by the system which would not meet some of the child's needs or protect him from abusive behaviour from others. His abuse would take a different form. Whilst the declared intention of state statutes is to protect the child, how this is interpreted and managed leads us to believe that the element of control is a constant factor.

The intervention suggested by his teacher would have been based only on the project of regulation and control. The Children Act 1989, through its priority to the interests and welfare of the child, can provide the opportunity - if not always the resources - to take a more child-focused approach. A plan to engage in partnership with the child and his parents, to understand the personal and social causes of the child's behaviour, to find ways of responding to it which can be effective, promote the child's development to autonomy without the use of punishment which is harmful and can be defined as abusive, would be compatible with the requirements of the Act. It could also show respect for the difficulties, dilemmas and distress of all concerned. Modi and Pal (1992) argue that the lack of referrals of Black children who may be experiencing abuse may be related to common perceptions that the role of social services is one of policing rather than support.

The child protection case conference

The case conference provides a framework for all agencies' practices and views about families to converge. How we exercise our authority can have a significant impact on the partnership with the carer. The Department of Health guidelines, 'Working Together' suggest that successful partnerships can be achieved within a context which:

1. provides the means for overcoming any barriers which may arise as a result of communication requirements.
2. values, supports, monitors and rewards participatory practice which is sensitive to 'racial' origins, religious persuasions and cultural and linguistic backgrounds.

In addition to the above we suggest that the following questions ought to be addressed:

- are arrangements made to communicate effectively with parents whose first language is not English before, during and following conferences; do they reflect customer care policy guidelines?
- how are parents prepared for what must be an ordeal for them?
- what factors influence decisions made about Black children?
- are Black people adequately represented amongst the professional participants - police, teacher, health visitor etc?
- are Black people represented amongst Chairs of conferences?
- what information is available to ACPC, Children and Family Teams, Social workers, about how procedures are working for Black children, how the children and their families experience them and about the availability of ethnically sensitive services which can enhance social work practice?
- how is The UN Convention on the Rights of the Child used to inform agency policy and practice?
- does your department children's plan systematically address the above issues ?

In spite of well documented evidence of inequality, inequity, prejudice and discrimination against Black people (Fanon, 1968; Sivanandan, 1982; Jordan ,1987; Roys, 1988; Solomos, 1989;) there has been a recent and sustained backlash against the commonly accepted view of Britain as a racist society. We maintain the view articulated in CCETSW paper 30, (p.46, 1991) adopted by the Council, which sparked debates about 'political correctness' which continue to be used to deny the strength of the problem:

> *CCETSW believes that racism is endemic in the values, attitudes and structures of British society, including those of social services and social work education. CCETSW recognizes that the effects of racism on black people are incompatible with the values of social work and therefore seeks to combat racist practices in all areas of its responsibilities. (Annex 5, Paper 30 CCETSW's Statement on Antiracism)*

In response to pressure this statement was taken out of more recent CCETSW publications. The report into the death of Stephen Lawrence took an unusually strong position in drawing attention to institutional racism (Macpherson, 1999). It echoes the original CCETSW view.

It has been our experience that racist overtones can be found in all agency and individual practices irrespective of the various statements of intent or policies. We argue that these often influence the process in child protection conferences and unless all professionals involved, particularly the chairperson, are mindful of this fact, there is a danger that liberal or punitive measures may be suggested, leaving the Black child either unprotected from further abuse or indirectly exposed to secondary abuse.

Deployment of black social workers

A relatively recent development in Social Services is the deployment of Black workers, who have made a substantial contribution in putting race matters onto their agency agendas. A big assumption, however, is made - that this in itself can offer protection for Black children and encourage real participation by Black parents in child protection. In our experience this is a long way from the current reality. Many of these workers struggle with issues of professionalism, because of expectations of their agencies, expectation of their communities and their own values and beliefs. They are expected to be experts on cultural matters above all else. They are trained and work with euro-centric models which disempower Black people and deny them equal rights or status. With growing numbers of individuals from war-torn nations, the problem increases.

Modi and Pal (1992) suggest that they struggle, without a shared theoretical basis for practice. They can end up being intermediaries in the state's own project by providing the surveillance necessary for regulation and control. For example, a white social worker goes out to investigate an alleged case of abuse of a child in a Pakistani family. The Social worker later asks an Asian welfare officer to call a meeting of Asian parents in the locality to 'tell them that over chastisement is not accepted in Britain'. This assumes that the whole community is guilty and that it is the duty of the welfare officer to deal with the issue; that the worker is acceptable to the community, and that there is no differentiation between Asian and Pakistani. It ignores possible religious sensibilities and impact on the elders' role within the community.

On a more personal level, the deployment of Black women social workers in the child protection field ignores the power relationships which exist between Black men and Black women and the difficulties that this causes them. This difficulty is particularly pronounced where sexual abuse is alleged because of the taboo that surrounds the subject between men and women within some Black communities. How does a Muslim woman investigate an allegation that a 14 year old Muslim girl is pregnant as a result of being sexually abused by her paternal uncle, when her father does not know about this?

A Black woman's professional responsibility to investigate may not be recognised by the family. She may be seen by the Black family as someone who has lost her way. Yet, it might be possible to work with families who come to the notice of the agency at an earlier stage if there were strategies in place to consult groups, inform and empower the families to participate in partnership with all agencies. Issues and dilemmas could then be considered outside situations of crisis.

Development of child centred services

The concerns expressed earlier cannot be underestimated by agency policy makers, managers and practitioners, all of whom have a role to play in the development of child-centred services. This role extends to social work educators, health practitioners and non governmental agencies whose functions and activities in the current climate of change increasingly impact on social work tasks. When a Black child is referred to a local social services department as a result of suspected abuse, the situation needs to be explored within a social and economic context as well as in the social and familial circumstances.

Invoking Child Protection Procedures without taking account of wider aspects, hidden needs and stresses, may set the family on a spiral, over which we have little control. In seeking to punish the alleged perpetrator, the instrument of oppression, who may be an unemployed male or a step- parent in a reconstituted family, or in some cases the mother, we can on occasions ignore the impact of racism and other forms of discrimination which impinge on coping mechanisms. Child centred services should have the ability to address holistically all the conditions that affect the Black family.

June Jordan, (1987) describes society's misplaced perception and judgements of Black mothers. A mother is likely to be blamed for all the ills that may befall her child. She cites the conditions in which many Black families live, work and play, as well as their state of health, mental and physical. She further suggests that in the Black family, child abuse may not be the only problem for the child.

We are not suggesting that Black families do not on occasion abuse children nor that we should not respond when children are harmed. We are arguing that a significant percentage of Black children are brought up in households with little or no support, parented by single Black women. June Jordan suggests that we often fail 'to give credit where it is due.' The implication of this perspective is that we must improve our ability to distinguish between responsibility for and the consequences of the system's response to Black families in economic , social and spiritual difficulties. We argue that the state currently fails Black children and their parents in these matters.

Agencies may turn attention to the passivity of Black males, their position within the family and over exposure in the media. These concepts and images need to be understood and addressed if we are to promote the identity and well -being of all Black children and their families. To deny what has been and is happening to Black males, to fail to address their particular conditions, is to deny significance to Black children and their families (Cress Welsing 1991). As Black males and females become more and more alienated, as levels of divorce and separation increase the impact of distrust, anger, loss of self esteem and mental anguish, social and personal needs may be side tracked by attention to the rights and wrongs in child abuse.

There are problems also in mixed relationships. Black children and their families are neither responsible for nor the creators of injustices which the state endorses. DuBois and Miley (1992) suggest that through intolerance a social worker may blame and label the client as resistant to change. This is a conclusion often reached about Black families who challenge assumptions about the family unit. The Code of Practice on Race and Child Protection (REU 1990) along with Ahmad (1990) addresses the difficulties agencies face where they have policies but are without clear strategies to influence outcomes.

These publications highlight a number of issues requiring attention by educators and social welfare agencies, in statutory and voluntary sectors and by social work practitioners and others involved in the management of child protection. They emphasise the importance of recognising and working with the strengths of Black families. They challenge the dominance of euro-centric values and practices in current social work thinking and child rearing practices.

The United Nations Convention on the Rights of the Child seeks to demonstrate the importance of difference and the value that should be placed on it. If these values underpin practice, the essence and focus of child centred services will ensure that the needs of Black children and their families will be met.

We have throughout this chapter provided a number of practical suggestions to assist agencies and relevant personnel involved in this difficult task. Cress Welsing (1991) however reminds us that over '75% of the world's population are non-white, yet subjected to domination throughout their lives either directly or indirectly, by a tiny minority who class themselves as white'. Her theory of colour confrontation- and the responses and reactions which it arouses - can be a creative tool for those involved in responding to child abuse, to scrutinise and reflect on their thinking. Our aim and responsibility in social work intervention is to effect positive change rather than limit it. The social reality in which we live begs us to not affront the strengths of Black families, their social and economic position, the stresses that afflict their daily lives and their attempts to cope with the struggle. Those involved in responding to child abuse should scrutinise what informs their thinking. It might be useful for students, managers and educators to explore Cress Welsing's theory of colour confrontation as well as the responses and reactions it arouses.

She asks us to reflect on the following concepts; when engaging in work with families whose life course may be traumatised by racism and oppression:

The psychogenic and social dynamic of racism (white supremacy).

Genetic factor: colour inadequacy state (white) and albinism or variant.

Individual and group psychological response: development of psychological defence mechanisms.

Compensatory logic system: white supremacy.

Compensatory behavioural practices: (economics, education, entertainment, labour, law, politics, religion, sex, war).

White supremacy behavioural 'system' and culture on world-wide scale.

Systematic oppression, domination and inferiorisation of all people with the capacity to produce significant amounts of melanin skin pigment: Black, brown, red and yellow peoples of the Earth'.

(Diagram 1 p11 The Isis Papers 1991)

She emphasises the importance of understanding the societal dynamics associated with prejudice, power and supremacy.

In cases where poor assessment has been implicated in the death of a child, understanding of these dynamics is crucial. These concepts can help move beyond an exploration of individual blame towards an understanding of the pathological assault of inequality.

The Code of Practice (REU 1990) emphasises the need for awareness of the interconnectedness of children's and families' experiences with key players- individuals and organisations-and with societal factors. The degree of tension which may exist needs to be recognised and attempts made to respond. These interconnections in

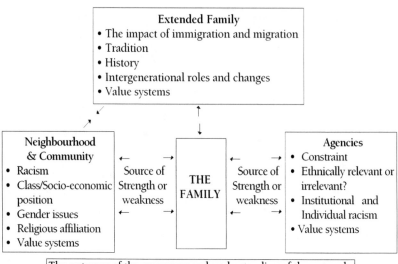

The outcome of the awareness and understanding of the network, is relevant information which assists the intervention.

R.E.U. Seale et al 1990 A Code of Practice p22)

families' networks are an essential focus of assessment.

Agencies need clear lines of responsibility and accountability and all policies procedures and implementation strategies require regular scrutiny, to see how far they help to create an environment for effective dialogue with families and communities and help to ensure meaningful action and outcomes.

If we analyse realistically the conditions in which Black families are bringing up their children, we may wish to reappraise our policies and strategies in child protection. All too often agencies' policies state an intention to act, which is let down by procedures which hamper an environment for meaningful action and dialogue. Students in training need opportunities to engage in debate that will help them to understand fully what is required of them as they begin their practice learning. We suggest that discourse is needed on a number of levels, including the political environment in which child protection takes place. Issues of change and its impact, and the adversarial role of social work, need to be addressed.

Creating learning environments which will promote the welfare of Black children and families.

The anti-racist lobby, having struggled to get racism on the agenda for social work and social work education, has been accused of zealousness. We argue that the journey has just begun - for all on the receiving end of policies, attitudes and practices which damage Black families and limit children's opportunities to achieve their full potential.

Practitioners and students alike need opportunities to learn, through continuing debates, and sensitive and relevant practice opportunities, what is required to develop the competencies needed for practice. This is needed throughout all levels of the training continuum, pre-qualifying, qualifying, post-qualifying and advanced.

The impact of the 'Shame and Blame' phenomenon experienced by all Black groups is relevant to practitioners, students and users of services. Historical coping strategies based on pride in the family name, or standing within the community, and on managing the problem from within, are all under continuing threat. This historical and social picture needs to be understood in relation to the needs of learners and users. The UN Convention on the Rights of the Child recognises that the family, 'as the fundamental group in society and the natural environment for the growth and well being of its members and particularly children, should be afforded the necessary protection and assistance so that it can fully assume its responsibilities within the community.' (Article 9). Article 19 sets out the duty of the State to protect children from all forms of abuse, neglect and exploitation.

A study of the interconnections and self perpetuating relationships of economic disadvantage, poverty, unemployment, lack of educational and training opportunities, poor housing and other destructive encounters with racism, should be a priority in academic and practice curricula. Questions about who are the key abusers of Black children and the context in which harm and abuse occurs need to be at the forefront of childcare education and training. Family members may be the instrument of abuse, but are they the cause? A brief hypothetical case study illustrates the issues.

Harry is a 36 year old Black man. He is a product of the environment described above. His current employment status is plagued by insecurity, inability to fulfil his obligations as breadwinner, father, etc. In a fit of anger he hits out at his demanding son. The boy is subsequently injured and taken to hospital where the child protection machinery comes into operation.

Should we come to a judgement about his violence and his fitness to maintain custody of his child on the severity of the injury alone or should we enquire into his life course? Responsible professionals will make a holistic assessment of risk and need before identifying aspects of a protection plan.

To encourage such an overview, Devore and Seale (1993) suggest that social work curricula should attempt 'to provide students with a greater awareness of life in other more distant worlds.' This is particularly relevant when dealing with refugee families, for whom a main tool to help retain a sense of self may be the pattern of child rearing practised in their country of origin, or the maintenance of strict religious beliefs and practices. These social situations provide opportunities for students to explore the tensions and opportunities of working together with families.

Devore and Seale encourage educators to help students break free of insular positions by emphasising cross cultural perspectives. The impact of migration, immigration, political persecution, can be studied, providing a useful backdrop to theories of life course and development. Within such an approach, students can be encouraged to develop understanding of their own life course. In particular, this will provide opportunities to consider negative interactions they have experienced, including how Black and white students deal with their experience of earlier negative interactions with Black and white people.

Cress Welsing (1991) on Black male passivity within the family, suggests that in order to explore this phenomenon we need to address the 'total dynamic of racism, the different levels of imposed power and cruelty towards Blacks by white men'. As a child, born into the conditions stated above, he experiences through his life course 'the process of inferiorisation', and as such may only ever experience a sense of preciousness within the family or community. Experience suggests that the value placed on Black children outside the family is a pecarious one.

Urie Bronfenbrenner (1979) suggests that human development is affected by four systems, which he defines as:

1. Microsystems, the immediate setting in which development occurs
2. Mesosystems, comprising the relational linkages between the micro, for example, the family and school-peer connection
3. Exosystems, extensions of the mesosystems embracing other specific social structures both formal and informal, that do not directly include the developing person but nonetheless affect their development, and
4. Macrosystems, the ' overarching institutional patterns of culture and subcultures' which impact on the person's well-being.

For example the combination of social policy programmes, fiscal and economic strategies, housing and health policies which determine the quality of existence, the ability to fulfil their potential and the life span of Black people, directly impacts upon the well being of Black children. Of paramount importance to any state should be investment in all its people, regardless of their racial origins and social class. We argue that the life course of Black children and their families, determined by systems which exclude them from achieving their fullest potential, should be a focus of study and action.

Child abuse within the community can provoke a level of numbness which leads to withdrawal. Electric waves triggered by the media's response to a tragedy can dispel the numbness. However, too often, well meaning interest is not grounded, and the child's voice may not be heard. The over dramatisation of a perpetrator's life course often takes precedence when abuse relates to Black people: the perpetrator is condemned before the facts are known. Black individuals are often described in the most horrific terms in the popular press. In this process, the long term effect on the victim, family, or community fades, in a system which is more concerned with managing today's events than considering the long term implications of child abuse.

These dynamics are commonly reflected in state responses to child abuse within the indigenous white community, so what hope can we have for Black children and their families? Those involved in the administration and management of child abuse need to recognise and work on these dynamics if they are to develop a partnership which is just and has meaning to under-served Black groups.

Earlier we argued that agencies could make better use of available literature to inform practice, ensure insights into different family forms and child rearing practices and evaluate the most effective services for Black children. There is a need to reframe normality beyond that which is formulated within a euro-centric model. The need to plan for effective partnership involves valuing the individuals concerned. Even where a member of the family has been accused of abuse, we are not required to condemn, nor does the family unit or the entire group warrant condemnation.

We would like to re-emphasise the need for clear criteria for evaluating the quality of service offered to Black families and their communities. Services should demonstrate to communities that social workers are there to assist rather than judge. If this can be achieved, the intervening social worker is more likely to develop a good rapport and relationship with all concerned.

Conclusion

In conclusion, we should like to revisit some key issues. Modi and Pal (1992) in their article 'Beyond Despair', highlight the complexities of getting the first stage right, particularly when sexual abuse is the main area of concern. They urge that agencies need to become sensitised to cross-cultural issues. Burke (1991) in a paper on stress amongst Black women, for Kirklees Metropolitan Council, advised that agencies must educate practitioners on the bi-culturation process for Black families as it affects their life course. It is our view that only when this occurs, can we truly begin to respect and respond to individuals in psychological and emotional trouble. Devore and Seale (1993) suggest the there is a duty to ensure that the social work curriculum explores cross cultural issues in individual and family development, and that we 'consider the impact of immigration.' We would also include migration due to war or political persecution. Adopting an insular position limits the effectiveness of practice.

In the United Kingdom we have a unique opportunity within our Diploma in Social Work and post qualifying educational partnerships to capitalise on the current responsibility to develop Children's Services Plans. Models of practice can be developed which take account of dysfunction beyond family units. Teaching on child abuse has for too long centred on psychological issues. Agencies have focused on reactive, crisis remedies. Current educational and agency partnerships provide the opportunity to engage in a dialogue of prevention and family support.

Research and evaluation can play a very important part in the process. We need to make more use of the information we obtain from family histories to assist planning for prevention. In the current atmosphere of measuring impact and outcome of investigations, we could ensure that this area of social work makes a difference in focusing expenditure where it is most needed. We would suggest that whilst we may not eradicate child abuse we might reduce its incidence and improve family life for children.

We can look at the comparative effectiveness of different strategies and services - for example comparing the value of support and prevention with families we are currently involved with, with preventive work with potential abusers. Schools of Social Work in equal partnership and dialogue with Black communities should influence the learning outcomes set for students by drawing together research on practice. Representatives from Black communities could be co-opted onto course committees, and be involved in programmes with academic staff.

This approach will ensure that preventive work is emphasised in parallel with crisis responses to abuse and harm. Educational partnerships need to use and promote, 'real world research' (Robson 1993) to ensure that students engage with the life course of Black communities and understand its relevance to the experiences of abuse. It is particularly urgent for academics, practice teachers and managers within agencies to gain a better understanding of Black communities' belief systems, values and attitudes to sexual issues and their common practices in physical and emotional engagement with children. Biographies such as Jonathan Kozol's books 'Savage Inequalities' and 'Death at an Early Age' can provide dramatic portraits of Black children's lives. A fourteen year-old girl tells how:

> *Every year in February we are told to read the same old speech of Martin Luther King. We read it every year. 'I have a dream....' it does begin to seem — what is the word? she hesitates and then she finds the word: 'perfunctory'. I ask her what she means. 'We have a school in east St Louis named Dr King, she says. 'The school is full of sewer water and the doors are locked with chains. Every student in that school is Black. It's a terrible joke on history. (Kozol 1992)*

Improved understanding and recognition of the issues will enhance the quality of children's services plans. By ensuring assessments and interventions are free of Eurocentric values, attitudes and misdirected use of political correctness, agencies may begin to achieve real change. This will provide the confidence needed to engage fully with families in exploring their histories, discipline, affection and attention, providing earlier support and prevention, so as to promote children's well being.

The concept of partnership could be creatively extended if educational and practice agencies committed themselves to ensure that Black communities were involved in research with them. How we develop strategies and implement action will determine our effectiveness to advocate and change current organisational responses to child abuse and to engage in partnership with Black families. Finally we need to avoid pious rhetoric and organisational rituals about equality and communicate more effectively with people who have too few reasons to believe that state agencies act in their best interests or the interests of their children.

References

Ahmad, B. (1988) 'The Development of Social Work Practice and Policies on Race', *Social Work Today* on Race. Jan Issue.
Ahmad, B. (1989) 'Child Care and Ethnic Minorities' in Kahan, B. (ed) *Child Care Research,, Policy and Practice*. London: Hodder and Stoughton.
Ahmad, B. (1990) *Black Perspectives in Social Work*, REU NISW, Birmingham, Venture Press.
Barn, R. (1993) *Black Children in the Public Care System*. Batsford (in association with BAAF).
Barn, R., Sinclair, R. & Ferdinand, D. (1997) *Acting on Prinicple; An examination of race and ethnicity in Social Services provision for Children and Families*. London: BAAF.
Bhat, A., Carr-Hill, R. & Ohri, S. (1988) 2nd ed. (Radical Statistics Race Group). *Britain's black population, a new perspective*. Aldershot, Hants, England, Brookfield, Vt., USA: Gower.
Brindle, D. (1993) 'The Women Child Abusers', *The Guardian*, 7th June.
Bronfenbrenner, U. (1979) *The Ecology of Human Development*. Cambridge Mass: Harvard University Press.

Buzawa, E.S.. & Buzawa, C.G. (1990) *Domestic Violence: The Criminal Justice Response.* London: Sage.

CCETSW (1991) Paper 30.

CCETSW (1993) *Improving Practice with Children and Families.* Northern Curriculum Development Project. Leeds: CCETSW.

Channer, Y., Parton N. (1990) 'Racism, Cultural Relativism and Child Protection' in *Taking Child Abuse Seriously: The Violence against Children Study* Group. Unwin Hymen.

Chaner, Y. & Parton, N. (1990) 'Racism, cultural relativism and child protection' in *Taking child abuse seriously, contemporary issues in child protection theory and practice*, the Violence Against Children Study Group. London: Unwin Hyman.

Creighton, S. (1987) *Child Abuse.* London: NSPCC.

Devore, W. & Seale, A. (1991) 'Anti-Discriminatory Practice', *Journal of Social Work.*

DoH Abstracts, *Partnership with Families in Child Protection*, Practice Guide DOH.

DHSS (1988) *Working Together: A guide to arrangements for interagency cooperation for the protection of children from abuse.* London: HMSO.

DuBois, B. & Miley, K.K. (1992) *An Empowering Profession.* Allyn & Bacon.

Dutt, R. (1989) *Towards Black Perspectives in Child Protection.* London: REU-NISW.

Fanon, F. (1969) *The wretched of the Earth.* Harmondsworth: Penguin.

Fryer, P. (1984) *Staying Power:* Pluto Press.

F.S.U. (1992) 'African Religion and Philosophy' in *Confronting the Pain of Sexual Abuse.* London.

HMSO (1989) *Children Act.*

Jordan, J. (1987) *Don't Talk About my Mama.* Essence.

Kozol, J. (1967) *Death at an early age: the destruction of the hearts and minds of Negro children in the Boston public schools.* Boston: Houghton Mifflin.

Kozol, J. (1988) *Rachel and her children: homeless families in America.* New York: Crown Publishers.

Macauley, M. (1989) 'Telling a child they are black', *Social Work Today.* Jan. Issue.

Macpherson, W. (1999) *The Stephen Lawrence inquiry. Report of an inquiry by Sir William Macpherson of Cluny advised by Tom Cook, The Right Reverend Dr John Sentamu, Dr Richard Stone.* Presented to Parliament by the Secretary of State for the Home Department by Command of Her Majesty, February 1999. Stationery Office.

Modi, P. & Pal, J. (1992) *Beyond Despair Looking after Children: Confronting the Pain of Child Sexual Abuse.* Family Service Unit.

REU, Baldwin, N., Johnson, P. & Seale, A. (1990) *A Code of Practice: Race in Child Protection.* REU/NISW.

Robson, C. (1993) *Real world research, a resource for social scientists and practitioner-researchers.* Oxford: Blackwell.

Stone, M. (1990) *Child Protection Work: A Professional Guide.* Birmingham: Venture Press.

UN Convention on the Rights of the Child (1989). Articles 3,6,9 & 19.

Vittachi, A. (1989) *Stolen Childhood: in search of the rights of the child.* Cambridge: Polity Press.

Welsing, F.C. (1991) *Isis (Yssis) Papers.* Chicago: Third World Press.

Williams, E. (1981) *Forged From the Love of Liberty*, compiled by Sutton, P.K. Harlow: Longman Caribbean.

Williams, R. (1988) 'The Black Experience of Social Services', *Social Work Today*, 14.1.88, pp. 14 - 15.

6
Issues in education

Tricia David

Teachers might be considered pivotal in child protection work, as the professional group which comes into almost daily contact with all children aged over four, and a significant proportion of those aged three-to-five years. In this paper I will explore some of the issues and dilemmas facing teachers, and others in the education service with different professional training and at different levels, as they struggle to define their own role in both the reactive and proactive processes of child protection in the current context of changing services.

Taking an ecological systems approach based on the work of Bronfenbrenner (1979), I will show that participation of teachers in the process of child protection is vital and requires attention to the dual responsibilities of: a) improving direct responses, raising awareness of children's rights and being alert to behaviour which might indicate current abuse; and b) ensuring the centrality of education in the supportive network which seeks to prevent abuse and which acknowledges children's needs holistically. However, I will also discuss the ways in which teachers and schools may have colluded to some extent in their own exclusion from the main networks visibly involved in child protection. A variety of factors have been involved, including the socio-medical model of child abuse which has dominated thinking in the past.

Under-representation

Anyone combing available material for evidence of the levels of involvement in child protection activity and training by those employed in the education sector will be struck by the low profile of teachers, whether primary or secondary trained.

For example, the report by Elizabeth Butler-Sloss (1988) following the Cleveland Inquiry mentioned not one teacher, and gave the impression that any input there had been from the education sector was from an Education Welfare Officer (EWO). While it is important to recognise the important role EWOs play in providing services to families and schools, it is vital to recognise also that EWOs have a background in social work, not classrooms. They are not in the same kind of daily contact with children.

Further questions could arise from an examination of NSPCC referral statistics (eg. NSPCC 1989; Susan Creighton 1993). During the period covered by the first set of statistics, teacher referrals appear to have fallen by 50 per cent. In any case, these were largely made up of referrals of suspected physical abuse to children under five by nursery staff. In the later statistics schools and preschool institutions account for eleven per cent of referrals, higher than in the previous period but still not up to the levels of the early eighties.

There is little available research evidence about schools and child protection, but one exception is Corinne Wattam's (1990) study about teachers' experiences of children who have or may have been sexually abused. Outstanding features of the results of this study are:- the teachers' anxieties, lack of confidence and self-confessed lack of knowledge.

Another example of the low profile of the education sector can be found in the attendance lists of multi-professional conferences. These feature little, if any, representation by educationists (eg. ISPCAN 1993; BAPSCAN 2000).

Further, in 1992-3 a socio-medical committee of experts was convened by the European Commission, to debate the situation in EC countries concerning child abuse and protection. That committee had no representation from the education sector. This may seem logical since it was intended, after all, to have a socio-medical focus. However, a judge sat on that committee, and prevention of abuse was reported to be the committee's highest priority (Christine Hallett 1993).

Teachers and schools alone cannot change society, there are aspects of children's lives upon which those in the education sector can have little immediate impact, such as poverty and housing, for example.

However, it is my view that the less teachers are represented in the field of child protection, the more it will be seen as a reactive process, responding to crisis, rather than as a proactive, preventive function of a caring society which sees children as citizens, who can be educated about their rights and their responsibilities towards others. Further, schools can be at the centre of their communities, facilitating the development of supportive networks for families.

What may actually hinder teachers in their perception of themselves as central in this process may be their understandings of the family, discipline, and the influence of social or economic circumstances (Rosonna Tite 1993), as well as the permeation of the ecological system in which they live and work by a socio-medical model of the causes of abuse (Tricia David 1993b).

The more we learn about the early roots of bullying behaviour (Manning et al 1978; Randall 1991) and about the proportion of abusers who are teenagers (Bentovim et al 1991), the more we may come to recognise that not only the inequalities in society leading to stress must be addressed, but so too must the learning and development needs of children, from their earliest years, particularly their learning concerning their own rights and the way in which the rights of others impinge on their actions.

We have to ask then, why is education sector involvement so problematic?

A teacher's role is to teach

First it is perhaps necessary to examine the argument that a teacher's role is to teach, that child protection falls in the realm of social work rather than education. If one looks for pointers to Governmental expectations of teachers in the massive documentation which resulted from the 1988 Education Reform Act and other subsequent legislative changes, there is scant recognition for children's personal, social and emotional needs. The particular curricular model adopted for the National Curriculum, conceived as a collection of disciplines/ subjects, hardly reinforced the idea that one teaches 'whole children'.

Although 'cross-curricular themes' concerning topics such as health and citizenship appeared to have been tacked on as an afterthought, the documents concerning *Health Education* (NCC 1990) and *Education for Citizenship* (NCC 1990a), did contain aspects which indicated an expectation that teachers would address child protection issues as part of the entitlement curriculum. However, the National Curriculum proved too 'large' and a review led by Sir Ron Dearing was instituted to prune it. The cross-curricular themes did not survive the review process (see Dearing 1993; 1993a for the Interim and Final Reports), but schools are still advised to use the ideas put forward in the NCC (National Curriculum Council) documents.

There are also expectations that teacher training establishments will incorporate detection of abuse and awareness of health and safety in their courses (DfEE 1998). In addition, teachers, like other professional and voluntary workers offering a service to children and their families, come under the remit of the Children Act 1989, and have a strong obligation to be involved in child protection.

The excuse that teachers teach subjects and have no responsibility for either the *reactive* or the *proactive* aspects of child protection can no longer be sustained. Teachers have a responsibility under the Children Act 1989 and as a legal requirement relating to the curriculum, to promote the well-being of today's and tomorrow's children and to work to prevent abuse.

What other factors may be affecting levels of teacher involvement?

Issues relating to training

For some teachers their reticence will be the result of lack of awareness and /or lack of training in the teacher's role in child protection. Like many older teachers, I reflect on my years as both a class teacher and a head with some sadness, because I now realise that (in the reactive sense) I must have failed to help some children, maybe even children who would have disclosed to me had I been able to 'see' and to 'hear' appropriately. What we define as abuse may be an ever evolving set of concepts, but at least now there is much more extensive knowledge available to help us recognise a need for support for children, and in many cases their families too.

Within the context of certain and variable conditions resulting from reforms to initial teacher education there is already so much that students must cover, little time is left for developing child protection work in a meaningful way. Trainers need to explore how each year of a course, in the case of degree courses with QTS (Qualified Teacher Status) will build on what students have already studied in ecological approaches to the child within the family and society, childhood as perceived and lived in that community, and child protection as prevention as well as 'rescue'. In the one year PGCE and some of the new routes into teaching, such careful interweaving of experience, theoretical input and reflection may not be possible, and students need to be reassured that there will be ongoing in-service training, while being offered some basic points about their responsibilities. Local authorities will need to address this issue as part of their present responsibility for the well-being of children under the Children Act, in spite of funding problems and the uncertain future of LEAs themselves in a world where school budgets are increasingly devolved.

A further issue related to training is the dearth of material aimed at the education sector, in research and publications concerned with child protection and the teacher's role, or appropriate curriculum materials for use in practice (David 1993), although the NSPCC is developing new materials. There is a good deal of scepticism about the effectiveness of current child sexual abuse prevention programmes (see for example Webster 1991); in general teachers who are aware are looking for material which could help them embed child protection into the everyday activities of the school. This is particularly true of child sexual abuse protection (csap) at primary school level, where children's understanding of adult sexuality is likely to be very limited. Research carried out in Scotland indicates that children of primary school age do not fully understand the concept of a 'stranger' and while this calls into question much of the preventive work by police units visiting schools with films to warn against abduction, the Home Office video 'Think Bubble' (Home Office 1993) still incorporated this problem. Further, it has been criticised (Angela Phillips 1994), in the wake of the Jamie Bulger murder, for promoting children's fear of anyone they do not know.

Issues in individual schools

It could be that as far as the statistics are concerned levels of teacher involvement in referrals are actually higher than specified. This could be so for two reasons. Firstly, teachers, or rather schools, may prefer that certain parents do not realise that a referral originated from the school, because of potential backlash in a community.

Secondly, where headteachers have refused to accept the suspicions of a member of staff, so that the teacher was forced to act as an independent person and report privately, the record will mask the fact that the referral was made by the child's teacher. The reasons why headteachers refuse to accept a teacher's request for consultation or referral to social services (or NSPCC where appropriate) may be varied, but years of building up home-school links may be an important underlying factor, as may be the individual head's lack of training in child protection.

Further factors which could be preventing schools from performing effectively in child protection processes, whether concerning reactive detection and responses to current abuse, or proactive developments in the curriculum in school plus involvement in supportive networks in the community, include:- time and pressure to fulfil curricular requirements; and the style and expectations of the new inspection teams following the inception of privatization and the hiving off of HMI from the DofE (Department of Education, now DofEE - Education and Employment) into Ofsted (the Office for Standards in Education) . Schools where children will feel valued and where there are private places and times at which one could disclose, and staff who are willing and able to listen - in other words a whole ethos which enables disclosure and promotes the development of self-esteem, knowledge about rights, responsibility, etc - must be able to foster high standards in *achievements and relationships*. Indeed, schools where time is spent nurturing supportive relationships are likely to be those in which parents are valued as partners, and where the school has become the centre of a community network helping protect *parents* from the kind of isolation and stress which could lead to child maltreatment. While the previous Government claimed its reforms were enacted in order to wrench power from the providers (teachers) and place it in the hands of the consumers (parents, according to education legislation), parent groups have argued that it is Central Government itself which has been the beneficiary of all the new legislation relating to schools, passed during the last decade.

Having said this, there are still many relationships in individual schools where power imbalances can result in difficulties relating to the development of child protection policy and action.

Further, at secondary school level, the 1980s development of personal and social education, taught more overtly than in the primary sector, was threatened by the National Curriculum overload. Additionally, there are new complications arising from the Education Act 1993 and the right of parents to have their child withdrawn from sex education. It is virtually impossible under such circumstances to debate essential protection issues such as sexist harassment in the way Carrie Herbert's (1989) research indicated. In her discussion of her work, Carrie Herbert indicates that disclosures need to be matched by honesty, openness and reciprocation on the part of the researcher. The regulations applying to parental rights that their child be excluded from any sex education could mean that a child wishing to explore, through conversation with a teacher, the possibility that she, or he, had been sexually abused, would be forbidden.

The effects of messages generated by the hidden curriculum of the school may also contradict and over-ride a policy of openness. For example, a school with a strong hierarchical structure, with high profile male domination of the upper echelons of management and an authoritarian rather than authoritative regime speaks volumes. It may also be a sign that in the school and the community there exists a persistent belief in the traditional family. At a three-day training event which I attended, a male deputy head expressed his concern that schools could be undermining 'the natural authority of the father of the family'.

The establishment of strong home-school and community-school links is important, because when issues of child protection are raised parents and governors will already know and trust the school's ethos and policies. Indeed, in schools where parents are truly respected as partners (Pugh and De'Ath 1989), they will have participated in formulating the policies and will therefore appreciate the school's part in the supportive preventive network.

While the development of parent-teacher links is seen as essential, there is a further dilemma for teachers to consider here, again relating fundamentally to power differentials. There have been instances where children did not approach their teacher to disclose abuse because they perceived the teachers as their parents' allies rather than their own. This has sometimes meant that children have preferred to confide in a student or 'dinner lady' (school meals supervisor), yet for in-service training and policy discussions the teaching staff may exclude these very people. What such instances illustrate is the children's recognition of a powerful adult alliance between parents and teachers, and their identification of two groups (meals supervisors and students), who, like themselves, are excluded from this 'club'. (Meanwhile, headteachers who do wish to include mealtime supervisors in training and policy sessions may have difficulty finding funding to pay supervisors for their extra hours.)

For some teachers there may also be dilemmas related to a power imbalance between professionals and parents when it comes to confidentiality and record-keeping. The issue of a teacher's right to pass on confidential information about children and their families has not been helped by the fact that the profession has no General Teaching Council, nor a Code of Conduct. Although the majority of records kept about a child must be made available to parents, any records being made concerning suspected abuse may be kept privately by a teacher. When a child is moved to another school, that teacher will be deeply uneasy, being in some cases unable to decide whether to notify the new school of suspicions.

In addition to all this, some school staffs may be aware that in developing the *proactive* aspects of child protection within school they will be using curricular content and teaching methods which are likely to promote in children concepts and attitudes which will result in their challenging authority. They will no longer be taught to 'do as they are told'. This is another reason why it is vital for parents and community members to be involved in the discussions about the school's position, about the principles underpinning the ethos of a non-oppressive school, in fact, a school operating according to the principles of the Children Act and ensuring that the child's voice is heard. Otherwise the repercussions for some families could be counterproductive, as parents struggle to maintain what they see as their right to be obeyed unquestioningly.

For some teachers this is made even more difficult by the fact that their own expectations of children at particular ages and stages, based on their knowledge of child development, may be at odds with parental expectations. They may also have different views about what is suitable television and video material for children. As one teacher I interviewed put it 'It's sometimes difficult to tell what's been happening to a child in real life, what is the result of television. Sometimes I see them humping about in the home corner and I think, goodness, when we were little we just made tea.' What teachers can contribute to the debate with both parents and professionals from other services is their wide knowledge of children's development and behaviour, its similarities of sequence and pattern, as well as its range, variety and uniqueness through the effects of environment. This means that teachers can play a key role in observing any alterations or aberrations in children's behaviour.

Some issues besetting LEA officers, advisers and coordinators

In some local authorities in-service training, both within the education service and multi-professionally, has been excellent, but it seems to depend upon the priorities of the Chief Education Officer (CEO) in question, who may (or may not) endorse the appointment of a Child Protection Coordinator for the Education Authority. This person will then have the responsibility for the provision of courses and for fostering the development of networks, as well as being someone to whom teachers can turn for advice and support. Many CEOs will claim that their ability to initiate and to maintain such an appointment is increasingly limited, as funding to Education Authorities is cut back. Can one be sure that schools which no longer come under the influence of a local authority will buy in expertise for training in child protection, or even continue to promote equal opportunities policies which relate directly to progress towards a non-abusive society? Will Ofsted inspections pick up on these aspects of a school's effectiveness?

In a number of local authorities where Child Protection Coordinators do exist, they have been appointed from the ranks of EWOs rather than the teaching force. There are positive arguments for this practice - EWOs usually have a social work background and are therefore already au fait with social work practices, as well as being confident in dealing with representatives from other professions (eg. police, health). However, there are also arguments in favour of teachers with classroom and school experience being appointed to such posts, because they will have firsthand understanding of the professional identity of members of the teaching force, and the constraints likely to impede classroom practice and school development, etc.

Issues relating to educational support services

The many and varied types of support services which have been available under the auspices of LEAs, such as home language teachers, special needs advisers, educational psychologists, have been cut back or, in some cases, privatized, under the new funding systems. Market forces and competition may be seen positively, because schools appear to have opportunities to exercise choice. However, under the earlier LEA system the work of different teams within the same agency at least held the potential to adopt a coordinated approach, now one wonders whether the fragmentation hinders a view of the whole child.

Further, another negative aspect is that where budgets are tight, or other spending prioritized, expensive support services will not be called on despite need, or schools will adopt strategies to discourage certain pupils from enrolling or continuing attendance.

The issue of abuse by a colleague

Whenever a case of suspected or proven abuse of children by a member of staff in a school comes to light, there is quite naturally a review of both the appointment of that person and everyday procedures. Teachers' unions report that allegations of abuse against teachers are on the increase (Croall 1993). For example, the National Association of Schoolmasters and Women Teachers recorded 71 cases in 1971, and 134 in 1992, but in the first six months of 1993 alone 91 serious allegations involving their members were reported, 54 concerning physical abuse and 37 sexual abuse. Yet 63 of the 69 cases completed by mid-1993 were found to have no case to answer.

The six teachers' unions and local authorities' organisations have been working together on this issue, because they recognise the need to develop nationally agreed guidelines on good practice which will protect both children and those teachers who have been falsely accused. Union representatives argue that the Children Act has created a climate in which the definition of abuse 'is too broad' and where 'the pendulum has swung too far in favour of the child's testimony.' (Croall 1993, p.7). On the other hand there have been cases where abuse by a member of staff has gone unrecognised by colleagues who did not wish to 'see' what was happening, so that they unconsciously colluded, until a child dared make explicit allegations (See Jacqui Halson's chapter in this volume.). Clearly the profession as a whole needs to debate the issues so as to provide some sound procedural guidelines which do not renege on the advances made through the Children Act, in accordance with the UN Convention on Children's Rights.

Meanwhile, child protection work in schools can be a sensitive area, especially for male teachers. They may become aware that some children are frightened of men, they may have had limited or indeed no experience of gentle male role models - all the more reason then that we ensure a plentiful supply of caring, trustworthy male teachers at all levels of our education system, and that we educate each new generation of males to respect those less powerful than themselves (Christine Harrison 1993 and chapter in this volume). Unfortunately, the looming crisis in teacher recruitment (*Sunday Times* 2000) does not bode well in this respect.

Some thoughts on a way forward

Perhaps the most important element in the development of child protection work in the education service is more time for discussion, thought, courses, and with it the acknowledgement that for the present we must accept uncertainty (Esther Saraga 1994). Part of that uncertainty relates to the increasing awareness in society of children as people in their own right, so that the question of what constitutes abuse is changing. Protecting children has traditionally meant ensuring they were freed from the risk of physical, emotional, sexual maltreatment and neglect. Since the ratification of the UN Convention on Children's Rights, child protection can be seen to have a much broader remit, meaning the protection of children's rights, including for example, freedom of association (Article 15) and the right to leisure, play and cultural and artistic recreation (Article 31). There are no quick answers, there is no body of absolute knowledge that teachers can be 'given' to enable them to detect and stop current abuse or ensure a future abuse-free society, and besides, each case of suspected abuse is unique. However, there are some measures which could begin that process.

Teachers need access to more training and support relating to:- working with parents; reactive child protection and links with other services; teaching survivors; curricular development for proactive child protection/prevention, including work on children's rights. With the advent of the Children Act 1989, and the need to make assessments rapidly if an order has been made, a teacher's ability to make a careful, factually based contribution to that assessment is vital, so training in this type of recording and reporting is also needed. At least teachers have been helped by the publication of Circular 10/95 (DfEE 1995) and the Ofsted inspection system could have a more positive role in the future.

By discussing their dilemmas intra- and inter-professionally in workshops and seminars, teachers may become confident in the kinds of expertise they can bring to professional networks (for example their observation and assessment skills in settings which are familiar to children; knowledge, expertise and experience relating to the patterns in children's development), while at the same time benefiting from a greater understanding of the skills and roles of others and a recognition that the whole field is complex and controversial.

Schools and the teachers who work in them have traditionally acted as agents of the state, socialising the next generation. What kind of children and what kind of childhood, or childhoods (Jenny Kitzinger 1990), is our society now promulgating? Time to debate and define underpinning values and principles is seen as a luxury professionals from all services cannot afford while coping with rapid changes, yet it needs to be found. For example, what one worker may see as an appropriate way to work with parents, another may consider an imposition of white middle class values.

If, as the Children Act 1989 and the UN Convention on Children's Rights would demand, the child's voice must be heard, someone must be able to hear - and if necessary act as advocate for that voice. Teachers are in an ideal position to be those advocates (Tricia David 1993a). Perhaps, understandably, they have colluded in their own relative exclusion from child protection work because they have accepted the socio-medical model of child abuse and neglect which developed out of early theorizing in this field (Tricia David 1993b). If a new model is being developed, one based on recognition of children as people with their own rights under the UN Convention and through the implementation of the Children Act, both of which have influenced the macro-level climate (Bronfenbrenner 1979), then teachers will find they have a clearer role. The new General Teaching Council could take a lead in such work.

The centrality of the school, as a potential community resource and as a place where children can experience a mix of age-groups, engaging in children's culture, learning to make their own decisions, to be both independent and inter-dependent, caring about others, means that the education service in this country has a significant part to play in protecting children. The expertise and knowledge about children which teachers bring to the field, needs greater recognition so that their special role can be acknowledged and developed within a multi-professional framework.

References

Bentovim, A., Vizard, E., and Hollows, A. (1991) *Children and Young People as Abusers: an agenda for action* London, National Children's Bureau

Bronfenbrenner, U. (1979) *The Ecology of Human Development* Camb. Mass., Harvard Universiy Press

Butler-Sloss, E. (1988) *Report of the Inquiry into Child Abuse in Cleveland in 1987* London, HMSO

Creighton, S. (1993) *Child Abuse Trends in England and Wales 1988-90* London, NSPCC

Croall, J. (1993) 'The harshest accusation' *Guardian Education* 5.10.93, p.6-7

David, T. (1993) *Child Protection and Early Years Teachers* Buckingham, Open University Press

David, T. (1993a) 'Families and child protection: the role of the early childhood educator' *International Journal of Early Childhood* 25, 2, p.8-12

David, T. (1993b) 'Teachers and child protection' Paper presented at the University Autonoma de Barcelona, 9 December 1993.

Dearing, R. (1993) *The National Curriculum and its Assessment: an interim report* London-York, SEAC/NCC

Dearing, R. (1993a) *The National Curriculum and its Assessment: the Final Report* London, SCAA

DfEE (1995) *Protecting Children from Abuse: The Role of the Education Service.* Circular 10/95. London, DfEE

DfEE (1998) *Teaching: High Status, High Standards. Requirements of courses of initial teacher training.* Circular 4/98. London, DfEE

Hallett, C. (1993) 'Council of Europe Guidelines on child abuse: themes and issues' Paper presented at the 4th European Conference on Child Abuse and Neglect, Padua-Abano Terme, Italy, 28-31 March 1993

Harrison, C. (1993) 'Young men, power and sexuality - educating for change' Paper presented at the 4th European Conference on Child Abuse and Neglect, Padua-Abano Terme, Italy, 28-31 March 1993

Herbert, C. (1989) *Talking of Silence: the sexual harassment of schoolgirls* Brighton, Falmer

Home Office (1993) *Think Bubble* (video, audio cassette and leaflet) London, Home Office-Roar Talent Picture Company

ISPCAN (1993) *Proceedings of the 4th International Conference on Child Abuse and Neglect* Padua Italy, ISPCAN

Kitzinger, J. (1990) 'Who are you kidding? Power and the struggle against sexual abuse' in A.James and A.Prout (eds) *Constructing and Reconstructing Childhood* London, Falmer Press

Manning, M., Heron, J. and Marshall, T. (1978) 'Styles of hostility and social interactions at nursery school, at school, and at home: an extended study of children. in L.A. Hertsov and M.Berger (eds) *Aggression and Anti-social Behaviour in Childhood and Adolescence* New York, Pergamon Press

NCC (1990) *Health Education* York, National Curriculum Council

NCC (1990a) *Education for Citizenship* York, National Curriculum Council

NSPCC (1989) *Child Abuse Trends in England and Wales 1983-1987* London, NSPCC

Phillips, A. (1994) 'Video nasties' *Times Educational Supplement*, 21 January 1994, p.22

Pugh, G. and De'Ath, E. (1989) *Working Towards Partnership in the Early Years* London, National Children's Bureau

Randall, P. (1991) 'Bu;llies and their victims' *Child Education* 68, 3, p.50-51

Saraga, E. (1994) 'Living with uncertainty' in T.David (ed) *Protecting Children from Abuse: Multi-professionalism and the Children Act 1989* Stoke-on-Trent, Trentham Books

Tite, R. (1993) 'How teachers define and respond to child abuse' *Child Abuse and Neglect*, Vol. 17, 5, p.591-604

Wattam, C. (1990) *Teachers' Experiences with Children who have or may have been Sexually Abused* London, NSPCC

Webster, R. (1991) 'Issues in school-based child sexual abuse prevention' *Children and Society* 5, 2, p.146-164

7
The abuse of disabled children

Margaret Kennedy

Information about abuse of disabled children

There are few systematic studies and investigations in the field of child protection in relation to disabled[1] children. The paucity of statistical data is compounded by the fact that most social services reports on child abuse do not specify whether an abused child has an impairment or not. Disabled children have only become a main focus of concern relatively recently (Kennedy & Kelly 1992).

The paper reviews key issues in trying to ensure that disabled children will be effectively protected from abuse.

Most of the statistical data come from America and Canada. To date no large scale analysis of the lives of disabled children in relation to abuse has been undertaken in the UK. Sobsey and Varnhagen (1989), estimated a 50 per cent increased risk to disabled children. Ammerman (1989), found 39 per cent of a group of children with multiple impairments showed evidence of abuse. Doucette (1986) found that 67 per cent of disabled women, compared to 34 per cent of non-disabled women, reported childhood experiences of being physically abused. A 1978 study of deaf children showed 50 per cent of deaf children at residential school reported sexual abuse (Sullivan, Vernon, Scanlon 1987). Kennedy (1989) surveyed 156 teachers and social workers in the UK and they reported 136 confirmed cases of abuse and 262 suspected cases.

Anecdotal evidence from disabled people themselves suggest serious problems, with a range of additional abusive behaviours perpetrated against them, not generally found in documented cases of non-disabled children. Stories are told of practices perceived as humiliating, such as medical photography, in which their bodies were photographed by unknown male photographers in hospitals. Physiotherapy, speech therapy and surgical interventions were not always perceived as benevolent and therapeutic by disabled adults in retrospect. Many felt the constant pressure to become 'normal' was eroding and detrimental to positive self-identity, confidence and self-esteem. A proportion of both disabled people and professionals are beginning to question intrusive and prolonged therapies, such as the Peto and Doman methods of physiotherapy, or surgery. Such people consider that the emotional and psychological

---

1. The word 'disability', or 'disabled', will refer to the process of oppression: dis-abled by society. The word 'impairment' will be used to describe conditions such as cerebral palsy, deafness, spina bifida and so forth. This follows the social model of disability.

well-being of the disabled child is sacrificed to the concept of looking and functioning as 'normal'.

Other forms of abuse have been recognised. I have information about children sleeping in cots with lids on them, children being locked into bedrooms at night and children having 'nappies' on when in fact more age appropriate incontinence devices should be utilised. Restraint of disabled children with 'challenging' behaviour has not yet been fully discussed in the child protection literature (Lyons 1994). Over medication has been consistently documented as a means of control (Newport 1991). Some current practices are regularly deployed without awareness that they are against the law.

Definitions of abuse

There are dilemmas in the definition of abuse since standard definitions do not embrace practices such as discrimination, segregation, financial and property abuse or humiliating service provision. Other forms of abuse such as 'market forces neglect', or 'service created neglect' is conveniently overlooked in the child protection field (Kennedy 1997). In the former, disabled children are seen as expensive, requiring additional resources which put pressure on service provision for others deemed more worthy of these resources. Thus we see a burgeoning dialogue around 'allowing to die', euthanasia (Kennedy 1995) and termination of pregnancies of disabled foetuses.

'Service created neglect' arises when poor service provision to families of children creates impossible care dilemmas and stresses, increasing the likelihood of parents abusing their disabled children (Beresford 1995).

Whilst stress can never be an excuse for abuse, it seems a travesty of justice to find parents subjected to child protection procedures and the providers not called to account. Social workers are aware of these double standards.

Children's rights and needs

We need to examine more closely how disabled children feel about their lives. The UN convention on the rights of the child (1989) states, 'The child has the right to express his/her opinion freely and to have that opinion taken into account in any matter or procedure affecting the child'. This right has been enshrined in the Children act 1989 and the Children (Scotland) act 1995. Unfortunately 'child' here does not necessarily mean *disabled* child. Rarely are their wishes and feelings ascertained. Assumptions are made that:

1. They don't understand.
2. They have no communication system.
3. They won't know what is 'good for them'.

In the case of communication, this generally means that they do not use voice. Many disabled children have *good or excellent alternative communication systems*. However because they use British Sign Language, blissymbolics, makaton, rebus, sign and say, or computer aided systems, professionals in a hurry (who may not know how to use these systems) cannot *find the time* to engage in dialogue. It is easier to ask the parents.

In some cases disabled children have not been given the most advanced communication systems, such as computer-aided technology, as this is 'too expensive', and are reliant on antiquated, inadequate methods which cannot allow full expression of their wishes and feelings: a clear case of market forces or service created neglect. This becomes the equivalent of gagging a speaking child.

The impact of segregating children

Segregation - splitting off this group from children as a whole - has many causes and consequences. It continues in the use of language and in the way children are put into categories. Disabled children are seen as being in such a different category that separate rules apply. For example the Association of Metropolitan Authorities Report in 1994 was entitled *Special Child: Special Needs*. A very useful report, it is nonetheless discriminatory in its segregation into a 'special' group. The Children Act places disabled children automatically in the category of 'children in need'. An unfortunate description, as it is also applied to an annual charitable television appeal, thus linking 'Disability' with 'cap in hand' begging! Such language portrays disabled children as less able, less capable, somehow different, in need of charity not rights.

Philosophy and values

Other messages portray disabled children as less valuable. The 1984 In vitro fertilisation Bill reduced the gestation date for termination of pregnancy to 24 weeks in the case of a 'normal' foetus. However if the foetus is deemed disabled or seriously 'handicapped', then abortion is allowed up to term ... 9 months! (Morris 1993). Polly Toynbee castigated Brian and Melanie Astbury for going ahead with their pregnancy of con-joined twins. Letters to the Daily Mail following her article include the following:

> *Polly Toynbee deserves thanks for her logical look at the wilful production of handicapped children.*
> *I sincerely hope Mr and Mrs Astbury will give every penny of the money they receive for their story to St Mary's hospital to help pay for the high cost to the tax payer of their Siamese twins over the next few years. (Daily Mail, September 21, 1997)*

The 'logical look' described in the first letter is prevalent in all service provision. How do you protect disabled children if there is a scramble for their death? 'Deathmaking' is reality. With a health service led by market forces, disabled children's lives are at great risk for they may in future be refused treatment just as they are now refused life. For no other group of children do we have to consider whether euthanasia is child abuse. For the disabled child the option is frequently discussed. For non-disabled children there would be no hesitation in considering it as abuse.

Where do these debates 'fit' in child protection? Termination of disabled children, 'allowing to die', euthanasia has not been addressed as a major child protection issue. There are commonly held attitudes which have so de-personalised, even de-humanised disabled children, that they are rarely fully and comprehensively considered in 'ordinary' child protection processes and services. These debates around life or death must be addressed as part of the child protection remit for disabled children.

Marchant (1991) helped us conceptualise why disabled children were left off the child protection agenda:

- They would not be targeted as they would not be attractive or because people would feel sorry for them.
- Sexual abuse is not as harmful because they don't understand it or because they don't feel it. (Learning disabled and paralysed children respectively).
- Disabled children make false allegations.
- Disabled children cannot benefit from specialist help.

De-humanising and negative attitudes are associated with vulnerability for disabled children. Senn (1986) says; 'Society has created a situation in which children with disabilities have been taught to be good victims'.

The ABCD pack (Kennedy 1993), looks at this 'created vulnerability' and how discriminatory practice across all services leaves disabled children vulnerable. It is not the disabled child's impairment or condition that creates the vulnerability, something that is falsely assumed. It is the sort of mentality that can allow a child protection policy maker to publicly pronounce, in answer to a question on disabled children's protection: 'Let me sort out the normal child first.' A great deal still remains to be done.

Child protection policies

Policies must reflect the disabled child's additional (not special) requirements. Guidance to child protection workers needs to be specific and helpful. Broad statements such as, 'If the child is disabled they may need extra help', is totally unsatisfactory when in a crisis situation. There are specialised guidelines in relation to deaf children (Kennedy 1993, 1995). The ABCD pack is a valuable resource for child protection workers. Chailey Heritage has further guidance on intimate care, same sex/opposite sex carers and child protection procedures for the multiply impaired child.

Safety and prevention materials

Books, videos, worksheets, must reflect the specific needs of disabled children. Disabled children need to be seen in the material to act as role models for disabled children. Only then may they realise this material is 'speaking' to them. It is about their lives, their experiences. Materials need to be in Braille or audiotaped for blind and partially sighted children. Children who are learning disabled often benefit if the English text has superimposed makaton symbols/signs. To date only two books have been produced for deaf children, 'Secrets' and 'You Choose', both available from the National Deaf Children's Society. These books have both English text and visual representation of sign language. LDA, Cambridge, has produced an enormous amount for learning disabled students. Unfortunately schools which do not allow deaf children to sign will not use these safety and prevention books. It appears that for these schools, producing so-called 'normal' children is more important than producing safe ones!

Recognising, picking up abuse of disabled children

There are many problems in investigation, assessment and response. Key workers are too ready to assume that the signs or indicators one might normally attribute to abuse are in fact features of impairment. For example, comments such as; 'Oh she self-injures because she is learning disabled' or 'she masturbates because she is learning disabled' are common, in my experience. These generalisations can be applied to all disabled children such that even serious signs of abuse are attributed to the impairment. Soiling, bed wetting, fears, sexual behaviours or soreness in a non-disabled child can be spotted easily, a pattern of indicators which may ring alarm bells. With disabled children the alarm bells don't ring quite so easily or quickly. Disabled children's abuse is therefore missed (Kennedy ABCD).

Once a child protection concern is picked up by staff, they may find it very difficult to take it further. This is sometimes out of loyalty to parents whom they see as having *'done a wonderful job'* or *'they are under enough stress already'*. The bond between worker and parent is often very strong and parents are often perceived as *part* of the professional team looking after the child. This closeness, usually of years standing, means that objectivity is not so acute and boundaries and roles are blurred. Collusion with parents may result or the parents become the focus of protection. If the suspicions are serious and are moved forward to investigation, problems may arise when child protection workers are fearful of the disabled child and disability workers are fearful of child protection issues. Both sets of professionals may feel utterly de-skilled and unprepared, untrained to deal with a suspected case of an abused, disabled child.

There can be considerable panic in the planning process for interview and investigation. The practicalities of interview are further complicated by access issues. Often a child in a wheelchair cannot get into the interviewing suite and may be precariously carried up and down flights of stairs. This is extremely disempowering and frightening for the already disempowered and frightened child. If the child uses another form of communication, British sign language, blissymbolics, makaton, the interviewer will need the skilled help of a trained interpreter in sign language. There are now British sign language interpreters who have undergone child protection training. Facilitators help with augmentative communication systems. These should always be independent, qualified persons, not teachers or family members (Kennedy ABCD).

Following the interview, generally the criminal process ceases as the Crown prosecution service rarely sees disabled children as 'credible witnesses', especially if the child does not use voice for communication. For many of these children, going to court to give evidence is extremely unlikely, unless they have British sign language or other *fluent* system. This means that there is a considerable justice issue. Even though the criminal process may not carry through, the interview should be done and videotaped as cases have succeeded in civil courts based on these interviews. The Home Office is now looking again at the Memorandum (Home Office 1992) guidelines in relation to disabled children giving evidence.

Survival and therapeutic work

Supportive, survival work is crucial for disabled children just as it is for non-disabled children. Disabled children have to work through the dual oppression of disabilism and abuse. These two oppressions coming together can be devastating for the child, with a corrosive dis-empowering effect. The child has had to deal with the subliminal messages constantly given out that she/he is 'wrong', 'different', and not even supposed to be alive. If on top of this the child is sexually abused, for example, by (most commonly) a non-disabled adult, they may believe they were abused because they were disabled. They may think

If I wasn't disabled I would have been loved and not abused.
If I wasn't disabled I would not have been sent away from home to a residential school and been abused there.

Such thoughts are based in reality for many disabled children. The level of distress and pain can be extreme. For the worker helping the disabled child survive his/her experience, the emotional pain can also be great. The worker can also realise that the training and skills previously used with non-disabled children may be inadequate or inappropriate for working with disabled children. Imagination and sensitivity is required to develop and transfer techniques used with non-disabled children. For example, how does one help a child with Athetoid Cerebral Palsy vent and express rage and anger when limbs and voice may be restricted? How does one help the disabled child work through the discrimination and bullying they may have experienced in addition to the abuse? Imagination, sensitivity and commitment are needed from supervisors and managers to support workers in engaging with these combined oppressions. Training is needed on a much wider scale.

We are in the very early days of our professional work of child protection with disabled children. In taking account of pressure to move from investigation to protection and family support we must not cease to investigate what is truly happening to disabled children. We must guard against collusive alliances with parents or carers which may have developed because the child is disabled.

'No one would abuse a disabled child,' is a myth. Disabled children have not been given sufficient attention in child protection. Their voices have not been heard, because we have not asked and have not listened. The voices of disabled children have been silenced. Now is the time of listening, of paying attention so that new work can be developed. Only when we know about and understand the abusive experiences of disabled children can we begin to challenge attitudes, practices, caring and service provision which cause so much harm.

References

Ammerman, R.T. et at (1989) 'Abuse and neglect in psychiatrically hospitalised mutihandicapped children', *Child Abuse and Neglect, 13,3; 335-343.*

Association of Metropolitan Authorities (1994) *'Special Children - special needs'.*

Beresford, B. (1995) *Expert opinions a National survey of parents caring for a severely disabled child.* York Community Care/Joseph Rowntree Foundation.

Doucette, J. (1986) *Violent Acts against Disabled Women.* Toronto, Canada: DAWN.

Home Office (1992) *Memorandum of Good Practice.* London: HMSO

Kennedy. M, (1989) 'The Abuse of Deaf Children', *Child Abuse Review* 3,1; 3-7.

Kennedy, M. (1993) 'Created Vulnerability', in Kennedy M and Gordon, G. Eds. *The ABCD pack: Abuse and Children who are Disabled: Training and resource pack.* ABCD Consortium.

Kennedy, M. (1993) 'Confusion of signs and indicators'. In ABCD Pack, Kennedy, M. & Gordon, G. (eds) 1993.

Kennedy, M. (1993) 'Human aids to communication'. ABCD Pack.

Kennedy, M. (1995) Protecting Deaf Children: Policies and procedures. Disability and Child protection training and consultancy service.

Kennedy, M. (1995)'Euthanasia and Disabled Children. *Childright* No 119. September.

Kennedy, M. (1997) 'Are children who are disabled neglected?' Conference Papers: 'A focus on neglect', NSPCC Northern Area child protection committee. Co. Antrim. N. Ireland.

Kennedy, M. & Gordon, G. (1993) The ABCD Pack: Abuse and Children who are Disabled: Training and Resource Pack. ABCD Consortium.

Kennedy, M. & Kelly, L. (1992) Inclusion not Exclusion: *Child Abuse Review* 1 (3) 191-193.

L.D.A. Abbeygate House, East road, Cambridge CB1 1DB - Resource material for Learning Disabled Children.

Lyon, C. & Ashcroft, E. (1994) *Legal issues arising from the care and control of children with learning disabilities who also present severe challenging behaviour: a guide for parents and carers.* Mental Health Foundation.

Marchant, R. (1991) 'Myths and facts about sexual abuse and children with disabilities'. *Child Abuse Review, 5,2 22-24.*

Morris, J. (1993) *Pride against prejudice - transforming attitudes to Disability.* The Women's Press

Newport, P. (1991) *Linking child abuse with disabilities.* Harmondsworth: Barnardos.

Senn, C.Y. (1986) 'Vulnerable: sexual abuse and people with intellectual handicaps'. G. Allen Roeher institute, quoted in: *Interagency information and awareness programme on sexual abuse.* Subiaco, Western Australia. (1991).

Sobsey and Varnhagen (1989) 'Sexual Abuse and Exploitation of People with Disabilities: Towards prevention and treatment'. In Csapo, M. and Goughen, L. Eds *Special education across Canada.* Vancouver: Centre for Human Development and Research.

Sullivan, P.M., Vernon, M. & Scanlon, J.M. (1987) 'Sexual abuse of Deaf Youth', *American Annals of the Deaf, 3,* 256-262.

'You Choose', 'Secrets', two books in sign for Deaf Children. National Deaf Children's Society, Dufferin Street, London EC1Y 8PD.

8
Myriad Voices: Feminist and poststructuralist understandings of childhood sexual abuse

Sara Tibbs

It is critical that those who were sexually abused as children talk about what happened to them and that those who are concerned about it listen. In this paper I will examine the uneasy relationship between feminism and poststructuralism suggesting that, while there are deep theoretical divisions between them, they can also be of use to one another, in making sense of experiences of childhood sexual abuse. Poststructuralism, particularly the work of Michel Foucault, can offer a sensitive and complex analysis of power and feminism can offer poststructuralism a view of systematic gender inequality.

This text includes personal tales of childhood sexual abuse. The main themes I will explore in relation to them are power, gender and discourse (for poststructuralists, the process by which we give meaning to experience). Both feminists and poststructuralists have accounts of power although poststructuralism usually has little to say about gender. Broadly speaking, each settles on a different site of power relations: poststructuralism concerns itself with the specific and immediate, while feminism tends to concentrate more on systems of inequality. As most of the literature on childhood sexual abuse is informed either by psychodynamic or by feminist theories, poststructuralism may offer an alternative position from which to examine critically these perspectives.

Diversity and commonality in relation to power

According to Foucault, power can be, exercised where difference can be turned into inequality; it is not a commodity to be owned but a relationship (Foucault, 1976). Power is infinitely diverse: experience and knowledge are built up for the individual from innumerable small incidents and are constantly changing and being renegotiated. This view of power can seem inappropriate to a discussion of the sexual abuse of children, where adults are experienced as all-powerful. The adult-child relationship, as constituted within discourse, is automatically one of power and of inequality, because childhood is discursively constructed in opposition to adulthood. Adult power is crystallised by absolute notions of authority and exercised through the overt use or threat of physical violence, through surveillance and through covert forms of emotional manipulation. Differences in the way power is understood are key to the philosophical parting of the ways between feminism and poststructuralism.

Diversity and commonality in relation to gender: Feminism

Sexual abuse is committed primarily by men. Virtually all data collected show this male preponderance. (Finkelhor, 1984)

There is a major gender bias to childhood sexual abuse. A theory of gender inequality, therefore, which sees childhood sexual abuse as an expression of gendered domination, is often crucial to understanding what sexually abused children go through. Men's sexuality is culturally privileged and in most societies, sees the equation of masculinity with sexuality, aggression and dominance.

Feminists have focused on male sexuality as the problem, and it was feminist activism which first made the sexual abuse of children a political issue. Most of the support schemes that are now fairly widespread were feminist innovations: incest intervention centres, telephone helplines, counselling and self-help groups for those sexually abused in childhood. However, feminist theory has tended to limit its focus only to masculinity and this has left it with an underdeveloped analysis of the significance of age and generation, and unable adequately to explain abuse which occurs outside the particular context of a male abuser within a family situation.

Elizabeth Ward, author of *Father-Daughter Rape*, sees the sexual abuse of children as an effect of the patriarchal 'rape ideology' which determines 'that male sexuality is innately active, aggressive and insatiable, that female sexuality is innately passive, receptive and inhibited' (Ward, 1984).

She assumes a direct causal relationship between ideology and sexual violence, which predetermines that females will always be in positions of powerlessness in relation to males. In her deference to the 'patriarchal metanarrative' (Barrett, 1987), she can argue that sexual agency is the exclusive realm of men. Diana Russell follows a similar ideological train of thought which leads her to dismiss the power wielded by female perpetrators. '[N]ot only was incestuous abuse by female perpetrators very rare, it also appears to have been less traumatic and serious than incestuous abuse by male perpetrators' (Russell, 1986).

Who quantifies the trauma of childhood sexual abuse?

Another tendency in radical feminist analysis is to tell a simplistic tale of gender socialisation: a gender identity is imposed on us and we passively internalise it. The view does not allow much room for resistance: for the children, women and men who reject conventional subject positions of masculinity and femininity. Patriarchal ideology does construct masculinity and femininity in relation to each other. It associates male sexuality with dominance, offering men sexual agency above women, whom it constructs as passive. Whether people accept this construction of gender, and to what degree, involves more than merely being offered it, however. Socialisation explanations do not need to be rejected entirely but neither do they help us to understand a woman's behaviour when she steps out of expectations for her gender's behaviour. Despite conditioning, we could say, women do sometimes sexually abuse children.

The feminist perspective I criticise here is only one of many but it has been very influential in the area of feminist research on the sexual abuse of children. In so far as feminism offers theoretical explanations of those involved in sexual relationships it is helpful, but when it becomes, 'the radical feminist project of understanding sexuality and biological reproduction solely in terms of male supremacy' (Barrett, 1987), its generalising limits its credibility. To hold up women's oppression as a way of understanding all forms of oppression is exclusionary. Having said this, the concept of structures of inequality, whether according to gender or to 'race' are nevertheless necessary for perspectives which look for commonality in experience.

In common with psychodynamic theory, the feminism which informs much literature on the sexual abuse of children defines it in relation to the family. All childhood sexual abuse is assimilated as incest and the biological and family context is seen as the main site for analysis. Mary McIntosh points to this as a weakness. Cultural representations of childhood (ie child pornography), the sexual exploitation of children by strangers and child prostitution are, she says, separate arenas and should be given specific theoretical consideration (McIntosh, 1988). The value of feminist analysis can be limited without a willingness to address directly the sexual abuse of children outside of relationships which resemble the father/daughter one.

Psychodynamic theory

Criticised as 'the orthodoxy' by MacLeod and Saraga (1988), the psychodynamic approach informs conceptual accounts of childhood sexual abuse such as the 'cycle of abuse' and 'family dysfunction' theories. It underpins much social work practice as well as many versions of therapy and counselling.

Psychodynamic theory shares with feminism an over-emphasis on the family as the site of the sexual abuse of children. However, the family they describe looks very different from the two perspectives. Because its paradigm is the opposition of a so-called normal, healthy family with a dysfunctioning one, family dysfunction pathologises all families in which childhood sexual abuse occurs, and fails to interrogate the distribution of power within the family unit. Feminists criticise the unsophisticated gender politics of this theory. Frequently interrogating the role of the mother rather than the actions of the father, family dysfunction theory takes the heat off the perpetrator and promotes, 'ideas of uncontrollable male urges, female responsibility to control men, the collusive wife and the absent, withdrawn or neglecting mother' (MacLeod and Saraga, 1988).

Poststructuralism

It can be useful to apply poststructuralist theories of discourse and subjectivity to an analysis of the 'telling' of childhood sexual abuse, as the way experience is given meaning is a very complex issue, and poststructuralism can correct essentialist tendencies in this area. Poststructuralism can provide a useful focus to accounts because it takes heterogeneity as its starting point, unlike psycho dynamic and radical feminist theories which seek to unify by stressing commonality. A poststructuralist analysis of subjectivity can, says Chris Weedon (1987) dismantle existing unrecognised modes of domination, thus addressing the gaps in theories of social structures. Rather than looking at overall systems of inequality, poststructuralism interrogates their make up, emphasising the complexity of power relations from the most immediate site of power: the child's body.

Poststructuralists have, argues Rosemary Tong, (1992) 'thematised the many'. Discourse theory seeks to modify absolutism. In the realm of philosophy it takes enlightenment thought, the 'hallmark of modernity', and the basis of liberal humanism, as its 'other'. Enlightenment thought revolves around the Cartesian framework (from Descartes, seventeenth century philosopher). The Cartesian framework is a quest for certainty, order and clarity of thought. It informs the modernist way of making sense of the world, based on dualistic ontologies such as culture/nature, mind/body and, particularly, object/subject. Poststructuralists would locate family dysfunction and radical feminist theories firmly in the modernist tradition.

Poststructuralism has its roots in the work of Nietzsche. It rejects all dualistic, oppositional thought as inevitably dependent on a belief in 'universal signifiers' (Foucault, 1990) and the existence, somewhere, of absolute 'truth'. Discourse theory insists that people are made, not born. We are constituted socially by language and do not exist outside of it. This is called, in the argot of poststructuralism, a non-unitary approach to knowledge. It is a kind of pluralism which totally rejects the idea of indisputable facts or final answers, replacing the 'will to truth' with an in-depth exposition of diversity and difference. It rejects theoretical overviews, or metanarratives, and its organising principle is discourse: the accumulated written spoken knowledge on a given issue.

Discourse is, says Foucault, plurality of meaning . In this instance, childhood sexual abuse would be defined as the discursive field, the sum of all the specific discourses on it. The discourses themselves are the various, competing ways in which it is given meaning. Examples of discourses on the sexual abuse of children are psychiatric, legal, libertarian and feminist. Although meaning is always plural, there is a hierarchy of discourses. In the hierarchy of discourses currently engaged in producing the social meanings of childhood sexual abuse, the 'family dysfunction' and legal discourses, for example, carry more weight than feminist ones.

Discourse is, according to Foucault, a structuring principle of society because it is where actual and possible forms of social organisation are both constituted and resisted; it is the site of social transformation. All meaning is constituted by language, there is no meaning outside language. Therefore, instead of looking to structures of inequality to explain power reactions, we look to language.

What an event means to an individual depends on the ways of interpreting the world, on the discourses available to her at any given moment. (Weedon, 1987)

One of the most significant concepts in the process of assigning meaning to experience is subjectivity. Poststructuralism sees the subject of a text as fragmented and contradictory, always in a state of change and always changing meaning. In the poststructuralist world, we can do no more than create a 'truth' for a moment, in discourse. We actually constitute the subject by the act of naming her. In poststructuralist interpretation then, those who have been sexually abused, like all subjects, do not have the final word about the meaning of their experiences because there is no truth to be found and there will never be a final word.

By locating feminism in a modernist framework, radical feminism would be seen by poststructuralism as a falsely unitary approach to subjectivity. The implication in much feminist literature on this subject is that the abused child, from her own standpoint, speaks unquestionable fact and holds the secret to her own, possibly to all sexually abused children's experiences. An example of this essentialist approach to knowledge is in the extremely popular handbook for women survivors of childhood sexual abuse by Ellen Bass and Laura Davis, 'The Courage to Heal'. In this book, Bass and Davis (1988) treat 'survivors' as a homogeneous group, their differences overlooked in favour of their 'shared' experiences. From this assumption of the archetypal survivor comes a step-by-step guide to 'healing' which says that once you have gone through your denial, self-hatred, anger (the backbone of healing), etc , then you will be healthy and healed. As Ellen Bass says in the introduction,

this book is based on the premise that everyone wants to become whole, to fulfil their potential. That we all, like seedlings or tadpoles, intend to become our full selves and will do so if we are not thwarted. (Bass and Davis, 1988)

Clearly, the gap between feminism and poststructuralism on the interpretation of experience is vast. Poststructuralism would say that there is no full self, that our experiences and knowledge are fragmented and cannot be otherwise.

Childhood sexual abuse as diversity of experience: Introduction to accounts

Two of the accounts that follow are from a series of interviews. During the interviews with 'Hannah', she gave me a copy of a text which she has written, recording all she can remember about the abuse of her childhood. The parts which I have used are a very small section of this. The third account, Richard's, is from a book, 'Rescuing the Inner Child' by Penny Parks (Parks, 1990). The reader may find the accounts that follow distressing but a direct, felt engagement with such stories is an essential influence on theory.

Apart from illustrating the diversity of experiences that are called 'child sexual abuse', these accounts are also included to highlight the complexity of ways in which power is abused and as examples of childhood sexual abuse occurring in very different contexts.

Hannah

(M is her mother, SF is her father, Lee is her sister.)
Hannah was born to a German mother in Portsmouth and was immediately taken into care. The abuse began the first time she was sent to stay with M and SF in Germany.

> SF always bathed me. The water was too hot as he poured it over my head and body. When he soaped me he would interfere with my genitals. If I objected he would slap or hurt me in some way... What scared me more was when he would lift me by the ankles so that my head slid under the water. He would hold me like that until the bubbles appeared, then he would let me up...
>
> At night I would be tied by my wrists to the bed. If I wanted to go to the toilet I couldn"t. I often woke to find my bed wet and cold. This would always result in a beating...
>
> SF would come at night and take me into his/their bed. Pushing my head beneath the covers, he forced his penis into my mouth. I was frequently sick afterwards...
>
> SF is sitting in an armchair, he lifts me up and sits me, astride him. His 'knife' enters me. He pushes a cushion onto my face, I am screaming into the cushion...

The second time Hannah was removed from M and SF was when she was found beaten and locked in a cellar. She had been there for days. She lost speech entirely between the ages of seven and ten. At ten, she was again returned to them.

> Prior to my going, I had been given a live baby rabbit that I called "Rupert Thumper". He was wonderful. I would take him for walks and talk to him. When I was returned to M and SF I took Rupert with me. It was a mistake. One day on my return from school, he met me at the door, holding a white blood stained skin in his hand... That evening there was a place set for me at the table. I was terrified, but I knew I could not eat what was being served... Pushing me back into the chair, he got M to hold my head and began to force feed me. M held my nose so that I would open my mouth if only to breathe. When I did, he forced a spoonful of the pie into my mouth and held it shut. I refused to swallow it. When I spat it out, he became more and more angry and began hitting me. As I fell around the room, he followed, raining punches. Somehow, I didn't mind being hit, I was glad I hadn't eaten my friend.
>
> The usual pattern of starving and abuse began again. M. was often ill and spent quite a lot of time in bed. I remember holding Lee's crucifix and wishing she would die.
>
> He, (SF) would get M to hold me down as he inserted objects into me. He had a small dog, a Dachshund. He would hold my legs apart and let the dog interfere with me. If the dog made me cry, he would praise it.

Hannah was not finally removed from M and SF's custody until she had been hospitalised as a result of injuries inflicted by SF for the second time.

> The visit drew to a close with the most awful event of my life. I was locked in the bedroom, not dressed although it was daylight. M and Lee had gone out, only SF was in the flat. I heard him come up the stairs and unlock the door of the bedroom. I stood in the

middle of the room, rigid. He was sweating, his face was red and angry. He pointed and began to shout at me, 'you bastard'. I don't remember what came next. Then he began to beat me, one hit would send me flying across the room. He continued until I could stand no longer. Then he lifted my nightdress over my head. He secured my hands. I lay and watched him, thinking I was in for a thrashing. I closed my eyes. The next thing I feel is the weight of his body on top of me and his hand around my throat, pinning me down. He, was hot and smelled. I kept my eyes closed and remember my heart thudding in my chest. I couldn't breathe, he was so heavy. He was moving on top of me, he opened my legs wide I could feel him pushing. There is a terrible pain as he forces himself inside me. I feel I am burning all over and I feel sick, I can't breathe. The pain is awful. I begin to vomit and everything goes black...

Hannah was abused in many ways by M and SF. They held the power of life and death over her and, reading Hannah's account, it seems amazing that she did, in fact, survive.

Hannah's story is of having her body constantly controlled and violated. As well as being powerless to prevent the abuse, she was not allowed to express any resistance. When M and SF were trying to force her to eat her beloved pet rabbit, her resistance was met with extreme violence. The violence and sexual abuse were accompanied by SF's ever-present threat that he would kill her if she told. Instead of telling an adult what was happening to her (twice she had been 'rescued' only to be sent back), she spent several years of her life in a state, of 'elective mutism'. She says of this now 'If you get something like elective mutism, I think that's sort of the ultimate in pulling away resources because what is the point of communicating with the world?' Her elective mutism shows her complete isolation. M and SF repeatedly told Hannah that she was hated, they called her 'bastard' rather than by her name. She, in turn, held her sister's crucifix and prayed for her mother's death. But she had no other trusted adults to turn to and she was left in their power entirely for most of the first ten years of her life.

I have analysed Hannah's account in its most immediate context, her home life, in terms of the power relationships between her and her perpetrators. In this account it is subjectivity with which I am most concerned. There is another power relationship in Hannah's account, between M and SF, M could be seen as his accomplice rather than his equal. This is part of a broader context of gender inequality but in terms of this analysis, the powerlessness I am focusing on is Hannah's. M, like SF, must be held responsible for her actions. To Hannah it is irrelevant which adult was the more powerful.

Tasmin

In this account Tasmin talks about being sexually abused at two different times of her life, as a young child up to the age of eleven, and then between the ages of sixteen and eighteen. When she was a child, her father raped her mother regularly and sexually abused her sister. She also has two brothers. He was physically violent with all of them. The text below comes from the transcripts of interviews with Tasmin.

The whole thing was quite confused really, for me it wasn't obvious. Basically I have enormous gaps in my memory. The whole environment that I was living in was so abusive that I'm not clear what was sexual abuse, what was emotional abuse, what was violence.

My father used to massage us. It was an Indian custom, he said, of putting mustard oil onto the children. He used to do that a lot. I have one memory, I must have been six. I was standing by a big window, the sun was coming in onto me and I was completely naked.. I'd been covered in oil by him and I was feeling so uncomfortable, I was really unhappy. He'd made me stand there. I don't know how much he touched me, he must have touched me all over to massage me and I know I didn't want to be standing by that window and knew that basically whatever he said, we did. My body was his, just no question, because I was so scared of him. It was so life and death really, considering all the violence that was going on at the time, it was just so much about my body being completely touched and exposed.....

The first time I had penetrative sex was with this teacher and I was just sixteen at the time. I just knew about sex, I felt so old. I feel very confused about it all because I felt adult but I'd felt adult for years. At the time it felt so expected. Clandestine, silent. We were always hiding, we were always going for walks. And I mean sex outside in a park on the heath. Part of that was exciting and yet part of that was really degrading in a way. I remember one time, the first time he actually came inside me was outside. He said something like, 'it's gonna be wet' or something and I stood up and I was really embarrassed. All this kind of stuff was dribbling down my leg and I didn't know what was going on. And that level of unawareness meant I was a child, I didn't know, didn't have a clue.

He asked me whether I wanted to sleep with him and I said 'yes' I did. Because, I did. It was just so expected, you know. And in some ways I was a child, in some ways I wasn't I suppose. When I look at my diary, I was a teenager, I was coping with O-Levels. I took on a very serious, difficult relationship which went on for two and a half years. What I was dealing with was not, I wasn't adult enough to deal with.....

He was very powerful. He was a director and I was really into theatre. And he was my biology teacher. We were doing reproduction in biology, sitting in the class room with him as a teacher, with my class mates and we'd just had sex. I went through a whole phase of 'am I a survivor or not?' and I just know without a doubt that I am..

Tasmin's account raises the question of how narrowly or broadly we define the sexual abuse of children. In her experiences before the age of eleven, she does not have any memories of specific incidents. She defines the abuse in a context wider than specific incidents in her home environment, what was going on with other members of her family. She also connects her early years to her sexual relationship with her teacher which began when she was sixteen. She is more clear about what happened here but does what she experienced constitute childhood sexual abuse?

Tasmin and Hannah's experiences are very different. This difference shows the importance of avoiding prescriptive judgements. Tasmin 'knows' she is a survivor of childhood sexual abuse even though her memory is often vague, 'all those kind of contradictions and silences, I feel like I embody them, I feel that's truth'.

By focusing on Tasmin's story, in her own words, I am putting her 'truth' above her father's or her teacher's. They would have different versions. Tasmin's father, for example, denied sexually abusing her. She thinks this is because he did not rape her:

I asked my father if he sexually abused me, in a very stupid way and he, said 'no'. And it hasn't left me feeling any clearer about it. He admits my sister's abuse but to a certain extent he'll stop short of what happened. I mean her story's different from his, basically.

The law draws the boundary between childhood and adulthood at the age of sixteen for heterosexual sex. Legally then, Tasmin was not a child at the start of her sexual relationship with her teacher. He could not at that time have been prosecuted for sexually abusing a minor, though there are now changes in the law relating to teacher/pupil relationships. In this case, seeing the line as sixteen is too simplistic. As Bob Franklin says, 'the term "child" has a connection less with chronology than with power' (Franklin, 1986).

In relation to her teacher Tasmin was in many ways still a child. She was many years younger than him. He had considerable authority over her. The responsibility which he abused was based on both his age and authority.

Richard

The third account I will look at in this chapter is of a male survivor, Richard. Penny Parks introduces it.

There are fewer examples of female abusers but what is known shows that they use the same blackmail techniques as their male counterparts. The myth that they would be more loving and kind...should be shattered by this example. (Parks, 1990)

Richard was sexually abused by his aunt Ellen for five years, from the ages of eight to thirteen.

After the time in the bathroom, I was told to go and sit on the bed and wait for her. When she came in she was holding a book and a newspaper. She sat next to me and asked if I had enjoyed what happened and I said 'yes' because if you say 'no' to her then you are punished. She said did I know what I had just done? I said 'had sex'.

She said, 'yes but do you know what incest means?'

She passed me the book and found it and told me to read what it meant. I read some of it but I couldn't read it all so Aunt Ellen read if out for me. I still didn't understand so she said it meant having sex with a relative could send you to jail. She then asked me if I knew what rape was. Without waiting for an answer she looked it up and read it out. It sounded like what I had done with her. She then opened the newspaper and showed me a story about a man who had been jailed for ten years for rape. I thought I was going to jail and started to cry. Aunt Ellen put her arms around me and told me not to worry, she would never tell anyone. But she said I had to promise that every time my willy got hard I had to tell her by saying, 'I need to rape you again Auntie'.

She said that way I wouldn't rape anyone else and go to prison. Every time I got hard I was so scared I would tell her and we would have sex.'

Aunt Ellen uses her knowledge and authority to put Richard into a position where he is unlikely to tell anyone about the abuse. She manipulates her knowledge, to make

Richard believe that he is raping her, that he is responsible for the sexual abuse and that he will go to jail for it if he is found out. Under guise of teaching him about incest, Aunt Ellen manipulates his limited knowledge on the subject, his difficulties in reading and his fear of her. She 'proves' to him that he is raping her by showing him a newspaper story about rape. She offers him identification with the rapist in the story through their shared masculinity. To Richard, 'It sounds like what I had done with her'. It was like what he had done with her, except that it would be more accurately described as 'what she had done to him'. She was in control, he did not fully understand what was going on and was not allowed to refuse her.

After she has told him that he could go to jail, Aunt Ellen puts her arms around Richard to comfort him. In this short extract we see emotional treachery. At the start of the account Aunt Ellen has sexually abused Richard and then made him say he enjoyed it. Her manipulation is successful: she makes possible her intention to sexually abuse Richard again. 'Every time I got hard I was so scared I told her and we would have sex.

> In sexual abuse, you're absolutely on your own. I mean that's quite an incredible thing isn't it? If you think of a child having to depend entirely on themselves?' (Julie, from another interview).

Survivors begin to break their isolation by telling someone what happened to them. What they share is that they have been sexually exploited as children. This statement stresses commonality, connecting them by acknowledging suffering, whatever form it takes, without rendering contradictions and differences invisible. In order to move on, to claim power, there must be a concentration on what are the common aspects, a connecting of personal suffering with social relations. Trying to make sense of the actual complexity and multiplicity of situations is the theoretical project and it requires grouping people together on the basis of experiences. A poststructuralist theory which can refute the concept of social relations altogether could lead to the dismissal of the categories 'survivor' and 'perpetrator' entirely, rejecting them as oppositions and products of dualist thought. The feminist/poststructuralist tension is between 'local' and 'total' arrangements of power. It is not sufficient merely to say that there are systems of power, they must be analysed. When power is socially sanctioned, it moves beyond the individual.

Conclusions

Feminism and poststructuralism represent complex and changing approaches and there is no imminent synthesis likely. I have tried to carry them as elements which are in tension. Accounts of childhood sexual abuse can be approached through poststructuralism and can themselves, in turn, underline aspects that poststructuralism obscures.

Discourse can become a site of resistance. We do not need to take established meanings, values and power relations for granted. Survivors' discourse is a discourse of resistance to the overwhelming power of perpetrators. It is cumulative, it involves the coming together of many voices, but they speak of diversity because they speak for themselves. Power is invested in those who speak and it is crucial that survivors speak out, given their long history of being silenced. Another dimension of power is personal power, the resistance that comes from the motivation to survive. The other side of power, says Michel Foucault, is always resistance,

> *there is a plurality of resistances, each of them a special case: resistances that are possible, necessary, improbable, others that are spontaneous, savage, solitary, concerted, rampant or violent. (Foucault, 1990)*

At the time of abuse, the children in the accounts seemed completely powerless and yet they survived: a resistance in itself. Power is productive, positive as well as negative. Abusers hold it in the moment they are sexually abusing a child but it is always resisted, which means that experience does not destine that child to the life of a victim. Discourse can create new positions for survivors to assume, encouraging them to speak for themselves and to occupy resistant positions.

> I remember when SF was sort of having a go and one of his aims was to make me cry I can remember even from being quite small, being absolutely determined that I wasn't going to give him the satisfaction of seeing me, cry. And he never did. He never succeeded. (Hannah)

References

Barrett, M. (1987) 'The Concept of Difference'. *Feminist Review*,26, 1987.

Barrett, M.(1988) *Women's Oppression Today*. London: Verso.

Bass, E. & Thornton, L. (1983) *I Never Told Anyone: Writings by Female Survivors of Childhood Sexual Abuse*. New York: Harper.

Bass, E.& Davis, L. (1988) *The Courage to Heal. A Guide for Women Survivors of Childhood Sexual Abuse*. New York:Harper & Row.

Finkelhor, D. (1984) *Child Sexual Abuse*. London: Macmillan.

Firestone, S. (1971) *The Dialectic of Sex: the case for feminist revolution*. London: Cape.

Foucault, M. (1976) *Histoire de la Sexualité*. Paris: Editions Gallimard

Foucault, M. (1990) *The History of Sexuality. Volume One*. Harmondsworth: Penguin.

Franklin, B. (ed 1986) *The Rights of Children*. Oxford: Blackwell.

Frost, N. & Stein, M. (1989) *The Politics of Child Welfare: Inequality, Power and Change*. London: Harvester/Wheatsheaf.

McIntosh, M. (1988) 'Introduction to an issue: family secrets as public dramas.' *Feminist Review*. Issue 28 pp6-15.

MacLeod, M. & Saraga, E. (1988) *Child Sexual Abuse: towards a feminist professional practice*. Polytechnic of North London.

Parks, P. (1990) *Rescuing the Inner Child: therapy for adults sexually abused as children*. London: Souvenir.

Russell, D. (1986) *The Secret Trauma* Basic Books.

Tong, R. (1992) *Feminist thought : a comprehensive introduction*. London: Routledge.

Ward, E. (1984) *Father-Daughter Rape*. Women's Press.

Weedon, C. (1987) *Feminist Practice and Poststructuralist Theory*. London: Blackwell.

9
Sexual harassment in everyday life: Protection in the context of power relations

Jacqui Halson

Introduction

This chapter describes some girls' everyday experiences of 'sexual harassment'. I draw on my own interviews with 16 young women who were 13 and 14 year olds attending a co-educational school which I call Henry James Comprehensive. The research explored girls' perceptions and negotiations of sexual harassment, as well as documenting the form it took (Halson 1992)[1]. Like Mahony (1985, p.53), I discovered that, through style and gesture, use of language and physical molestation, 'boys are active in structuring relationships of dominance and subordination'. Since the young women collaborated in defining what the research was about by relating their experiences of heterosex, I heard ample evidence of oppressive continuities between these more intimate encounters and sexual harassment in everyday life (Halson, 1991), forming what Kelly (1988) has called a continuum of sexual violence. I found that young women discussed experiences which evidently humiliated and frightened them as if they were 'natural' and 'only to be expected' - they said they 'don't mind', they 'get used to it' - and that the school does little to challenge this state of affairs. Thus, sexual harassment, though common and coercive, is largely taken for granted. The young women were neither protected, supported nor empowered to resist this form of oppression.

I supplement the qualitative data from my small sample with quantitative data drawn from surveys of larger samples of both sexes by Lott et al (1982) and Anderson et al (1990a). Surveys on the prevalence of sexual harassment in the working lives of adults have shown substantial variations, depending on definitions used, response rates and so on. However, many of these indicate that sexual harassment is or has been a problem for more than 50% of women respondents.[2]

This chapter addresses just one dimension of the multifaceted, lived reality of young women's lives. It has a particular purpose. Accepting that there are a variety of ways in which children's rights *as children* need to be promoted, it asserts that there are some *gender specific* ways in which girls experience human rights abuses which call for gender-conscious strategies of rights promotion and protection. Such a view accepts that the concept of children's rights is itself contested.

I argue that sexual harassment is a routine, but still harmful, experience, continuous with more *obviously* harmful experiences such as rape and child sexual abuse. I consider all of these to be features of relationships of power in society, and hence political issues. 'Political' is here understood as referring to the myriad ways in which power is *exercised* in social life and to how it is socially *structured*. In this sense, the social conditions of everyday lives in which questions about protection and the promotion of 'rights' are raised are political conditions.

I have chosen to focus on power relations for 'down to earth', as well as more abstract reasons. During a training day on sexual harassment at my own institution in 1994, it became evident that several members of the group, all voluntary advisors on sexual harassment, viewed the phenomenon as the aberrant behaviour of a tiny minority of 'deranged' individuals, rather than as a more ordinary feature of heterosexual interaction which constitutes an abuse both of masculine power and of the privilege afforded 'the lecherous professor' by the pedagogic relationship (Dziech and Weiner 1984; Purkiss, 1994). More abstractly, I am interested in the problematic influence upon social theory of Foucauldian perspectives which propose the absence of discernible structures or patterns to power relations and a *neutrality* to power, a view which speaks from a position of privilege based on the suppression of violence (MacCannell and MacCannell, 1993). I would argue that support and protection for women and children demands theory and analysis which can inform action, and that neither of the views above, because they neutralize power, are successful in this regard.

Many theoretical perspectives inform a more generally inclusive understanding of politics than is conventional but all recognise that power is ubiquitous (Foucault, 1980); it is integral to social interaction at all levels of social life (Giddens, 1981, 1984). The range of verbal and non-verbal communications which constitute the micropolitics of human interaction in everyday life (Goffman, 1967; Argyle, 1967; Henley, 1977), and in particular within organisations (Ball, 1987; Hearn and Parkin, 1987), are well documented. The personal (or inter-personal) fabric of our everyday lives is political, as feminists have long argued (Hanisch, 1971, cited by Humm, 1989; Ramazanoglu, 1987). In particular, the threat and use of violence by men has been considered central to the maintenance of power (Jones and Mahony, 1989; Dobash and Dobash, 1992).

My own understanding of power draws on the critical sociological tradition of Lukes (1974) and Giddens[3] on the feminist sociology of Ramazanoglu (1989) and Davis et al (1991). These feminist and sociological perspectives share the idea that individuals are active subjects and that their experiences are varied but also that they are influenced - constrained or empowered - by the way society as a whole is structured: there is agency and diversity *and* structure. In essence, Giddens' theory suggests that structured relations of power involving domination and subordination are produced and reproduced (though they may be subverted, transformed and changed) through the situated practices of individuals. An abstract 'grand theory', it needs to be grounded or 'anchored in our experiences' with full recognition that, although power is ubiquitous, it is 'always and everywhere *contextual*' as Davis (1991, p.83) observes. Contemporary feminist theory recognises itself as a *partial* theory of society which highlights the gendered dimensions of power, fully cognisant of the fact that these forms of power are 'enmeshed in all the other forms of oppression that people have created' (Ramazanoglu, 1989, p.178).

Power, then, is *exercised* in everyday situations and these processes *simultaneously* reflect and reconstruct or re-produce power *relations* or social structures. Sexual harassment is understood in these terms, as the situated and routine power practice of individuals and groups in gendered forms of domination and subordination. My consideration of power and structure unfolds in the second section of this chapter, grounded by means of illustrations of some concrete processes described by the girls of Henry James School. I begin, however, with a definition of sexual harassment.

Defining sexual harassment

Attempting to capture the complexities of social phenomena with 'neat' definitions - precise meanings, precise boundaries - is fraught with problems, as any student of 'crime' (Box, 1983) or 'violence' (Tutt, 1976) will be aware. The term sexual harassment covers a wide range of behaviours which may involve *physical contact* such as being 'felt up', held, or grabbed. It may be *verbal or vocal* such as sexual remarks and propositions, name-calling and appraising whistles and 'grunts'. *Non-contact and non-verbal*, *visual or 'psychological'* sexual harassment includes staring, leering, 'standing too close for comfort'; being followed; threatening body postures and obscene gestures, including 'flashing'. It is not the discrete behaviours, some of which can feature as harmless and pleasurable components of friendships nor the intentions of the perpetrator which define the above as harassment. Rather, it is the structural *context* in which it occurs and the *consequences* of the behaviour. Even though the business of 'drawing lines' is inevitably a precarious one, it can be observed that sexual harassment differs from friendly sexual banter, flirtation and so on in that it is *not* mutual or welcome or pleasant. Rather it is imposed, offensive, embarrassing, humiliating, invasive, threatening and, therefore, *harmful*. It has become conventional within organisations which have formally responded to sexual harassment to do so under the rubric of 'equal opportunities' or 'sex discrimination'. However, it could equally well be considered under the rubric of 'health and safety', since distress, fear, anxiety, depression, associated physical symptoms such as insomnia and tension headaches, are often the result of persistent harassment, amongst adult women workers. According to the European Commission (Rubenstein, 1988), sexual harassment is the most common and least discussed occupational *health* hazard for women. Sexual harassment creates a damaging and *unsafe* environment.

Drawing on elements of others' definitions of sexual harassment (notably those of Farley, 1978; Grahame 1985) and Kelly's (1988) definition of sexual violence, I define sexual harassment as:

> *any non-reciprocal, unsolicited, sexually oriented physical, visual or verbal act, (excluding assault and rape), that is experienced, at the time or later, as humiliation, imposition or invasion, that has the effect of degrading the person so victimised in the eyes of others and/or frustrates or denies her capacity to control sexual intimacy.*

There is a problem of distinguishing between sexual harassment and sexual assault. Kelly (1988, p.103) argues that there is a considerable overlap in the definitions of harassment and assault used by the women she interviewed. Only one distinction emerged: whereas 'sexual harassment involved a variable combination of visual, verbal and physical forms of abuse; assault always involved physical contact'. Sexual harassment and sexual assault are continuous with one another. Similarly, although legal boundaries are drawn, there are no *precise* boundaries to be drawn between sexual assault, attempted rape and rape, which can equally well be understood as on a continuum (Box, 1983; Kelly, 1988). In cases of sexual harassment where the perpetrator is an adult and the invaded or threatened person a child, we are clearly discussing behaviours which are continuous, if not co-terminous, with child sexual abuse. Notwithstanding these difficulties of 'overlap', the key terms in my definition highlight the importance of understanding that all such behaviours amount to non-reciprocal invasions which undermine a person's capacity to *control* whether, when, where, how and with whom sexual interactions occur. It is the ability, or otherwise, to control heterosexual intimacy that defines sexual harassment as a power relationship.[4] Children's ability, at different stages of development, to comprehend the meanings of such interactions, and their capacity to give informed consent, complicates this relationship further.

Power, gender and sexual harassment: Power as agency

Foucauldian conceptualisations of power reject the 'commodity' view of power which proposes that some groups *have* power which is in some sense a form of domination (Ramazanoglu, 1993, p.22). Foucault focuses instead on power as a mechanism or process which is diffused in everyday life, having few discernible patterns or 'fixed' structures. The idea that power is ubiquitous, is one shared by interactionists, organisation theorists and 'non-postmodern' feminists cited earlier. The idea that power is *exercised* rather than simply 'possessed' is also widely accepted. Since power is therefore widely viewed as being involved in the very constitution of social life, it cannot logically be viewed as *inevitably* negative, coercive or repressive in its consequences, a theme which Foucault is particularly keen to emphasise: 'throughout Foucault's work ... power is in the realm of freedom, the field of possibilities no one owns' (MacCannell and MacCannell 1993, p.203-3). Although feminists have focused attention on the illegitimate and repressive aspects of men's power, it is accepted that power, when deployed responsibly, has a productive or enabling or transformative capacity which the later works of Foucault emphasise and which, in different ways, feminists have explicitly brought into focus in our use of the concept of empowerment and our emphasis on women's agency. In its most *general* sense, power *is* agency: it is the 'can' and the 'could have done otherwise' which is implicated in even the most restrictive and oppressive situations (Giddens 1976, p.11). It is the ability or capacity to 'do something', to challenge others, to change things, without fear of dreadful repercussions.

Consider in this context the following girls' statements about one of their teachers, Mr. Ryder:

Pauline: He's a right Casanova. I hate him ... It's the way he sits on the table with his legs up. It's just the way he sits there with his feet on the table, givin' you really sly smiles. It really bugs me! ... Makes you feel a bit uneasy.

Lynn: When I was in (the lesson) he just kept lookin' at me all the time and it was embarrassing!

Fiona: He sort of stands too close.

Lorna: He gives me the creeps.

My interpretation of the girls' comments is that they are articulations of the way Mr. Ryder exercises power. More specifically, they are accounts of the way in which he routinely uses gestures and postures which subtly but effectively 'sexualise' his non-mutual and non-reciprocal interactions with the girls, such that they feel embarrassed, repulsed or disgusted and fearful, uneasy, unsafe. For the most part, Mr. Ryder engages in non-contact and non-verbal forms of harassment: he stares or leers; he invades their physical space with his proximity; he uses the classroom table like a sofa, spreading his body out, prone, in front of them, 'giving really sly smiles'. However, on one occasion, Liz explains, 'he sort of put his arm round me ... I don't think he meant it but I didn't like it ... It shocked me a bit'.

Given Mr. Ryder's status as an adult, a man, and as a teacher it comes as no surprise to learn that the girls do not, despite their discomfort, feel empowered directly to challenge his behaviour:

Liz: You can't tell him to get lost.

Fiona: As soon as you see Mr. Ryder, you think 'oh dear'. You don't say anything.

Thus, the girls are both humiliated and denied the capacity to control the non-reciprocal, sexualised interactions - to 'do something' effective about his routine invasions. They are silenced, though not completely for, despite their relative powerlessness, the girls use such resources as they have to help one another cope with teachers who sexually harass them. Their resources are each other, the 'grapevine' which they have created and employ to pass along warnings or rumours from older to younger girls: 'people tell you to watch out for him'; 'he kept a girl in after school and had sex with her'. The girls do not tell their male peers ('they'd just laugh') but the warnings and rumours help girls define which teachers they can trust and which they have just cause to feel unsafe with. This does not prevent them from being harassed, but it at least forewarns them about the possibility and affords them a measure of protection. 'It makes you think what teachers are like when you're on your own with them', Liz explained. In view of information on attempted and actual sexual abuse of children by teachers provided by Kitzinger (1988) and Herbert (1989), Liz and her peers are astute in reading into Mr. Ryder's public expressions of power, the threat that this relatively subtle behaviour might be less subtle in more private circumstances. A thirteen year old girl, for example, told me that her twenty-five year old uncle, then lodging at her mother's house, 'comes downstairs in his grundies (wearing underpants only) ... and he goes 'Swivel!'", the meanwhile gesticulating at her with his extended middle finger, indicating penetration. Is such joking 'just harmless fun?' Or does it 'have a serious point to it' (Fox, 1990, p. 434)? The gesture, in and of itself has no fixed or inherent meaning - it can be funny and non-threatening. In the context of a partially clad adult man and his young niece, as was evident from the manner in which this young women mentioned these interactions, such 'humour' discomforts and threatens.

Mr. Ryder was protected by the *public silence* which surrounded his behaviour. There was no sexual harassment policy at the time within the school which could have helped promote the girls' rights, nor any designated persons to whom they could have gone for advice, support or intervention on this matter. Thus Mr. Ryder could do what he does, with relative impunity. He is thereby empowered. The girls are not. There is no evidence here of major psychological trauma; these are dripping tap experiences which can grind one down, in part because of the absence of opportunities to talk about them:

> *It is now known that many children have suffered silently through being sexually abused. That silence is the silence of the (relatively) powerless victim who feels and knows something is wrong but who has no-one to turn to; who has no words to speak that can communicate the hurt, the wrong, the mistreatment; who has little hope that the situation will change. So too with sexual harassment. (Orbach, 1994, p.226)*

In addition to the intrusive, if occasional, touching by Mr. Ryder, the various other forms of *physical* sexual harassment which the young women described to me ranged from short-lived but persistent one-on-one skirt lifting, bra strap twanging, bottom pinching and crotch grabbing by peers, in school and out, to more prolonged experiences of being chased, pushed to the floor and groped by *gangs* of lads outside school. In these latter cases, the touching was particularly intrusive: boys' hands were everywhere, skirts were pulled up and attempts were made to remove underwear. The encounters described involved older and, in some cases, considerably younger boys. In one case, 'they just sat on me and pulled my skirt up 'n' all that. An' it was horrible 'cos I was right in the middle of the street'. In another case, a girl was at her friend's house. Her friend's brother 'had all his mates in as well'. She said, 'they got me on the grass'. What shocked her most was 'when it was Pamela's *brother* that got his hand up me - tried to get his hand up me. It really shook me up that did'. The shock was that an *acquaintance* rather than the other boys, whom she did not know, should invade and humiliate her thus. In another case, an assault occurred in the house of an acquaintance who was having a birthday party. Liz, together with a girlfriend, had gone round to deliver his birthday card and they had been invited in, only then to discover that they were the only girls amongst a group of some twelve boys. Almost immediately:

> Liz: they were all on top o' me, trying to get me knickers down 'n' everything. I hated it. I was screamin', kickin' everybody. Can't do nothin' about it ... They didn't properly get 'em down ... cos I was kickin' everywhere. I just blew! They were teasing me about it at school 'n' everything.
> Jacqui: What were they saying afterwards?
> Liz: Calling me 'knickers'. Things like that.

Here, then is evidence that the use of force and violence remain central to the everyday exercise of power. As MacCannell and MacCannell (1993, p.212) observe, Foucault's discovery of 'capillary power' operating throughout the body politic is essential but it should be accompanied by an understanding of 'capillary violence'. This becomes evident when the perspective of victims/survivors is adopted in preference to a perspective of privilege.

The teasing or repeated taunt, 'knickers', which Liz describes, can be understood as verbal harassment which served to remind her of the humiliation she experienced at the time of the assault and to embarrass her further by making her humiliation more public. This name calling has the effect, if not the intention, of threatening further violence: the lads have assaulted her once; they *could* do it again. Such verbal harassment, in the form of joking and name calling, was commonplace. 'Jokes' took a variety of forms, from the barely concealed contempt of one young man who said, 'dirty little fucker!' as Jill and I passed him in the corridor ('he was only joking', she said) to the more prolonged 'polo joke' with which Lindsey was repeatedly taunted ('polo hole') following an episode in which a boy had failed to achieve penetration: '*she* got called names because *he* couldn't get it up', Janet explained. Briefly, the most common names with which girls were taunted were 'slag' and 'dog'. The girls in my study confirmed Lees' (1986 and 1989) observations that 'slag' is defined so imprecisely and covers such a range of 'female misdemeanours' that it effectively condemns *many* girls and women and 'functions as a form of generalised social control', setting limits on young women's capacity to control sexual intimacy and sexual identity. 'Dog' does this too: a girl is either dissipated or boring; she's damned if she does and she's damned if she doesn't; she is punished for being 'too sexy' and for being 'insufficiently sexy'. The abusive power of words should not be underestimated; names do hurt.

The lads whom the girls know are far less subtle than the 'creepy' Mr. Ryder in their techniques of subordination, which deny the capacity of young women to control whether, when, where, how and with whom they engage in sexual interactions. Both can be understood as exercising, and abusing, power. The lads do it with more obvious violence. The creation of an unsafe environment in which the girls live their everyday lives is the consequence of *both*. It must also be observed that the fear and threat of rape exists during many of these more obviously violent manifestations of sexual harassment. As Linda expressed it: 'you don't know how far they're gonna go before they stop'. Sexual harassment in everyday life is continuous with rather than fundamentally different from the more obvious violence of events like rape, sexual assault and coerced sex by acquaintances. Two illustrations will suffice. Liz reluctantly told me that she had gone round to a would-be boyfriend's house ('he asked me to go out with him'). They were in the kitchen when he attempted to force her to fellate him:

> And he wanted me to gob him off an' I kept sayin', 'No'. He goes, 'Wank me off. An' what he did, he got really vicious then cos I wouldn't gob him off. He kept tryin' to put me head down an' I wouldn't do it. I was really upset about it.

The gestures which accompanied Liz's words indicated that he had grabbed her by the back of her head, reinforcing his verbal demands with physical force. This disclosure was made amidst great and uncharacteristic embarrassment and fear - that I would 'hate' *her* because of the event. That is, she was more ashamed for having almost fellated the young man than angry at having been forced.

Another of the young women, Vicky, described how she had been raped in not dissimilar circumstances, when she was thirteen. She and Lindsey had been invited to the house of a 'friend', a boy some two years older than herself, who was there with his brother and another lad. Speaking very quietly, she explained how she had gone upstairs to the toilet. When she came out, the three boys 'jumped out on (her) and dragged (her) to the bedroom', whereupon, despite her struggling and her screaming for help from Lindsey, which was not forthcoming, two of the boys raped her, taking turns to hold her legs. The third boy sat on her chest. Echoing Liz's phrase, you 'can't do nothin' about it', Lindsey said, matter-of-factly, 'there weren't much you could do really'. Such phrases underline young women's perceived and real powerlessness. Although the girls adopt routine precautions, avoidance and self policing strategies in an attempt to protect themselves (Stanko, 1985 and 1990), such as 'going the long way round' and not going out alone after dark, the social and political context in which the abuse occurs does little to empower or protect them. Whatever they do to try to avoid or cope with particular encounters, they feel powerless because they cannot change the general state of affairs. For power is not simply exercised in specific interactions, it is backed up with the use of force and violence and it is socially structured by both material and ideological conditions.

Power as structure

In contemporary sociological, as opposed to poststructuralist and postmodern theory, 'structure' is understood as 'rules and conventions which 'stand behind' observed regularities in social activity' (Giddens, 1992a, p.349) and power is understood as much as a 'commodity' or 'resource' as it is a 'mechanism'. That is, power is something which some people, more so than others, 'possess', are privileged by and at liberty to abuse by virtue of their being members of certain groups. Power *is* agency but agency in the context of relations of hierarchy, dependence, domination and subordination. People engaged in interactions 'do not have equal access to resources for effecting the outcome of the interaction. Resources are asymmetrically distributed in accordance with structures of domination' (Davis, 1991, p.73). As Bauman (1990, p.113) expresses it, 'different people have different degrees of freedom'; this is "the essence of social inequality"'.

The unequal distribution of economic resources profoundly structures power relations, affecting individuals' degrees of freedom, their power to act effectively. Agency and freedom are also facilitated or constrained by other structures or relations of power, based not on what people have but on what they *are* or are deemed to be: ethnicity, sexuality, age and gender resource people differentially. Social conditions of relative advantage and disadvantage - power relations - are created and reproduced most markedly when power is abused in physically violent ways in circumstances where the capacity to defend oneself is hindered by differences of size and/or physical strength. But *ideas* about what specific groups of people 'are' - the conventions or rules about what they can and cannot do - also differentially resource individuals and affect their capacity to do things. Structures of power or hierarchical social relations are always, from my perspective, accompanied by cultural power - the development and dissemination of ideas which differentially empower groups within the system. Ideologies are here understood as a means of representing material relations of domination and subordination as natural and legitimate, even desirable, thereby concealing and mystifying conflicts of interest. Ideologies are the *dominant* ideas of what is normal, natural and desirable - dominant in the sense of being 'most available' in the media. Adults hit children and 'get away with it' not simply because adults are bigger but, in part, because of the still widespread, though contested, idea that hitting children isn't wrong. The ideological construction of children as (non) persons who 'need' to be physically disciplined, perhaps 'for their own good', conveniently absolves adults from the responsibility of finding alternative ways of negotiating outcomes with children.

Similarly the young women of Henry James School are sexually harassed, coerced and raped not simply because young men are differently 'resourced' in a material (bodily) sense but because, in this context, they 'can' with a high degree of impunity. Sexism and sexual harassment cannot be reduced to the wilful acts of individuals; they are embedded in organisational life and society (Ball, 1987; Ramazanoglu, 1987; Herbert, 1994; Mac an Ghaill, 1994). The individual exercise of power in specific interactions is facilitated by largely taken for granted rules and resources in given locations at given times. Ideas like 'boys will be boys', 'men can't help acting on impulse', 'you can't do anything about it', women 'ask for it', are component parts of the ideological construction of gender and heterosexuality for these young women. How convenient these ideas are for those who harass and rape since they neatly, if simplistically, represent their own interests either by representing the problem as one of 'nature' and/or by deflecting responsibility onto victims/survivors. This context also clearly structures women's and girls' silence, self blame and shame, as I, and others, have argued elsewhere (Kelly, 1988; Halson, 1991; Orbach 1994).

Gender and power

I have asserted a connection between power and gender through my focus on the sexual harassment of girls by men and boys. I want now to argue that there is a systematic connection between gender and power which makes it meaningful to consider children - and their rights and their protection - in terms of their gender and emerging heterosexuality as well as in terms of their age, class and ethnicity. The relationship between gender and power is far from simple. The 'gender of power' is not simply a matter of 'haves' and 'have nots'; a matter of 'us' and 'them'. The social experiences of being a woman or man in a given culture at a given time are diverse, complex and often contradictory. Definitions of 'masculine' and 'feminine' vary across cultures and historically. There are gendered divisions *amongst* men and amongst women; variations which fall within a socially accepted range and 'stigmatised outgroups': hegemonic and non-hegemonic forms (Connell, 1987 and 1995). Further, gender cross cuts with other attributes such as age, class, ethnicity and sexuality, which differentially structure power relations as they are lived. Gender and power cannot be conflated. To be a man is not inevitably always to be powerful or to have limitless 'degrees of freedom'. To be a woman is not inevitably to lack power in social life.

Viewed critically, then, gender is a descriptive rather than an explanatory concept (Oldersma and Davis, 1991). It is appropriate to 'deconstruct' gender, to appreciate diversity and evidence of transformations and to explore the complexities of its interrelationships with other attributes which construct a variety of life experiences. However, there is evidence that it is appropriate also to engage in the 'hazardous strategy of reconstruction' (Cain, 1990). That is, accepting that the relationship between gender and power is not simple, that there is diversity, we have to have some means of describing and analysing social and cultural patterns, gendered power processes, interactions and structures, when they can be seen as enduring and significant features of social life. I take it as given that although the power of men 'is not spread in an even blanket across every department of social life' (Connell, 1987, p. 109), it is institutionalised. Patriarchal social relations is as good a phrase as any to describe the institutionalised power of hegemonic masculinity and the institutionalised subordination of women. Patriarchy is viewed as an historical product, recreated by the situated activities of people in the course of their everyday lives. Whilst in some cases, the gender dimensions of an interaction or phenomenon will be far less clear or significant than other dimensions such as class and ethnicity, in other cases, gender is of the most crucial significance.

In sexual harassment, the evidence for 'reconstructing gender' in the analysis of power is, in part, empirical. Quantitative data indicates that in the overwhelming majority of cases it is men/boys who harass women/girls. Lott et al's (1982) university based study provides clear evidence of this in their analysis of the genders involved as victims and as perpetrators of sexual assault and sexual intimidation.[5] The incidence statistics are low in each category of offence (6% and 26% of the sample reported sexual assault on and off campus respectively) but the victim/offender statistics are startling: 95% of those with personal experience of assault *on* campus were women; in 95% of the reported cases, the perpetrators were men; 88% of those with personal experience of assault *off* campus were women; in 97% of the reported cases, the perpetrators were men. There are difficulties associated with accepting statistics at face value. However, Lott et al's data are supported by a wealth of other data on the gendered nature of comparable interactions. For example, Kelly et al's (1991) study of sexual abuse showed that frequencies of abuse experienced by women and men were 81% and 19% respectively and men were the abusers in 85% of experiences of abuse by peers and 95% of experiences of abuse by adults.

Sexual harassment, even for those, like Lott et al, who do not prejudge the phenomenon as, by definition, masculine behaviour, is demonstrably an overwhelmingly masculine activity. The argument that 'women do it too' hardly supports a 'neutral' analysis of power with respect to gender. This is not to assert that all men sexually harass, still less to assert some causal relationship between masculinity and sexual harassment. It is simply to note the characteristics of connections so that specific interactions, specific life experiences such as those described by the girls of Henry James School, can be understood *in their structural context*. It is not to assert that men and boys cannot be subject to intimidating and *comparable* behaviours, which I discuss shortly.

Empirical data on attitudes or 'ways of seeing' the world can also be employed in support of the argument about 'reconstructing gender' in the analysis of power: gender is 'the factor that most consistently predicts variation in people's identification of what constitutes sexual harassment' (Thomas and Kitzinger, 1992). Lott et al describe, as one of their most striking findings, evidence that 'women and men differ substantially in their perceptions and attitudes regarding acceptable sexually inviting behaviour and in their perception of each other as sexual objects .... men consider sexually related behaviour on the job and at school more natural, more to be expected, and less problematic and serious than do women ... (there is a) greater acceptance by men than women of sexual harassment' (Lott et al, 1982, p.311-3). Helen Watson's (1994) discussion of some fundamental differences in the narrative accounts of women (who had brought complaints) and men (alleged harassers) adds further weight to these observations. Thomas and Kitzinger (1992) argue that whilst many of the women they interviewed stressed the sheer pervasiveness of the problem, viewing it as problematic but routine or a normal feature of social interaction, 'many of the men expressed the view that such routine incidents could not be sexual harassment on account of their frequency' (p.5). Thus they argue,

> *the very same feature of sexual harassment - its sheer pervasiveness - is used in feminist discourse to stress the importance of acting to stop it, and in an anti-feminist discourse (here endorsed primarily by men) to discount it (p.6).*

Thus, although we need to be wary of transforming average differences into *categorical* differences (Connell, 1987), it seems clear from the above that, on average, women and men have very different experiences of being in the world and differing perceptions of or ideas about some phenomena. They are differentially located within structures of power and they take different things 'for granted'. Following on from this is the observation that the exercise of power is not *necessarily* the outcome of the self conscious or *intentional* activities of individuals. As Cain (1990) argues, there are unthought about realities and relationships or 'unacknowledged conditions' which may constrain our capacity to reflect critically on our experiences of being in the world, to see ourselves 'in context' and to appreciate that less powerful 'others' might have a valid point. Phenomena such as sexual harassment and structured relationships of class, ethnicity and gender may be part of our experience and identity but we may not be self conscious about them. For this reason it is not sociologically justifiable to define sexual harassment in terms of the consciousness or intentions of the perpetrator: 'I didn't mean to offend' and 'I was just being friendly' are evidence more of unselfconsciousness or recklessness than of 'non occurrence'.

The very concept of sexual harassment is one which 'challenges the meanings of taken-for-granted behaviours embedded in heterosexual relationships' (Schneider, 1982, p.75) - the meaning of touching, comments, jokes and so on. The specific power effects of the 'discounting' are that it recreates the 'licence' to harass and undermines attempts to resist it.

Thus, when women speak out about and attempt to resist sexual harassment and to change the environment in which it occurs, it is no great surprise to find that they (we) are represented as 'extreme', and their (our) campaigns are in practice 'transformed into a female assault on the rights of men' (Ramazanoglu, 1987). Our ongoing 'interaction rests upon taken-for-granted techniques and rules ... When these techniques and rules are not followed disorder, confusion and *anger* result (Craib, 1992: 22, my emphasis). Disorder, in this sense refers not to 'anarchy' but to disruptions of the *established* order. Promoting the 'rights' of girls and women to control sexual intimacy and arguing in favour of strategies which would afford them a greater measure of protection from abuses of power, constitutes a threat to the established order. People who have an investment in the established way of doing things are understandably angry.

Can boys and men be sexually harassed by girls and women?

In view of the fact that this volume is about protecting children, whilst the focus of my research was girls' experiences of sexual harassment, one question remains: does this argument, that the exercise of power through the mechanism of sexual harassment is *gendered* power, mean that men and boys cannot experience sexual harassment? It is clear from some of the survey data on adults that some men regard themselves as victims of sexual harassment by women. I will cite here just two illustrative case studies of men apparently being sexually harassed by women. Edward, a 30 year old executive of a car manufacturer:

> *I started working here when I was 16. It was my first job working on the factory floor. After I'd been here a few days the women on the production line put me through (what I learned afterwards was an) initiation ceremony. I was literally chased down the production line by the crowd of female workers, all shouting very rude things and banging hammers ... (it) was very frightening. Then one of them took down my pants and put them on her head. They all thought it was great fun ... Afterwards they let me go, but for weeks they all whistled and shouted at me whenever I walked anywhere round the factory, just the way that men whistle at women. I was very embarrassed. I suppose when I stopped shaking I thought it wasn't too bad. (Read, 1982, p.82)*

Rayner (1992) recalls an incident which occurred when he was 18 and travelling on a bus in Turkey. An 'older woman' (mid/late thirties), sat next to him and began to chat him up and to touch him on the arm and knee. Eventually, feigning sleep, she slid her hand under his clothes and, whilst he was 'frozen', grasped his penis. Rayner states that he was 'unnerved' and thought: 'this is a gross invasion of my personal space', 'I am being assaulted'. More or less immediately, his assaulter 'opened her eyes, cackled with laughter and let go'.

In both of the above incidents, the young men concerned felt justifiably disconcerted, as did the male lecturers discussed by Dziech and Weiner (1984) who found themselves subjected to the unwanted sexual attention of female students. Any observer who has witnessed boys being verbally bullied by means of name calling which, for example, draws hostile attention to their perceived sexuality or perceived lack of masculinity (poof, queer, cissy, wimp), especially when accompanied by physical assaults, might well object that this is a directly equivalent phenomenon which, therefore, constitutes sexual harassment. At the level of subjective experience, I readily appreciate that the resulting feelings of humiliation, invasion and degradation are directly comparable and that some boys are vulnerable and as much in need of protection from such behaviour as girls.

As distressing as such incidents are for individual boys, there are some fundamental differences in the nature - or contextualized meaning - of the interactions. In the first place, as Rayner notes, although he *realised what it must be like to be a woman groped by a strange man who won't take no for an answer ... for a man it is no threat at all ... What it never was, was physically threatening. I never felt out of control about what was happening to my body for, at the back of my mind, there lay the knowledge that I was bigger than she was, that I could throw her off ... Sexual harassment works one way: it is something men do to women. Women only feel men up.* (Rayner, 1992)

It is not size alone, or even most significantly, which renders women's unsolicited sexual advances relatively less threatening, it is the *context* of men's socially constructed and institutionalised power as men. Women's power is not institutionalised, nor is it abused with violence, anywhere near so frequently, as the degree that men's power is so abused. The 'likely degree of escalation' (Connell, 1987, p.132) is therefore predictable for men. They do *not* live in a culture in which men are, alarmingly frequently, violently assaulted *by women* (sexually or otherwise). Unlike the girls cited earlier who fear rape and who are raped, the young men cited above have every reason to expect that they are not 'in real danger' *from women*. 'There is no balance in the fear' (Zahavi, 1992, p.108).

Another difference is that incidents such as those described by Edward and Rayner are 'one-off' incidents. They do not constitute one element of a continuum of behaviours, including coerced heterosex and rape, which serve repeatedly to deny men control over sexual intimacy. They do not constitute part of the fabric of men's lives *as men* (although comparable forms of behaviour may constitute the fabric of some men's lives as *gay* men for example). There is an obvious non-equivalence about what happens in girls' and boys' everyday lives. In my research I came across *no* cases of women teachers subjecting boys to sexualised staring, remarks or touching, nor any accounts of gangs of girls subjecting boys to intrusive groping; no instances of girls coercing boys into sexual acts;[6] nothing resembling 'rape' of boys by girls.

Age is of crucial importance however. It is the relative *youth* of Edward and Rayner which rendered them susceptible to 'sexual hassle' (Dziech and Weiner, 1984; Herbert, 1989 and 1994) not the simple fact of their gender. Women are susceptible to sexual harassment well into, if not throughout, their adult lives. Such quantitative data as exists suggests that not only are there gender differences in the sexual victimisation rates of young people but also that the incidence of such victimisation of men decreases with age, with adulthood. In relation to harassment of an overtly sexual nature *by adult males*,[7] Anderson et al (1990b) found that

overall, 26% of girls and 9% of boys had been victims of this at least once. For boys, victimisation fell with age (15% of 12 year olds compared with 3% of 15 year olds), while for girls it rose from 17% of 12 year olds to 30% of 15 year olds.

That is, whereas boys 'grow out' of having to cope with this form of abuse, girls *increasingly* have to cope with it. Avoiding it, coping with it, surviving it - becomes embedded in what it means to *be* a woman in this society at the present time.

Accepting that boys are subject to humiliating and intimidating behaviour of a sexualised nature by other boys, adult men and, to a lesser extent by women and girls, that has some correspondence with sexual harassment, *some* equivalence at the level of individual discomfort or degradation, and accepting that boys are deserving of protection from and support in dealing with such behaviour, I would argue that 'de-sexing' sexual harassment *over-individualises* the phenomenon. Defining sexual harassment as something which some 'people' do to other 'people' ignores the empirical evidence about the systematised direction of the abuse and neglects the structural context within which interactions occur. It deconstructs it beyond recognition so that the gendered dimensions of the phenomenon are made invisible. It would be like arguing, on the grounds that some individual children demonstrably manipulate their individual parents, that parents (adults) and children have equal resources to produce desired outcomes. Sexual harassment of girls and women by boys and men, is an institutionalised mode of conduct; sexual harassment or sexual hassle of boys and men by women and girls is *not* institutionalised behaviour. This is not to deny that some boys suffer from coercive or embarrassing sexual behaviour initiated by women. It is simply to argue that the latter goes against the grain, the former goes *with* the grain - part of the fabric of the structured relations of gender domination and subordination which the word 'patriarchy' describes. This analysis does not deny that some boys suffer coercive, intrusive sexualised behaviour initiated by other males. Again, there are indications of the inter-connectedness of patriarchal, homoerotic and homophobic social relations. The focus of my concern has been to establish that girls, like adult women, experience subordination, in their everyday lives, on the basis of their gender, and that this needs to be understood as an additional concern when recognising the vulnerability of children and protecting children from sexual exploitation by adults, particularly adult men.

Conclusion

I have discussed ways in which everyday experiences of sexual harassment can be understood as abuses of power which diminish, harm and oppress young women. Sexual harassment is worthy of consideration in its own right, for, even where girls are not *also* forced into sexual activities, such events as being called names, being stared at, being groped, constitute the fabric of girls' and women's lives. They can become woven into the tapestry of our identities as, disrespected, despised and abused individuals. These experiences are located and analysed primarily within the context of patriarchal social relations, although the significance of age structures which render boys vulnerable to comparable experiences is noted. Thus, in accordance with the themes of this volume, I consider that the business of protecting young people and more fully promoting their rights can only be effective through an exploration of the social conditions of power within which harm occurs and through which their rights - to go about their everyday lives unmolested - are quite systematically abused.

The task of specifying strategies intended to create resistances and changes and to protect children is not easy. Nevertheless, there are a range of discrete and interconnected possibilities for actions which aim a) to stop, deter or prevent, b) to protect and support and, c) to empower and help create strategies of resistance, through reinforcing the idea that change is both possible and desirable.[8] The formulation of policies, guidelines, statements of unacceptable conduct in schools, youth clubs and elsewhere together with networks of adult or peer advisors is an obvious and now more commonplace strategy. More is needed than formal complaints procedures, positive action, and legalistic burdens of proof however. The creation of a safe forum within which young people can simply talk about what's happening to sympathetic and well informed helpers and explore solutions - even if only at the level of subjective feeling, so that they don't have to suffer in silence is, I think, a necessary strategic response. Group work with girls and boys is another. Education and training for teachers, social workers, youth workers and others which highlights the significance of sexual harassment and abuse has a role in creating a more protective and supportive environment in which children and young people can survive with dignity and, thereby, thrive.

Notes

1. Given the difficulty of determining precisely when children become adults, I use the terms girls and young women interchangeably.
2. Herbert (1994, p.36) provides a useful summary of survey data from 1981 to 1993. The highest rates cited are 72% (National Union of Teachers, 1987) and 73% (Labour Research Department, 1987).
3. Giddens has formulated what he calls 'structuration' theory in a variety of ways. See his introductory works: Giddens 1982, 1989 and 1992a. See also Giddens 1984 and 1992b. Davis (1991) provides a useful summary, Craib (1992) a more extended discussion and critique.
4. Implicitly 'sexual harassment' has referred to heterosexual harassment. I do not have the space here to explore the interconnections between (hetero)sexual harassment and homophobic harassment but would agree that the term heteropatriarchy, as used by Kitzinger et al (1992), highlights the necessity of recognising the inter-connectedness of structured social relations which subordinate women and those which subordinate lesbians and gay men. See also Connell, 1995.
5. The data resulted from a random, stratified 14% sample of all staff and students at the University of Rhode Island in 1980. 1954 questionnaires were distributed. The response rate of 47.7% produced a sample of 927. Their definition of sexual assault approximates my understanding of physical sexual harassment.
6. On the contrary, when the subject of 'muff-diving' (cunnilingus) arose the girls affirmed that they neither force nor demand it. Further, lending weight to the idea that heterosexuality is traditionally constructed around men's and not women's sexual pleasure, they also 'don't expect it' and they 'sort of don't *want* it'.
7. It may be that further research on the subject of sexual victimisation of boys by women reveals more of such abuse than is currently thought to occur. Although Anderson et al's questionnaire did not pose questions on this, one of the authors commented that 'it cropped up quite regularly in the interviews with boys' (personal communication with Richard Kinsey, June 1994). But see Kelly et al's (1991) statistics cited earlier.
8. There are now some valuable texts which focus on 'eliminating' sexual harassment in

schools and workplaces (Herbert, 1992 and 1994). Chris Harrison's chapter in this volume develops this theme.

References

Anderson, S., Kinsey, R., Loader, I. and Smith, C. (1990a) *Cautionary Tales: A Study of Young People and Crime in Edinburgh*, University of Edinburgh: Centre for Criminology (since publ. by Avebury)

Anderson, S., Loader, I. and Smith, C. (1990b) 'Happy Days', *New Statesman and Society*, 16 November.

Argyle, M. (1967) *The Psychology of Inter-Personal Behaviour*, London: Cox and Wyman

Ball, S.J. (1987) *The Micro-Politics of the School: towards a theory of school organization*, London: Methuen.

Bauman, Z. (1990) *Thinking Sociologically*, Oxford: Basil Blackwell.

Box, S. (1983) *Power, Crime and Mystification*, London: Tavistock.

Cain, M. (1990) 'Realist philosophy and standpoint epistemologies or feminist criminology as a successor science', in L. Gelsthorpe and A.Morris (eds.).

Connell, R.W. (1995) *Masculinities*, Cambridge: Polity Press

Connell, R.W. (1987) *Gender and Power: Society, the Person and Sexual Politics*, Cambridge: Polity Press.

Craib, I. (1992) *Anthony Giddens*, London: Routledge

Davis, K. (1991) 'Critical Sociology and Gender Relations' in K. Davis, M. Leijenaar and J. Oldersma (eds.).

Davis, K., Leijenaar, M. and Oldersma, J. (eds) (1991) *The Gender of Power*, London: Sage.

Dobash, R.E. and Dobash, R.P. (1992) *Women, Violence and Social Change*, London: Routledge

Dziech, B.W. and Weiner, L. (1984) *The Lecherous Professor. Sexual Harassment on Campus*, Boston: Beacon Press.

Farley, L. (1978), *Sexual Shakedown. The Sexual Harassment of Women on the Job*, New York: Warner Books.

Foucault, M. (1980) *Power/Knowledge: Selected Interviews and Other Writings 1972 1977*, edited by C. Gordon, New York: Pantheon Books.

Fox, S. (1990) 'The Ethnography of Humour and the Problem of Social Reality', *Sociology*, 24(3).

Giddens, A. (1976) *New Rules of Sociological Method*, London: Hutchinson.

Giddens, A. (1981) *A Contemporary Critique of Historical Materialism*, London: Macmillan.

Giddens, A. (1982) *Sociology: A Brief but Critical Introduction*, London: Macmillan.

Giddens, A. (1984) *The Constitution of Society*, Cambridge: Polity Press.

Giddens, A. (1989) *Sociology*, Oxford: Polity Press.

Giddens, A. (ed.) (1992a) *Human Societies: An Introductory Reader in Sociology*, Cambridge: Polity Press.

Giddens, A. (1992b) *The Transformation of Intimacy*, Cambridge: Polity Press.

Goffman, E. (1967) *Interaction Ritual*, Garden City, N.Y.: Doubleday.

Grahame K.M., (1985) *Sexual Harassment* in C.Guberman and M.Wolfe (eds.) *No Safe Place: Violence Against Women and Children*, Toronto: The Women's Press.

Halson, J. (1991) 'Young Women, Sexual Harassment and Heterosexuality: Violence, Power Relations and Mixed-Sex Schooling', in P. Abbott and C. Wallace (eds.) *Gender, Power and Sexuality*, Basingstoke: Macmillan.

Halson, J. (1992) Sexual Harassment, Oppression and Resistance: A Feminist Ethnography of Some Young People from Henry James School unpubl. PhD thesis, University of Warwick

Hearn, J. and Parkin, W. (1987) *Sex at Work. The Power and Paradox of Organisation Sexuality*, Brighton: Wheatsheaf.

Henley, N. (1977) *Body Politics: Power, Sex and Non-verbal Communication*, London: Prentice-Hall.

Herbert, C.M.H. (1989) *Talking of Silence*, Basingstoke: Falmer Press.

Herbert, C.M.H. (1992) *Sexual Harassment in Schools: A Guide for Teachers*, London: David Fulton Publishers.

Herbert, C.M.H. (1994) *Eliminating Sexual Harassment at Work*,London: David Fulton Publishers.

Humm, M. (1989) *The Dictionary of Feminist Theory*, London: Harvester Wheatsheaf

Jones, C. and Mahony, P. (eds.) (1989) *Learning Our Lines: Sexuality and Social Control in Education*, London: Women's Press.

Kelly, L. (1988) *Surviving Sexual Violence*, Cambridge: Polity Press.

Kelly, L., Regan, L. and Burton, S. (1991) *An Exploratory Study of Sexual Abuse in a Sample of 16-21 Year Olds*, ESRC End of Award Report

Kitzinger, C. (1988) 'It's Not Fair on Girls': Young Women's Accounts of Unfairness in School, Paper presented at the British Psychological Society Annual Conference, University of Leeds 15-18 April.

Kitzinger, C., Wilkinson, S. and Perkins, R.(1992) 'Theorizing Heterosexuality', *Feminism and Psychology* vol. 2 no. 3

Lees, S. (1986) *Losing Out: Sexuality and Adolescent Girls*, London: Hutchinson.

Lees, S. (1989) 'Learning to Love: Sexual Reputation, morality and the social control of girls', in M. Cain (ed.) *Growing Up Good*, London: Sage

Lott, B, Reilly, M.E. and Howard, D.H. (1982) 'Sexual Assault and Harassment: a campus community case study', *Signs*, Vol.8, No.2.

Lukes, S. (1974) *Power: a Radical View*, London: Macmillan.

Mac an Ghaill, M. (1994) *The Making of Men: Masculinities, Sexualities and Schooling*, Buckingham: Open University Press

MacCannell, D. and MacCannell, J.F. (1993) 'Violence, power and pleasure: a revisionist reading of Foucault from the victim perspective in C. Ramazanoglu (ed.) *Up Against Foucault*, London: Routledge

Mahony, P. (1985) *Schools for the Boys: Coeducation Reassessed*, London: Hutchinson in association with The Explorations in Feminism Collective.

Oldersma, J. and Davis, K. (1991) 'Introduction', in K. Davis et al (eds.).

Orbach, S. *What's really going on here?* London: Virago

Purkiss, D. (1994) 'The Lecherous Professor Revisited: Plato, Pedagogy and the Scene of Harassment in C. Brant & Y.L.Too (eds.) *Rethinking Sexual Harassment*, London: Pluto Press

Ramazanoglu, C. (1989) *Feminism and the Contradictions of Oppression*, London: Routledge.

Ramazanoglu, C. (1987) 'Sex and Violence in Academic Life, or You Can Keep a Good Woman Down, in J. Hanmer and M. Maynard (eds.).

Ramazanoglu, C. (ed.) *(1993) Up Against Foucault*, London: Routledge

Rayner, J. (1992) 'A woman put her hand down my trousers ...', *Cosmopolitan*, February.

Read, S. (1982) *Sexual Harassment at Work*, London: Hamlyn.

Rubenstein, M., Commission of the European Communities (1988) *The Dignity of Women at Work: a report on the problem of sexual harassment in the member states of the European Communities*, Luxembourg: Office for Official Publications of the European Communities.

Schneider, B.E. (1982) 'Consciousness about Sexual Harassment Among Heterosexual and Lesbian Women Workers', *Journal of Social Issues*, Vol.38, No.4.

Smart, C. (1989) *Feminism and the Power of Law*, London: Routledge.

Stanko, E.A. (1985) *Intimate Intrusions: Women's Experience of Male Violence*, London: Routledge and Kegan Paul.

Stanko, E.A. (1990) *Everyday Violence*, London: Pandora.

Thomas, A.M. and Kitzinger, C. (1992) 'Contesting 'Sexual Harassment': an Analysis of the Rhetoric and Denial', Paper presented at the British Sociological Association Annual Conference, University of Kent, April 6-9.

Tutt, N. (ed.) (1976) *Violence*, London HMSO

Warshaw, R. (1988) *I Never Called it Rape*, New York: Harper and Row.

Watson, H. (1994) 'Red Herrings and Mystifications: Conflicting Perceptions of Sexual Harassment in C. Brant & Y.L.Too (eds.) *Rethinking Sexual Harassment*, London: Pluto Press

Zahavi, H. (1992) *Dirty Weekend*, (a novel) London: Harper Collins.

10
What do children need by way of child protection? Who is to decide?

Mary MacLeod

For many years now, child-centred has been a word used by agencies and by professionals to authenticate their credentials in the area of child protection – as if it were obvious what child-centred means and what it might imply for child protection activity, both what is done and how it is done. It is a term with which no one can disagree. But what does it mean in practice?

On the face of it, putting the child at the centre of the endeavour. But do actual children have a place in this? Do children and young people themselves have any role to play in naming their own needs; in defining what is unacceptable to them; or in describing the kind of help they themselves could use? And whose conception of children's needs and rights predominates? For notions about the best interest of children – of what harms them and how best to educate, care for and protect them – are culturally defined as well as being differently theorised; and they are hotly contested in the adult world.

My concern here is to argue for the inclusion of children in the processes of both defining child abuse and child protection and discovering what is therapeutic and helpful to them. But this is not easy to achieve. Despite the constant use of such phrases as 'the voice of the child' and 'listening to children', examination from the child's point of view is extremely hard to do.

First, there is not one 'voice of the child' but many. Children are no more homogeneous than adults, so both the diversity of their experiences, feelings and views, and the variety of responses they seek need to be discovered. And what a child wishes for in the present might be deeply regretted by the adult looking back with hindsight; equally a child might have quite different views at different points in their childhood, as research on stepfamilies and divorce has discovered (Reibstein, 1996). Thus, I am not arguing that children are the only ones who know or who know best; only that their views, experiences and feelings ought to be taken into account when adults are organising help around them.

Secondly, children's own perceptions, understanding and their experience are inevitably mediated through adult lenses with adult preoccupations. Two dominant media preoccupations are children as 'innocents' or 'demons' – territory constantly explored and argued over as if children's moral impulses were distinct from those of adults. These representations have their impact, too, on the way abuse of children is constructed: witness the swings between 'they are making it up' and 'every statement must be believed'.

Thirdly, primarily, in service provision, children are conceived of as passive. They are done to, they receive, they are organised, confined and regulated – for their own good. In the new language of welfare: are children ever users? Recipients, yes; but participants? Can they be consumers, customers, resisters, complainants? Or are they not just needy, mere 'objects of concern'? In consequence, their views are unlikely to have been canvassed and recorded and so are inaccessible.

In addition, researching children is difficult because of methodological and ethical issues: can you really ask the questions you want the answers to? How can children be protected from the consequences upon them of being researched? Can they consent? Is it fair to use controls? How does one achieve either a representative sample or a truly comparable control? Can the research point of view be explained? How are children's voices to be mediated in the research? Are the researchers self-conscious about their positions as mediators?

Traditional research practice also confines children to passivity. It is only recently that attention has been paid to researching children as actors in their worlds (ESRC programme on 5-16-year-olds). And if there are ethical issues in researching children generally, how much more so when the research focus is child abuse? Apart from the moral dilemmas involved about confidentiality of information and disclosure, the very fact of being 'researched' might compromise the scope of an individual child's freedom of action (such as it might be); and the researcher's own beliefs on children's rights to autonomy will affect those researched as it does the research outcomes. Furthermore, children might have too much to lose in being frank about the outcomes of the interventions that they have experienced. These are direct quotations from children's calls to ChildLine.

'I didn't want to go into care again; so I just told the social worker everything was OK.'
'He said he'd beat me if I told again so I just said nothing ... they took me home again anyway. I knew they would.'
'My mum has enough on her plate ... she's not well. I don't want to worry her more.'
'If my mum knew it would kill her. I can't tell her'

Even given the difficulties, the attention paid to children's perceptions of child abuse and child protection has been disappointing. Instead, much research consists of researching cases, trends, adults, parents and families. Commonly, in reports of research studies, one cannot easily discover whether children have been surveyed or interviewed and, if so, under what conditions, because the methodology refers to interviewing 'families' (DoH, 1995; Wilding and Thoburn, 1997). And even when they have been interviewed, they are usually reported as objects of adult behaviour rather than subjects with a point of view or even a role in the action taking place.

This leaves an absence at the heart of the research enterprise, demonstrated sharply in the summary discussion of definition in the DoH research compendium, *Child Protection: Messages from research* (DoH, 1995). Among the eminently sensible questions about 'normal' behaviour in families, and what is bad for children, there was no discussion of how children might define abuse. The question was not even posed, though professionals were urged to take account of 'children's perceptions of what constitutes abuse'. How are professionals to establish children's perceptions when research has yet to be done? We are then left with a space which can be filled with the researcher's or commentator's views.

The absence of the child in research practice mirrors a muteness in actual child protection practice. Parton, Thorpe and Wattam (1997) reported the absence of children's voices from the social services files they studied to discover the dynamics of the decision making process in child protection referrals. Birchall and Hallet (1995) found that far from the assumed prevalence of repeated and intrusive interviewing of children in child protection inquiries, there was evidence that children were not actually being directly spoken to, leading to a lack of both information and evidence for decision making at conferences, which, in turn, affects what is 'counted' and defined as abuse.

It has become fashionable for social work academics to allude to child abuse as an unstable category (Thorpe, 1994; Parton et al., 1997), as if the difficulties involved in defining child abuse had only just been recognised. In fact, feminist research has long argued the complexities of naming and counting as they applied to domestic violence, rape, sexual assault and child sexual abuse, as have theorists of racism, and, more recently, of bullying (Russell, 1984; Nelson, 1987; Kelly, 1988, MacLeod and Saraga, 1988; Kelly et al., 1991; MacLeod and Morris, 1995; MacLeod, 1996a).

Few categories are stable except perhaps 'alive' and 'dead', and modern medicine has rendered even these problematic. In quibbling over whether the category is stable or not, the glaringly obvious may be masked: children are beaten, cruelly treated, sexually assaulted, raped, prostituted and even killed by adults, usually within their families; they cannot easily defend themselves; and (unless one takes the position that children may be assaulted with impunity) something must be attempted to prevent or end the violence, safeguard the child and promote his or her future well-being.

If we, just for a moment, consider viewing women subjected to domestic violence in the way we do children who are physically assaulted in their families, the gulf between adult's human rights and children's are revealed. Can we imagine ascribing domestic violence to family stress and arguing for assaulted women to be described as women in need? How would we define being hit on a daily basis for such a woman? In grappling with the question of definition, the culpability of fathers and mothers, the level of intention involved, the adults' need for help rather than punishment and the impact of family stress or impoverishment are irrelevant to the process of describing children as having been abused or at risk of harm, though they are highly relevant to the process of offering help.

Central to the debate about how abuse should be defined is a recognition that naming happens from a number of points of view – one of which ought to be the child's. This is not simply a matter of semantics, for research into the use of physical discipline in parenting found that adults who defined their own childhoods as abusive reported using less physical punishment towards their own children, than did those who, though assaulted as children with similar frequency (more than daily), did not define it as abuse (Hemenway et al., 1994).

So, it is not good enough to retreat from complexity into some conspiracy theory about how the term child abuse may be used to authenticate the work of 'rabid', unreflexive child protectionists. No one can claim immunity from the processes of social construction. In finding post-modernism, theorists of child abuse must include their own position in the process of deconstruction to which they lay claim. As Atmore says: academic work does not '..simply address the problem of child sexual abuse as already formed 'out there', but helps construct its very parameters (Atmore, 1997).'

The major contribution that cultural studies has made to child welfare is to undermine ideas about certainty, ideas that there is but one subject of a story and that subjectivity is fixed and stable. This creates a space, perhaps, for children to be the subject, even the tellers of the story of their lives, and for their meanings to be complex and multi-dimensional.

Their stories lead away from comfortable conclusions that

> .....the current system does essentially do the work demanded of it. There is little evidence that children are being missed and in many ways practitioners are very good at detecting the few (my emphasis) who might suffer injury. But this is at a cost. (Parton et al., 1997)

It depends what you mean by 'missed' and 'few'. This conclusion seems optimistic indeed if you think of the 15 per cent of children subject to serious physical punishment (Smith et al, 1995) and the thousands of children who call ChildLine each year saying they have not told anyone about what is happening to them at home. Their voices only emerge later in their lives as they write to the NSPCC Commission to describe abuse (mainly undisclosed) or give statements to police or evidence to tribunals about sexual and physical assaults suffered in care, or respond to anonymous surveys.

Children's own accounts lead into territory that is almost entirely uncharted. How do children define themselves as assaulted? What kind of protection do they want? How can their views change what we do when we do child protection work?

Normally, children enter the welfare frame when others designate them as needy. One point of entry in examining what children want by way of child protection is to interrogate children's use of services which are accessible and which they approach directly. What do children say about their lives when they are reporting on them? What do they name as bad treatment? How do they interact with each other and with adults to organise their own surroundings to their advantage or safety? What are their preferred ways of satisfying their social and emotional needs? ChildLine, the telephone helpline for children and young people, is such a service. What follows is an account of children's use of that service to talk about child abuse.

Children and young people calling ChildLine about child abuse

There are obvious limitations in any study which reports what children say outside the ambit of strictly controlled research. But the sheer numbers of children who have talked to ChildLine means that it has spoken to more children complaining about abuse than any other organisation. In its first ten years of operation, 198,000 children and young people talked with counsellors about physical and sexual abuse. This amounts to 1.16 per cent of the child population over these years (MacLeod, 1996).

In the year up to 31 March 1997, as in other years, 18,263 children and young people (19% of the total counselled) said physical or sexual assault was their main reason for calling (ChildLine Annual Review, 1997) as did 1,500 adults worried about a child (MacLeod, 1997). A further 6,000 youngsters described physical or sexual assault as a difficulty contributing to the immediate reason for their call – having run away, feeling suicidal, suffering acute emotional distress or family relationship problems, among others (MacLeod, 1996). For example, over 30 per cent of the children calling because they had run away said that they had run from physical abuse or sexual abuse (Barter et al., 1996). Finally, over 3,500 young people called because one of their friends was being abused and they did not know what to do (Keep, 1997). Thus, in that year, as in other years, ChildLine heard directly or indirectly about around 30,000 children and young people suffering assault currently or in the past. The majority of these calls (90%) were from children and young people aged between ten and 15 years; but many children were talking about assaults which were ongoing over many years (one in five of those who reported duration, described assaults going on for more than five years).

Far fewer children (less than 1% of callers each year) and just over two hundred adults called about emotional abuse and neglect – possibly because in talking about assaults children describe events, whereas emotional abuse and neglect are more like diagnoses. A much higher proportion would emerge if calls from youngsters about family relationship problems were analysed to discover the frequency of types of parental behaviour which have been identified as emotionally abusive in recent research – for example, terrorising, verbal abuse, vindictive teasing, denigration and humiliation (Doyle, 1997, Glaser and Prior, 1997).

The overwhelming majority (90%) of the children and young people calling about abuse had not yet been in touch with any authority. Many (three-quarters of children who gave us information) had, though, told others about what was happening to them. In the 1996/97 year, friends were the most common confidantes of children (48% of those describing sexual abuse and 30% of those complaining of physical abuse who gave information), then came parents, mainly mothers (around 26%), then other family members (12%). Teachers were the most likely professionals to be told (up to 5%). Only around 4% had told social services, though around six per cent of youngsters described some contact with social services or the police.

Against this backdrop of thousands of confidential and 'informal' conversations, lie the official statistics about registers: in the year up to 31 March 1997, the names of 32,370 children in England and Wales were on child protection registers. During the year around 29,000 names were added and as many were deregistered (Source: Government Statistical Office). This is out of an estimated 160,000 initial referrals in each year (DoH, 1995): around 20 per cent.

Public and media want to know definitively how many children are abused in the UK. This is not something that can be known; not merely because of the problem of definition and therefore counting; but also because the processes of validation or substantiation of the complaints which emerge into the light of day are incapable of establishing the truth, or are deeply flawed. We cannot even distinguish for certain between all babies who have died of natural causes and those who have died at the hands of their parents (Hobbs and Wynne, 1996, Parton et al., 1997).

The most influential factor in substantiating a child protection referral, for children who can communicate, is whether a child confirms that he or she has been assaulted (Gibbons et al., 1995). But the quotations given earlier from children themselves indicate that denials may not be freely given. It would be a very optimistic commentator who would assume on the basis of the official statistics, that because most inquiries did not lead to registration, therefore most children involved were not assaulted.

Naming the problem

Calls to ChildLine are categorised as being about sexual or physical abuse when children say they are being sexually or physically assaulted. It is not possible to be specific about the exact extent of violence experienced; but the words and phrases they use are telling. Children are usually quite explicit about physical assaults: they use words like 'battered', 'hit all the time', 'beaten', 'beaten up', 'given a kicking'; but less so about sexual assaults, where children often use phrases like, 'doing something he shouldn't', 'touching me where he shouldn't'. The context given usually confirms the nature of the complaint.

The overwhelming impression received from children is their clear sense that what is happening to them is not right, whether or not they use the term abuse – often they do not. Some children are angry and wanting to act; others hesitantly wonder whether they should or can complain. Mainly, they approach the business of naming through describing their distress or through their tone of voice, tears or breathing. But they all communicate a powerful sense that there is another way to be cared for; a way that would not involve assaults; and that is the way they would like it to be for them. Some voice their longing to be in a different family; others talk about wanting to go in a children's home.

The authority to communicate on children's behalf rests not only on numbers but also on the kinds of conversations that take place. Children talk privately to people whose primary function is to listen to them, helping them to say what they want without attempting to influence the story or rushing to take control. Callers are concerned about confidentiality. They usually wish to remain anonymous. They can talk outside the conventions of family, peer or community loyalty and outside the child protection frame. In doing so, they are not necessarily threatening their families. If, in talking, they are contravening an injunction or threat, no-one need ever know.

They are also free of face-to-face contact – a freedom vitally important in enabling children to talk. If we compare how adults talk to children with how they talk to one another, one aspect of this freedom becomes clear: adults look at each other and then look away, but tend to fix children with a gaze. It is a measure of their power. Though that is disincentive enough to children and young people struggling to put the unspeakable into words; how much more so for young people who have been fixed by adult gazes when they have been abused, or controlled and threatened by glares and looks? For such children, being looked at can be unbearable.

The evidence produced from these conversations, then, is unique. It gives the opportunity for a view from the other side. Here, children may be subjects of their own stories, experts on their own lives.

Physical abuse

'Dad is beating me with a belt. It leaves bruises and marks. My sisters get beaten too. My mum knows but she can't stop it. I get on well with Dad at other times, other than the beatings ... .. I think I want to go in a children's home.' (an 11 year old boy)

'He only hits when other people aren't there. He pulls my hair ... he's really violent to me and my brother. He hits me really hard and leaves marks and he fights with my brother as well. I used to get on well with my mum and dad. But Mum doesn't seem to have noticed what's going. She's working an awful lot.'

'I can't tell anyone. I'm frightened of my dad. He gets so angry. He's given me a black eye and a split lip. I just want the beatings to stop ... Can you just take me from the house? I don't see my mum that often. Maybe I could go in a children's home.'

'Mum keeps hitting me off the wardrobe. It's really sore. She says afterward she doesnae mean it, that she loves me. She says she only does it 'cause she's under strain.'

The final quotation was from a 7-year-old boy, one of more than 10,000 children and young people describing physical assaults in the year up to 31 March 1994 – a similar number to those in recent years (ChildLine annual review, 1995, 1996, 1997).

It was difficult to establish the extent of injury from a telephone conversation, but children generally talked about assaults which marked them – bruises, cuts, nose bleeds, black eyes, belt marks and broken limbs. They described slaps, kicks, punches, being kicked out, across the room down stairs, being shaken, strangled or burned, being locked in rooms and cupboards. They used phrases like 'battered', 'always hitting me', 'hits me for nothing', 'has beaten me up'. They described being struck with all kinds of implements – belts, straps, cable, tools, billiard cues, for example.

Physical assaults were commonly accompanied by being locked in rooms, by meals being withheld, toys taken away or broken and also by yelling, threats and verbal abuse: 'I'm going to dig a grave and put you in it'. Callers also told of their parents saying they wished they were dead or had never been born. American research confirms that yelling and hitting frequently go together (Hemenway et al., 1995). And in the children's view, the verbal abuse could be as bad as, and often worse than physical abuse – a view that also emerges from calls to ChildLine about bullying and racism (MacLeod and Morris, 1995, MacLeod, 1996).

Those responsible for the assaults were overwhelmingly the immediate family (89%) and mainly their parents or parent figures. Most assaults were by fathers (43%), then mothers (23%). The proportions differed according to the sex of the child: girls were assaulted more by mothers than boys were. If numbers assaulted by all father figures totalled, then father figures were responsible for 61% of assaults reported by boys and 50% of the assaults reported by girls in that year. Eight per cent of the children reported assaults by both parents.

Assaults by teachers were rarely reported (around 1%), as were assaults by brothers and sisters (around 4% by brothers and 1% by sisters) and friends and relatives (around 4%). A significant proportion of girls (6%) rang about abuse by boyfriends – often punishment for a misdemeanour: looking at another boy; or to persuade them into having sex. Here domestic violence is seen in its beginnings.

The majority of child callers were aged between 11 and 15. Only ten per cent of the callers were ten years and under. Girls use helplines more than boys. Generally, at ChildLine, four girls ring for every one boy; in calls about physical assaults the ratio changed to 2.5 girls to one boy. Twenty per cent of all boy callers rang about physical abuse, compared with 11 per cent of all girl callers. This suggests either that boys are assaulted more commonly than girls, or that they consider physical assault something they can call about, or perhaps both.

Some children did ring because they had just been assaulted for the first time; but that was unusual. The picture was rather of assaults happening frequently and over a long period of time: only 16 per cent in the review year called about abuse ongoing for a month or less; while 30 per cent talked of the abuse having gone on for up to a year; 34 per cent for from one to five years; 20 per cent said the assaults had been happening for more than five years.

The most usual time for assaults to happen was when one parent, fathers more commonly than mothers, was alone with the child. But children said they could not talk to the other parent about what was happening in their absence. Some children described a violent world where sudden outbursts happened unpredictably and terrifyingly. Others could predict danger times and a significant proportion linked assault with their parents' drinking (MacLeod, 1996, Houston, et al., 1997).

Children offered a number of other explanations for the beatings: parents' taking feelings out on them; family rows; siblings getting them into trouble; being scapegoated within the family or another child being favoured; discipline getting out of control; or recent stressful changes in the family circumstances, like unemployment, bereavement, parental ill-health or parental separation. They also talked about the context of domestic violence. Among children ringing about domestic violence, 35 per cent described being assaulted themselves (Epstein and Keep, 1994).

Sexual abuse

It is difficult to assess public perceptions of sexual abuse because media reporting is, perhaps understandably, wildly contradictory: on the one hand castigating the authorities for inventing it; and, on the other, declaiming the horror of it; pursuing paedophiles at one turn, and making much of every alleged false allegation the next. The role of child sexual abuse in popular culture is also confusing. Having the plot of so many soap operas and crime stories turning on sexual abuse makes it at one in the same time commonplace and fictional. By contrast, what children say is very straightforward, though chilling.

'It happens when I come home from school. Mum doesn't know, I feel desperate, I hate him.' (An 11-year-old girl describing abuse by her father)
'Dad does things. It happens when Mum is working in the evening. When I ask him to stop, he just hits me and carries on. I want to tell my mum, but I'm scared.' A boy aged nine years. (It's more common for boys than girls to complain of physical abuse accompanying the sexual violence.)
'Daddy's in bed with me and R. He does a lady and man kiss. He's got no clothes on. I don't

like it. I told Mum, but she said, "Daddy doesn't".' (A nine-year-old girl.)

Over 9,000 girls and nearly 2,000 boys rang about sexual assault in the review year (1993-94): 13 per cent of all boy callers to ChildLine in that year, and 14 per cent of all girls. Four girls called for every one boy, the same ratio as for all children calling.

The vast majority of children (94%) were abused by someone they knew: 56 per cent described abuse within the immediate family; the remainder were abused by neighbours, acquaintances and relatives (29%), teachers (4%) and other authority figures (5%). Only four per cent described stranger abuse and two per cent did not specify.

The father was the most common assailant (32% of girls and 30% of boys), followed by male acquaintances (13% of callers), stepfathers (8%), brothers (6%), uncle (5%), and mother's boyfriend (4%). Mothers were responsible for assaulting one per cent of girls and 20 per cent of boy callers.

Some children reported one-off assaults, but generally abuse was ongoing: 16 per cent under a month; 30% up to a year; 34% from one to five years; and 20 per cent of children more than five years.

The experiences described ranged from flashing and touching through to rape, violent and sudden assaults; being made to watch pornography, to copy what had been watched; being photographed and videoed. Some described being threatened and beaten. Others being prostituted to father's, mother's, or brother's friends. There were few calls from children selling sex for money, but the majority were from girls, usually in the context of other problems like fear of pregnancy or AIDS, or homelessness. The involvement in selling sex was a way of getting money, or a roof over their heads for children and young people who had run away frequently from families where they were being assaulted. Some girls talked about boyfriends pushing them into prostitution; they did not see the boyfriends as pimps; the importance to them of being 'wanted' trapped them.

The depth of children's confusion can hardly be overstated. There was much less explanation about sexual assaults than physical assaults. Indeed an inability to find an explanation was a marked feature of the calls.

Asking for help

Perhaps as disturbing as the physical and sexual violence they described was the inability of children – and the adults in their worlds – to organise secure protection for them. So deeply feared were the consequences of approaching police or social services that these sources of protection were shunned. To what extent does this fear arise from real and likely consequences, to what extent from representations of practice in the media? What can be done to make services less fearsome? How can children's and adults' perceptions of satisfactory outcomes be communicated? Though the messages from adult survivors is that they wish they had told, or told earlier (NSPCC, 1996), children get precious few messages that help will be feasible and bearable. We have not yet been able to encourage either children or adults to see this as a 'way out'. Few child callers had or were prepared to contact 'the authorities'. Most would only consent to giving us their names so we could call social services or police to their assistance as a last resort because they had run way or been thrown out of home or were suicidal.

In consequence, many children felt hopeless of changing anything in their lives. Some talked of suicide attempts, self-harm, running away, behaving in self-destructive. Some thought about dramatic solutions – about killing their father, going to live in a new and different family; or their abuser suddenly changing into a good parent. Children, in effect, decided that tolerating the violence was the price that they had to pay for keeping things organised in the same way around them, often for keeping their family.

> 'Maybe I could go in a children's home. Mum hits me all the time. I don't want to tell anyone. I don't want to get her in trouble.'
> ' I don't want the family to break up.'
> 'I found him drunk. I thought to myself, 'Should I kill him or shall I kill myself?'

Though all callers wanted assaults to stop, they were not in any position to organise this for themselves. Most had either been explicitly threatened by the abuser or were in no doubt about the consequences for them should they ask for help.

> ' He said he'd kill me if I told anyone.'
> ' I don't want him to go to prison.'
> ' It would kill my mother if she knew.'
> ' I can't tell anyone, I'm so terribly frightened of my dad. He gets so angry.'

Adult survivors of sexual abuse have shown how extremely hard it is for children to talk about sexual abuse (NSPCC, 1996). It is also difficult for children to talk about physical abuse. Fear of the consequences of telling, fear of the consequences of not being believed, or taken seriously, silences them too.

It is seventeen years since the publication of Roland Summit's groundbreaking article, *The Accommodation Syndrome*, describing the emotional entrapment of victims within abusive relationships (Summit, 1983). It is like the so-called 'Stockholm' or hostage syndrome and has, more recently, been described in these terms (Doyle, 1990, Goddard and Stanley, 1994). The children described here were indeed hostages in their families.

But that is not to say they did not tell or try to tell. Though it is usually assumed that children tell no-one, in fact, most child callers about sexual and physical abuse who give ChildLine information about whether they had told or not, had done so – mainly telling their friends.

Children not only confided in their friends, they also used their friends to organise protection for them. Some described trying to organise a stay with a friend when they knew a danger time was coming up, for example when one parent was away or likely to get drunk; others ran away to friends, or had friends to stay to keep the parent under control. Sometimes the friend and the friend's family were fully in the picture as shown in the calls from adults asking to find out what the legal position is when their children's friend does not want to return home for fear of assault (MacLeod, 1997). While children do try to escape violence by these mechanisms, those who help them are in a precarious legal position. Adults are almost as reluctant as the children to involve the authorities, fearing the consequences, but also not wanting to have to get involved.

Telling mother is obviously the first try for protection made by many children – and one in four callers had done so. But mainly, child callers were frightened of doing it. ChildLine encourages children to think through their reasons for fearing it and to consider whether it might be an option, neither assuming that it always will be nor that mother knows and is 'colluding'. Some children are convinced the other parent must know and is closing her eyes to it or is scared to do anything. Sometimes children are silent to protect the other parent from violence, but they also want to avoid the upset they know it will cause, so they protect the parent from knowing. But they also find indirect ways of telling, as this call from an adult woman shows:

> 'I've come across a letter from ChildLine, When I talked to Alice she admitted she was being sexually abused by her stepdad. I confronted him. At first he said it wasn't true, but then he admitted touching her. I just don't know what to do.'

This mother's anguish shows that adults are as baffled as children about what to do and how to get help, which is part of the reason children find that sometimes telling their mother does not work for them. Though mothers are the frontline of child protection – unless they themselves are responsible for the abuse – they are often left to get on with it with very little support (Farmer and Owen, 1995) or in the context of a child protection investigation which, in itself, has been likened to an abusive process (O'Hagan and Dillenburger, 1995), or through civil family law proceedings where their reluctance to accept contact or residence orders on grounds of risk to their children can be viewed as their being malicious.

Only six per cent of callers about physical or sexual assault had told or were in contact with social services or the police. Most children's and adults calls about legal or statutory intervention were complaints because it had been traumatic, ineffective in preventing further abuse or in providing children or adults with what they perceived as justice. It has to be remembered that ChildLine is likely to hear about what is wrong rather than what has gone right. Nevertheless, there were few reports from children about receiving therapy or counselling. Children often remarked that they were not supposed to talk about what had happened because of going to court. For some children this is a relief, they are not ready; but for many it is another kind of punishment. So it was heartening to find that where children had been interviewed by police or social workers, or both, following an allegation, they had usually found that person kind, sympathetic and supportive. It does seem as if we are getting that part of the process right.

What can we learn about child protection from children's calls?

The clearest message is that what is 'good' for the family cannot necessarily be assumed to be 'good' for the child. That is something which must be borne in mind whenever child care policy changes are being considered. We cannot just assume that a service designed to help families deal with stress will assist children to be free of sexual or physical assault. Or that adults' and children's views of what constitutes reasonable chastisement and what is abuse concur. We need to make room for children to have assistance explicitly aimed at stopping assaults, without invoking the whole child protection juggernaut, and to provide them with much greater access to therapeutic help.

Family conferencing offers some possibilities here (Freeman, 1996, Morris and Tunnard, 1996), as does family mediation and the provision of short-term crisis refuge (Houston et al, 1997), though none of these help children where a family is 'in complete denial'. Equally, some children need to be 'rescued' – an unacceptable word in may social work and counselling quarters, but not from a human rights perspective. And, whatever the outcome of civil or criminal legal processes, there should be access to therapeutic help for children and families.

Children's use of a service they can access themselves has shown that there is no place in their diverse, complex lives for a monolithic, inflexible system or for help which is only offered on the helper's terms. The challenge now is to widen children's access to help. Here, I have been writing for the most part about those youngsters in a position to communicate, at the very least, their need of help. Addressing the needs of young children and those with less access to the outside because of disablement, communication difficulties, emotional and even actual 'imprisonment' is that much more of a challenge.

Much child protection practice derives from a view of child sufferers as victims. Viewing them thus does children injustice, denying the remarkable resilience, strength of mind and determination which many children reveal. Their capacity to discuss possibilities and assess options in calls to ChildLine was considerable. They were imaginative and very resourceful in their attempts to protect themselves, their brothers and sisters, and their mothers. When they were prepared to disclose abuse, they faced the processes of intervention with courage. What their experience attests is that there is no one solution, no single route to preventing and stopping abuse. It requires a variety of responses with children an integral part of defining what might work for them.

Though the help children wanted the most, and adults most want to give them, is for the violence to end, they also required and valued emotional support, the opportunity to be attended to, and offered comfort. Calling ChildLine or talking confidentially to a friend can have an important connotation to children as an act of resistance that is safe to make. Safe resistance can give them a feeling that they are succeeding. And that, in turn, can help in their taking other, riskier steps to secure more consistent protection. They can perhaps begin to feel that they are not passive recipients of abuse, but resisters.

Prevention, we might not be able to do comprehensively; protection, we might not be able entirely to succeed at; but help for children who are troubled we can always offer. In offering therapeutic help, we have to be imaginative too, offering flexible, responsive help, available when required; not hidebound by the conventions of orthodox counselling or therapy; but certainly governed by rules of professional good conduct: that helpers ' ... adapt themselves to (children's) needs and do not live out their own frustrated urges in their contact with them'. For these young people, according to Winnicott (1961), ' ... need human contact and real feelings and yet need to place an absolute reliance on this relationship'.

References

Atmore, C. (1997) 'Conflicts Over Recovered Memories – Every Layer of the Onion', *Feminism and Psychology*, vol. 7, London: Sage.

Barter, C., Keep, G. and MacLeod, M. (1996) *Children at crisis point*, London: ChildLine.

Birchall, E. and Hallet, C. (1995) *Working Together in Child Protection*, London: HMSO.

ChildLine (1993, 1994, 1995, 1996) *Annual Reviews*, London: ChildLine.

Dempster, H. (1993) *The Aftermath of Child Sexual Abuse, in Waterhouse, L.* (ed) (1993), *Child Abuse and Child Abusers*, London: Jessica Kingsley Publishers.

DoH (1997): *Children and Young people on Child Protection Registers Year Ending 31 March 1996 England*, London : Government Statistical Office.

DoH (1995) *Child Protection: Messages from research*, London, HMSO.

Doyle, C. (1990) *Working with Abused Children*, Basingstoke: Macmillan.

Doyle, (1997) 'Emotional Abuse of Children: Issues for Intervention' *Child Abuse Review*, Vol. 6, No. 5, 330-342, London: John Wiley.

Epstein, C. and Keep, G. (1994) 'What children tell ChildLine about domestic violence' in Sanders, A *It hurts me too*, London: NISW.

Farmer, E. and Owen, M. (1995) *Child Protection Practice: Private Risks and Public Remedies – Decision Making, Intervention and Outcome in Child Protection Work*, London: HMSO.

Freeman, I. (1996) *Social work Intervention in Child Abuse – an ever widening net?*, Child Abuse Review Vol 5: 181-190.

Gibbons, J, Conroy, S and Bell C (1995) *Operating the Child Protection System, Studies in Child Protection.* London: HMSO.

Glaser, D. and Prior, V. (1997) 'Is the term child protection applicable to emotional abuse?' *Child Abuse Review*, Vol 6:315-329.

Goddard, C. R. and Stanley, J.R. (1994) 'Viewing the abusive parent and the abused child as captor and hostage: the application of hostage theory to the effects of child abuse', *Journal of Interpersonal Violence*, Vol. 9: 258-267.

Hemenway, D., Solnik, S. and Carter, J. (1994) 'Child-rearing Violence', *Child Abuse and Neglect*, Vol. 18: 1011-1020.

Hobbs, C. J. and Wynne, J. M. (1996) 'Child Abuse and Sudden Infant Death', *Child Abuse Review* Vol. 5: 155-169.

Houston, A., Kork, S. and MacLeod, M. (1997) *Beyond the limit: Children who live with parental alcohol misuse*, London: ChildLine.

Keep, G. (1996) *Going to Court: child witnesses in their own words*, London: ChildLine.

Keep, G. (1997) *Children helping their friends*, London: ChildLine.

Kelly, L. (1988) *Surviving sexual violence*, Cambridge: Polity Press.

Kelly, L, Burton, L and Regan, S. (1991) *An Exploratory Study of the Prevalence of Sexual Abuse in a Sample of 16-21 Year Olds.* London: University of London.

MacLeod, M. and Morris, S. (1996): *Why me?*, London: ChildLine.

MacLeod, M and Saraga, E (1991): 'Child Sexual Abuse: Challenging the Orthodoxy' in Loney et al: *The State or the Market*, London: Sage.

MacLeod, M. (1996) *Talking with children about child abuse*, London: ChildLine.

MacLeod, M. (1996a) *Children and racism*, London: ChildLine.

MacLeod, M. (1997) *Child protection: everybody's business*, London: Community Care.

MacLeod, M. and Barter, C.(1996) *We know it's tough to talk*, London : ChildLine.

Morris, K. And Tunnard, J. (Eds.) (1996), *Family Group Conferences: Messages from UK Practice and Research*. London: Family Rights Group.

NCH Action for Children, (1996) *Fact File 1996/97* London: NCH Action for Children

Nelson, S (1987) *Incest: Fact and Myth*, Edinburgh: Stramullion.

NSPCC (1996) *Childhood Matters: Report of the National Commission of Inquiry into the Prevention of Child Abuse*, London: The Stationery Office.

O'Hagan, K and Dillenburger, K., (1995) *The Abuse of Women within Childcare Work*, Buckingham: Open University.

Parton, N. Thorpe, D. and Wattam, C. (1997) *Child Protection: The Risk and The Moral Order*, Basingstoke: Macmillan.

Reibstein, J. and Bamber, R. (1997) *The Family through Divorce*, California, Thorsens.

Russell, D (1984) *Sexual Exploitation*, London: Sage.

Smith, M.., Bee, P., Heverin, A., and Nobes, G. (1995) *Parental Control within the Family: The Nature and Extent of Parental Violence Towards Children*, Thomas Coram Foundation

Summit, Roland C., M.D. (1983) 'The Child Sexual Abuse Accomodation Syndrome', *Child Abuse and Neglect*, Vol. 7 pp 177-193, Pergamon Press, Ltd.

Thorpe, D. (1994) *Evaluating Child Protection*, Milton Keynes: Open University Press.

Wilding, J. and Thoburn, J (1997) 'Family Support Plans for Neglected and Emotionally Maltreated Children', *Child Abuse Review*, vol 6, Number 5, 343-256, Chichester: John Wiley.

Whipple, E. E. and Richey, C. A. (1997) 'Crossing the line from physical discipline to child abuse: how much is too much?', *Child Abuse and Neglect*, Vol. 21, No 5, 431-444.

Winnicott, . (1961) *Home is Where We Start From*, Harmondsworth: Penguin.

11
Young men, power and sexuality: Challenge and change

Christine Harrison

Introduction

This chapter is about preventive work in the field of child sexual abuse. From the basis of feminist theoretical perspectives which attempt to account for child sexual abuse and other forms of violence towards women and children, it will argue the need for preventive strategies which are broadly based and at a societal level. This acknowledges that reactive child protection services, although clearly necessary, will on their own achieve little in reducing the appalling levels of child sexual abuse we know exist (Kelly, Regan and Burton 1991, Pilkington and Kremer 1995). These services will only ever have contact with a small proportion of those children and young people who have been the subject of sexual abuse (Kelly, Regan and Burton 1991, Report of the National Commission of Inquiry into the Prevention of Child Abuse 1996). The chapter also assumes that the primary responsibility for preventing sexual abuse should not be placed with children, who are the potential or intended victims, nor with mothers who may themselves be effectively disempowered or the subject of abuse (Hooper 1992, Hooper and Humphreys 1998).

The starting premise is that preventive child care is about promoting the well-being of all children and young people and that this requires a recognition of the range of oppressions which impact on them and their healthy development. This premise is well supported by the diversity of issues explored within this collection, which spans both the wide range of conditions that are harmful to children and correspondingly varied forms and levels of intervention in response. As Baldwin and Spencer (1993) argue: 'The logic of what is known about the needs of children suggests that community wide strategies to support families, promote children's health, development and well being must be the foundation of child care and child protective services' (p.358). The recent Report of the National Commission of Inquiry into the Prevention of Child Abuse, amongst its many recommendations, emphasises the role of local communities in the prevention of abuse, suggesting that 'central government, local authorities should.....develop explicit strategies to facilitate stronger and permanent neighbourhood support and service networks' (Report of the National Commission of Inquiry into the Prevention of Child Abuse 1996 p.82). The Report drew substantially on the experiences of survivors, who, it has been argued, could play a much more centrally recognised role in the development of preventive strategies (Sanford 1991, Browne 1996).

Such considerations cut across private and public domains and areas of professional responsibility. As well as cautioning against a reliance on or confidence in statutory intervention and expertise to deal with child care and child protection issues, they set out imperatives for all of those involved in the care and upbringing of children. Parents, carers, teachers, health workers, youth workers, nursery workers, social workers and local communities all have responsibilities. Collectively and cooperatively, all of these can be involved in the challenge and change which is necessary to reduce the incidence and impact of oppression and abuse on children and young people.

Applying this logic to the prevention of child sexual abuse suggests that strategies need to be identified and implemented which:

- fully recognise the societal context of child sexual abuse, the sexual exploitation of children and the social conditions and oppressions which allow them to exist;
- are based on an awareness of the attitudes and power relationships which generate and sustain child sexual abuse and other forms of violence against women, children and young people;
- place at the centre the relationship between gender, power and sexuality and appreciate the critical significance of male socialisation within this;
- promote ways of working within educational and welfare fields which challenge and shift commonly held beliefs about gender, power, 'race', sexuality and disability.

It also implies that 'short term protection strategies need to be combined with longer term primary protection initiatives *and a vision of a society in which child sexual abuse no longer exists*' (Kitzinger and Skidmore 1995 p.82 – my emphasis). This vision is crucial, although like the eradication of other forms of oppression such as racism or homophobia, it is difficult to imagine its full achievement. However, it is consistent with a radical tradition in social research, welfare theory and practice (Langan and Day 1992, Humphries and Truman 1994). It is the combination of theoretical rigour with a vision of something different which enables feminists to talk with some authority about prevention, not just protection; about prevention, not just reduction . For, 'if we do not even start from the ideal of preventing abuse, rather than protecting children, we lose opportunities for developing explanations and therefore limit our possibilities of helping' (Saraga 1994 p.118). This perspective is the result of joining with women and children who have been sexually abused and asking insistently, and often in the face of discreditation, *why has this happened?* (Kelly 1988, Saraga 1994, MacLeod 1996).

This chapter will review some distinctive contributions of feminist perspectives to our understanding of child sexual abuse, in theoretical, policy and practice terms. It will use this knowledge base to evaluate the concept of prevention, particularly as it applies to child sexual abuse. It will try to identify the parameters of strategies which could contribute to the prevention, as well as the reduction, of child sexual abuse.

Theoretical context

In Britain and Europe, the 1980s witnessed an upsurge of awareness, a burgeoning of professional knowledge and of theoretical accounts of child sexual abuse. The accounts of survivors, from women strong enough to 'break the silence', made an unrivalled contribution to raising public awareness of both the extent and the destructive impact of sexual abuse (Spring 1987, Feminist Review 1988, Hall and Lloyd 1989): They are a testament to women's and children's strengths and resilience. At a theoretical level, distinctive contributions from feminist writers such as Mary McLeod, Esther Saraga, Liz Kelly, Sarah Nelson, Judith Herman, Melba Wilson, challenged the predominance of individual and family dysfunction accounts of child sexual abuse. By taking as their starting point the sheer scale and prevalence of the sexual abuse of children and young people within and outside the family and the lived experiences of women and children, they showed that sexual abuse is distributed across the class spectrum, across geographical areas, across racial and cultural groups. Even on the most conservative estimates, the vast majority of perpetrators are men (Kelly, Wingfield, Burton and Regan 1995) and the majority of victims are girls and young women. This means we cannot take refuge in the idea that sexual abuse is the product of a 'sick' individual or of a 'sick' family. The uncomfortable probability that sexual abuse is perpetrated by apparently normal men in normal families and in the organisations in which we work - schools, residential homes, foster care, social services departments, has to be confronted (Pringle 1992/93, Carter 1992, Kent 1997, Utting 1997).

Research by Kelly, Regan and Burton (1991), for example, found that 59% of the young women and 27% of the young men they interviewed had experienced at least one sexually intrusive incident before the age of 18. Sexual abuse was defined as what the young person considered to be abusive and included flashing, being touched, being pressurised into sexual activity, attempted and actual assaults, including rape. 14% of abusers were close relatives, 68% were distant relatives and 18% strangers. One quarter of the abuse described was committed by other young people under 18. Most abusers were men (95% where the abuser was an adult, 85% where the abuser was a peer).

This evidence fundamentally challenges explanations which rely on the models of individual or family pathology (as well as those explanations which rely on cycles of abuse or addiction models of behaviour) which have predominated in shaping interventions with children who have been abused, with their mothers and with offenders themselves. Through these explanatory models men's responsibility for abuse can be minimised or transferred to the women and children who have been victims (Milner 1994), as 'the mother steadily became the focus both of responsibility and of condemnation for the abuse' (Humphreys 1997 p.531).

Feminist writers have established a theoretical framework within which gender is central to our understanding of power in general and abuse is viewed as a betrayal of trust. It scrutinises a pervasive ideology of masculinity in which power and sexuality are inextricably linked (MacLeod and Saraga 1991). Work undertaken with male abusers by the Faithful Foundation confirms that the men involved are wholly responsible, know what they are doing, know what they have done, and use societal messages to further their abuse. This is evident not just in the use of threats, bribes, and force, but also in processes of targeting and grooming which may have occurred years before any event of sexual abuse has taken place. Sexual abuse is not a singular event, but includes all processes instigated by the abuser in order to abuse a child. It may also have included the disempowerment of the child's mother (Hooper 1992, Mullins 1997).

The experience of sexual abuse as a form of oppression in relation to age and gender may be compounded by the experience of other oppressions, in relation to 'race', sexuality, disability (Kennedy 1989, Kelly 1992, Wilson 1993, Sinason 1994, Morris 1996). Such factors not only shape a child's experiences, but may make it even more difficult to tell.

The range of feminist perspectives and individual accounts referred to supports attempts to interrogate the relationship between patriarchy, masculinity, power and sexuality (Segal 1990, Abbott and Wallace 1991). There is great diversity amongst feminist perspectives. What is common, however, is a concerted endeavour to establish how patriarchal power is created, maintained and exercised; the institutional and personal manifestations of this exercise; the social, political and legal discourses which operate across the public and private divide. In these theoretical examinations, neither women nor children are constructed as passive and their resistance to dominant discourses and the forms that this resistance can take are also acknowledged. Their concentration is not just on the formal mechanisms and institutions implicated in the distribution of power, but includes a consideration of the everyday interactions within which 'sexuality emerges repeatedly as the instrument by which power over women is maintained and exercised because it serves to define them in particular ways' (Abbott and Wallace 1991 p.xii).

Attempts are made, therefore, to consider how the sexual abuse of children and women is related to other forms of violence, for example domestic violence, stalking and rape and to other forms of oppression, such as racism and homophobia (Kelly 1989, Mullender and Morley 1994, Mullender 1996). Not only is the familial and societal context scrutinised, but a global context also (Barry 1995). The relationship between sexual abuse (of women and children) and slavery, warfare, domination and colonialism cannot be ignored.

A relevant example of the close consideration of everyday interactions is given in Jacqui Halson's examination of young men 'doing masculinity' (Halson 1991). In her intensive research study over a nine month period in a secondary school, she draws in the connections between masculinity, heterosexuality and sexual harassment in the relationships between young men and young women. She finds that sexual harassment is embedded, ranging from the commonplace and subtle through to overt and brutal; blurring into and often indistinguishable from normal and routine interactions of day to day life; evident in both public and private domains. A consequence for young women is that they find it difficult to register actively their experiences as offensive or oppressive. They must either become inured or appear to have become inured to direct and indirect forms of sexual intimidation which humiliate and disempower them and create a hostile environment for their development. Powerful parallels are to be found between this and studies of sexuality in organisations which reveal what Harlow, Hearn and Parkin refer to as the 'ever-present exercise of power through gender, which is crucially underpinned by the power of the male sexual narrative' (Harlow et al 1991 p 134).

Feminist perspectives have been crucial, not just in trying to raise the issue of child sexual abuse and its extent and impact, but in asking the question *why?* (MacLeod and Saraga 1991). As MacLeod and Saraga argue, sexual abuse may be a gross or extreme manifestation of the relationship between gender, sexuality, age and power, but it can only exist because of the acceptable or 'normal' forms of these relationships. Forms of relationship which, though they may be questioned, are difficult to challenge and which are supported, encouraged and legitimated in the everyday, taken for granted interactions described by Halson (1991 and also in chapter 9 of this Reader).

At the same time as this questioning by feminists and survivors, there have been systematic attempts to undermine, erode and marginalise their concerns and accounts. Indeed, if taken in historical context, as Herman has shown, a pattern emerges of knowledge and evidence of sexual abuse and other forms of violence periodically emerging into the public domain and then being suppressed (Herman 1981, Masson 1992). The concept of backlash has been used to encompass the complex, diverse and diffuse ways through which this submerging occurs. The existence of women who abuse and the 'discovery' of false memory syndrome have both been used over recent years to discredit feminist accounts and analysis, and to distract attention from the scale and impact of child sexual abuse (Armstrong 1995, Armstrong 1996). This may have the effect of silencing many children, young people and women struggling with the pain and costs of child sexual abuse.

Issues for social work practice

The accounts of survivors, the development of theory, the continuance of research are unfinished business. Most professionals accept that our knowledge base must increase and that other painful areas will need to be confronted. What we know so far has forced us to evaluate systematically the ways in which statutory services and social work practice have responded to children and young people who have been sexually abused (Bray 1991, Bannister 1992, NCH Action for Children 1994).

Statutory intervention in child protection has, of course, continued to be the focus of media attention, public scrutiny and considerable opprobrium over the decades since the Maria Colwell inquiry (Parton 1991, Langan and Clarke 1994, Parton 1996, Parton 1997). The unprecedented ideological, legal and organisational change of the last decade and a half has not only resulted in increased fragmentation, proceduralisation and bureaucratic control over practice, but has attempted to shift the nature of social work practice itself (Langan and Clarke 1994). One result of this 'legalism' (Parton 1991) is that social workers across both child care and community care have experienced the kind of demoralisation which can precipitate a search for certainty within a procedural framework (Saraga 1994). Another consequence is the fear of exercising judgement or developing innovative work when the cost of perceived failure can be high.

Despite very real difficulties and pressures, efforts continue to improve practice and to counteract the sometimes abusive impact of the child protection system itself (NCH Action for Children 1994). 'That the picture is not more grim is due in great part to the strengths of individual children, women and men who try to find ways to struggle with the consequences of abuse and the practice of social workers who struggle to offer help to troubled people, despite the constraints of resources, policy etc..' (MacLeod and Saraga 1991 p.33).

The challenging of myths and stereotypes that has come through the persistence of those who have experienced, lived with or worked with child sexual abuse has enabled us:

- to be more aware of what a slow and painful process talking about abuse may be for a child;
- to be willing to listen actively to children and to try to understand the meaning for them of their experiences;
- to recognise the extent of abuse of children with disabilities;
- to be aware of the longer term effects of abuse;
- to work at responding more appropriately and sensitively throughout the processes of investigation;
- to appreciate the need for supportive intervention after an investigation is complete;
- to appreciate that the operation of child protection procedures and implementation of guidelines, like the 'Memorandum of good practice' (HMSO 1992), can be abusive.

Feminist writers have challenged at theoretical, policy and practice levels the view that mothers invariably collude with sexual abuse (Hooper 1992, Humphreys 1997). Indeed, there has been a recognition that working with mothers as well as young people is perhaps the best way of ensuring that a child's future needs are met.

Understanding the relationship between the child protection system and effective work with children who have been sexually abused is vital, if best practice is to be achieved and progress made in reducing the incidence of abuse or preventing its occurrence. Child sexual abuse is a thread which runs right through the fabric of the lives of many thousands of children, many more than has been previously acknowledged. Statutory services will only ever have contact with a small proportion of those young women and men who have been the subject of abuse (Report of the National Commission of Inquiry into the Prevention of Child Abuse and Neglect 1996). Some children will find a trusted friend or adult to tell and the majority of work and recovery in child sexual abuse, like that in domestic violence, occurs outside the statutory services. Some will make use of confidential helplines like ChildLine, which research has indicated children and young people value because they are able to retain some power and control (Butler and Williamson 1994, MacLeod 1996). Others will never tell anyone because they fear they will not be believed, fear they are responsible, or because they fear that if they tell, intervention will only make the situation worse (NCH Action for Children, 1994). The strategies employed by abusers with the specific aim of silencing them, may generate complex feelings for children and young people. Victims have to develop their own strategies to cope with the impact of child sexual abuse in both child and adulthood (Bass and Davis 1989, Hall and Lloyd 1989, MacLeod 1996).

This brings us to the area of preventive work, both generally and specifically in relation to child sexual abuse; to an evaluation of what currently constitutes preventive work in this area and to consider what might be effective strategies in future.

Preventive strategies

Preventive work in child care has historically been the subject of varied and tendentious interpretations. The concept has a high level of use but a low level of meaning and 'part of the problem may be the concept itself. It is one of those dangerous words that we all understand and think we agree on but then use in different ways' (Gough 1988 p.107). Many writers have recognised this multiplicity in meaning and have usefully represented prevention as a continuum of provision (Hardiker et al 1995, NCH Action for Children 1996):

- *Primary prevention*
  Provision of universal services to promote the health and well being of all children and young people, including strategies aimed to reduce the impact of oppression and discrimination, avoiding attempts to identify risk factors or risk groups;
- *Secondary prevention*
  Provision of services to individuals and families who may have been identified or have identified themselves as experiencing a level of distress and or difficulty;
- *Tertiary prevention*
  Epitomised by attempts to identify the 'high risk' (individual adults, children, families or groups of adults, children or families) in order to target services and interventions.

The Children Act was heralded as making greater provision for preventive services, that is support services for children in need and their families as described in Section 17 and Schedule 2 of the Act. Its implementation and interpretation through local authority policy, procedure and practice has, however, effectively created a hierarchy of preventive provision, with a concentration on the interventive, child protection, or tertiary, end of the continuum (Audit Commission 1994, Report of the National Commission of Inquiry into the Prevention of Child Abuse 1996). There have been renewed debates about the relationship between preventive and interventive child protection provision more recently, in part generated by the publication of the DOH Child Protection: messages from research (DOH 1995, NCH Action for Children 1996).

The debate takes place against the backdrop of the unprecedented ideological, legal and organisational change in the provision of welfare services already noted, which supports the narrower interpretation of prevention being synonymous with child protection, an interpretation reinforced by budgetary constraints. Continuing predominance of theoretical understandings of child abuse rooted in individual or family pathology are exemplified by the framework for assessment provided in Child Protection: a guide for social workers undertaking a comprehensive assessment (DOH 1988), in which prevention was equated with prediction.

This conflation of a narrow concept of prevention with child protection has undermined the broader concept of prevention in child care and contributed to the erosion of any work which cannot be identified as core business. It has had the effect of stigmatising services, making them more difficult for people to identify with and make use of (Parton 1991, Stevenson 1992, Masson 1992, Baldwin and Harrison 1994). Social workers themselves are aware of the over-riding priority given to child protection work and feel frustrated in their attempts to develop innovative, more preventive work (Masson, Harrison and Pavlovic 1997).

Prevention and child sexual abuse

The implications of the feminist research and theoretical perspectives outlined are for the development of coordinated, comprehensive preventive strategies to tackle the societal, as well as the individual dimensions of child sexual abuse. Whilst acknowledging that 'planners of sexual abuse prevention are faced with trying to prevent a social problem of enormous proportions that seems endemic to most identifiable social groups' (Melton 1996 p 171), critical questions need to be posed about the current range of provision. Where is the responsibility for preventing child sexual abuse located? Is it informed by research, theoretical understandings and the experiences of survivors? Is it aimed at stopping abuse rather than just reducing levels? Does it tackle the risk of re-offending and treating the effects of child sexual abuse?

The strategies currently being promoted in relation to child sexual abuse can be summarised as follows:

- Campaigns aimed at school aged children which focus on reducing their vulnerability to sexual abuse, enabling them to be assertive and 'say no' and to avoid or resist abuse;
- Campaigns or strategies aimed at adults and parents to alert them to possible dangers such as the recent NCH campaign about abuse and the internet;
- Screening of people working with children;
- Rehabilitative/therapeutic work with known abusers;
- Identification and registration of children who have been the subject of sexual abuse and the formulation of child protection plans;
- Therapeutic work with victims of child sexual abuse;
- 'Self protection' work with victims of child sexual abuse.

This range does not fully take account of feminist theoretical considerations and only partially addresses the questions posed. There is much concentration on prevention through avoidance, through emphasising 'stronger danger' and through 'treating' the effects of sexual abuse. In evaluating current children's charities responses to child sexual abuse, for example, Julie Browne found that these were 'largely directed at responding to government initiatives, trying to improve the position of children appearing in court, and providing treatment facilities for children, abusers and families' (Browne 1996 p.42), mirroring what has happened in the USA (Melton 1996). 'Stranger danger', 'avoidance' and 'treatment' are concepts reinforced in media representation of prevention, where 'reports drew on a narrow repertoire of strategies.....' (Kitzinger and Skidmore 1995 p.49). Reporting tends to be reactive; there is little evidence of theoretical consideration of underlying causes, a broader social and political context or analytical connections with other forms of violence towards women and children. Official (government) agencies, rather than grass roots organisations representing women and children, were the preferred source of information and there was a 'disproportionate focus on abuse outside the domestic, home and family network' (Kitzinger and Skidmore 1995 p.50). This also confirms feminist concern that an acknowledgement of the extent of child sexual abuse inherently confronts the nature of masculinity and patriarchy and powerful interests ensure that questions are consistently reframed to obscure this.

Work at the primary end of the continuum has largely been through efforts in the education system to raise children's awareness of sexual abuse and better equip them to be able to 'say no'. This is integral to the care and education of children and having this knowledge and information may be considered an issue of children's rights (Gough 1993, Elliot 1994). School-based programmes which attempt to make children and young people responsible for avoiding or protecting themselves from abuse are, however, criticised on a number of points and evidence suggests that they may be of only limited value (Bagley and Thurston 1996). Not only do they constitute a 'strange and unique way of considering the problem' (Browne 1996 p.40), but studies of pre-school children show that they are too young to appreciate the concepts dealt with in preventive programmes (Gilbert et al 1989). Programmes for older children aimed at helping them avoid assault may reinforce the behaviour of those already confident and do little for those with low self-esteem (O'Donahue and Geer 1992). Most programmes cannot take account of the broader social and individual contexts in which abuse takes place, the processes of targeting, of grooming, the pressure exerted to maintain secrecy etc (Tutty 1996). The young people that Kelly et al (1991) interviewed had unsuccessfully tried to use a range of strategies to prevent, limit or avoid the abuse they suffered; they had said no but this had not stopped the abuse. Research in America, where school-based sexual abuse programmes have been longer established and evaluated, also suggests that trying to alter the behaviour of potential victims can do little to prevent sexual abuse and assault (Wald and Cohen 1986, Trudell and Whately 1988 Finkelhor and Dzuiba-Letherman 1995). An approach which concentrates on altering the behaviour of children may inadvertently 'blame the victim' when abuse does occur.

This is not to say that school-based programmes should be abandoned. Benefits, even if they are limited, have been identified. In raising awareness amongst children, for example, they may facilitate talking about sexual abuse (Finkelhor and Stapko 1991, Finkelhor et al 1995, Bagley and Thurston 1996). There are examples of school based preventive strategies which are viewed as being more progressive: approaches which are accepted as being a legitimate part of the curriculum; are well integrated within it; are well resourced; have the support of students, teachers, parents and the local community; consider the many and varied forms that the abuse of power takes, including racism, sexism and bullying; attempt to challenge attitudes, particularly those of young men; and, finally, directly involve survivors or organisations run by survivors.

In Canada, broadly based anti-violence programmes, extensively piloted in Ontario, are widespread. They have a prominent position in the curriculum (for example a whole week in a school year in many elementary schools) and a range of media and support materials are used. The involvement of survivors or groups representing users and substantial training for teachers implementing the strategy are particular strengths (Mullender 1994).

In Australia, strategies to prevent child sexual assault have been common for more than ten years. These have been multi-faceted, considering primary, secondary and tertiary levels of prevention. In New South Wales, for example, a four year Child Sexual Assault Programme was initiated with the aim of reducing the incidence of child sexual assault as well as improving child protection intervention when it was believed that a child had been the subject of sexual abuse. This was preceded by a major public consultation exercise and the campaign involved the orchestration of community-based and statutory agencies, central and local government and the implementation of legal and policy reforms. It was accompanied not just by an increase in resources, but statewide interdisciplinary training (Calvert 1990). As part of a community education campaign, the media was actively harnessed to challenge, with adults, 'the secrecy which surrounds child sexual assault and people's attitudes regarding responsibility for child sexual abuse' (Calvert and Humphreys 1995).

There are few examples in this country of even the most basic preventive provision. Audrey Mullender (1994 p.257). notes that initiatives abroad make 'the relative inactivity here look inexcusable'. Kidscape is an exception and a notable local authority example is the Zero Tolerance campaign, originally launched by the Women's Committee of Edinburgh District Council in 1992 (Foley 1993). This latter was a deliberate attempt to promote prevention of child sexual abuse (and other forms of violence against women and children) without targeting potential victims. Rather, appreciative of the extent of child sexual abuse and the need to tackle the social context of abuse, it avoided the limitations of much preventive work in this field, and was 'the first major advertising campaign in Britain with the stated aim of attempting to challenge social attitudes to physical and sexual assaults against women and girls' (Kitzinger 1994 p.247). In challenging attitudes and values and focusing on the problematic of male sexuality, it is more consistent with feminist research/theory and the requirements of preventive work outlined earlier than many of the school based strategies which rely on changing the behaviour of intended or potential victims. Other authorities in Scotland and some authorities in England have taken up this initiative.

In response to concern about the focus and emphasis of preventive efforts and the paucity of materials which would enable carers and workers to explore issues related to young men, power and abuse, the University of Warwick Child Protection Resource Centre commissioned a pack of training materials from the Faithful Foundation (funded by Coventry Safer Cities Project). Materials were devised which would support community based, strategic interventions within the care and education of children and young people. The materials provide a framework within which to explore issues, enhance workers' and carers' awareness and increase their confidence in direct work with young people. Focusing on the societal context of sexual abuse, they identify those trends in society which underpin abuse and enable it to occur, and encourage users to identify key societal messages, how they impact on people in general and children and young people in particular, how they can be abusive and how abusers use them (sexual myths and stereotyping, media images, peer group pressures, pornography etc). They are intended to help workers transfer increased knowledge and awareness into their direct and indirect work with young people. Piloting of the materials has confirmed that both carers and workers need support in challenging attitudes and values, in moving towards a preventive approach characterised by community awareness (University of Warwick/Faithful Foundation, unpublished). It has also confirmed that connections need to be made with other campaigns which emphasise links between sexual violence and abuse and other forms of violence, like racist bullying.

Conclusions and key points

Children can learn to say no until the cows come home, but until men stop abusing them sexual abuse will continue .. whether we like it or not, prevention has to mean intervening in the way that boys learn to be sexual and use their sexuality. (MacLeod and Saraga 1991 p.42).

Feminist perspectives have sought to demonstrate that the sexual abuse of children occurs within a patriarchal ideology of masculinity in which sexuality and power are inextricably linked. It depends on associated views about women, children and childhood itself (Jenks 1996, Gittens 1998). Comparison of the socialisation of boys and girls is needed. Questions about the ways in which boys are socialised, how aggression and expectations of dominance are encouraged or discouraged are central (Wolfe et al 1997).

These perspectives and accounts of survivors of child sexual abuse have not only taken apart many myths and stereotypes and allowed a critique of current services, they have more importantly provided both a theoretical and experiential base which gives direction to the development of preventive initiatives. When considering the social and political context, important connections are made between various forms of violence against women and children and child sexual abuse, which supports the need for broadly based interventions.

Prevention is a long term objective that will require community-based strategic interventions, not just in the education of children, but in their day-to-day care. In trying to develop more progressive practice at the universal/primary prevention end of the continuum there are at least some signposts to the direction that might be taken:

1. Widespread social action including community education relating to child rearing practices and the promotion of non-violent relationships;
2. Broad, community-based anti-violence campaigns which consider sexual abuse alongside other forms of violence against children (like racism) and women and children (like domestic violence) and make the connections between them, eg the Zero Tolerance Campaign, and local inter-agency initiatives to confront domestic violence;
3. Attempts to integrate, as a significant and legitimate part of the school curriculum, strategies to counteract sexual and other forms of violence, focusing on the behaviour of potential perpetrators not just potential victims, and ensuring that teachers have appropriate training and support;
4. Acknowledging that sexual abuse education cannot be tackled without also properly addressing areas which have traditionally been considered controversial in educational terms, ie sex education, sexuality, children's sexual development;

5. Ensuring that school-based programmes are not only developmentally appropriate but take account of ethnic and cultural diversity;
6. Drawing on models of similar campaigns against violence and sexual assault from Australia, Canada and America;
7. Making extensive use of the experiences of survivors (both adults and children) who have demonstrated that they are not only experts on their own experiences but have something to contribute to the development of more adequate services.

These are consistent with the view that preventive work should mean the promotion of well-being in its broadest sense, challenging attitudes and values to generate change. It means taking away from children and young people the responsibility for preventing abuse. All of us working directly with children and families must take responsibility for addressing these issues. A reduction in child sexual abuse is contingent upon such developments.

References

Abbot, P. & Wallace, C. (eds) (1991) *Gender, Power and Sexuality*. London: Macmillan.
Audit Commission (1994) *Seen But Not Heard: co-ordinating community child health and social services for children in need*. London: HMSO.
Armstrong, L. (1996) *Rocking the Cradle of Sexual Politics: what happened when women said incest*. London: Women's Press.
Armstrong, L. (1995) *Of Sluts and Bastards: a feminist decodes the child welfare debate*. US: Common Courage.
Bagley, C. & Thurston, W. (1996a) *Understanding and Preventing Child Sexual Abuse: critical summaries of 500 key studies, Volume 1*. Aldershot: Arena.
Bagley, C. & Thurston, W. (1996b) *Understanding and Preventing Child Sexual Abuse: critical summaries of 500 key studies, Volume 2*. Aldershot: Arena.
Baldwin, N. & Harrison, C. (1994) 'Supporting Children in Need: the role of the social worker.' in David, T (ed) (*1994 b*).
Baldwin, N. & Spencer, N. (1993) 'Deprivation and Child Abuse -Implications for Strategic Planning in Children's Services'. *Children and Society*, Vol 7 No. 4 pp 357 - 375.
Bannister, A. (ed) (1992) *From Hearing to Healing*. Harlow: Longman.
Barry. (1995) The *Prostitution of Sexuality: the global exploitation of women*. New York: University Press.
Bass, E. & Davis, L. (1989) *The Courage to Heal; a guide for women survivors of child sexual abuse*. London: Cedar.
Bray, M. (1991) *Poppies on the Rubbish Heap*. Edinburgh: Cannongate.
Browne, J. (1996) 'Policy Developments in Child Sexual Abuse', *British Journal of Social Work* 26: 37-52.
Browne, K., Davies, C. & Stratton, P. (1988) *Early Prediction and Prevention of Child Abuse* London: Wiley.
Butler, I. &Williamson, I. (1994) *Children, Trauma and Social Work*. London: NSPCC/ Longmans.

Calvert, G. (1990) 'Using Mass Media Campaigns to Prevent Child Sexual Assault in Australia' *New South Wales Prevention of Child Sexual Abuse* pp 23-39.

Calvert, G. & Humphreys, C. (1995) 'No Excuses: primary prevention strategy for child sexual assault' *Oral presentaion to V European Conference on Child Abuse and Neglect,* Oslo 1995.

Carter, P., Jeffs, T. & Smith, M.T. (eds) (1991) *Changing Social Work and Welfare.* Buckingham: Open University Press.

Carter, P. (1993) 'The Problem of Men : A Reply to Keith Pringle', *Critical Social Policy* Issue 38, Autumn 1993 pp.

Child Line (1995) *Annual Report.* London: ChildLine.

David, T. (ed) (1994a) *Protecting Children from Abuse.* Stoke on Trent: Trentham.

David, T. (ed) (1994b) *Working Together for Young Children.* London: Routledge.

DoH (1995) *Child Protection: messages from research.* London: HMSO.

DoH (1988) *Protecting Children: a guide for social workers undertaking a comprehensive assessment.* London: HMSO.

Driver, E. & Droisen, A. (1989) *Child Sexual Abuse: Feminist Perspectives.* London: Macmillan.

Elliot, M. (1994) 'Evaluation of 'Protective Behaviours' and 'Keeping Ourselves Safe': commentary on 'Choosing Between Child Protection Programmes', by Briggs and Hawkins (*Child Abuse Review* Vol 3: 272-284)' *Child Abuse Review* Vol 3 Issue 4: p 284.

Feminist Review (1988) *Family Secrets: child sexual abuse.* Issue 28 Spring 1988.

Finkelhor, D. & Stapko, N. (1991) 'Sexual Abuse Prevention Education' in Willis (et al) *A Review of Evaluation Studies'.*

Foley, R. (1993) 'Zero Tolerance' *Trouble and Strife* No 27 pp16-20.

Gilbert, N., Berrick, J.D., Le Prohn, N. & Nyman, N. (1989) *Protecting Young Children From Sexual Abuse.* Massachusetts: Lexington.

Gittens, G. (1998) *The Child in Question.* Basingstoke: Macmillan.

Gough, D. (1988) 'Approaches to child abuse prevention' in Browne, Davies and Stratton.

Gough, D. (1993) 'The Case For and Against Prevention' in Waterhouse, L. and Stevenson, O. (eds) *Child Abuse and Child Abusers: protection and prevention.* London: Jessica Kingsley.

Hall, L. & Lloyd, S. (1989) *Surviving Child Sexual Abuse.* London: Falmer.

Halson, J. (1991) 'Young Women, Sexual Harassment and Heterosexuality: violence, power relations and mixed-sex schooling' in Abbott and Wallace.

Hardiker, P., Exton, K. & Barker, M. (1996) 'The prevention of Child Abuse: a framework for analysing services' in *Report of the National Commission of Inquiry into the Prevention of Child Abuse.* London: The Stationery Office.

Harlow, E., Hearn, J. & Parkin, W. (1991) 'Sexuality in Social Work Organisations' *in Carter et al (eds).*

Herman, J. (1981) *Father-Daughter Incest.* Massachusetts: Harvard University Press.

HMSO (1992) *A Memorandum of Good Practice.* London: HMSO.

Hooper, C.A. (1992) *Mothers Surviving Child Sexual Abuse.* London: Tavistock/Routledge.

Hooper, C. A. & Humphreys, C. (1998) 'Women Whose Children Have Been Sexually Abused: reflections on a debate' *British Journal of Social Work* 28: 565-580.

Humphries, B. & Truman, C. (1994) *Rethinking Social Research: anti-discriminatory approaches to research methodologies.* Aldershot: Avebury.

Humphreys, C. (1997) 'Child Sexual Abuse Allegations in the Context of Divorce: issues for mothers' in *British Journal of Social Work* 27: 529-544

Jenks, C. (1996) *Childhood.* London: Routledge.

Kelly, L. (1989) *Surviving Sexual Violence.* London: Polity Press.

Kelly, L. (1992) 'Case Study II: Can't Hear or Won't Hear? The Evidential Experience of Children With Disabilities' *Child Abuse Review* Volume 1 Issue 3: 188-190.

Kelly, L. (1996) *Women, Violence and Male Power: feminist activism, research and practice.* Buckingham: Open University Press.

Kelly, L. Regan, L. & Burton, S. (1991) *An Exploratory Study of the Prevalence of Sexual Abuse in a Sample of 16-21 yr olds.* London: Polytechnic of North London.

Kelly, L. Wingfield., Burton, S. & Regan, L. (1995) *Splintered Lives: sexual exploitation in the context of children's rights and child protection.* Barkingside: Barnardo's.

Kennedy, M. (1989) 'The Abuse of Deaf Children' *Child Abuse Review* Spring, 3-7

Kent, R. (1997) *Children's Safeguards Review.* Social Work Services Inspectorate, Scottish Office. London: Stationery Office.

Kitzinger, J. & Skidmore, P. (1995) 'Playing Safe: media coverage of sexual abuse prevention' *Child Abuse Review* Vol 5.

Kitzinger, J. (1994) 'Challenging Sexual Violence Against Girls: a social awareness approach' *Child Abuse Review* Vol 3: 246-258.

Langan, M. & Clarke, J. (1994) 'Managing in the mixed economy of care' in Clarke J (ed) *A Crisis in Care? Challenges to social work.* Milton Keynes: Open University Press.

Langan, M. & Day, L. (1992) *Women, Oppression and Social Work.* London: Routledge.

MacLeod, M. & Saraga, E. (1988) *Child Sexual Abuse: towards a feminist professional practice.* London: PNL Press.

MacLeod, M. & Saraga, E, (1991) 'Clearing a Path Through the Undergrowth : a feminist reading of recent literature on child sexual abuse' in Carter P et al (eds) *Social Work and Social Welfare Yearbook.* Buckingham: Open University Press.

MacLeod, M. (1996) *Talking to Children About Child Abuse.* London: ChildLine.

Masson, J. (1992) 'Managing Risk Under the Children Act 1989; diversion in child care' *Child Abuse Review* Vol 1: 103-122

Masson, J., Harrison, C. & Pavlovic, A. (1997) *Working With Children and 'Lost' Parents.* York: Joseph Rowntree.

Melton, G. B. (1991) 'The Improbability of Prevention of Child Sexual Abuse' in Willis et al (eds).

Milner, J. (1994) 'Men's Resistance to Social Workers' in Featherstone et al (1994).

Morris, J. (1995) *Gone Missing: a research and policy review of disabled children living away from their families.* London: Who Cares? Trust.

Mullender, A. (1994) 'School-Based Work: education for prevention' in Mullender, A. & Morley, R.

Mullender, A. & Morley, R. (1994) *Children Living With Domestic Violence.* London: Whiting and Birch.

Mullender, A. (1996) *Re-Thinking Domestic Violence: the social work and probation response.* London: Routledge.

Mullins, A. (1997) *Making a Difference: working with women and children experiencing domestic violence.* London: NCH Action for Children.

NCH Action for Children (1994) *Messages From Children.* London: NCH.

NCH Action for Children (1996) *Children Still in Need: refocusing child protection in the context of children in need*. London: NCH.

Nelson, S. (1981) *Incest: fact and myth*. Edinburgh: Stramullion.

O'Donahue, W.& Geer, J. (1992) 'The Primary Prevention of Child Sexual Abuse' in O'Donahue, W. and Geer, J. (eds).

O'Donahue, W. & Geer, J. (eds) (1992) *The Sexual Abuse of Children: clinical issues Volume 2*. Hillside: Erlbaum.

Parton, N. (1991) *Governing the Family: child care, child protection and the state*. London: Macmillan.

Parton, N. (1996) *Social Theory, Social Change and Social Work*. London: Routledge.

Parton, N. (1997) *Child Protection and Family Support: tensions, contradictions and possibilities*. London: Routledge.

Pilkington, B. & Kremer, J. (1995) 'A Review of the Epidemiological Research on Child Sexual Abuse' *Child Abuse Review* Vol 4: 84-98.

Pringle, K. (1992/3) 'Child Sexual Abuse Perpetrated by Welfare Personnel and the Problem of Men' *Critical Social Policy* Issue 36.

Report of the National Commission of Inquiry into the Prevention of Child Abuse (1996) *Childhood Matters: Vol 1 The Report*. London: The Stationery Office.

Report of the National Commission of Inquiry into the Prevention of Child Abuse (1996) *Childhood Matters: Vol 2 Background Papers*. London: The Stationery Office.

Sanford, L.T. (1991) *Strong at the Broken Places: overcoming the trauma of childhood abuse*. London: Virago.

Saraga, E. (1994) ' Living With Uncertainty' in David, T. (1994 a).

Segal, L. (1990) *Slow Motion: changing masculinities, changing men*. London: Virago.

Sinason, V. (ed) (1994) *Treating Survivors of Satanic Abuse*. London: Routledge.

Spring, J. (1987) *Cry Hard and Swim*. London: Virago.

Stevenson, O. (1992) 'Social Work Intervention to Protect Children: aspects of research and practice' *Child Abuse Review* Vol 1: 19-32

Trudell, B. & Whatley, M. H. (1988) 'School Sexual Abuse Prevention: unintended consequences and dilemmas' *Child Abuse and Neglect Vol 12 pp103-113*.

Tutty, L. (1996) 'Prevention Education: an integrative review' in Bagley, C. & Thurston, W. (eds).

Utting, W. (1997) *People Like Us: the report of the review of the safeguards for children living away from home*. Department of Health, Welsh Office. London: Stationery Office.

Wald, M. S. & Cohen, S. (1986) 'Preventing Child Abuse: What will it take?' *Family Law Quarterly* 20: 281-302.

Waterhouse, L. & Stevenson, O. (eds) (1993) *Child Abuse and Child Abusers: protection and prevention*. London: Jessica Kingsley Publishers.

Willis, D.J., Holden, E.W. & Rosenburg, M. (eds) (1991) *Prevention of Child Maltreatment: developmental and ecological perspectives*. US: John Wiley and Sons.

Wilson, M. (1993) *Crossing the Boundary: black women survive incest*. London: Virago.

12
Strategic planning to prevent harm to children

Norma Baldwin & Nick Spencer

Introduction

This chapter focuses on the importance of a strategic approach to planning services in child care and child protection. We have argued elsewhere the importance of the association between material and social deprivation and child abuse and neglect (Baldwin and Spencer, 1993), an argument further developed in Tuck's chapter. Building on this perspective, here we emphasise the value of preventive strategies based on community-wide approaches, to complement services which focus on individual needs and risks. Such strategies are not only more likely to be effective than strategies based on individual risk but are more consistent with the philosophy of the UN Convention on the Rights of the Child and the 1989 and 1995 Children Acts. They are compatible with and should link closely to national and local initiatives to combat social exclusion and enhance opportunities for young children (Sure Start DfEE1998; HM Treasury 1999). Some of the policy and practical implications for national and local government and for professionals working in the area of child abuse and neglect are considered.

UK preventive strategies

In spite of known links between the circumstances and conditions in which harm of various kinds arises (Browne & Madge 1982, Browne 1983, Becker & MacPherson 1988, Bebbington & Miles 1989), child care and family services have traditionally been focused on *individual* need, failing, risk, as though the causes of problems lie within families. Services whose main focus is on individual manifestations of problems are unlikely to be successful in preventing harm (Holman 1988, Blackburn 1991, Melton & Barry 1994, Henderson 1995, Garbarino 1995, Acheson 1998, Baldwin & Carruthers 1998). Yet a major emphasis in strategies in the UK employed to prevent child abuse and neglect has been the identification of individual families thought to be 'at risk' based on 'risk' criteria identified around the time of the child's birth (Ounsted et al. 1982; Browne & Saqui, 1988).

Despite widespread use for a number of years there is little evidence that individual 'risk' strategies have been successful in preventing abuse (Gough, 1988 & 1993). Risk checklists have serious limitations as screening instruments and are open to serious criticism on philosophical and theoretical grounds.

Initially these strategies were based on loosely derived criteria which were not individually weighted and often depended on the judgement of experienced practitioners (Ounsted et al., 1982). In the system employed in a Sheffield hospital and administered for a time by one of the authors (NS), health visitors were asked to indicate whether they agreed with risk status based on an assessment made by ante natal clinic staff, using criteria such as 'young unsupported mother' and 'lack of preparation for the birth of the infant' as well as 'previous history of abuse'. More sophisticated systems have been developed in recent years (Browne and Saqui, 1988, Ware & Browne 1996) based on weighting of criteria and tiered assessments carried out by health visitors at predetermined times.

Even the most developed screening procedures however have major difficulties related to their very low positive predictive value (PPV). PPV is a measure of the validity of the screening test; the lower the PPV, the less valuable the test in distinguishing true positives (those correctly identified by the test) from false positives (those falsely identified by the test as positive). PPV is derived using the following formula:

$$PPV = \frac{\text{Number of true positives}}{\text{Number of all positives on screening}} \times 100$$

Identifiable abuse and neglect are relatively uncommon events and the complexity of the causative pathways minimises the usefulness of checklists, however sophisticated, administered at one time in a complex and changing reality.

The problem can be illustrated using figures from a prospective study in Surrey of the prediction of child abuse reported by Browne and Saqi (1988). 14,238 births were screened of which 949 (6.7%) were identified as high risk using a weighted checklist (p.68). 83(5.8/1000) children were subsequently identified as 'abused'. Of these, 56 (67.5% of those abused) were in the high risk group. Thus, there were 885 false positives and 27 false negatives (those abused children who were in the low risk group). Using the above formula, the PPV is 5.9%. This is unacceptably low for a screening test.

Browne and Saqi (1988) are aware of this limitation and propose a second level of screening based on parent-child interaction, in order to improve the predictive value. Agathonos - Georgopoulou and Browne, (1997) suggest that 'prediction is feasible but there is need to improve the procedures for the assessment of risk, possibly by using a standardized clinical assessment' (p 723). However, even in the unlikely event that such measures would be successful in narrowing the high risk group down to 200, of whom 50 would be abused, the PPV would remain unacceptably low at 25%.

Of equal importance with the statistical inadequacies of predictive systems is the potential damage caused by inappropriate 'labelling' of families as potential abusers (Gelles, 1982; Guterman 1999). The lack of evidence that interventions with individual families actually reduce the incidence of child abuse (Gough, 1988 & 1993) raises major questions about the approach. However sensitive and well-designed, predictive systems cannot avoid inappropriate 'labelling' because, as Gelles points out, there is no precise and acceptable definition of abuse and the process of prediction is influenced by factors other than those that cause a parent to maltreat a child. 'Labelling' may have the opposite effect for stressed and uncertain parents; a self-fulfilling prophecy may be created and maltreatment be made more, rather than less, likely as a result of predictive interventions (Gelles, 1982). The likelihood is that in families identified as 'high risk' behaviour which might be seen as falling below the ideal would be more likely to be diagnosed as abuse than would the same behaviour in so-called 'low risk' families.

The widely differing proposed interventions arising from 'at risk' identification (Gough 1988 & 1993) indicate the lack of clarity as to which interventions actually have any measurable effect. The type of intervention chosen seems to be more related to availability of personnel and resources than to clear theoretical frameworks based upon causal pathways.

Risk prediction, based on the identification of single variables at specific times, cannot account for the complexity of the causal pathways leading to child abuse. These require an approach, similar to that proposed by Rutter (1988), in which causal relationships are examined in the form of chains and of linked sequences involving several different short-term effects. What we can identify - as Tuck has shown in an earlier chapter - are some of the conditions, circumstances and characteristics associated with high risk of harm of various kinds. There are practical as well as moral arguments for trying to promote conditions which help children thrive. The strategic objective is to try to bring about the optimum environment for children.

The UN Convention on the Rights of the Child recognises the importance of state and government provision of support to families in the care of children and a level of housing and living standards sufficient to ensure the proper development of the child. Signatory states are charged with the responsibility of ensuring that such provision is available for children within their national boundaries. The 1989 Children Act and 1995 Children (Scotland) Act give local authorities the task of providing communal services to meet the needs of children and to support families in providing adequate care for children. In spite of continuing debates about definitions of 'children in need' there is an increasing emphasis on the prevention of harm (Tunstill 1995 and 1997). The Audit Commission report 'Seen but not heard' (1994) and Messages from Research (DoH 1995) have both emphasised the need for services to change the balance between current individualised and investigative interventions and those aimed at supporting families. The NSPCC sponsored National Commission of Inquiry into the Prevention of Child Abuse draws together arguments and evidence for such a shift (1996). Preventive strategies compatible with the philosophy of the UN Convention and the Children Acts must move to positive communal services, community-wide strategies, aimed at raising the general level of child care, health, and safety within an area, in parallel with attempts to improve sensitivity and effectiveness of those services which must continue to focus on a small minority of families and children where harm is already apparent.

Chamberlin (1988), reviewing the most successful programmes, argued that preventive strategies work best when they are concentrated on defined geographical areas, where there are substantial numbers of people in a middle range of social and economic disadvantage. Support for children and families in such areas can strengthen community supports, prevent families becoming over burdened with stress (Chamberlin 1988; Schorr 1988; Gibbons (ed) 1992; Melton & Barry (eds) 1994; Garbarino 1995).

In one of the few types of early intervention which has been thoroughly researched - visiting the homes of pregnant women and mothers of very young children with the aim of supporting parenting and preventing child abuse and neglect - Guterman (1999) shows that 'the most robust outcomes come from programmes which rely on demographically based involvement criteria'. He argues the need for services which take account of factors such as 'economic impoverishment, social network deficits, and neighbourhood exigencies' and attempt to match services with the needs of the populations they serve.

In the remainder of this chapter we shall consider some community-wide preventive strategies which are philosophically aligned with the UN Convention and the Children Acts and which recognise the important role of material and social deprivation in the causative pathways of child abuse and neglect.

Community wide approaches to promoting the health and well-being of families and children

A familiarity with current research and theory and a critically evaluative approach to policy and practice can be fostered through training programmes, but organisational and management commitments within local authorities and between them and health and other welfare agencies are needed to support realistic and effective preventive and supportive strategies and services. Support and prevention challenge the dominance of crisis management and investigation driven child protection services (Gibbons 1995), demanding a recognition that culture, structures and procedures need to change and that agencies need to provide increased support for their front line practitioners and for voluntary agencies and groups. The emphasis in Messages from Research (DoH 1995) on the need for *professionals* - particularly social workers - to change their emphasis ignores the limits on the autonomy and discretion of individual professionals, who have been carrying out agency and national policy.

Here we consider some examples of projects which have tried to develop community wide strategies. Such projects tend to be partially evaluated at best. However, valuable experience has been gained and characteristics associated with successful outcomes have been identified, providing a useful basis for planning strategies for primary prevention.

Three examples from the USA: the Addison County Parent Child Center, Vermont, the FAST project, Wisconsin and the Head Start Project USA wide, are explored. The Newpin Project in the UK is also discussed. Broad lessons for community wide strategies will be drawn from these and similar projects.

The Addison county parent child center

Addison is a rural county in Vermont with a high level of rural poverty and isolated families headed by young, single parents. The Center, based in the largest town (population 7,800), was established with the broad aim of increasing self-esteem and communication skills of both parents and children and to develop a sense of community. Communal facilities for education, entertainment and 'household chores' such as laundry are available. Child care programmes and support groups to help people through stressful life situations (divorce; first-time parenting; single parenting) have been developed and the Center coordinates various State agencies. Outreach activities are organised. Community participation in the running and management of the Center is an essential element of the approach. Joint public/private funding supports the Center and the community is actively involved in fund-raising.

Though no formal evaluation has been undertaken, the following changes in adverse outcomes have been attributed to the activities of the Center (Chamberlin, 1988):

1. Teenage pregnancies reduced from 70/1000 in 1979 to 45/1000 in 1986.
2. Of those teenagers becoming pregnant in 1986:
    a. 90% received ante natal care compared with 49% in the rest of State.
    b. <1% had infants weighing <2,500 gms. compared with 8.9% in rest of State.
    c. Infant Mortality Rate was 5.6/1000 compared with 11.6/1000 in rest of State.
3. Amongst families served by the Center:
    a. Welfare dependency fell from 40% in 1983 to 17% in 1987
    b. Child abuse incidence fell from 21% to 2%
    c. Only 4 families had a child placed in permanent care
    d. Adolescent parents receiving high school diplomas increased from 30% to 71%.

FAST (Families and Schools Together) programme, Maddison, Wisconsin

This programme offers school based family support: a preventive programme for children 6-9 at risk for future problems because of behaviour, attainments, apathy, depression etc. The approach used 'can be viewed as a bridge between active community development and therapeutic interventions and used to connect both endeavours' (p.141 McDonald et al 1997).

Families referred to the programme are under stress and socially isolated, living on benefits, most are single mothers, some suffer depression, many are substance or alcohol abusers (McDonald & Billingham 1990; McDonald et al 1997). All are invited as whole families to join the programme - all are volunteers. They agree to attend eight weeks of family group meetings, accompanied by outreach work.

The programme attempts to provide intense support for families and for individual children, whilst taking account of immediate and future practical demands, such as child care. Trained workers work with parents (usually mothers) both as individuals and in their parental role, trying to increase the quality of interactions and the rewards for positive parenting.

Families are recruited in their homes (often by a FAST Graduate). Families are picked up from their homes and driven to meetings, where a free meal is provided for the whole family. Child care is provided for infants and toddlers. Monthly meetings, for whole families who have graduated, continue, along with child care support, for the next two years.

The programme attempts to avoid stigma. FAST supports parents while engaging active, voluntary participation in all levels of the Programme - deciding future work, recruiting new families, running meetings, fund raising. Some parents go on to become paid staff.

It has a partnership model, with parents and professionals collaborating with other health and welfare agencies. It develops parent support networks through individual 'buddies' and groups.

Evaluations have shown increases in self esteem, family closeness and support networks, attention span at school and also improvements in classroom behaviour, and parent-child interactions.

Parents believed it helped them to enjoy time with children, get closer to them, understand them better, deal with school problems more effectively.

Head Start

The Head Start initiative in the USA began in 1965 as a widespread development programme for low income children and their families. Programmes provide pre-school support as well as paying attention to parents' needs for support and opportunities to improve social networks and environmental conditions. Early childhood education and support is found to be effective over long periods in improving educational achievements, in avoiding the need for remedial placements, and in promoting social adjustment. (Barnett 1995 & 1998; Raver & Zigler 1997). Parents are involved in the day to day work of the programmes with the children, in training, in management and in broader aspects of social change. Zigler (1993) associates effectiveness of programmes such as Head Start with their attention to the whole child, over time, in their environment, and to the emphasis on full parental involvement.

Newpin

The Newpin project, started at one centre in South London in 1980 and subsequently developed centres nationwide. It shares many of the same aims as the projects described above. Newpin aims to break the cyclical effect of destructive family behaviour by raising the self-esteem of individual parents who are suffering from depression or loss of identity and to inspire parents to recognise the value of consistent good practice in caring for children. Referrals come from health visitors, social workers and other professionals.

The focus is on individual parents in contrast to the community wide approaches of two of the US projects but there is a similar emphasis on developing the resources of families for the benefit of the whole community. Newpin approaches this by the development of a network of befrienders, women from the neighbourhood who themselves have experienced child care difficulties and have been assisted by Newpin, who are assigned to newly referred mothers. In addition, Newpin have developed a training programme for mothers allowing them to become coordinators within the project.

Mothers are seen as a positive resource rather than 'risky' mothers whom the services must police. Partnership is an essential principle.

Evaluation has been limited. Newpin claim a clear reduction in abuse and neglect among the children of mothers referred but it is not yet possible to assess the effect within a community. Mothers in the greatest adversity were the most likely to continue with the programme. They 'showed striking improvements in self esteem and control over their lives. The greatest improvement occurred between seven and twelve months involvement' (Gibbons, 1995, p.95 referring to Cox 1992). A more recent study (Oakley et al 1998) found that 62% in their sample believed that Newpin had made a positive difference to their lives. Oakley et al were concerned however that a high proportion of those who were referred did not take up the offer of support from Newpin and there was no follow up for them.

A similar but health service based approach is described by Barker et al (1987 & 1992). As a result of the Bristol Child Development programme a number of health authorities have trained Health Visitors and volunteers to offer supportive visiting to first time parents in areas of high risk. They concentrate on increasing self esteem, reducing conflict and improving confidence in parenting. Evaluations suggest that referrals for child abuse reduced in those areas.

Extensive research into programmes of parental and early years home visiting in the USA (Olds et al 1988, 1995, 1997, Kitzman et al 1997) has shown substantial health and welfare gains for mothers and children involved in these projects and reductions in anticipated numbers of cases of abuse, neglect, home accidents and criminal behaviour, for up to 15 years.

Supportive evidence

In her study of preventive work in local areas, Gibbons (1990) said:

The results of the research lend support to the hypothesis that parents under stress more easily overcome family problems when there are many sources of family support available in local communities.

Unfortunately, few longitudinal studies have been done in this country which evaluate the outcomes of preventive work. Many of the evaluations which have been done have substantial methodological flaws (Gough 1995; Macdonald & Roberts 1995; Oakley & Roberts (eds) 1996; Oakley et al 1998; Finkelhor 1999). Nevertheless there is a substantial body of demographic, public health research, which demonstrates the pervasive and harmful effects of disadvantage *when supportive and preventive services are not available* (Acheson 1998; HM Treasury 1999).

Schorr (1988) describes a large number of evaluations of the impact of preventive programmes in the USA. She identifies common characteristics of the successful programmes:

Common elements of successful programmes

- comprehensiveness;
- intensiveness;

- family and community orientated;
- staff with time and skills to develop relationships of respect, trust and collaboration;
- offer broad spectrum of services - social, emotional and concrete help;
- recognise needs are untidy, cross professional and bureaucratic boundaries;
- flexible, user friendly, easy access.

> 'They see the child in the context of the family and the family in the context of its surroundings. Services take account of parents' needs, help them to gain access to support and help for their children.'
>
> 'The partnership model is not just one of professionals across their voluntary and statutory agencies, but one of partnership with users.'

The shape of services comes from the needs they serve, rather than precepts of professional or bureaucratic boundaries.

Evaluations of American Head Start programmes add further evidence that these characteristics are associated with effectiveness (Zigler & Styfco 1993).

Approaches which focus on family support do however need to recognise tensions between children's rights and their need for protection and between the rights of children and the rights and needs of families. The explicit priority in the Children Acts to the welfare of the child, whilst emphasising family participation and cooperation, recognises such tensions. Safeguards for children and young people, along with ready access to services in their own right, will need to be considered as part of any strategy. A realistic appraisal is needed of the range and type of services needed to protect children and as far as possible to promote their rights.

The planning context

Current government attention to the importance of early childhood and family support (Meeting the Childcare Challenge: Scottish Office 1998; Our Healthier Nation: DoH 1998; Sure Start: DfEE 1998; Towards a Healthier Scotland: Scottish Office 1999) along with broader social inclusion developments, provides an opportunity for health and social work organisations to review their childcare and child protection plans. A more balanced portfolio can be developed, of individualised and community wide initiatives - the 'downstream' and 'upstream' policies recommended in the Acheson Report (1998). The need for a wide range of community based projects appears to have been recognised (Family Policy Studies Centre (1999)). However problems remain in ensuring that these will be adequately linked together, integrated in a long term strategic plan. These problems are highlighted in the chapters on 'Promoting effective child protection and family support for Asian children' (21) and the 'Henley Project' (22).

The positive potential for linkage can be illustrated by a small creative initiative in Dundee. A Young Women's Project - linked with Rape Crisis Centres - has developed training materials for work with young children on issues of safety (Young Women's Project (1999)). This is part of a programme to support parents and young children in identifying situations of risk such as bullying, violence and sexual abuse. A priority is to help parents communicate well with their children. The workers pay attention to the different needs, expectations and behaviour of girls and boys. Work is done in schools and neighbourhoods. It is a programme which can be used as a stepping stone to other outreach work in communities, to educate about child safety, to back up parent training courses and family support initiatives. It can help to involve local people in thinking about positive strategies to promote child safety and well being. Such work, *as part of an ongoing community strategy*, can improve responses to the threat posed in communities by sexual offenders. Local people can work together with professionals and the media to encourage neighbourly responsibility for children's care and safety and help avoid fear and panic which is leading to vigilantism in some areas. Children can be encouraged to share with each other and with adults their knowledge or fears of dangerous adults, for the sake of other local children, so avoiding the stigma and difficulties associated with more direct investigative approaches. Where partnership and community outreach is backed up with long term planned resources for child care and family support, the likelihood of increasing resilience, confidence and well being in disadvantaged neighbourhoods may be enhanced.

Planning: A long term process

There are numerous examples of imaginative, creative, effective community based initiatives (Henderson (ed) 1995; Cannan & Warren (eds) 1997; Family Policy Studies Centre 1999). Many of them have enormous problems, however, because of the short term nature of funding. Short term initiatives can be successful in stimulating energy, focusing attention, bringing in new ideas, but they are very expensive in start up and run down costs. They are costly too in human stress when funding is under threat. Strategic, long term planning, which takes account of the need for a range of parallel but linked and coordinated initiatives is essential to best value - in financial terms, but more importantly, to best value for children.

Long term, flexible partnerships, can draw in and support short term projects, and can ensure that objectives evolve and change to meet changing needs and priorities. Partnerships across agencies, with community groups, involving adults and children, are essential to any comprehensive, strategic plan.

Parallel initiatives will need to draw on differing views and definitions of communities, such as those based on neighbourhoods and those based on community of need or experience. Some initiatives ('downstream') will be intensive, rehabilitative, controlling. Others ('upstream') will be developmental, preventive, promotional. Strategic planning will ensure that they can be developed together, not in competition, that they complement and connect. All depend on high levels of skill in gathering, assessing and analysing individual and community needs and risks. (See overleaf).

Analysis
- ▲ Economic and social processes
  - Group and individual needs, cultures, attitudes
  - Social problems
  - Organisational and institutional arrangements
- ▼
Planning and evaluation

- ▲ Connections between plans focused on individuals, groups, schools, localities
  - Plans continuously updated in light of changes in situations, resources, knowledge
  - Realistic time scales which take account of long-term processes
- ▼
Action

Conclusion

We have emphasised the major links between deprivation and harm to children and questioned strategies which rely mainly on identifying risk in individual families. We have drawn attention to some of the characteristics of programmes which have been successful in improving life chances for children.

Whilst recognising that the fundamental problems need major political and economic interventions, we argue that there is a substantial body of work which demonstrates that the worst consequences of deprivation can be lessened by community and family supports, making it more likely that parents will cope with their own and their children's needs.

Our analysis leads us to support broadly based initiatives, multilayered, aiming to support families and children without stigma. The projects we have described could form effective foundations for more systematic planned strategies, aiming to fulfil local authorities' responsibilities under section 17 of the Children Act 1989 and section 22 of the Children (Scotland) Act 1995, based on the principles of the UN Convention on the Rights of the Child. Such strategies will need to draw on national and local data about the material resources, social supports, and services available to children and families. They are relevant to the broad spectrum of children's needs, as well as to issues of juvenile crime (Audit Commission 1994 & 1996). They will also need to take account of current attitudes to children, to expectations on mothers, to the particular strengths and needs of minority groups, and recognise the potential for responsibility and partnership within communities, if they are to be effective in preventing harm to children.

References

Acheson. Sir D. (Chair) (1998) *Independent Inquiry into Inequalities in Health Report.* London: TSO.

Agathonos-Georgopoulou, H. & Browne, K.D. (1997) 'The Prediction of Child Maltreatment in Greek Families' in *Child Abuse and Neglect*, Vol 21 No. 8.

Audit Commission (1994) *Seen but not Heard*. London: HMSO.

Audit Commission, (1996) *Misspent Youth*. London: HMSO.

Baldwin, N., & Carruthers, L. (1998) *Developing Neighbourhood Support and Child Protection Strategies: The Henley Safe Children Project*. Aldershot: Ashgate.

Baldwin, N., & Spencer, N. (1993) 'Deprivation and child abuse: implications for strategic planning in children's services'. *Children & Society* Vol. 7 No. 4: 357-75.

Barker, W. et al. (1987) *Community Health and the Child Development Programme*., University of Bristol.

Barker, W.E., Anderson, R.M., Chalmers, C. (1992) *Child Protection: The impact of the Child Development Programme*. Evaluation Document No. 14 Early Childhood Development Unit, University of Bristol.

Barnett, W.S. (1995) 'Long term effects of early childhood programmes on cognitive and school outcomes'. *Future of Children* Vol. 5 No. 3 pp 25-30.

Barnett, W.S. (1998) ' Long term cognitive and academic effects of early childhood education on children in poverty'. *Preventive Medicine* Vol. 27, No. 2 pp 204-207

Bebbington, A. and Miles, J. (1989) 'The background of children who enter local authority care', *British Journal of Social Work*, 19(5).

Becker, S. and MacPherson, S. (eds.) (1988) ' Public issues, private pain', *Social Services Insight*.

Blackburn, C (1991) Poverty and Health: *Working with Families*, Milton Keynes: Open University Press.

Brown, M. and Madge, N. (1982) *Despite the Welfare State*, London: Heinemann Educational Books.

Brown, M. (1983) *The Structure of Disadvantage* SSRC/DHSS Studies in Deprivation and Disadvantage. London: Heinemann.

Browne, K. Davies, C. and Stratton, P. (eds) (1988) *Early Prediction and Prevention of Child Abuse*. Chichester: Wiley.

Browne, K. and Saqi, S. (1988) 'Approaches to screening for child abuse and neglect' in Cannan, C. & Warren, C. (eds) (1997) *Social Action with Children and Families: a community development approach to child and family welfare*. London: Routledge.

Browne, Davies and Stratton (eds) *Early Prediction and Prevention of Child Abuse*. Chichester: Wiley.

Browne, K. (1988) 'The nature of child abuse and neglect: an overview' in Browne, Davies and Stratton (eds) *Early Prediction and Prevention of Child Abuse*. Chichester: Wiley.

Chamberlin, R. (ed) (1988) *Beyond Individual Risk Assessment: Community Wide Approaches to Promoting the Health and Development of Families and Children*. Washington DC: The National Center for Education in Maternal and Child Health.

Cox, A., Pound, A., Pickering C,. (1992) 'Newpin - a befriending scheme and therapeutic network for carers of young children' in J.Gibbons (ed) *The Children Act 1989 & Family Support: Principles into Practice*, London: HMSO.

DfEE (1998) *Sure Start: Making a Difference for Children and Families*.

DoH (1991) *Child Abuse: A Study of Inquiry Reports* 1980-1989. London: HMSO.

DoH (1995) *Child Protection: Messages from Research*. London: HMSO.

DoH (1998) *Our Healthier Nation: a contract for health*. London: TSO.

Family Policy Studies Centre (1999) *Transforming Children's Lives: the importance of early intervention*. Occasional paper 25.

Finkelhor, D. (1984) *Child Sexual Abuse: New Theory and Research.* New York: Free Press.

Finkelhor, D. (1999) 'The Science' in *Child Abuse and Neglect* Special Issue *Convening a National Call to Action: Working Towards the Elimination of Child Maltreatment.* Vol 23 No. 10. pp 969-974.

Garbarino, J. (1995) *Raising Children in a Socially Toxic Environment.* San Francisco: Jossey-Bass.

Garbarino, J. and Crouter, A. (1978) 'Defining the community context for parent-child relations: the correlates of child maltreatment'. *Child Development,* 49, pp. 604-16.

Garbarino, J. and Sherman, S. (1980) 'High-risk neighbourhoods and high-risk families: the human ecology of child maltreatment', *Child Development,* 51, pp. 188-98.

Gelles, R. (1982) 'Problems in defining and labelling child abuse' in Starr, R. (ed.) *Child Abuse Prediction.* Cambridge, Mass: Ballinger.

Gibbons, J. (ed) (1992) *The Children Act 1989 and Family Support: Principles into Practice.* London: HMSO.

Gibbons, J. (1995) 'Family Support in Child Protection' in *Supporting Families* (ed.) Hill, M., Hawthrone Kirk, *Part D,* Edinburgh HMSO.

Gibbons, J., Thorpe, S. and Wilkinson, P. (1990) *Family Support and Prevention: Studies in Local Areas.* London; HMSO/NISW.

Gough, D. (1988) 'Approaches to child abuse prevention' in Browne, Davies and Stratton (eds.) *Early Prediction and Prevention in Child Abuse* . Chichester, Wiley,

Gough, D. (1993) *Child Abuse Intervention: A Review of the Research Literature.* London: HMSO.

Guterman, N.B. (1999) 'Enrolment Strategies in early home visitation to prevent physical child abuse and neglect and the 'universal versus targeted' debate: a meta-analysis of population based and screening based programmes. *Child Abuse and Neglect* Vol. 23 No. 9 pp863-890.

Henderson, P. (ed) (1995) *Children and Communities* London. Pluto Press in association with the Children's Society and Community Development Foundation.

HM Treasury (1999) *Tackling Poverty and Extending Opportunity* No. 4. The Modernisation of Britain's Tax and Benefit System. London.

Holman, R. (1988) *Putting Families First: Prevention and Child Care.* London: Macmillan Education in association with Children's Society.

Holman, R. (2000) *Kids at the Door Revisited.* London: Russell House.

Kitzman, H., Olds, D., Henderson, C.J., Hanks, C., Cole, R., Tatelbaum, R., McConnochie, K., Sidora, K., Luckey, D., Shaver, D., Engelhardt, K., James, D., Barnard, K. (1997) 'Effect of infancy home visitation by nurses on pre-natal pregnancy outcomes, childhood injuries and repeated childbearing. A randomized controlled trial. *JAMA* 278(8), 644-652.

Macdonald, G. & Roberts, H. (1995) *What Works in the Early Years: Effective Interventions for Children and Families in Health, Social Welfare, Education and Child Protection.* Ilford: Barnardo's.

McDonald, L. and Billingham, S. (1990) Families and Schools Together, Programme Evaluation. FAST Project: Madison, Wisconsin.

McDonald, L., Billingham, S., Conrad, T., Morgan, A., Payton N.O. (1997) 'Families and Schools Together (FAST): Integrating Community Development with Clinical Strategies', *Families in Society: The Journal of Contemporary Human Services,* Families International, Inc.

Melton, G.B. & Barry, F.E. (eds) (1994) *Protecting Children from Abuse and Neglect: Foundations for a New National Strategy.* New York: Guilford Press.

National Commission of Inquiry into the Prevention of Child Abuse (1996) *Childhood Matters*. London: Stationery Office.

Oakley, A., Roberts, H. (eds) (1996) *Evaluating Social Interventions: a report of two workshops*. Ilford: Barnardo's.

Oakley, A., Rajan, L., Turner, H. (1998) 'Evaluating parent support initiatives: lessons from two case studies' in *Health and Social Care in the Community* Vol. 6(5) pp 318-330.

Olds, D., Henderson, C.R.J., Tatelbaum, R., Chamberlin, R. (1988) 'Improving the life-course development of socially disadvantaged mothers: a randomized trial of nurse home visitation'. *American Journal of Public Health* 78(11), 1436-1445.

Olds, D., Henderson, C.J., Kitzman, H., Cole, R. (1995) 'Effects of prenatal and infancy nurse home visitation on surveillance of child maltreatment.' *Pediatrics* 95(3), 365-372.

Olds, D., Eckenrode, J., Henderson, C.R., Kitzman, H., Powers, J., Cole, R., Sidora, K., Morris, P., Pettit, L., Luckey, D. (1997) ' Long term effects of home visitation on maternal life course and child abuse and neglect: 15 year follow up of a randomized trial.' *JAMA* 278(8), 637-643.

Ounsted, C., Gordon, M., Roberts, J. and Milligan, B. (1982) 'The Fourth goal of perinatal medicine', *British Medical Journal*, 184, pp. 8789-82.

Raver, C.C., Zigler, E.F. (1997) 'Social competence: an untapped dimension in evaluating Head Start's success.' *Early Childhood Research Quarterly*. Vol. 12 No. 4 pp 363 - 385.

Rutter, M. (1988) 'Longitudinal data in the study of causal processes: some uses and some pitfalls', in Rutter, M. (ed.) *Studies of Psychosocial Risk: The Power of Longitudinal Data*. Cambridge: European Science Foundation, Cambridge University Press.

Schorr, L. (1988) *Within Our Reach: Breaking the Cycle of Disadvantage*. New York: Anchor Doubleday.

Scottish Office (1998) *Meeting the Childcare Challenge: A Childcare Strategy for Scotland*. Edinburgh: TSO.

Scottish Office (1999) *Towards a Healthier Scotland*. Edinburgh: TSO.

Tunstill, J. (1995) 'The Concept of Children in Need: The Answer on the Problem for Family Support', *Children and Youth Services Review* 17.5/6 pp 651-664.

Tunstill, J. (1997) 'Implementing the family support clauses of the 1989 Children Act: legislative, professional and organisational obstacles' in Parton, N. (ed)) *Child Protection and Family Support: tensions, contradictions and possibilities*. London: Routledge.

United Nations Convention on the Rights of the Child.

Ware, J.& Browne, K. (1996) 'Research into Practice - C.A.R.E. (Child Assessment Rating and Evaluation)' Eleventh International Congress on Child Abuse and Neglect, Dublin

Young Women's Project (1999) *The Wee VIP Project*. 28 South Tay Street, Dundee.

Zigler, E. & Styfco, S.J. (1993) *Head Start & Beyond: A National Plan for Childhood Intervention* Yale. New Haven.

13
Towards user friendly assessment

Chris McCarrick, Adrian Over, Pam Wood

This chapter describes a project to develop a framework for the assessment of children and families where there are child protection concerns. As three generic workers in Coventry Social Services Department, we shared a common interest in assessment and a common dissatisfaction with models available to us. None of the frameworks gave adequate guidance, we felt, about how to go about assessment in practical, tangible ways, which would feel participative and real to family members and would be genuinely child focused.

We explore here some of the literature we used and how our ideas and work developed. We describe the main aspects of the assessment framework which we developed and some of the exercises and materials it contains. The complete framework is set out in chapter 14.

The framework has been used by social workers and nursery officers undertaking Child Protection Assessments in Coventry Social Services Department.

Background to the assessment framework

The Policy Development Officer for child care in Coventry was asked to develop practice guidelines on assessment in the year in which we were undertaking the Child Protection Course at Warwick University. We negotiated with him, with senior managers in the department and the Area Child Protection Committee to take responsibility for consulting widely within the department, developing a framework which could be used alongside the Department of Health Guide (DoH 1988), and piloting the framework.

Our focus was to be on the type of child protection cases in which *social workers* are expected to undertake assessments. It was not anticipated that the framework would be a replacement for comprehensive assessments, undertaken with some specialist input, in the most complex cases. We did envisage, however, that the emphasis on participative methods, which was a key element of our work, would have relevance for those undertaking comprehensive assessments. Part of our motivation for the work came from our sense of being left 'empty handed' by the Department of Health Guide (op cit) and other frameworks. We felt that they gave very little guidance about *how* to gather information, engage families and undertake assessments. It seemed to be assumed that question and answer, verbal exchanges are always effective between professionals and all service users, an assumption which our experience brought into question.

The tone of the Department of Health Guide (op cit) suggests a process in which assessment is *done to* families rather than *with* them. We believe that co-operation from parents, in making agreed plans, is more likely from a perspective which takes account of their needs and concerns and those of their children than from a focus purely on incidents and likelihood of harm. In this we anticipated the recommendations of 'Messages from Research' (DoH 1995).

We gained the agreement of a group of case conference Chairs to identify a representative group of cases for the pilot study, balanced according to ethnic origins, family size, disability, district of origin, status of the assessments and types of child protection concerns. They agreed to brief district team managers.

We wrote to all of the social work teams and operational managers in Coventry, inviting their comments on and contributions to the assessment framework. The common issues which we had identified - after a great deal of uncomfortable discussion and work together - and which we wished to address were:

- The difficulties for social workers in engaging parents when undertaking assessment work. There is often conflict and resistance which has to be overcome in order for the assessment to proceed and, in particular, in order to gain the parents' permission for work with the child(ren) to take place.
- The need to find ways for parents *to be involved in and part of* the assessment, rather than it being *done to them*. In short, the framework needed to be *user- friendly*.
- The child(ren) and their needs should always be the focus of any information sought in the assessment, including information about the adults' backgrounds and their relationships.
- The framework should be developed with district social workers, who have responsibility for leading and co-ordinating assessment, in mind. However the involvement of other professionals and agencies should be encouraged, based on clear agreements with the social workers and family.
- Unless absolutely impossible to achieve, all assessments should include some work with the child(ren) to gain an understanding of her/his perception of her/his world.
- The general *inquisitive* work of an assessment should take place before any judgments are made or conclusions reached about the *causes for concern* being due to the family's functioning.
- This inquisitive work should have as its starting point a shared appreciation with parents of children's needs.
- Assessment should always include a thorough analysis of the practical and economic circumstances of the family and of their social networks.
- An opportunity for members of the family to provide a self-assessment should be central to the process.
- The inquisitive work should involve reaching a substantial understanding of significant features, unique factors, rules and norms of the family.
- At some point during the assessment, direct observation of the interactions and dynamics in the family should be made.

Preparation for the framework

Our initial planning focused on eight main aspects of the family's current and historical circumstances:

- The actual causes for concern.
- Assessment of the parents' appreciation of the needs of any child from birth to young adulthood.
- Assessment of the family's practical and environmental circumstances.
- The child according to self perceptions.
- The child according to parents' perceptions.
- Assessment of the children's relationships with parents.
- Assessment of the adult relationships and the impact of those upon the care of the children.
- Assessment of the whole family as a unit.

Our intention was to provide a general introduction to the framework which would include philosophy, values, discussion about initial engagement with the family, the organisation and the process of the assessment. The connections between each of the eight aspects above in making an overall assessment would be stressed.

We considered at length whether or not to include a separate section focusing on class, ethnic, cultural, gender and sexuality issues in child protection assessment work. We concluded that these issues should not be 'packaged' separately, with the risk of marginalising them. It was decided that their importance and impact should be highlighted, wherever appropriate, throughout the framework.

We divided up the work, each of us taking responsibility for focusing on certain aspects of assessment. We exchanged our first drafts and met each other in pairs to discuss them. This process generated a great deal of energy, new ideas and further discussion, leading to some sections being combined, some having substantial adjustments made and additional material being introduced.

We were particularly influenced by a paper presented at the first NSPCC International Conference on 'Risk Assessment in Child Protection', in Leicester, by Dr Leonard Dalgleish, of the University of Queensland, Australia, entitled 'The Relationship of Child Abuse Indicators to the Assessment of Perceived Risk' (See also Dalgliesh 1997).

This paper convinced us that, although our framework could not include a mechanism for establishing degrees of risk in exact terms, it could and should *provide a means for practitioners and parents and children explicitly to set out the information* arising from an assessment which each of them regard as *significant* in evaluating the risk to a child. We therefore set about developing a format in which all of the information regarded as significant could be set out explicitly as perceived indicators of risk, as either significant *strengths* or significant *hazards* for the safe care of the child(ren).

We included in our introduction to the framework the suggestion that *strengths* and *hazards* should be used as headings under which significant information could be recorded by all parties at each stage of the assessment. *The overall emphasis on working with parents to identify their needs and their children's needs could be related closely to this.*

We believed that this process would be likely to encourage social workers to be open and explicit about their perceptions of risk to the child and the concrete information which relates to it. This militates against the trend identified by Dalgleish of the term 'at risk' being applied to children without definition or analysis. His research indicates that there is very little agreement between workers about the *meaning* and *levels* of risk. There is a need to be factual and descriptive, ensuring that particular situations, material hazards, behaviours and attitudes can be evaluated. Although our framework does not provide a scientific means for workers to assess risk, it is a means whereby evidence can be looked at in relation to each aspect of an assessment and judgements then made explicit. This then acknowledges the influence of individual values in assessment and guards against wholly unqualified and subjective judgements.

The second component of the framework as initially envisaged was an assessment of the parents' appreciation of the needs of any child, from birth to young adulthood. We believed that assessments should be conducted from the starting point of a shared appreciation of children's needs with parents. A number of assumptions and principles were associated with this view. One was the need to engage families successfully and secure their co-operation without alienating them, while practising in an open and honest way. The consultation exercise had identified this process as critical. We agreed that the social worker would be unlikely to engage a family successfully if the initial approach was to focus on the parents' culpability in the suspected abuse, or simply on factors associated with the incident causing concern. Not only would such an approach risk alienation but it contains an implicit assumption about child abuse as a product or symptom of dysfunctional personal and family relationships. What we wished to promote was an emphasis upon the *needs* and *rights* of children within a definition of child abuse something akin to that suggested by Gil (1975, p 347):

> Child abuse is: *inflicted gaps or deficits between circumstances of living which would facilitate the optimum development of children, to which they should be entitled, and their actual circumstances, irrespective of the sources or agents of the deficit.*

Such an approach clearly requires an initial discussion with parents around their understanding of the 'circumstances of living which would facilitate the optimum development of children', and then requires an assessment of their child(ren)'s 'actual circumstances'.

Returning to the issue of engagement of parents, we also felt that to begin the assessment with a general discussion about the needs of all children would remove the focus from child abuse as such, thus avoiding an accusatory or interrogative approach and providing more relaxed opportunities for the parents to begin to communicate with the social worker.

Assessments often begin - with these same objectives in mind - with parents being asked to talk about themselves, their own relationships and backgrounds. Our approach ensures that the assessment is *child centred* from the beginning, consistent with one of our core values.

The DoH Guide 'Protecting Children' (op cit) suggests beginning the assessment with a consideration of the Causes for Concern but, where these are contentious, it suggests starting with the parents and their backgrounds (Page 17 para 4.2 (C)). Our framework reflects the view that the latter can be equally contentious and requires a sensitive approach. Our framework *does* recommend that Causes for Concern should be made explicit when first engaging the family, by explaining that the need for the assessment has arisen because something has happened to the child. We suggest that it is this *outcome for the child* which should be emphasised at this stage and that the workers should do this in a non-judgemental and neutral way (Jones et al, 1987 pages 119-120). We agree with the suggestion in 'Protecting Children' (op cit) that any areas of agreement and disagreement between the parents, child(ren) and professionals should be noted at this early stage. However, we suggest that detailed discussion of the Causes for Concern and disagreements about them should take place at a later stage of the assessment (Section 7) by which time the process of the assessment might well enable parents to discuss disagreements constructively and they may possibly have shifted from their original position.

Following our initial writing, therefore, a section on the Causes for Concern was included in the introduction. The section looking with parents at the general needs of children comes next. It includes the assessment of the family's practical circumstances or what we have called external pressures and supports. We felt it important to include the analysis of the family's *practical* resources with their *intellectual* resources to understand their child's needs.

Related to Gil's definition of child abuse, the second section of our framework contains the first part of an analysis of the family's 'actual circumstances' along with an analysis of the parent's views of the 'circumstances of living which would facilitate the optimum development of (their) children'.

Sections 3 to 6 are designed to facilitate the rest of the assessment of the child/ren's actual circumstances and needs, from varying perspectives, including her/his own (section 5).

Our work in pairs after our initial writing helped to crystallise much of our thinking and to develop the structure of the framework in its eventual form. The process of feedback and discussion about each other's work led to many detailed amendments and clarification.

Our very different backgrounds, personalities and perspectives made the work awkward at times but healthy disagreements were stimulating and helpful for the production of work. We had to reach consensus in certain areas. This led to a development of core values for us as workers. Much of this human interaction provided valuable material for the framework, for example:

- Don't make assumptions.
- Clarify information; check out; feed back.
- Be aware of your values - they affect judgments and hence how small or great risk is perceived to be.
- There is a need for some basis for agreement - or openly acknowledged room for differing analysis and judgement.
- Participation means embracing *everyone*.

We explored what we thought an assessment was or should contain. From that came our categories of assessment. We discussed what information was really necessary in an assessment. Good practice came under scrutiny. Our work as individuals and together focused our collective thinking more clearly on risk, the needs of the child and practical work with families.

A number of the practical exercises for promoting discussion with families and gathering information arose from this exchange, as each of us was stimulated by the others' work. The 'Helps and Hindrances' exercise, designed to assess external pressures and supports, is a good example, arising directly from discussion about a simple, practical way to engage parents about these issues.

The final structure of the assessment framework was:

1. Introductory comments, values, preparation and engagement.
2. Meeting children's needs and the family's practical resources.
3. Assessment of the parent/child relationship.
4. Assessment of the relationships between adults in the family and their impact on the children.
5. The child, as seen by self.
6. Assessment of the whole family.
7. Final evaluation and assessment of risk and need.

Pilot study and training

After an initial distribution of the framework to 60 practitioners, we arranged to conduct a pilot study of the framework in use. Twelve cases, balanced in relation to family size, ethnic origin, district, type of assessment and particular family circumstances such as disability, employment etc. were selected. The framework was evaluated with the practitioners who took part, amended and reprinted. Training and consultation was offered to practitioners using the framework during the pilot phase and afterwards.

The framework was well received by practitioners and managers. Our emphasis was on working in partnership with parents and on being open and honest about child protection concerns, as well as the practical orientation of the framework. Caution was expressed about the length of time involved in working in this way. Some workers thought the time and resources involved were unrealistic for busy practitioners. The same might be said about any framework which attempts to engage in some depth with families experiencing difficulties where children may be in need or at risk. Our view is that children and families have a right to expect that decisions affecting their lives and futures will be made by workers who have the time, skill and resources to engage with them on their terms, in sufficient depth to ensure that children will be protected, their rights promoted and their well being safeguarded.

We hope that this account of our work in developing an assessment framework will be helpful to social workers who share this view, however busy and under pressure they may be.

Summary of literature which we found relevant

The DoH Guide 'Protecting Children' (op cit) was in common use throughout our department. We had all used it but thought it had a number of shortcomings. Whilst the Guide gives a clear idea of the areas which should be covered in an assessment, it gives very few ideas about the ways in which information can be elicited.

It very much relies upon verbal questioning. Many of the people we work with have limited verbal skills and children in particular do not respond well to this approach. Therefore, in the framework we have suggested a number of different methods, exercises and activities which may elicit the information required more effectively. To avoid assessments being made *about* people, and encourage them to be made *with* them, we have suggested methods and approaches which we hope parents and children will be able to participate in and consequently might help them to feel involved in their own assessment. The process should be one of partnership and should seek to achieve honesty.

The DoH Guide seeks to acquire a lot of information about different aspects of a family's situation, e.g. marital relationships, finances, networks etc., but it does not set out what the links may be between the information gathered and the effective, safe parenting of the child or the causes for concern. In our framework, we have attempted to place the child at the centre of the assessment and we only suggest that information which is directly relevant to the care of the child/ren or the ability of carers to provide for the child's needs should be considered. Hence the use of 'strengths' and 'hazards', 'strengths' being those things which reduce the risks to the child or protect her/him and 'hazards' being those things which increase risks to the child. In the final analysis, it is the balance of these factors and the magnitude of past or current harm that are considered in determining the overall perceived risk. All other information is considered to be extraneous. Our framework then provides an opportunity for a systematic assessment which should produce a degree of consistency across a number of cases. In addition, the child and family have an opportunity to disagree with the worker's analysis and can present their own views of the situation to a case conference or review.

When we began this piece of work, we felt the DoH Guide was both cumbersome and time-consuming. Acknowledging that fieldworkers have a limited amount of time available, we hoped to produce something that took less time. However, our final document was similar in length to the DoH Guide. It seems unlikely that effective assessment, undertaken in partnership with carers and children in distressing circumstances, can ever be a short and speedy process.

The DoH Guide was useful in helping us to appreciate the importance of planning and the need to clarify the respective roles and responsibilities of those people involved in the assessment. It was also influential in helping us to determine our core values. We believe that these values are implicit within the DoH Guide, whereas we have attempted to make them explicit through our style, approach and methodology.

We looked at a range of literature on the subject of assessment, to consider whether the approaches described would be suitable for our purposes. The work of the NSPCC team in Rochdale, documented in 'Dangerous Families' (Dale et al., 1989), was influential in a number of ways. It stressed the neutrality of the worker and the importance of being honest with the family about the causes for concern. It emphasised the need for clarity about the roles and responsibilities of various workers and highlighted the need for contracts. In particular, it stressed the importance of working with the whole family and understanding the abuse within the context of family dynamics. This was extremely influential in our section on family relationships. However, we were not able to adopt this model wholesale for a number of reasons. Their work relied heavily on the use of sophisticated technical equipment such as video cameras and one-way screens. These resources were not readily available to us in fieldwork teams. To undertake their work they relied on a therapeutic team of three or more workers, using consultation extensively. Whilst we are able to draw on other workers to assist in the assessment process, e.g. health visitor, day nursery, etc., this could in no way be considered a 'therapeutic team'.

The NSPCC team worked with what could be described as 'heavy end' cases, where a child had been removed from home and was placed on a Care Order. Co-operation in the assessment would provide the family's sole opportunity for their child/ren to be returned. In contrast, we were focusing on social workers required to make assessments in a range of situations, often where children are still living at home. The use of authority to secure co-operation from the family is not appropriate in all of these situations. We needed to consider other ways of engaging the family.

We also considered the Thurlow House Assessment Programme (Gawlinski et al. 1988). The programme stressed the importance of observation and was influential in our decision to use this method as an integral part of our framework. Like NSPCC, it also relied heavily on the use of contracts. It stressed the participative nature of assessment and the parent/child contribution to the process. However, as with the NSPCC format, we were not able to adopt this approach wholesale because of the reliance on technical equipment, a therapeutic team and the need for a statutory order before work could begin.

We also considered the assessment profiles contained within 'Good Enough Parenting' (Adcock & White 1985). On the whole we felt these operated with middle class concepts of parenting and that it would be inappropriate to make judgments about the parenting abilities of many of the people that we work with, based on the criteria that were used. However, the authors did stress the importance of undertaking assessment *with* parents and children rather than *about* them. They also stressed the importance of demonstrating a causal link between the parents' behaviour and the child's development. They suggest that if it is not possible to demonstrate a link, that particular information is irrelevant to the assessment.

A literature search undertaken by the NSPCC revealed a number of short articles on particular forms of assessment. Orten and Rich (1988) in their model for assessment of incestuous families made it very clear that the workers needed to look at both the strengths and weaknesses within families in order to ascertain the level of risk. Hewitt, Powell and Tate (1989), in considering assessments undertaken by health visitors, acknowledge the importance of parental perception of the problem. This influenced our emphasis on eliciting parents' views of their children.

General literature

There was other literature, not always on assessment, that was influential in our thinking in a general sense. The reports of the Inquiries into the deaths of Jasmine Beckford (London Borough of Brent 1985) and Kimberley Carlile (London Borough of Greenwich 1987), and also into Child Abuse in Cleveland (Secretary of State for Social Services 1987), emphasised that the needs and welfare of the child must always be at the forefront of considerations. The Cleveland Report in particular emphasised the importance of listening carefully to what the child has to say and taking him/her seriously: "the child is a *person*, not an *object* of concern". This heavily influenced our approach to the section on the perceptions of the child and the emphasis we have placed on respect for the child. This was underlined by a range of literature published by the Children's Legal Centre. The Cleveland Report also emphasised the need to work in partnership with the child's parents through honest and open communication. Our emphasis on sharing the causes for concern and making a shared evaluation of the strengths and hazards at each stage was influenced by this.

The need to develop ethnic-sensitive practice in assessment work was highlighted by Devore and Schlesinger in 'Ethnic Sensitive Social Work Practice' (1987). They examine the inter-relationship between class and ethnic group (eth-class), and how this will directly influence things like child rearing practices and problem resolution. Therefore any assessment that involves a family from a minority ethnic group should take into consideration how 'eth-class' has influenced child rearing and causes for concern. It will be important for any worker from a different cultural group to seek consultation in this area. Workers must also recognise that ethnic reality can be a source of strength as well as a source of discord and this must be taken into consideration in the evaluation of risk. In each section workers are encouraged to consider the relevance and effect of ethnic identity and experience and ask the family how culturally-based beliefs might relate to the problem, rather than considering this as a separate item and therefore merely a token gesture. Workers need to acknowledge how people from a minority ethnic group may feel about seeking help from an agency controlled by the dominant ethnic group in society.

In order to help families feel comfortable, the assessment will need to be conducted in the language of the child and family. Ideally, a worker from the same culture should be involved, but lack of personnel in this area might mean an interpreter must be sought. The assessment will need to be conducted in a place where the family feel comfortable and the worker may need to include relevant people from the family's local community. The assessment must be sensitive to the race, culture and religion of the family but workers must ensure that this sensitivity does not lead to a failure to protect the child.

Finally, in a general sense our work was also influenced by Dingwall, Eekelaar and Murray (1983) in their comparative study of child protection work and decision making. They made us aware how much a worker's own values will influence the way in which she/he interprets information and makes decisions. Consequently, workers are urged to be aware of their own values. Regular structured supervision is important to check out these influences in our work. The fact that parents and children are also substantially involved in the evaluation process, and have an opportunity to present their own assessment, acts as a further check on the subjectivity of the exercise.

Literature which influenced specific sections of our framework

Specific sections of the framework were influenced by particular writers. The section 'Meeting Children's Needs' considers parents' awareness of the needs of their children and how well they consider they are able to meet those needs. In this section we drew on the work of Pringle (1974) and Cooper (1985) to define the general needs of children. However, because we wished to involve parents in this exercise we attempted to express the needs in everyday language and added to the list where we felt it was deficient.

In this section we also acknowledge that parents' ability to meet the needs of their children may be impaired by external factors beyond their control. Many assessment models have concentrated on individual characteristics and the relationship between parents and children and have given external factors much less attention. Parton (1985) and Cooper and Ball (1987) were influential in convincing us that the impact of wider social factors should be taken into account in an assessment. The exercise on 'Helps and Hindrances' reflects this.

The DoH Guide was helpful in developing the section on 'Parent/Child Relationships'. The exercise on the child's most and least favourite things is included in the guide. However, we believe that discussion alone is often insufficient to give workers a sufficiently full understanding of parent/child relationships. Our decision to include a period of observation was influenced by the 'Thurlow House Assessment' (Gawlinski et al. 1988) 'Dangerous Families' (Dale et al, 1989) and Cooper and Ball (1987). Workers can explore and observe particular areas of concern, involving themselves with parents in tasks, particularly where alternative responses have been suggested. The observational element of the assessment can then be extended to consider parents' ability to change.

The 'Declaration of Self Esteem' from Virginia Satir (1978) set the tone and influenced the approach in the section on 'The child, as seen by self'. It stresses the uniqueness of each individual child. We believe that assessment, like any other work with child/ren, must be based on respect for the individual child and a desire to understand things from her/his perspective.

'Windows to our children' (Oaklander 1988), BAAF Workshop books 'In touch with Children' (1984), and 'In Touch with Parents' and the teaching methods of Maria Montessori, all influenced the choice of exercises and methods of work suggested.

The section on 'Work with the Whole Family' draws many of its ideas from family therapy and systems theory. Problems are located both within the relationships between people and between people and wider social systems, rather than solely within individuals themselves. This charges us to look at relationships within the family where the abuse occurred and the family's relationship with the outside world. In the literature there are a number of perspectives that consider the issues of responsibility. Those individuals who support a 'family dysfunction' model (Bentovim 1988) propose that it is the relationships between people within the family that are dysfunctional and have led to the abuse occurring. Therefore all family members have to accept some responsibility for what has occurred. Family relationships then have to be re-aligned to enable the family to function more appropriately. Others, who write from a feminist perspective (Driver & Droisen, 1989), have severely criticised this approach for failing to take into consideration the wider influences of patriarchal society. As a result of this it is men who are usually the more powerful within relationships and who go on to abuse their power. Responsibility for the abuse lies fairly and squarely with the perpetrator. While it is important to recognise that individual workers may have differing views about this, it is important that these issues are discussed within supervision. Workers must acknowledge their own value system, and the way it will influence their perspectives and approaches to assessment.

The exercises used in this section are designed to elicit information; how that information is interpreted will be for individual workers to judge and justify. Theories of family therapy were influential in the choice of exercises such as the Genogram and Family Rules. The family task was devised to enable workers to observe the whole family together and was an extension of the exercise suggested in the section on 'Parent/ child relationships'.

Unlike some other assessment frameworks we have not included a section to consider the individual histories of the adults in a family. However, this is referred to in the framework and workers are encouraged to pursue this area if they see it as relevant. Our decision not to include this as an essential part of the framework was made for a number of reasons.

Our own experience of attempting to gather this information in the past had been that parents could rarely see the usefulness of engaging in the exercise when they felt the information bore no relationship to the causes for concern. An insistence on continuing often lessened their motivation to co-operate. We felt it far more important and relevant to concentrate on day-to- day relationships in the here and now and how these had contributed to the causes for concern. We suggest that workers should only probe historical information where it appears to be of vital importance. In our experience, parents are more motivated to talk about their present circumstances.

Finally, the literature on predictive studies convinced us of the dubious causal link between individuals' earlier experience and the abuse of their children. Predictive studies are an attempt to identify a population at risk by identifying those characteristics in and between individuals that are more likely to cause them to abuse their children. They suggest that if we know the factors that are most likely to contribute to child abuse, we can target that group of people for preventive work. However, there are major problems with the reliability of predictive studies as well as ethical problems of labelling (Starr 1982; Baldwin & Spencer 1993). There are people wrongly identified (false positives) and a number of people who are a risk to their children who are not identified at all (false negatives). We felt that to identify individual characteristics or experiences from a parent's past may lead us to draw the wrong conclusions. Browne et al. (1988) in 'Early Prediction and Prevention of Child Abuse' recognised the importance of mediating factors: those more recent experiences or relationships of a positive nature which may reduce the effects of negative past experiences. We took the view that it is important to concentrate on the more recent relationships between adults and their relationships with their children.

It is important to note, however, that parents have opportunities to make connections with their own experience and histories when giving their views on children's needs, as well as when describing their relationship with their own children.

Risk analysis: The literature

The framework should enable workers to gather varied information about the child/ren, the family and social circumstances. However, questions remain about how to use the information to determine the degree of risk.

How should we determine the relative importance of factors? How should we balance positive and negative factors in a particular set of circumstances? How should we include the parents and children in this evaluation? We wanted to develop a framework that would enable us to do this, rather than relying solely on the value judgements of individual workers. On the other hand, we wanted to avoid the "rule of optimism", identified by Dingwall et al. (1983), based on the social work value of benevolence which leads workers to attribute the best possible motives to their clients. Our search of the literature did not reveal anything that we felt happy with.

However, we were interested by a chapter in 'Social Work and Child Abuse', Cooper and Ball (1987), on the 'Evaluation of Risk'. They quote the work of Brearley (1982) who drew heavily on material from the world of insurance to look at the concept of social work and risk. Risk was seen as the relative variation in possible loss outcomes. This was measured by 'hazards' minus 'strengths'. 'Hazards' are those things which introduce or increase the probability of an undesirable outcome. 'Strengths' are those things which introduce or increase the possibility of a desirable outcome.

Dalgleish's model for the 'Assessment of Perceived Risk in Child Protection' made explicit the components of risk assessment, with a definition of the component parts. He started with Brearley's (1982) equation for risk and added to it past case information, information about the nature and severity of the abuse and information about the co-operation of the parents and therefore the potential for change. Dalgleish then produced a model to collate and evaluate this information.

Whilst we liked the model because it was based on a retrospective analysis of case records, it did not include the views of the parent(s) and child/ren in the evaluation. In order to facilitate this we produced a simplified model wherein the most significant strengths and hazards from each section could be identified with the family. The family can be encouraged to produce their own list if they disagree with that of the workers.

The most significant strengths and hazards, along with past case information, the current causes for concern and level of co-operation and potential for change, were considered to be the risk components. The overall perceived risk can then be calculated by the following equation:

Magnitude of past/current harm to child/ren	+	Most Significant Hazards	-	Most Significant Strengths	=	Overall Perceived Risk

We are aware that this process will still involve value judgments about what is or is not important, the level of co-operation, the nature of concerns etc. Workers will always need to check these out in supervision. A check will also be kept on these by having to discuss each stage with parents and child/ren and ensuring they have the opportunity to make their own representation to case conference/review. It will be the task of the case conference, not solely of the assessment process, to decide whether the overall perceived risk is an acceptable level of risk or not. The specific factors, behaviours and incidents will at least have been set out and evidence relating to them evaluated.

From whence they came - we knew not where!!

There were a number of things which we included in the framework to which we cannot attribute a source, either because we came across them as useful methods or exercises so long ago that we cannot remember their origin, or because they were products of our own lateral thinking. Sometimes we knew the sort of information that we wished to elicit but could find nothing in the literature that would enable us to seek this information *with* parents. On these occasions we attempted to recall things that we had used in the past and found effective. If this failed, we tried to devise something which we felt would be appropriate, and this was then devleoped by the process of discussion and negotiation. The Relationship Happiness Scale, Daily Diaries, Trigger Cards, Holiday Camp and Blame Cake are all examples of useful things that one or more of us have used in the past. The Helps and Hindrances exercise, the use of photographs, self-portraits and clocks were ideas of our own.

The assessment framework does not rely on one approach or methodology. It draws material from many different sources. We have chosen those methods that enable the child/ren and family to be involved as much as possible in the assessment process. Workers are also encouraged to add or substitute other methods that they have found useful in their own experience. The assessment evaluation process is continuous and involves the family. We hope that this will make it possible to reach consensus about the overall perceived needs and risks and ways forward at the end of the assessment. Unlike most other assessment frameworks in the literature, we believe that this one can be undertaken from a generic fieldwork base, accepting that it will be not only desirable but essential to involve other professionals in the process.

The framework is presented in full in the next chapter. We hope that it may be useful to social workers in a wide variety of settings, concerned to improve the quality of services to children.

References

Adcock, M. & White, R. (eds) (1985) *Good Enough-Parenting - A Framework for Assessment.* London: BAAF.

BAAF (1984) *In Touch with Children and In Touch with Parents.* London.

Baldwin, N. & Spencer, N. (1993) 'Deprivation and Child Abuse: implications for strategic planning.' *Children and Society.* 7.4.

Bentovim, A. (ed) (1988) *Child Sexual Abuse within the Family; Assessment and Treatment:* Wright.

Browne, K., Davies, C, & Stratton, P. (eds) 1988. *Early Prediction and Prevention of Child Abuse.* Chichester: Wiley.

Cooper, D.M. & Ball D. (1987) *Social Work and Child Abuse.* London: Macmillan

Dale, P., Davies, M., Morrison, T. & Waters, J. (1989) *Dangerous families: Assessment and Treatment of Child Abuse.* London: Routledge.

Dalgliesh, L. (1997) 'Risk Assessment and Decision Making in Child Protection'. Dept. of Psychology, Brisbane.

DoH (1988) *Protecting Children - A Guide for Social Workers undertaking a Comprehensive Assessment.* London: HMSO 1988.

DoH (1995) *Protecting Children: Messages from Research.* London: HMSO.

Devore, W & Schlesinger, E. (1987) *Ethnic Sensitive Social Work Practice.* Columbus Ohio: Merrill Publishing Company.

Dingwall, R., Eekelaar, J., & Murray,T. (1983). *The Protection of Children: State Intervention and Family Life.* Oxford: Blackwell.

Driver, E. & Droisen, A. (ed) (1989) *Child Sexual Abuse.* London Women in Society: Macmillan.

Gawlinski, Carr, McDonnell & Irving (1988) 'Thurlow House Assessment Programme for Families with Abused Children'. *Practice Journal BASW.* Vol. 2 No. 3.

Gil, D.G., (1975) 'Unravelling Child Abuse'. *American Journal of Orthopsychiatry, 453, 346-356.*

Hewitt, K., Powell, I. & Tait, V. (1989) 'The Behaviour of Nine-Months and Two-Year Olds as Assessed by Health Visitors and Parents.' *Health Visitor* Vol. 62 No. 9 pp52-55.

Jones, D.N., Picket, J., Oates, M. & Barbour, P. (1987), *Understanding Child Abuse.* London: Macmillan Education.

London Borough of Brent (1985): '*A child in Trust,*': The report of the Inquiry into the circumstances surrounding the death of Jasmine Beckford

London Borough of Greenwich (1987), *A Child in Mind: Report of the Commission of Inquiry: Kimberley Carlile.*

London Borough of Lambeth (1987): '*Whose Child?*': Report of the Public Inquiry into the death of Tyra Henry.

Oaklander, V. (1988) *Windows to our Children.* Utah Real People Press.

Orten, J. & Rich, L. (1988) 'A Model for Assessment of Incestuous Families.' *Social Casework - Journal of Contemporary Social Work.* Vol. 69 No. 10 pp611-619.

Parton, N. (1985) *The Politics of Child Abuse.* Macmillan.

Pringle, M.K. (1974) *The Needs of Children.* London: Hutchinson.

Satir, V. (1978) *People-Making.* London Science and Behaviour Books, Souvenir.

Secretary of State for Social Servies (1987) *Report of the Inquiry into Child Abuse in Cleveland.* London: HMSO.

Secretary of State for Social Services (1988): *Report of the Inquiry into Child Abuse in Cleveland 1987.* London: HMSO.

Starr, R. (ed) 1982 *Child Abuse Prediction.* Cambridge Mass: Ballinger.

14
A framework for assessment in child protection

Chris Mccarrick, Adrian Over and Pam Wood

Section 1 - Introduction

Purpose and Principles

The purpose of any assessment in child protection work is to obtain information about the child/ren and family in order to understand them and their needs, how the causes for concern came about, to evaluate the risks involved in this situation for the future, to act as a sound basis for decision-making about the child/ren, to produce longer term plans for the protection of the child/ren and to establish the assistance required by the child/ren's family.

Core Values

1 All children have rights, in particular a basic right to have their needs met.
2 Assessment must be child centred; its prime focus must be the child. Where there is a conflict of interest between parents and children the child's interests must have priority.
3 Honesty with both parents and children is important. Parents and children have the right to respect.
4 Assessment should take place with the parents and children, it should not be something that is done to them.
5 Assessment should be undertaken in a way that is sensitive to race, culture, class and disability. However, sensitivity to these issues by the worker must not result in a failure to protect the child.

 All workers must be aware of their own class, race, cultural, religious and gender values and how these might influence an assessment. It should be an ongoing process to check out these areas in supervision.

Engagement/contract

It is important to make clear to the parents the reasons why the assessment needs to take place, that is the fact that an unacceptable outcome has occurred for the child/ren, for example child is not gaining weight; child has been injured; there has been a disclosure of sexual abuse. However, while the causes for concern need to be made explicit, the worker should be careful to do this in a non-judgemental and neutral way in order to leave the maximum scope for a full assessment of possible causes for the concerns and of family needs.

Dealing with conflicts

Parents may deny or dispute the causes for concern expressed by workers, thus making it difficult to establish a common basis for work. If this is the case, parents can be encouraged by stating that the assessment will be an opportunity for them to demonstrate to the workers concerned that the causes for concern are unfounded.

We acknowledge that resistance can be difficult for workers to cope with. If parents persist in their refusal to co-operate, workers need to be honest about their powers and responsibilities in relation to the protection of the child/ren. The worker needs to be direct about stating that there can be no room for negotiation about whether an investigation or assessment will be carried out; but that there is plenty of scope within that as to how it will be undertaken, with an emphasis being on completion of an assessment with the family rather than about them.

If there is still a refusal to co-operate from any of the parties, workers need to be clear with the family that the assessment will still proceed, and what the legal basis for this is. Refusal to co-operate will of necessity mean exclusion from the decision-making process through lack of involvement. For example, if all parties refuse to co-operate, only monitoring of the situation is possible through the available resources such as school or day nursery, or where some parties participate and others refuse to do so, assessment proceeds on a partial basis with those who are prepared to co-operate.

If parents locate the blame for the abuse or harm outside the family, eg lack of money, lack of play space etc, workers need to make this the starting point of the assessment; consider the parents' view seriously, and then lead on to examine how these particular problems have impinged upon family life and affected family relationships.

 It will be useful to consider with a family how they have attempted to deal with the problems. This will give the worker a picture of their problem solving capacities and their capacity to bring about change. (See section on External Pressures and Supports)

Agreements about assessment

It is important to establish a common understanding about the assessment, both with the family and with the other professionals concerned. A written or taped agreement should be made with both groups of people. The agreement with professionals might include the following:

a) The purpose of the assessment and what is being assessed.
b) Who will undertake each aspect of the assessment. It is recommended that a minimum of two workers be involved in each assessment, with other professionals as appropriate.
c) Which family members and others are to be involved in each aspect of the assessment.
d) Where, when and how the assessment will take place.
e) How the assessment will be recorded.
f) Timescale and resources required.
g) Supervision and lines of accountability of all the workers involved.
h) How the information will be evaluated.
i) How the results will be shared with the family and how the family can make additions or register disagreements.

A similar agreement should be drawn up with the family, which they might write themselves or add to. It is expected that this agreement will be negotiated with the family before the substance of the assessment is dealt with. The family should be asked who else they would like to contribute to the assessment, other than the professionals that have been identified, when and where each session will take place, who needs to attend and which workers will be present. The family need to know the overall timescale and how the information gathered will be evaluated. This process of negotiation may help to engage a family which is reluctant or uncertain.

The worker may need to include a worker who speaks the same language as the family or an interpreter. Letters need to be written in the family's own language. The worker may involve a person who has influence with the family in encouraging them to attend, eg relative, teacher, community leader. The worker may need to provide transport for the family.

 There may need to be arrangements for a worker who speaks the language of the family, or interpreter with specialist communication skills to be involved. These arrangements are central to initial plans.

Style and Methodology

This assessment framework does not rely on any one methodology. It is eclectic in its approach and chooses those methods which enable workers to involve the child/ren and the family as much as possible in the assessment process. Accepting that many of the families we work with find communication difficult, we have attempted not to rely solely on the spoken word, discussion and dialogue all the time. The tools that we have chosen to assist workers should be seen as examples; workers should feel free to add or substitute other methods from their own experience.

 The sections do not need to be used in the order in which they appear - workers should use the framework flexibly to help them respond to the particular families and situations.

Ongoing evaluation of causes for concern and perceived risk

The evaluation - like the assessment process - should be shared with all those individuals concerned. Whilst ultimately the workers have to make the final recommendations concerning the degree of risk, the family should be given every opportunity to be involved in this process and register any disagreement.

It is recommended that during the assessment sessions, the workers and the family members find a way of recording each significant piece of information that may be a STRENGTH or a HAZARD in assessing the level of risk to the child/ren.

- HAZARDS would be those things that are likely to increase the risk to the child/ren, for example dad's problem in controlling his temper, or mum's problem drinking.
- STRENGTHS are those things which are likely to protect or reduce the risks to the child/ren, for example both parents attending meetings at the child's school, or a good local playground if the family have limited play space for the child/ren.

Exercise 1.1 - Strengths and Hazards

The STRENGTHS and HAZARDS could be colour coded like Traffic Signals
One sheet recorded with RED pen for HAZARDS
One sheet recorded with GREEN pen for STRENGTHS
An AMBER pen could be used to highlight disagreements on either or both of these sheets of paper, according to the views held by each person in the meeting.

It should be made clear which particular person(s) hold these views by initialling the item. For example,

STRENGTHS	HAZARDS
1. Carol gives children a lot of cuddles when they are upset	1. John easily loses his temper with kinds.
2. Have regular bedtimes and mealtimes for children.	2. John and Carol often smack children as a punishment.
3. Attend parents' evenings at school.	3. John and Carol find it hard to say good things about Simon.
4. John spends a lot of time out with his mates.	4. John spends a lot of time out with his mates (Dave, Sue, Carol)
(John)	5. John and Carol argue a lot in front of kids. (Dave, Sue)

At the end of each section of the assessment, with all the participants involved, there should be an attempt to list all the STRENGTHS and HAZARDS as they offset or confirm the causes for concern. The family should be give the opportunity to comment on the balance of STRENGTHS and HAZARDS. Any disagreements should be clearly recorded.

At the end of the assessment, there should be one or more concluding meetings with the family to attempt to draw together all the STRENGTHS and HAZARDS recorded at the end of each section, with a view to assessing the overall perceived risk to the child/ren. A model for organising this information and clearly demonstrating to the family and other professionals the basis of perceived risk is set out in the final section.

 Before moving on to the substance of the assessment, workers should make sure that the following work has been undertaken in the opening one or two sessions.

- An explicit sharing of the causes for concern with the parents, and the legal basis for the assessment.
- Negotiation of written agreements with the family and other professionals.

In the Process Flowchart we have attempted to provide a step-by-step guide to the process of:

- Identification of concerns
- Decision to undertake assessment
- Preparation
- Engagement/contracting
- Process of assessment
- Evaluation of overall perceived risk as suggested in this framework.

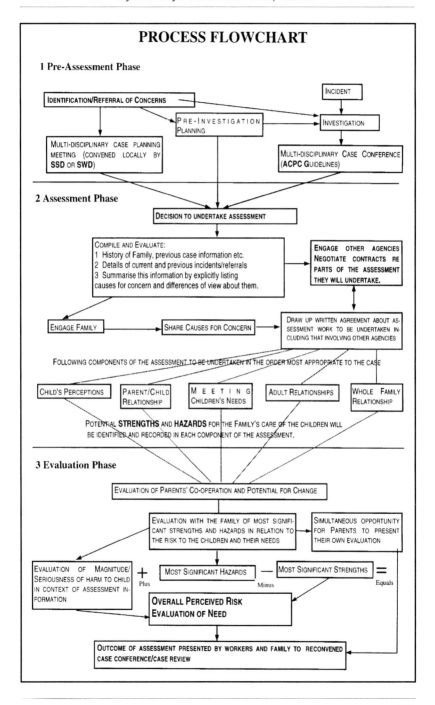

PROCESS FLOWCHART

1 Pre-Assessment Phase

INCIDENT

IDENTIFICATION/REFERRAL OF CONCERNS

PRE-INVESTIGATION PLANNING

INVESTIGATION

MULTI-DISCIPLINARY CASE PLANNING MEETING (CONVENED LOCALLY BY **SSD** OR **SWD**)

MULTI-DISCIPLINARY CASE CONFERENCE (**ACPC G**UIDELINES)

2 Assessment Phase

DECISION TO UNDERTAKE ASSESSMENT

COMPILE AND EVALUATE:
1 History of Family, previous case information etc.
2 Details of current and previous incidents/referrals
3 Summarise this information by explicitly listing causes for concern and differences of view about them.

ENGAGE OTHER AGENCIES NEGOTIATE CONTRACTS RE PARTS OF THE ASSESSMENT THEY WILL UNDERTAKE.

ENGAGE FAMILY

SHARE CAUSES FOR CONCERN

DRAW UP WRITTEN AGREEMENT ABOUT ASSESSMENT WORK TO BE UNDERTAKEN INCLUDING THAT INVOLVING OTHER AGENCIES

FOLLOWING COMPONENTS OF THE ASSESSMENT TO BE UNDERTAKEN IN THE ORDER MOST APPROPRIATE TO THE CASE

CHILD'S PERCEPTIONS

PARENT/CHILD RELATIONSHIP

MEETING CHILDREN'S NEEDS

ADULT RELATIONSHIPS

WHOLE FAMILY RELATIONSHIP

POTENTIAL **STRENGTHS** AND **HAZARDS** FOR THE FAMILY'S CARE OF THE CHILDREN WILL BE IDENTIFIED AND RECORDED IN EACH COMPONENT OF THE ASSESSMENT.

3 Evaluation Phase

EVALUATION OF PARENTS' CO-OPERATION AND POTENTIAL FOR CHANGE

EVALUATION WITH THE FAMILY OF MOST SIGNIFICANT STRENGTHS AND HAZARDS IN RELATION TO THE RISK TO THE CHILDREN AND THEIR NEEDS

SIMULTANEOUS OPPORTUNITY FOR PARENTS TO PRESENT THEIR OWN EVALUATION

EVALUATION OF MAGNITUDE/SERIOUSNESS OF HARM TO CHILD IN CONTEXT OF ASSESSMENT INFORMATION

Plus

MOST SIGNIFICANT HAZARDS

Minus

MOST SIGNIFICANT STRENGTHS

Equals

OVERALL PERCEIVED RISK EVALUATION OF NEED

OUTCOME OF ASSESSMENT PRESENTED BY WORKERS AND FAMILY TO RECONVENED CASE CONFERENCE/CASE REVIEW

Section 2 - Meeting Children's Needs

Before working with children when undertaking an assessment, it is necessary to engage parents in a meaningful way in order to:

i)   Gather real information which is an honest and accurate reflection of their world.
ii)   Gain their permission, co-operation and trust to work with their child/ren.

Where there are two parents or parent figures, workers will need to make a judgement about whether to undertake the suggested work exercises with both parents together or to do some work with them individually.

 Remember that fathers should not be left out of social work interventions; and also that mothers and children may need support to express their views.

Understanding the general needs of children with parents

In order to engage parents and to avoid immediately focusing on them and their family in a way which appears to place "blame" for the abuse or concerns totally with them, it is suggested that some discussion and understanding is developed with parents about what the basic and general needs of a child are, from birth to adolescence. Hopefully, this will establish a child-centred focus and will enable parents who have been reluctant to engage in the assessment to begin to do so.

The literature contains a number of examples of frameworks of children's needs, and there are many ways to help parents begin to consider these.

Needs of Children (Pringle 1974)
- Physical care and protection
- Affection and approval
- Stimulation and teaching
- Discipline and control which are consistent and age-appropriate
- Opportunity and encouragement gradually to acquire autonomy

---

Additional needs emphasised in more recent work might include:
- Sense of identity appropriate to social, ethnic, cultural and religious group.
- Security, stability, consistency.
- Resilience.

Exercises to consider children's needs with parents:

Exercise 2.1
Using a large nobo board or flip chart paper, write up a framework of needs, using everyday language as far as possible, for example
- Physical care and protection
  Care of child's body and keeping child safe.

- Affection and approval
  Showing love, cuddling etc and showing child you like what they do.
- Stimulation and teaching
  Helping child to learn through talking to them, reading to them, listening to them talk and read, telling them things, playing with them.
- Discipline and control
  Need to do something when child misbehaves so child learns to behave better and not to show you up!
- Responsibility
  Finding ways, bit by bit, to help child to grow to be able to look after her/himself when older.

Other examples might be:

- Developing the child's sense of belonging
  Encouraging the child to learn about family/group origins, culture, religion etc.
- Knowledge through experience
  Helping children to learn things by showing them and letting them try things while making sure they are safe.
- Order
  Letting children have freedom to explore and learn without being frightened of punishment, so they know you will guide them without stopping their need to find out.

*****

It may be necessary to experiment with and adapt these examples in order to find language which parents will understand but not feel patronised by.

At the beginning of the session, the worker should go through each need she/he has written up with the parent(s), checking their basic understanding of what each one means in simple terms. It might be helpful to ask parents if they would like to demonstrate - either in words or by acting a situation out - how they would respond to a situation outlined by the worker, in order to show how a parent might meet each need, eg how would they respond to a child's attempts to help to prepare a meal or wash up, which create a lot of mess, in a way which does not hinder growing independence.

Then, ask parent(s) to talk about how important they think each need is. Ask them to give examples of how each need can be met by a parent. Write these up next to the relevant need on the nobo board or flip chart. If they find this discussion difficult or they are resistant to it, a way to move forward is to ask them to score each area of need from 1-10 according to the relative importance of each need as they see them and then to say, in a few words, why.

Exercise 2.2
Ask the parents to think of the children of friends or relatives - they can choose whether to use actual or assumed first names.

What do they think is good and bad about the way these children are looked after and brought up?

How are the children helped to grow and develop?

In what ways could their needs be met better?

(NB Try to avoid parents talking about their own children and themselves as parents at this stage.)

*****

Exercise 2.3

Write on the nobo board or flip chart the following question:

"Where did you get your ideas about bringing up your children from?"

The worker may need to allow for and to hear about answers such as 'my parents/ relatives spoke to me about it', 'ante natal classes', 'child care course at school', 'trained as a nurse or nursery nurse', 'trained as a teacher' - but the question is designed to stimulate REFLECTION on how we know (or don't know!) what to do as parents.

Then ask parents to talk about their own childhood(s) and upbringing.

What were the good and bad things?

Similar questions as in Exercise 2.2 could follow.

What were the gaps, if any, in meeting their needs, or which needs were not met? What things were harmful?

(NB If workers feel that it is important to gain background/historical information about each parent, this exercise could be used for this as well, either at this stage or later in the assessment.)

*****

Exercise 2.4

Brainstorm with parents for 15 minutes about all the needs they can think of if a chld is to grow and develop into a happy, healthy, responsible and well balanced adult.

*****

An immediate record of the discussion in all the exercises used should be made and agreed with parents.

Process

The worker should help and encourage parent(s) to develop their thoughts and ideas without presenting their own to begin with.

The objective at the end of this part of the assessment is to agree a basic framework of needs which the parents can identify with and aim to meet, and also meet a minimum set of requirements acceptable to the worker.

This is one obvious stage at which it is crucial for the worker to be aware of and clear about their own values and "minimum standards". Any ambivalence or lack of clarity should be discussed in supervision.

As the parent(s) develop their ideas about needs, the worker needs to judge the appropriate stage at which to introduce areas of need which parents have not recognised as important or identified. Serious resistance to accept particular area(s) of need should be explored and reasons for this drawn out, made explicit, checked and recorded. A complete impasse or failure to agree either between two parents or between one or both parents and the workers should be noted.

Exercise 2.5

For each agreed need, the workers should ask the parent(s) to discuss, develop and agree a parental "duty" or "action plan" for that need, ie what might a parent (that is, any parent) need to do to meet each agreed area of need IN AN IDEAL WORLD, including all necessary equipment, resources etc.

Record examples and suggestions

* * * * *

External pressures and supports

The worker should recognise with the parents that we do not live in an ideal world and that there are all sorts of things that either help or hinder parents in their attempts to meet the needs of their children. There will be things that they find help them, but there will also be things that cause them stress and impair their parenting abilities. Contact with the extended family and wider community can be a source of strength and support or it can be a source of pressure for the family and the child. Absence of contact can lead to isolation which can be a major cause for concern. Likewise, financial problems, poor housing, lack of play space can all be pressures that affect the way parents are able to care for their children. Alternatively, good local services can enhance the quality of life for a family and positively influence the way that parents are able to meet the needs of their children.

 This is an area where workers have to be aware of their own identity, projections and values about the importance of some of these issues, as all individuals see them differently. However, it is most important to ascertain how the parents perceive their situation and how they feel it affects them and the care of their children.

To establish how the parents feel that external pressures and supports affect their ability to care for their children, the following exercise on HELPS AND HINDRANCES should be useful.

Exercise 2.6

Listed below are a number of people, organisations or circumstances that could either be seen as a HELP or a HINDRANCE by the parents in their attempts to meet the needs of their children. The item may be irrelevant, or perceived as irrelevant by the parents. All the items on the list should be included in a pack of cards which the worker will need to have made up, with a number of blank cards for the worker and the parents to add other things that are significant. The cards should be placed by the parents either on the HELP, the HINDRANCE or IRRELEVANT pile, and the worker should discuss why the parents think of each of these items in this particular way,

The state of repair of our house   The size of our house

Space for the children to play	Local shops
Furniture in our house	Nursery
Cooking equipment	School (3 cards)
My job (2 cards provided)	Toys
Money	Debts
Time I have for myself (2 cards)	Doctors
My partner (2 cards provided)	Police
The size of our family	Temple
Traffic	Vandalism
Sexual harassment	Garden
Neighbours (3 cards provided)	Clothes
Relatives (4 cards provided)	Transport
Children's Clubs	Noise
Income	Health Visitor
Social Security/benefits	Youth Club
Racial harassment	Adult Club
Friends (4 cards provided)	Social Worker
My hobbies (2 cards provided)	Temple
Sleeping arrangements	Mosque
Time spent with the children (2 cards)	Church
Time together as a couple (2 cards)	Clinic

Community Groups (2 cards provided: eg Tenants' Association etc)

More than one card should be provided for some items, eg neighbours, because there may be more than one neighbour who is a help or a hindrance to this particular family. Some blank cards should be available to allow parents to add things which they feel are important.

*****

Acknowledge with the parents that there will be some things in life that help them to meet the needs of their children and some things that hinder their ability to do so. Ask them to place the cards in the HELP pile or the HINDRANCES pile, or to put them on one side if they are IRRELEVANT. The worker will need to adapt the pack of cards in order to ensure they are in the family's first language and/or that they are accessible to parents with particular disabilities.

As they make their choices, discuss briefly why they feel that particular thing or person helps them or hinders them in the care of their children. For some categories, eg family, there are several cards, because there may be some family members who help and other family members who hinder, so that these will need to be placed on different piles. Identify which family members help or hinder, and discuss why.

When this part of the exercise is completed, check each pile and ask the parents to choose those things/people that help most of all and those things that hinder most of all and why. Discuss whether those things that hinder the care of their children have a particular link with the causes for concern. Explore how they have attempted to deal with those things or people that hinder them most. Consider with the parents how these things could be changed now, and what needs to be done.

If there are pressing problems in any of these practical areas, some short term intervention may be required during the assessment period, or a referral to another agency may be required. It may be necessary to do these things immediately rather than waiting until the assessment is completed.

Finally

Having now looked in considerable depth at the general needs of children and the resources and stresses (or helps and hindrances) with which these particular parents have to meet their children's needs, the following ground remains to be covered in this part of the assessment:

Exercise 2.7
- Ask which areas of need parents think they meet well and why
- What are they good at - and not so good at - as individual parents?
- And together as a couple?

* * * * *

 If specific management/behavioural difficulties are raised by parents, ask them to give examples of these and tell them that you would like them to point out any further examples when workers are observing them and their children together.

Apart from the stresses listed, are there any other reasons likely for the relative strengths and weaknesses? Discuss any areas of need they think they do not meet, or find hardest to meet. Help them to develop and produce an ACTION PLAN which would help them to start to meet each of these needs.

Exercise 2.7 is intended to help parents to begin to focus on the specific aspects of their parenting which are linked to the causes for concern. This may involve recognising practical and/or environmental stresses and helping parents to think imaginatively about meeting their child/ren's needs, but it is also the beginning of focusing on the parents' personal, emotional or relationship difficulties in meeting their child/ren's needs.

 Now record and evaluate all the STRENGTHS and HAZARDS identified in this section of the assessment with the parents.

 Working on the assumption that all relevant factual information and professional opinion has already been shared with the parents, they should be invited to nominate other people who they would like to comment on the nature and quality of their parenting, eg grandparent, friend, community leader, godparent, religious leader etc.

Section 3 - Parent/Child Relationship

Prior to starting this section of work, the parents should be briefed about the nature of the meetings/discussions and asked to undertake some preparatory work, for example:

- collecting as many photographs as possible of their children at various ages;
- they might be asked to provide "mental snapshots" of their children at various ages, by thinking about and being ready to record positive memories of their children.

Philosophy

All families are different and the individuals within each family are different.

In this section, workers need to gain an understanding of what these particular parents feel about these particular children, both now and prior to the intervention.

If there is more than one child it will be necessary to assess the parents' perceptions of each one, and how their attitudes to each one affect the others.

The activities in this section might stimulate greater interest in the parents which will benefit the child/ren. By talking about the child from babyhood, the joys of parenthood might be rekindled. The hard work of parenthood needs to be acknowledged, but if parents have lost sight of their role and aims for their child/ren, these need to be reidentified and embraced if there is to be a good prognosis.

The process of the assessment can also assist parents in recovering or increasing their power and ability to provide role models for their children. If this is done, parents may see their children in a new light and be more aware of how they have affected their children.

 Parents do not own children, but the child needs to be seen as a valued member of her/his family.

Exercises

A range of exercises follows. Some parents will clearly feel more comfortable with those exercises which involve doing things more than talking. The workers will need to choose those most appropriate to the circumstances of the case and to the particular parents involved.

Some of the exercises may mean that the worker has to arrange several items of equipment, child care facilities, transport, refreshments, and external surroundings conducive to parental co-operation in order for them to be productive.

Exercise 3.1

Ask the parents to bring a series of photographs of the child/ren at different stages of his/her life. Look at each photograph in turn.

Ask the parent(s) how they felt about the child at the time of each photograph and how they view those feelings now.

Did they enjoy caring for the child at that time?

What were the best and worst things at each stage?

(The worker will need to decide whether it would be most effective to do this exercise with parents together or separately)

NB If parents do not have any photographs of their children, it might be helpful to arrange to have some taken. If possible, supply parents with a camera and film and ask them to take pictures of their children. However, for the purposes of the exercise, where photographs are unavailable, parents can be asked to provide "mental snapshots" or memories of their children. Some parents might feel better able to participate by drawing or painting pictures of memories of things their children did at different stages.

*****

Exercise 3.2

Ask parents to write down five good and three bad things about each child (either phrases or descriptive adjectives). Note differences and similarities between each parent's list.

Ask each parent to talk about each feature they have identified; how it shows itself, why they like or dislike it; and how it affects them and other members of the family.

*****

Exercise 3.3

Ask parents if they can name the child's most and least favourite of the following:

food	TV programme	time of year
drink	adult	holiday
games	place to play	outing
activities	pet/animal	school lesson
clothes	room in the house	other child
friends	colour	sibling
day of the week	(add to these as appropriate)	

Ask them if they know why their child likes or dislikes certain things.

*****

Exercise 3.4

Ask the parents to give as detailed a physical description of the child as possible. Use a large or blown up photograph or a drawing or painting of the child, if one is available, to start the discussion.

Then, using this information and the information gathered from some or all of earlier exercises, the worker should describe the child in her/his own words as the parents have led her/him to understand their perception of the child. Each detail should be thoroughly checked out.

A detailed description of the child written on the board/flip chart should evolve. The parent(s) should eventually have before them a description of their child/ren which they are prepared to identify as their own.

For parents with learning difficulties or a visual impairment, the description could be recorded onto an audio tape.

When a description of each child has been agreed, ask each parent
- What are the six best things about being with your child/ren?
- What are the three worst things about being with your child/ren?
- What did you do to help your child learn to do the things you now like? What can you do from now on to encourage those things?
- What could you do to discourage/reduce the worst things?
*****

Exercise 3.5
With parents, prepare and complete a map or flow chart of the significant events in the child's life. Alternatively, ask the parents to identify significant events on a road map like the one used in working with the child. (see Section 5)
*****

Exercise 3.6
Ask each parent, separately, to complete a diagram of each child's world - identifying all the significant people, activities etc. Use this information to look with each of them at what and who they see as important to the child and how they each see the child's world. Explain how this can be helpful.

(We are cautious about the use of the term 'eco map' to describe this activity, as we do not believe it would mean anything to most parents.)

In combination with information gained from other exercises in this section, this exercise should give some indication as to how well each parent knows the child.

It might be particularly useful to compare the diagrams prepared by the parents with one completed by the child in another part of the assessment.
*****

Exercise 3.7
If parents have concerns about a child which centre around behaviour, ask them to complete a behaviour chart or a daily diary with good and not so good events recorded.

The worker can then see if the not so good behaviour weighs greater on their minds even if it does not predominate.

(NB It may be that some input about behaviour management is required promptly. This could become an integral part of the assessment, connected to the observations of family interactions, to see if parents can put advice into practice.)
*****

Exercise 3.8
Ask parents to act out or role play a situation with their child/ren. Alternatively provide dolls to represent their children for them to re-enact or act out certain situations or interactions.
*****

Exercise 3.9
Ask parents if they have ambitions for their child/ren.
What are they?
What do they think would need to happen for them to be realised?
What are they as parents able and prepared to do for them to be realised?
*****

Exercise 3.10
Parent message cards.
Workers can produce a set of cards each containing a statement/comment which any parent might make to a child eg
"I love you"
"You're very good"
"You're stupid"
"I haven't got time"
"Why don't you behave", etc.

These can then be used to explore the messages parents received from their own parents and now give to their own children, how these make a child feel, etc.

*****

Observation of Parent/Child Interaction

In addition to the exercises with parents, it is recommended that some observation of the parent/child relationship is undertaken. Workers may wish to do this specifically with the parent(s) and the child/ren deemed to be at risk, or they may wish to observe the family as a whole (see also Section 6). Some issues to be taken account of before undertaking observation are set out in Appendix 1.

Exercise 3.11
Ask the parent(s) and child/ren which games/activities/meal they enjoy sharing the most. Ask the parent(s) to plan for one of these in one or more sessions and to plan for the meeting of the child/ren's needs in those sessions, including materials, the arrangement of furniture etc.

Observe the session, trying to remain as unobtrusive as possible except in any situation where a child is at risk.

Observe and Record:
• Does the parent(s) talk to the child? In what tone? (Describe it)
• Does the child approach the parent?
• Does the parent respond to the child's approaches?
• Does the parent only relate to the child reactively, or does she/he initiate interaction?
• Bearing in mind the content of previous sessions about children's needs, is there evidence that the parent is aware of and makes provision for the child's needs?
• Does the parent have clear expectations of the child which the child understands? Are they realistic?
• Do the parent and child appear to enjoy each other's company?
• How does the parent respond to behaviour she/he/they do not like?
• Is this appropriate? Is it effective?
• If there are two parents, do they support or undermine each other's parenting efforts?

Either at the end of the session, or in the next one, the worker should feed back to the parent(s) the content of his or her observations and should explain why he or she has looked at/interpreted their interaction with the child in this way. The worker should also offer parents the opportunity to challenge his or her perceptions, and to explain to the worker why they do things in the way they do, and to ask the worker further questions about these issues as they wish.

*****

 Now record and evaluate all the STRENGTHS and HAZARDS identified in this section of the assessment with the parents.

Section 4 - Assessment of the relationship(s) between the adults in the family and the impact on the child/ren

Introduction

Where there are two parents or parent figures, assessment of the impact of the relationship on the children and on their care will be of primary importance in this section. However, there may be other significant relationships between the parent(s) and other adults in the family, household or care network which will also need to be assessed.

The first exercise suggested can easily be adapted according to the features of each relationship (ie according to whether the other adult is a grandparent, lodger, other relative or adult sibling of the child at risk) and for each separate one-to-one adult relationship that the workers decide to assess.

Relationship Happiness Scale

The "relationship happiness scale" is a tool designed to generate discussion between the adults in the family and the worker(s). A basic schedule is shown below but this can obviously be extended, adapted or reduced according to what the worker wishes to generate discussion about.

Exercise 4.1 - Relationship Happiness Scale

	Completely unhappy						*Completely happy*			
Housework	1	2	3	4	5	6	7	8	9	10
Looking after the children	1	2	3	4	5	6	7	8	9	10
Going Out	1	2	3	4	5	6	7	8	9	10
Money	1	2	3	4	5	6	7	8	9	10
Talking to each other	1	2	3	4	5	6	7	8	9	10
Sex	1	2	3	4	5	6	7	8	9	10
Employment/Unemployment	1	2	3	4	5	6	7	8	9	10
Freedom for yourself	1	2	3	4	5	6	7	8	9	10
Freedom for your partner	1	2	3	4	5	6	7	8	9	10
How you feel most of the time/General Happiness	1	2	3	4	5	6	7	8	9	10

*****

Possible ways of using the scale (Be ready to improvise and adapt)
- Give a copy to each adult in preparation for the next session. It often generates a sense of amusement and even absurdity and this should be anticipated by introducing it with a degree of humour!
  Ask each adult to complete it, thinking carefully about how they score each area and why, independently of each other, for the next session. It should be emphasised that they are asked to score how happy they feel about each aspect of their relationship as it is, not how well they do the housework, manage money, look after the children etc!
- Give each adult a second copy and ask them to complete it in the way they

anticipate the other adult will complete it, eg how happy will my partner say she/he is with the "going out" aspect of our relationship?

- If one adult tends to dominate or intimidate the other, or if there is so much tension between them that the worker(s) feel that one of them will find it hard to share or even complete the schedule(s), separate workers should spend time with each adult going through the schedule and preparing and supporting them to share the results in an honest way or helping them to complete the schedule, offering them the opportunity to talk through each issue.

  It should be recognised that this exercise could well be a very threatening and traumatic experience for people, especially for somebody frightened of, intimidated by, or worried about losing a partner or another adult. *It should be used with caution.*

- At the beginning of the following session, check whether they kept to working independently or whether they "compared notes". If the latter, this can be positive - it may have generated important discussions at home which have not taken place previously: use these to help them reflect on how they co-operate or battle with each other.

  Ask them to share the content and outcome of their discussions.

  Check why they decided to compare notes - did one or other apply any degree of pressure or coercion?

  Each adult can be asked to go through their entire schedule, talking about why they scored as they did, followed by the other, or else the feedback can be dealt with on an issue by issue basis.

- *Check*

  How they feel each aspect of their relationship impacts on the child/ren.

  How they each feel about the other's scores - are there any surprises?

  If all/any of the scores were significantly affected by a particular incident or mood.

Exercise 4.1 should give the workers a good overview of:

- How well the couple know each other.
- How in touch they are with each other's views/feelings.
- How aware they are of the effect of each other's views/feelings on their children.
- Areas of harmony and major disagreement and tension.

 The worker should then be able to extract from the information the important areas for further discussion, assessment and the need for change.

Exercise 4.2

Another useful exercise to use with parenting couples who appear to have difficulties in communicating with each other, or who appear to lack awareness of each other's needs, or who are not paying attention to each other in general or in discussion in the assessment work is to ask the couple to sit facing each other and to look at each other for a few minutes without talking. Then ask them to close their eyes and describe each other in as much detail as they can manage.

*****

Exercise 4.3

In preparation for the next session, ask parents to keep a diary, recording detailed events in their family life between this and the next session.

Where parents are reluctant or find it difficult to keep a written record, consideration could be given to providing a tape recorder, camera or drawing materials so that a different kind of record can be kept.

* * * * *

Developing the theme

In the next session, the worker should build on the information gleaned from the relationship happiness scale and the other exercises to form a detailed picture of the adults' relationships, their everyday lives and the arrangements for the care of their children. Further suggested exercises are:

Exercise 4.4

Ask them to talk through a typical weekday (school day) and weekend day. Write up on the flip chart or nobo board as much detail in chronological order as you can gather. Try to establish: WHO does WHAT, WHEN, WHERE and HOW in this family.

How were the routines in the family formed and decided? Who takes the lead and who makes suggestions?

What are the best and worst times and activities? Why? Are there any particularly fraught times?

Try to identify any "rules". Frame these explicitly and check with the adults that they are accurate.

* * * * *

Exercise 4.5

List all the tasks the adults in the household complete in one week, again using nobo board or flip chart - possibly using different coloured felt tip pens to indicate WHICH adult does which task.

Highlight who takes on which tasks.

Are they shared equally?

Are all the adults in the household satisfied with these arrangements?

* * * * *

Exercise 4.6

Ask each adult:

Which three things about your relationship with each adult in your household - WHICH AFFECT YOUR CHILDREN - worry you the most and would you most like to change?

What could YOU do to achieve these?

What could the other adults do to achieve these? CHECK how each adult feels about the other's responses.

THEN ask each adult to score on a scale of 1 - 5 how strongly motivated they feel to achieving the change the other(s) has identified as wanting them to make.

This can be done in a variety of ways - with a TV programme style quiz, with written questionnaires etc.

Explore the levels of motivation to change revealed by this exercise and give each adult the opportunity to express how they feel about the other's motivation to change.

*****

 Now record and evaluate all the STRENGTHS and HAZARDS identified in this section of the assessment with the parents.

Section 5 - The child as seen by self

The following is an extract from 'Declaration of Self Esteem' (in SATIR, Virginia, 1972 - *Peoplemaking*).

> *I am me. In all the world there is no one exactly like me, There are persons who have some parts like me but no one adds up exactly like me. Therefore everything that comes out of me is authentically mine because I alone chose it. I own everything about me, my body, including everything it does; my mind, including all its thoughts and ideas, my eyes, including the images of all they behold; my feelings whatever they may be - anger, joy, frustration, love, disappointment, excitement; my mouth and all the words that come out of it, polite, sweet or rough, correct or incorrect; my voice, loud or soft; and all my actions whether they be to others or to myself.*
>
> *Because I own all of me I can become intimately acquainted with me, By so doing I can love me and be friendly with me and all my parts. I can then make it possible for all of me to work in my best interests.*
>
> *I can see, hear, feel, think, say and do. I have the tools to survive, to be close to others, to be productive and to make sense and order out of the world of people and things outside of me.*
>
> *I am me and I am okay.*

*****

For the purposes of this section the word child will be used though it may be acknowledged that in a comprehensive assessment there may be more than one child who is deemed to be at some level of risk. This would obviously mean two, three or more child assessments, as the case may be. Sensitivity to the age of the child or young person should determine whether 'child assessment' or 'assessment of a young person' is the description given.

It is assumed that in the overall assessment the focus is child-centred. In this section it can be nothing else. The child has a right to be heard; a right to be protected. Her/his viewpoint is valid and it is important that the child knows that from the worker undertaking direct assessment work with her/him. In cases of suspected and actual abuse it has been said that children rarely lie - nor do they lie about their feelings though they may not always be able to express them freely and clearly. The task is to unlock the inner child and assist her/him in expressing views about how it is for her/him now.

Giving the message to the child that what they feel and what they have to say will be listened to and taken seriously does not mean that the worker assumes that their memories of events are always accurate but it does mean that their experiences and feelings are valid and real.

Many social workers deal almost wholly with adults; and are therefore likely to be more at ease in this sphere. It can be quite common to lose touch with the world of children. If the worker does not feel comfortable working with children he or she should arrange for someone who has substantial current experience or someone who already knows the child to do this work. Discomfort will be seen through by the child. The worker will not be accepted as honest or as an interested party and thus will not get a true reflection of the child's viewpoint.

Before undertaking work with the child, it may help to spend time in a nursery; play with toys, sand and water. Get back in touch. The emphasis should be on talking to children, remembering how they express themselves, what's important to them, and working at their pace. Preparing a range of appropriate materials to work with the particular child will be important.

The following general statements may be of some assistance:

1   *Go at the child's pace - let them control how fast you go.*
2   *"Listen" with all your senses - not just to what children say but to how they say it and to what they do not say bearing in mind what you already know of their situation. Don't be afraid to check out whether you've understood.*
3   *Record small details from one meeting to the next - the child will value the continuity and the fact that you continued to think of them.*
4   *Get alongside the child and come down in height.*
5   *Use an indirect approach rather than confronting or challenging with direct questions.*
6   *Provide a safe place free from interruptions.*
7   *Be clear about who you are and why you are there and any time constraints there may be on this.*
8   *Do something together - establishing what Claire Winnicott has called "a neutral zone of shared experience".*
9   *Find concrete ways of expressing yourself wherever possible and don't rely solely on verbal communication.*
10   *Get in tune with the child's own mode of self-expression.*
    (BASW 1986, *Creative Social Work with Families*)
                    * * * * *

The child needs to know who the worker is and why he or she is working with her/him. There has got to be something tangible in it for the child too. The practical work the child and worker produce together can be given to the child or partly shared and the worker can photocopy what is needed.

There are other areas where information can be gleaned about the child for the worker to incorporate as part of the assessment of the child. Written reports will need to be requested from hospitals, health visitors, doctors, schools, nurseries, psychologists etc, where applicable. An ongoing diary may be useful for nurseries, schools, foster parents etc to note observable changes since the commencement of the assessment. As indicated in Section 3 on "Parent/Child Relationship" it is also advisable that these reports are shared as openly as possible (given due regard to the age and understanding of the child). Open sharing of information can only enhance the working relationship and eliminate fantasies and blame. It is better still if information is shared from its direct source to the parent or child.

It takes time for a child to trust a stranger. As this is how the worker will initially be seen, she/he may be regarded as a threat too. A fair amount of informal time will need to be spent playing with equipment, toys, visiting places where the worker can be sure the child will feel safe. Issues of race and gender may play an important part in this.

The child's world evolves at a much slower pace; there is a different sense of time. It is therefore important not to rush the child or the work undertaken with that child. All children need help and guidance, though their desire for independence means they don't like being told what to do! A child's task in life is growing up and this should be as carefree as possible.

The child's mind is like a camera: it takes snapshots. The child copies those who are closest: role models are imitated. The child's sense of dignity will mean that if the child is treated with respect then this is likely to be returned to others.

It is easy to lose sight of the child's inner world as often the worker is under pressure to complete many tasks. However if the child's viewpoint is to be heard and their needs/ risks fully assessed then this can only be achieved by slowing down, looking and listening directly with the child.

The following is a list of some useful tools and exercises for ascertaining children's views, feelings, hopes and fears.

Books, Colouring books, identity books, games, toys, felt pictures.

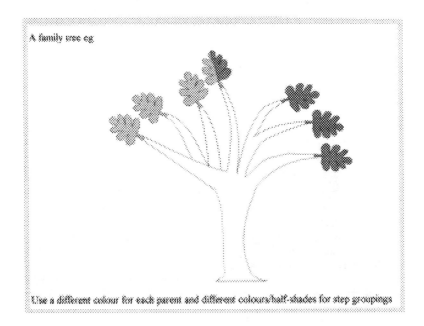

A family tree eg

Use a different colour for each parent and different colours/half-shades for step groupings

A road map

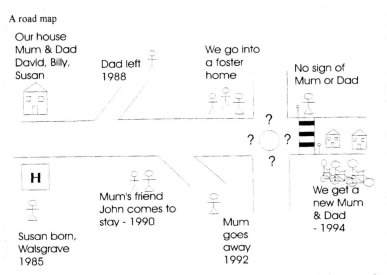

Our house
Mum & Dad
David, Billy,
Susan

Dad left
1988

We go into
a foster
home

No sign of
Mum or Dad

H

Susan born,
Walsgrave
1985

Mum's friend
John comes to
stay - 1990

Mum
goes
away
1992

We get a
new Mum
& Dad
- 1994

A 'genogram' is another way of setting out similar information. We would be extremely cautious of using this word - though not the basic concept - with many families, however.

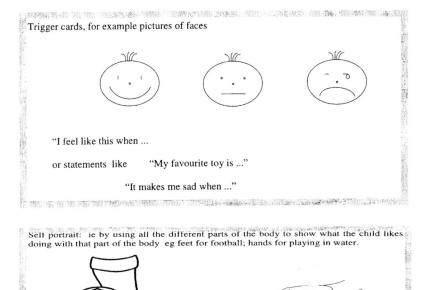

Trigger cards, for example pictures of faces

"I feel like this when ...

or statements like   "My favourite toy is ..."

"It makes me sad when ..."

Self portrait: ie by using all the different parts of the body to show what the child likes doing with that part of the body eg feet for football; hands for playing in water.

Holiday Camp: Ask the child to choose her/his own holiday camp anywhere the child wants it to be. The child writes down everyone they would like to take - friends, relatives, toys, pets. The child is told that there are only two chalets and as everyone cannot fit into one, then some will have to go into chalet 'A' with the child and the rest into chalet 'B'. This helps to ascertain who is "closest" to the child (or who they feel ought to go with them) but also when the final choice is made, who really is closest

Emily's holiday camp at the seaside

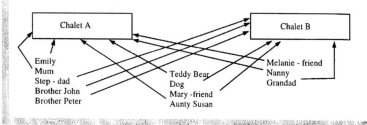

Blame cake: this will give an idea about how a child feels about an "incident". It gives an idea of the child's feelings about whose fault might have been. This can be done early on and then later to see if the blame has shifted

Mary

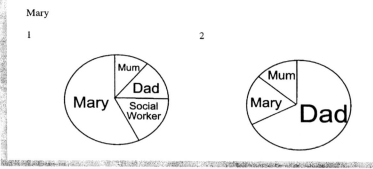

 Now record and evaluate all the STRENGTHS and HAZARDS identified in this section of the assessment with the parents.

The workers should attempt to reflect the child/ren's own views, wishes and feelings in the final evaluation of risk and need.

Section 6 - Work with the whole family

Introduction

Assessment work with the whole family can be a useful way to determine whether family relationships and dynamics have contributed to the causes for concern. However, in some situations it may not be possible to get the whole family together, eg when there is a stipulation of bail conditions, or where the children may find it difficult to meet with an alleged abuser.

If it is possible and desirable to work with the whole family, the worker will need to arrange to see all family members together and this should be a condition of the initial agreement. The worker should give the family some idea of the number of times she/he may want to see them.

To engage the family, the worker should explain that each family member will have a different point of view about what has happened and how things could be sorted out. The verbal and written invitation should be given to everyone in the family, stating how important it is to understand their point of view.

A number of different sessions are suggested below; workers can choose which ones are most suitable and appropriate.

Practical Arrangements

Discussion sessions should be away from the family home where possible to avoid distractions. They should be held at a venue that takes into account culture and disability. The observational session(s) could be in the family home if the worker feels it would be more appropriate. There should be two workers involved to manage the session and to deal with "process and content". Workers will need to negotiate ground rules with the family about the length of sessions, breaks, etc. If someone else lives with the family or is involved on a regular basis, workers may wish to involve them too.

The sessions should be at a time that is suitable for all family members. Have drawing materials, plasticine, lego etc available. The worker may need to include a worker who speaks the same language as the family or an interpreter. Letters need to be written in the family's own language. The worker may need to involve a person who has influence with the family in encouraging them to attend, eg relative, teacher, community leader. The worker may need to provide transport for the family.

If a family member fails to turn up for a session, the session should still go ahead, but the other family members present should be asked what the absent person might think, feel or do in a particular situation. The family can be given the task of getting that person along next time and/or the worker can write to or contact the absent member inviting him/her to the next session, stating that his/her valuable contribution was missed.

Exercise 6.1- Use of a family tree (or genogram)

First ask each person including the workers to introduce themselves. This should include everyone making a positive statement about themselves, eg "My name is John and I play in the school football team".

Explain to the family that you are going to look at who is in their family, and that together you will be considering some of the things that have happened in their family over the years and how they all see them. You will want to make a record with them of the main events etc. The worker will need to have large sheets of paper and felt tip pens available. The worker or a family member could undertake the drawing. Make sure each person does some of the talking. One worker should ask most of the questions and the other should observe the interactions.

Workers should observe how family members relate to each other in this exercise - how much they know about each other, who agrees with whom, whose views matter most, who takes the initiative, who decides what they write down. Workers should ask questions about their observations, for example "Do you two always disagree?" "How come you didn't know you had a brother who died?" If, during the process, the family indicate that other children have been abused or that the parents themselves were abused as children, the workers may need to discuss this further with the parents at a separate meeting.

Workers should bear in mind information that they already have about this family from files and other agencies. If significant information is not included in the construction of the family tree, map or genogram, workers may wish to raise it.

Workers should use their discretion based on the information they have obtained, as to whether they wish to discuss the causes for concern further at this stage. The family may well have raised important issues related to the causes for concern. In that case workers may wish to pursue these to hear the views of all family members.

*****

Exercise 6.2 - Family routines

The family could be asked to describe what happens on a typical day. This could be a school day or a day at the weekend or both. This would enable the workers to gain a better understanding of family routines and the role that various family members take on. It could be written up on a large sheet of paper or on a nobo board with felt tip pen.

A series of clocks showing different times could be used, and family members asked to describe what happens in their household at that particular time. Alternatively, the family could make drawings of what occurs in their household at that particular time of day.

A similar exercise may already have been undertaken with the adults in Section 4 (Exercise 4.4). In that case workers may choose not to repeat it or it might be useful as a comparison.

*****

Exercise 6.3 - Family rules and expectations

All families have rules about the way they live their lives together. These rules evolve over a long period of time. They may not have been made explicit within the family and not all family members may be clear what is expected of them. If this is the case or family members disagree about the rules it can lead to misunderstandings and conflict. A better understanding of family rules by the worker and the family may throw light on some or all of the causes for concern and help everyone to work towards change that they would like to bring about.

Ways of doing this with the family could include:

a) A series of questions that the family are asked to discuss, eg
    What does this family do when someone refuses to wash up?
    What does this family do when someone refuses to go to bed on time?
    What does this family do if someone stays out too late?
    What does this family do when someone tells lies?
    What does this family do when Mum is ill?
    What does this family do when Dad gets angry?
    What does this family do when they run out of money?

   Workers should attempt to devise questions which link directly to the causes for concern in the particular family they are assessing. It should be possible to think of many other questions to fit the individual family circumstances.

   Again, a similar exercise may already have been completed with the adults in Section 4 (Exercise 4.4). If so, the worker may wish to point out the differences in the perceptions of the parents and the children if these occur.

b) The worker could ask the family to list all the rules they can think of that operate within their family. The worker will need to give some examples first (as above), to start the family off.

At the end of (a) or (b), ask the family to make up some rules that they would like to have in their family. Give the family some possible examples to start them off, eg we would like everyone to say "thank you" to Mum when she cooks us a nice meal. The family could be asked to continue this exercise at home in preparation for the next meeting.

*****

Exercise 6.4 - Family tasks

Family relationships can best be understood by observation and feedback. Giving the family a task to do together will give the worker an opportunity to observe how family members relate to each other and how this might contribute to the causes for concern.

Guidelines for the use of observational work and feedback are given in Appendix 1. See also the checklist of things to observe and record in Exercise 3.11.

The worker will need to do some preparation with the family prior to the session. The family should be asked to choose something they would like to do together in the next session, eg playing a game, preparing a meal, going to the park, constructing something, etc.

Plans will need to be made about where and when the session will take place and how long it will last. Preparations for equipment and other resources required, eg transport, food, finance, etc will be needed. The worker and the family will need to decide who will take responsibility for these items; but the worker will need to take account of the possibility that the family may not have made all the necessary preparations.

The worker should also observe and record the following:

- how the family negotiate
- who makes decisions
- who initiates things
- who consults who
- how differences are resolved
- who misbehaves and how it is handled

At the end of the session the worker should check out with the family how they found the task and what they learnt. Then he/she should give feedback about his/her observations to the family, either verbally or by using audio or video recording of the session and using this to initiate discussion.

At the end of the session with the family, ask each family member to say two "good things" and one "not so good thing" about how they now feel about living in their family.

*****

Inclusion of foster family where children in care

Where a child has been removed from home and placed with substitute parents, the worker may need to consider how the child is relating to the foster family. One session with the whole foster family might include a discussion about how the child is settling in and whether there are any particular problems.   Any detailed work which might be needed should be planned carefully with the child and the foster parents, taking due account of their wishes and views and being sensitive to the rights of parents to know what is being done.

 Workers should now use this information to compile with the family their list of STRENGTHS and HAZARDS as they relate to the causes for concern.

Section 7 - Final Risk Assessment and Evaluation of Need

Two concluding sessions with the parents should be arranged. Whether the children are involved in these or not is open to the worker's discretion and will depend upon the child/ren's age and level of understanding. The parents should be informed that in these final sessions, the following tasks will be completed:

A) The work of the assessment to date will be reviewed by an analysis of the STRENGTHS and HAZARDS already identified at the end of each section.
B) The original causes for concern will be considered again along with any further concerns which have emerged. The parents' ability and willingness to understand the causes for concern will be discussed.
C) The worker(s) will give parents feedback about their co-operation and participation in the assessment. Parents will be invited to contribute their own analysis of this.
D) The parents' potential for effecting change in this family will be considered. This will involve consideration of the parents' receptiveness to advice and constructive criticism; their desire to achieve change; their capacity to bring it about; the help and resources they would need.

Exercise 7.1
At the beginning of the first of these final two sessions, the worker should write all the causes for concern on the nobo board or flip chart. The parents' views of the causes for concern at the beginning of the assessment should be recalled and the parents should be asked to comment upon them. Establish

•   Are their views still the same?
•   Have the causes for concern shifted in any way?
                                *****

Exercise 7.2
All the STRENGTHS and HAZARDS identified throughout the assessment should now be placed around the causes for concern.

(If these were originally recorded on flip chart paper which has been retained, the sheets can simply be put up again around the causes for concern. Alternatively, the worker will need to write them on the nobo board under the relevant section headings - Child's Perceptions, Adult Relationships, etc.)

Each individual (workers and parents) should be asked to go through all of the STRENGTHS and HAZARDS, identifying any they no longer agree with or which they feel no longer exist. If there is general agreement that a STRENGTH or a HAZARD is no longer relevant, it can be deleted.

Any disagreements should be fully discussed, and if they cannot be resolved, should be recorded and left on the relevant list. (Disputed STRENGTHS or HAZARDS should be clearly marked by an agreed symbol or by circling them with different coloured felt tip pens, in order to make clear which participant wishes to retain them.)

At the end of this process, all the STRENGTHS and HAZARDS still considered to be present in the family by at least one person should be listed in some way on the wall under the appropriate section headings.

THESE NOW REPRESENT A SET OF *INDICATORS OF RISK AND NEED*, WHICH NEED TO BE EVALUATED IN ORDER TO COMPLETE THE ASSESSMENT AND CONSIDER RECOMMENDATIONS FOR FURTHER ACTION.

*****

Evaluation of Parental Co-operation

A final indicator with its own STRENGTHS and HAZARDS should be explored at this stage. This is the PARENTS' CO-OPERATION AND POTENTIAL FOR CHANGE. As set out above, the factors in the assessment of this are:

A)   The parents' ability and willingness to understand and acknowledge the causes for concern as defined at this conclusive stage of the assessment.

B)   The level and quality of their co-operation and participation in the assessment process.

C)   Their potential for effecting change by consideration of their receptiveness to advice and constructive criticism; their desire to achieve change; and their capacity to bring it about.

The workers should give the parents full and honest feedback about these issues and the parents should be invited to respond and give their own evaluation of their participation in the assessment and their motivation to change.

Exercise 7.3
It should then be possible for all participants to identify further STRENGTHS and HAZARDS in relation to these issues and previous sections. These should then be discussed as before and recorded on a flow chart as further indicators of risk.

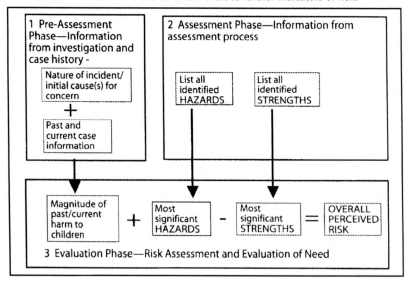

Flow Chart for final evaluation of risk and need
Exercise 7.4 - Use of Flowchart

Uncompleted copies of the flow chart should be handed to the parents. It should be explained that the chart is a model for setting out all of the case information and for clearly indicating how this information is used to formulate a FINAL RISK ASSESSMENT AND EVALUATION OF NEED.

The parents can then use exactly the same model or format as the workers for setting out the information (ie STRENGTHS and HAZARDS) they regard as significant from the assessment. The model provides a helpful basis for parents to make their own presentation to a future case conference if one is required, including their evaluation of the overall perceived risk.

The worker should have written on a large copy of the flow chart the main STRENGTHS and HAZARDS which have been identified, to leave with members of the family.

The chart should also include the following information, which should be explicitly shared with parents at this stage so that they can consider it prior to discussion in the final session:

(a) Nature of initial incident/initial cause(s) for concern.
(b) Significant past and current case information (eg history of abuse, previous conferences/registrations, information about children no longer in the family home etc).
(c) The magnitude of harm suffered by the child/ren, with hard information about events, incidents, disclosures, non-accidental injuries etc.

*****

Exercise 7.5

In preparation for the final session, all participants (parents and workers) should be asked to identify the STRENGTHS and HAZARDS which they regard as being most significant. They should arrange them in order of importance if possible. (Where there are a lot of STRENGTHS and HAZARDS to choose from, a maximum of ten of each is suggested in order to make sure the subsequent discussion is focused on the degree of risk).

*****

FINAL SESSION

Each participant should state which STRENGTHS and HAZARDS they have decided are most significant. Similarities or differences should be discussed. Everybody should have the opportunity to talk about why they have chosen and arranged their most significant STRENGTHS and HAZARDS in the way they have. This should facilitate considerable discussion and is an opportunity for the overall degree of risk to the child to be explored openly by all participants.

Exercise 7.6

At the end of the discussion, each participant should be able to record all the significant information as they see it on their own copy of the flow chart. This will include all the

STRENGTHS and HAZARDS they previously identified as being present: those which they regard as most significant; and their own evaluation of the overall perceived risk to the child/ren and any unmet needs.

* * * * *

At the end of this, it should be clear to the parents how the worker(s) perceive the overall risk to their child/ren, based on the information the worker(s) have explicitly identified as being most significant from their point of view.

The information on the flow chart should be the basis of the worker's presentation to a case conference if one is required. Additionally, the worker may be required to prepare a written report explaining the process of the assessment and the reasons for their perception of the risk to the child and their evaluation of need based on the significant STRENGTHS and HAZARDS. It is strongly recommended that parents should be given a copy of this report.

Even if the parents' view of the STRENGTHS, HAZARDS and overall risk to the child/ren is very different from the worker(s), they should be offered every assistance in completing their copies of the flow chart and in presenting and explaining this to a case conference.

Appendix 1 - Practical issues and decisions when undertaking direct observation with some or all of the family

Realistically, it may only be possible to undertake a small number of sessions of direct observation during the assessment. Ideally, it would be helpful to observe some or all of the family at different stages of the assessment. However, if problems of time, organisation and resources limit the number of observational sessions, the timing of them will depend on the nature of the causes of concern and the information already available.

Similar decisions will have to be made about the level of the worker's involvement in the session(s), about how they are recorded, and about planning their content. These decisions should be taken following consideration of a number of possible choices:

Whole family or parent(s) and certain child/ren

For instance, where concerns relate to emotional abuse, scapegoating or rejection of a certain child/ren, it would be most useful to observe the interaction of the whole family together.

Where it is indicated that a child has been injured or neglected due to various pressures of which large family size might be one, it would be logical to observe the way in which parent(s) organise to meet the needs of all their children. Alternatively, where there is concern about the way in which parent(s) meet certain clearly identified needs of a particular child (eg feeding and bathing a baby, responding to a toddler's exploration and inquisitiveness by being over punitive or controlling) it might be most useful to observe parent(s) in meeting those needs with that particular child.

Passive or active participation of the worker

If the observation is mainly designed to give the worker a view of interactions and processes in the family, it might be most appropriate for the worker to be very passive, not being drawn into the activity. EXCEPTIONS WOULD OBVIOUSLY BE ANY SITUATION WHERE A CHILD WAS PLACED AT RISK OF HARM DURING THE SESSION.

Alternatively, where certain aspects of parenting have been clearly identified and broadly accepted as linked to the causes of concern, it might be useful to summarise these in a list of simple tasks or behaviours which the parent needs to learn or change.

For example, where there is concern about hygiene and/or rough handling of a small baby, the parent(s) might be told that the sort of tasks to be observed would be:

- making sure the baby's feeding equipment is properly sterilised before use
- making sure milk/food is at necessary temperature
- making sure baby is allowed to feed at her/his own pace rather than being forced or denied food if she/he wants a break
- making sure bath water is correct temperature
- making sure the baby is held in a way which is both safe and comfortable for her/

him while being bathed.

Another example might be a case of emotional abuse of an older child. Examples of things to look out for might be:

- does the parent readily respond to the child's approaches or requests?
- does the parent promote or initiate interaction with the child?
- does the parent give the child any verbal, non-verbal and/or physical messages that she/he is loved and approved of?

Suitable joint activities between parent and child would need to be agreed.

Having broken the causes of concern down into simple tasks, activities and interactions as a basis for observation it will be possible to make parent(s) aware of the causes for concern as and when they occur in the observed session. This is also a way of measuring the parent's ability and motivation to use intervention and to achieve change.

NB Where the aspects of parenting being observed involve basic parentcraft, the worker(s) should ensure that the parent(s) involved have been shown how to undertake the tasks adequately.

Observation by Keyworker or Specialist Resource

Observation by one of the workers undertaking the bulk of the assessment gives her/him the opportunity to see parents and child/ren and to compare observed interaction with information gathered in other parts of the assessment. However, it has already been noted that the worker(s) may not have sufficient time to undertake direct observation on many occasions.

Where the potential for change needs to be assessed by direct observation of parents using a list of clear expectations or simple tasks as above, it would be useful to ask a day nursery, family aide/assistant or family centre to utilise their particular skills to undertake this part of the assessment over a number of planned sessions.

However, it is vital that these workers have clear written information about what they are looking for and what the nature of the concerns are. It is also important that the tasks to be observed are carefully explained and negotiated with parents so that they are aware of the expectations being placed upon them. Recording of observations must be factual, descriptive, related to actual incidents and interactions; interpretations and impressions should be clearly recorded as such and information given about alternative impressions of other workers or family members.

Use of Video or Audio recording

As an alternative to active participation or even physical presence in a session, worker(s) may seek the family's agreement to sessions being recorded.

The recording can then be used later to point out causes for concern to the parents or to make observations about interactions in the family and their parenting, hopefully stimulating discussion and insight.

Venue

Direct observation should take place in an environment in which the child is comfortable, able to play and move around, and familiar.

- The home, in most circumstances, may well give the most realistic picture of parent/child interactions. However, this may be problematic both in terms of distractions (television, telephone, visitors) and also difficulties for the worker in finding a space to be unobtrusive if she/he wants to be. The presence of a worker may make it very difficult for family members to be relaxed in their own home.
- A nursery, family centre or school room, with which the child is familiar, are possible alternatives and will usually be preferable to rooms in a social work office.

15
The Search for clarity in complex assessments

Jan Rushton

Introduction

Assessment, the process of gathering a mass of information and ordering it to facilitate decisions, is the starting point for most social work practice. Without assessment of need there can be no basis for planning the provision and delivery of services. In the field of child protection the Inquiries of the 1980s exposed the muddle and 'drift' that arose when systematic assessment failed to take place and in 1986 the Social Services Inspectorate reported on the general absence of comprehensive assessment in long term planning for children and families. As a consequence the DoH stressed the message of Adcock & White (1985) that:

> *A good assessment is an essential basis for planning work with parents to prevent children from entering or remaining in long term care. (p.7)*

The importance and purpose of assessment was reinforced in *Working Together* (DoH 1991b) which states that an initial plan should include a comprehensive assessment.

> *Its purpose is to acquire a full understanding of the child and family situation in order to provide a sound basis for decisions about future actions. (p.31)*

The Children Act places upon social workers the task of assessing not only the significance of any current harm that a child might be suffering but also the likelihood of future harm.

In this chapter I shall look at some of the problems associated with concepts and models of assessment. I will develop some of these themes in an account of an assessment of a family where there were concerns about sexual and emotional abuse.

Some problems with assessment

Problems associated with assessment include: lack of common standards, lack of clarity, paucity of models, research deficits and the effects of specialisation.

Lack of common standards

Assessment is a process of gathering information and making judgements against some yardsticks or requirements. For example in adult services we assess the requirements of individuals to enable them to achieve, maintain or restore an acceptable level of social independence or quality of life. This implies broad agreement about what contributes to an acceptable level of social independence, without which the assessment would have no meaning. In child care we make assessments against a yardstick of what are necessary requirements to ensure the safety and welfare of the child. Again there is an assumption that we can agree on a base line of adequate child care and good enough parenting. However, inter-agency training exercises such as that of Stainton Rogers (1989) and the comparative research of Christopherson (1988) indicate that there is considerable divergence in people's views as to what constitutes abuse and what is important in the rearing of children.

There is therefore an arena of professional debate which could be illuminated through research findings. However, Higginson (1990) suggests that personal values often distort perceptions and interpretations of research evidence. Moreover this process is likely to work against those families who are already marginalised or oppressed within society such as those who are poor and those culturally outside the norm (Bebbington & Miles 1989).

Lack of clarity

The emphasis on assessment within social work practice has led to a situation where it can be seen as a solution to problematic situations. Case Conferences, unable to formulate a plan of protection, may recommend an assessment as if that is a solution, rather than a part of the process of decision making. In such circumstances there is often a failure to clarify the level, the subject and the methods of assessment. It is essential to be clear as to whether the assessment is initial, comprehensive or multi-disciplinary. Is it an in-depth assessment, requiring major input within a short space of time or developmental, requiring work over several months? Are we being asked to assess risk, the nature of relationships, the potential for change? Who will be involved in the assessment and what model will be used?

Limitations of models

Where there is some clarity in the aims of the assessment there is still a problem over the paucity of models available for making the idea an operational reality. 'Good Enough Parenting' by Adcock & White (1985) provides an early model but is medical and individualistic in orientation and fails to take full account of the effect of structural factors in society on child welfare, cultural or gender perspectives. The Thurlow House programme (Gawlinski et at 1988) offers a detailed format for assessing families where physical abuse has taken place: again this is based on a medical model. Its depth, comprehensiveness and intensity means it could only be available to a few families. The

'Orange Book' or DoH guide for assessment (1988) offers a comprehensive guide to gathering information and a format for making sense of the material in order to make plans. It also provides some examples of possible methods, such as flow charts and eco maps. It addresses the problem of value laden judgements, stresses the need to seek objective evidence and states that:

> *Social workers must be aware of the cultural, racial, gender, class and religious values they bring to assessment ... particular importance must be given to issues of race and culture.*

However, as I shall demonstrate in the use of the guide in my own assessment, the underlying emphasis is on an assessment of a family based on the two parent model, without consideration of how the family is shaped by social factors, or the variety of modern day family structures, in particular the single parent family. For example the Orange Book acknowledges the problems caused by financial shortage but then sets guidelines for assessment based on judgements about individual capacities to manage, organise, prioritise (Section 8.7. questions 141 to 153). Some of these problems have been addressed in the new Framework (DoH et al 2000).

Research deficits

Having collected and ordered the information in the assessment there is a need to analyse and evaluate it before drawing conclusions. In some areas there is inadequate research to inform judgements in assessment. This is the case in the area of the short and long term effects of sexual abuse. Kieran O'Hagan (1989) highlights this defect, acknowledged by Finkelhor (1986). O'Hagan also points out the lack of consideration given to the multiple variables involved in sexual abuse. Evidence of what works to protect children from harm and help them recover from it is patchy and contested (Baldwin & Spencer 1993, DoH 1995, Macdonald & Roberts 1995). Where sound research is lacking judgements are made on the basis of subjective values and what might be called 'folk lore'.

Specialisation

Finally I want to highlight a problem that has arisen out of the shift towards intensification and specialisation in difficult areas of social work practice. Assessment, as it has come to be seen as central, has tended to become separated out as a specialist activity and a distinct phase of social work involvement. However, from the family's point of view it may be difficult to distinguish assessment from investigation or support and therapy. Assessment may become the job of a specialist worker or workers who will be involved with the family only for the duration of the assessment. There is an increasing trend towards a family being exposed to a series of workers, yet evidence (Thoburn 1990; DoH 1991a, DoH 1995) would suggest that a crucial factor in a successful outcome is the positive relationship between family and social worker existing over time from investigation through to therapy. I shall try to consider some of these issues and problems through an account of practice.

Background and choice of assessment

I shall describe my work in a basic comprehensive assessment of the Brown family. This is a case showing many of the characteristics which present themselves on a daily basis to the average social worker. There were concerns about risks of emotional and sexual abuse, combined with worries that a child might drift into long term care. Knowledge of children's needs and development together with risk analysis and knowledge of the short and long term effects of sexual and physical abuse were needed. The request for assessment came to me as a Social Services Department social worker immediately after a Case Conference. However, the family - a mother and two children - had become known to the Department through a request for help rather than as a result of a direct investigation. While the first duty of the Department was to consider the issues of abuse and safety, there were wider concerns of child and parental need. These issues in themselves were not wholly compatible, and raised questions around the desirability of rescue and safety from current risk as set against considerations of long term welfare and the stated principles of the Department:

that every effort should be made to support a child within her own family.

The Department became involved with Mary Brown and her two children, Sharon (5 yrs) and Tracey (2 yrs) when Mary came to the office to ask that Sharon be accommodated. Mary had recently moved into the area and was living in the home of a local family who had 3 children. Also present in the house was Mary's brother Pete. Mary complained that Sharon would not do as she was told, was very demanding and had threatened to kill Mary. The social worker visiting the household that evening was concerned about the crowded living circumstances and the apparent rejection of Sharon by all the adults. Sharon had in fact packed her own case and was sitting at the foot of the stairs awaiting collection. Sharon was accommodated in a short term foster home under Section 29 of the Children's Act 1989, to allow time for an initial assessment of family circumstances and for Mary to find alternative accommodation. The following day the Department received further information from a London social worker who had been working with Mary and her children for some time. Sharon's name had been placed on the Child Protection Register when she was a few months old for Failure to Thrive. Later she was said to have been sexually abused, allegedly by the father of Mary's second child Tracey. Further sexual abuse was suspected by another man a year later and a Place of Safety Order was obtained followed by an Interim Care Order. Sharon spent $5\frac{1}{2}$ months in a foster home.

As a result of this information, a Case Conference was held. There was a discussion around the ability of Mary, given her past history of changing partners, two of whom were suspected of child abuse, and current unstable life style, to protect her child from sexual abuse. At times of crisis it is not uncommon for workers to focus on the role of mothers to protect, which can scapegoat mothers, and allow attention to slip away from the person responsible for the abuse. There were also concerns around Mary's rejection of Sharon and whether it was more important to return Sharon home quickly for fear that a longer separation might further damage the relationship with her mother or whether a precipitate return home would expose Sharon to risk of sexual or emotional abuse. In the event the decision was for Sharon to remain accommodated pending an assessment. The wording of the minutes was somewhat vague, referring to the nature of the mother/child relationship and the risks of further sexual abuse. The Conference discussion had revealed divergent opinions as to Mary's capacities as a mother. The London social worker clearly had a big commitment to Mary based in part on evidence of Mary's achievements in the previous six months and in part on the strength of their relationship. The current local social worker was more concerned about Mary's apparent indifference to Sharon. What was clear was that while factual evidence was considered, personal values determined the way in which the evidence was viewed and there was no consensus on the relative importance of different aspects of Mary's parenting, thus supporting Higginson's (1990) findings. Mary was not present at the conference and was therefore not able to correct inaccuracies, state her point of view or be part of the decision making process. Divergent views as to the relative importance of needs and risks and whether Sharon should be with her mother or should be 'rescued' from a risky situation were reflected in previous Court reports.

Thus from the start, work with the Brown family illustrated some of the problems associated with assessment: its use as a solution to an impasse in decision making and the lack of common standards, combined with the power of value judgements, which make establishing the base line of risk and good enough parenting such a difficult exercise.

Choice of model and planning

I chose to base the assessment on the DoH model *Protecting Children* (1988) since it was the model accepted by my Department and the most comprehensive guide on offer for gathering and ordering information. However I consider that it has limitations because of a failure to address the structural factors in society which affect family functioning.

Protecting Children states that a planning stage - the who, what, where and how of an assessment - is essential if the process is to be effective. The Case Conference recommendations had been vague and I therefore found it necessary to clarify the aims of my assessment. In doing this I tried to move from a position of judging Mary to one which would focus on empowerment and on strengthening the bonds between her and her daughter. In doing this I believe I moved away from what MacLeod and Saraga (1988) describe as a 'mother blaming' position to one which, while acknowledging that mothers' and children's interests are not identical, recognises the difficulties of the mother and the importance of fostering the mother/daughter relationship. I decided that what I was assessing was:

• The capacity of Mary and the help she needed to be an adequate parent to Sharon, with respect to her emotional needs and protection from sexual abuse.
• The risks to Sharon of further rejection and sexual abuse.
• The nature of the relationship between Mary and Sharon and how it could be strengthened.
• What plans might be put into operation to allow Sharon to return home.

The Orange Book suggests that 6-10 sessions will be required to complete an assessment and that the time scale should be up to 12 weeks. Bearing in mind the research of Millham et al (1986) and Bullock et al (1993) stressing the importance of the early weeks of work in securing successful rehabilitation, I planned to complete the assessment in 4-5 weeks.

Who to include? I planned to have sessions with Mary, with Sharon, with Mary and Sharon and Tracey together. I included the foster parents of Sharon, the Health Visitor and Sharon's school teacher. I also included information from Court Reports prepared for Care Proceedings in London.

Of the four sessions which I had with Mary, three took place in her home and one at a Children's Centre. The observation session of Mary with Sharon and Tracey took place in Mary's home. The individual sessions with Sharon took place in a Children's Centre, in the same room on each occasion. The use of the same room and establishing a sequence of events - collection from school, arrival, working together time, free play with biscuits and drinks, return home - was to enable Sharon to feel secure.

Engaging the family

An assessment is something that should be done 'with' and not 'to' a family. It is then important that:

- The social worker should be open and honest about the causes of concern and the purpose of the assessment, the responsibilities and powers of the social worker.
- Parents should be allowed to challenge information held on them.
- Parents views should be sought and taken into account.
- Parents rights to help and support for themselves should be acknowledged.
- Parents understand that the assessment will be about the strengths and positives within the family as well as the areas of concern.

In my initial planning session with Mary we discussed past history, the way in which Sharon had been accommodated and our subsequent concerns. Mary acknowledged these, stated some of the things that had been said in the past that she disagreed with, and her own concerns for herself and for Sharon. We drew up an agreement. In the agreement we moved from the Case Conference emphasis on assessment of parenting capacities to focus on the identification of the supports and resources necessary for Sharon to return home. As Volume 2 of The Children Act 1989 Guidance & Regulations states:

the emphasis under the Act is on 'identifying and providing for the child's needs rather than focusing on parental shortcomings in a negative manner'. (p.8)

At this stage I was concerned that Mary was almost too compliant, as if she was going through the motions of previous involvement with social workers, indicative of her own sense of powerlessness. It was necessary early on to demonstrate on a practical as well as emotional level a concern for Mary herself and I did this by providing some assistance with furnishings for the privately rented accommodation Mary had managed to obtain.

It is also important to be honest with children involved in an assessment and to explain, in a way they can understand, what an assessment means. I asked Sharon why she thought she was in a foster home and why she thought I had come to see her. Her understanding was that Mummy needed to get settled in a new home and that she had been naughty. I talked briefly about some of the things that had happened to her in London, that this sometimes made it difficult for her and Mummy to be happy together but that this was not because she was naughty and that it was my job to try to find a way of making things better. I explained I would need her help to do this.

Having 'cleared the ground' I was able to embark on the assessment proper. In the following sections I shall describe the main stages and outcomes of the assessment, highlighting the positive aspects and limitations of the Orange Book model.

Initial session with Mary

During my first sessions with Mary we looked at the areas of concern about Sharon, considered differing views of these and Mary's view of her relationship with Sharon. We started from the point at which our Department had become involved and I clarified our concerns over the way in which Sharon had been accommodated, Mary's apparent lack of concern for her and Mary's comments that Sharon 'had an evil spirit in her'. Mary said that while she loved Sharon she found her difficult and added: 'She does not feel like my daughter'.

The main areas of difficulty with Sharon which she identified were:

- Sharon wet the bed.
- Sharon was loud and noisy.
- Sharon did not do as she was told and deliberately set out to upset her.
- Sharon sometimes seemed to compete with her to run the house and look after Tracey.
- Sharon did not respond to smacks.
- Sharon sometimes behaved in a 'sexy' way.

Mary felt that the cause of most of her problems with Sharon was the $5\frac{1}{2}$ months separation following a Place of Safety Order taken as a result of concerns about sexual abuse. She felt that the separation was wrong and unnecessary and had broken the fragile bond between herself and her daughter. We thus went on to look at the second area of concern - the past sexual abuse of Sharon and the risk of further abuse.

It became clear that Mary's view of events and risk to her daughter differed from that of previous professionals. The professional account, as revealed in previous reports, was that Mary reported that as a result of what Sharon was saying she believed her to be being sexually abused by Paul, her boyfriend and father of her unborn child. Subsequent investigation supported this, there was corroborative medical evidence. The allegations were: touching Sharon's vagina and digital penetration. Paul denied the allegations. Although Mary told Paul to leave her home she continued to associate with him and later indicated that she did not believe he was responsible for the abuse to Sharon. The London social worker had further concerns:

- Mary refused counselling help for herself or Sharon.
- Mary had a number of relationships with men about whom Social Services had concerns. She did not appear to assess their suitability as carers for Sharon.
- There were a number of drunken parties at Mary's flat and Mary was often not in a state to protect her child.
- Sharon continued to wet herself, use sexual language and exhibit sexually inappropriate behaviour.

These were the reasons for the Place of Safety Order and subsequent Interim Care Order.

Mary's view of events was that it was she who had reported concerns about Sharon to Social Services and Police, acting as a good protecting parent. She said that she had not refused but had not been offered counselling help. She had removed Paul from her flat but had continued to see him as he was the father of her second child. She said that over time Sharon had given the names of several people as possible perpetrators of the abuse, including one who was a known sexual abuser. She agreed that several people came and went in her London flat but denied that she had in any way exposed Sharon to risk. She was unsure of the reasons for Sharon's sexualised behaviour but associated it with the original sexual abuse and Sharon's association with an older cousin, also a victim of sexual abuse. It appeared that the London social worker judged Mary to be responsible for the sexual abuse of her child by another person and paid little attention to Mary's right to express her own feelings.

Towards the end of the first session we acknowledged the differences in accounts of the past and drew up a list of shared concerns. In doing this I hoped to reframe the assessment to acknowledge Mary's needs and concerns, while still maintaining focus on the conditions necessary for Sharon to be safe and secure in her home. The shared concerns identified were:

- The relationship between Mary and Sharon and whether they could live together.
- The past sexual abuse of Sharon and the problems that this left for Sharon and Mary.
- Sharon's sexualised language and behaviour and the risks associated with this as well as the difficulties it caused for Mary.

We also agreed that in the current situation there were problems of loneliness for Mary and unmet needs from her own past history which might be helped by counselling. In addition we noted and recorded the many positive aspects of Mary and Sharon's situation - Mary's abilities as a cook and home maker, Sharon's attachment to Mary, Sharon's intelligence, outgoing nature and beautiful appearance.

The mother - Mary

It had been clear in the first session that Mary needed to talk about her own history and this became the subject of the second session. The Orange Book stresses the importance of beginning with a detailed look at family structure and composition and points out that while some of this information may already be known it is likely to be incomplete or inaccurate. There were discrepancies in family names recorded so far. Between sessions 1 and 2 Mary did some work on gathering together the information she had on her background and together we drew up a Family Tree (See DoH 1988, Appendix 2) using this as a structure for sharing information and as an opportunity for the expression of feeling about people and events. Mary was the daughter of an English mother and Italian father. She was the youngest of 5, her four older brothers all having different fathers. Mary was taken into care when she was 3 weeks old as the result of her mother's mental health, varyingly described in her case notes as depressive and schizophrenic. Mary was placed with foster parents with whom she lived until the age of 16 and in whose care she suffered extensive abuse by her foster brother. In her teens Mary established some contact with her mother and her brothers, who themselves had spent some time in care. Mary's father had been murdered. Mary never knew him but had kept newspaper reports of his death. She expressed a romantic attachment for him and her unknown relatives abroad.

The Orange Book notes the need to be cautious about associating significant factors of parental background with child abuse but goes on to note Jones' et al (1987) list of significant factors and to quote Fraiberg (1980) on the importance of 'ghosts':

> the parent it seems is condemned to repeat the tragedy of her own childhood with her own baby in terrible and exacting details.

In the case of Mary it is perhaps most important to note her life in care, her abusive childhood, her underachievement at school, her unstable natural family, lack of support from relatives in bringing up her own children, the transiency of her adult relationships, as a means of understanding missing positives and unmet needs to be addressed in any future plans, rather than signs of her ability or otherwise to act as a good mother to her children.

The DoH Guide notes the importance of personality and attitudes. Mary's history revealed that while able to negotiate many of the practical difficulties of life she found it difficult to make long standing relationships or to live on her own. She described herself as 'a not very strong person' who needed men for 'comfort, love and sex'. She felt she was 'not very bright' and this view was a clear reflection of what she had been told about herself by others. At the same time, she was proud of her achievements - the rented house she had found and furnished, her sewing and cooking skills. She described herself as quiet but very open and willing to take a chance on all relationships. To professionals she presented as manipulative in terms of material things, vulnerable to manipulation by others and over ready to give confidences, seeming to want to reach a level of intimacy without going through all the social stepping stones. Central to an understanding of Mary's situation is an appreciation of her as a single parent and of her social networks. A weakness of the Orange Book is that while it acknowledges the existence of the single parent the focus is on families with more than one carer and there is no section for considering the particular circumstances and pressures of the single parent and in particular the single mother. The section on networks contains questions that personalise the parent's situation, for example:

> Do you take part in community or leisure activities (e.g. Church, Sports, Evening Classes).

The question does not look at what is available, affordable, relevant, nor how realistic participation is for the sole carer of two young children.

Mary's ecomap showed that she had few close relationships and that a boyfriend whom she had known for only two weeks could be as important to her as her children.

The Orange Book rightly notes that an absence of life-lines and support mechanisms at times of crisis leaves families under strain, but again suggests individual responsibility for this situation. It highlights personal difficulties in making relationships or self sought isolation, rather than any consideration of financial, geographical or social factors which might contribute to social isolation.

In gathering and ordering information from Mary about herself and her past the Orange Book proved useful in its comprehensiveness and the neutrality of some of its questions. It also offered a useful tool in the form of the genogram. However I would argue that by focusing on the individual, with minimal consideration of structural and societal factors, it would have led to an assessment of Mary's parenting capacities, which would further disempower her. I shall now consider the central person in the assessment - *Sharon*.

The child - Sharon

The assessment of Sharon was drawn from my own sessions with her, Mary's accounts, comments from the school and the perceptions of the foster mother. Again the Orange Book offered a useful tool in setting out the changes in Sharon's life in the form of a flow chart.

Mary described Sharon as 'lively, noisy, very active'. Sharon had not been planned, and Mary had felt ill through much of her pregnancy. In the first year of her life Sharon cried a lot, did not sleep and Mary was very depressed. Mary felt things had got better in Sharon's second year and she had enjoyed dressing her and being seen with her. At the present time she was worried that Sharon's sexual behaviour, which took the form of undressing and inviting inappropriate touching, would drive away any potential boyfriend.

The foster mother described Sharon as 'bright', 'affectionate and charming'. She found the most difficult aspect of Sharon's behaviour her use of sexualised language and behaviour. She also felt she was too friendly to strangers and would make physical contact with anyone without showing age appropriate caution.

I spent time with Sharon on three occasions and observed her with Mary, and in the foster home. In my sessions with Sharon I used material such as puppets, a doll's house and drawing materials. Sharon responded quickly to me as she had to a previous social worker and offered her affection very openly. She liked to establish some areas of control in the sessions, such as choice of room, and liked to be as active as possible. At the end of each session she liked to establish when I would next see her and when she would next see her mum. Sharon thought the reasons for her being in care were because of Mum moving from London and her being naughty. She was not sure how she had been naughty or why it was all right for her sister Tracey to be with Mum. She was clear that she wanted to live with Mum but wanted to be able to return to the foster home for holidays. Sharon enjoyed best playing with the doll's house. She identified figures for herself, Tracey and Mary and Mary's boyfriend. The only activities she identified for the male figures were sexual ones, such as lying on the settee 'snogging' with Mummy or 'sexing'. Using the dolls, she showed an awareness of what was involved in sexual activity. Using the dolls we talked about and positioned people close to her. Sharon clearly showed her attachment to Mary and Tracey but the lack of other significant people in her life. In observing Mary with Sharon I noted that Mary showed irritation at the noise and activity of Sharon and Tracey together and did not want, even when asked, to join in their games. She avoided physical contact. When the children needed correction she dealt with the situation in an appropriate way but had more confidence in her handling of Tracey.

Tracey - the sister

I observed Tracey on my visits to Mary and with Sharon. Tracey like Sharon was advanced for her age with a relatively wide vocabulary and showing good manual skills. She had an open, sunny disposition, played well on her own or with Sharon. Like Sharon she was indiscriminate in her affections and would make physical contact with anyone who showed her attention.

Financial and physical conditions

The weakness of the Orange Book assessment can be clearly seen in the sections on finance and physical conditions. On the one hand it notes the stresses and strains of financial problems and acknowledges the existence of low incomes. On the other it talks of poor budgeting and counsels against an over concentration on practical assistance. It comments on the effect of environmental factors being sometimes beyond control but refers to individual responsibilities for adequate shelter and suggests a detailed examination of the property including 'drainage, water, lighting and heating'. It does not give a realistic impression of the major practical and personal stresses of bringing up children in poverty.

In Mary's case she had in my view worked near miracles with her privately rented house as a single parent on Income Support. She had obtained furniture, furnishings, equipment beyond what could have been expected. In social work reports however she was described as unable to prioritise her spending and manipulative.

The planning phase

In the planning phase, the information from all stages of the assessment is brought together and ordered in terms of positive features, negative features, necessary changes, helping factors, blocking factors, time scales, resources and goals. It is one of the positive features of the Orange Book that it offers a model for planning. However a weakness lies in its assumption of a common standard of good enough parenting and shared acceptance of the boundary between 'good enough' and 'not good enough' and in its focus on individual failure or success. Problems in these areas are further exacerbated by research deficits.

Aspects of the Brown family assessment and plan illustrate these factors. The situation was extremely complex, concerned with assessing risks of emotional or sexual abuse and the prospect for successful rehabilitation. There were many positive aspects in Sharon's situation. She had been physically well cared for, well stimulated and she related well to other adults and peers. On the negative side she had been sexually abused and exhibited an inappropriate knowledge of sexual language and behaviour. She behaved in a sexually provocative manner and showed no caution in her affection towards strangers.

Mary was open towards the social worker, showed good practical parenting skills, had survived a grossly abusive childhood. On the other hand she was at times cold towards her child. She appeared to put her need for a loving relationship for herself above her responsibilities as a parent and take risks in her choice of male companions. She had not had counselling about her childhood experiences.

These illustrations of the situation of Mary and Sharon could lay emphasis on Mary's individual responsibility, without attempting to locate this in an analysis of the psychological, social and economic pressures that contribute to Mary's needs for a man. To be a 'good enough' Mum by the yardstick of Western society, Mary must cope with poverty, unshared child care, isolation. She must sacrifice any needs of her own for those of her child. It would perhaps be interesting to compare whether a single father seeking love and companionship from women friends would be judged in the same way as was Mary. Evaluating the risks of continued separation, the chances of rehabilitation, the risks of a precipitated return home, the risk of further sexual abuse and attempting to judge Mary's parenting capacities, highlighted the question of common standards and research deficits. There were in my authority current professional disagreements about Mary as a parent, reflecting earlier clashes in another authority. Mary was seen by one worker as irresponsible, feckless, unable to cooperate with professionals, unable to take proper precautions to protect her child. However a Guardian ad litem pointed out that Mary had reported the original abuse, had undergone difficulties to maintain contact with her child in care, had made efforts to get a home together and was the object of Sharon's attachment. On one side, the possible effects of a quick return home and a subsequent breakdown together with exposure to suspect male figures were cited and on the other, the risks of continued separation and the dangers of a life in care. 'Patterns and Outcomes in Child Placement' (DoH 1991a) and 'Going Home' (Bullock et al 1993) could be cited to support both the risks of prolonged care and a hurried rehabilitation. Discussion of local professionals on the subject of sexual abuse tended to be general, outside the family and social context. What research evidence was there to support the idea that Sharon would be at risk of sexual abuse? A study assessing risk of sexual abuse (Waterhouse & Carnie 1992) highlights the lack of research evidence for reliable predictions of risk and reinforces Higginson's (1990) findings that social workers are forced to use their own judgements, taking into account their experiences, observations and what factual evidence may exist. This process may be reasonable, but cannot be consistent. It is subject to a continuous effort to balance safety with general welfare and development. Individual beliefs and values will remain influential. The Orange Book cannot provide a solution to these problems.

In formulating the plan, in this case, I tried to draw on a feminist, empowering approach, rather than the individualistic and family dysfunction perspective which appears to pervade the Orange Book. My aim was to address Mary's unmet needs, recognise the structural aspects of her situation and plan to help her recognise those factors she shared with others at the same time as the individuality of her problems and gain strength through that understanding. The ideal plan would have included a swift return home for Sharon, with substantial daily support in the home. Limited resources ruled out this option. The final plan was for intensive short term work with Mary and Sharon before Sharon went home, then a substantial but less intensive support, for the family and for Mary in her own right. This plan was followed and Sharon returned home.

A final issue at the planning stage is the question of resources. A common argument and the basis of the purchaser/provider separation is that assessments should be made purely on the basis of need, without reference to availability of resources for the implementation of the assessment plan. However, in an assessment involving decisions about rehabilitation and risk of emotional and sexual abuse it would be unethical not to give consideration to the possibility of abuse arising from the inadequacies of the care system. All aspects need to be clearly evaluated in an assessment. A plan for achieving change must be based in reality, if it is to be of any use to those whose task is to carry it through. A balance must be sought between tailoring an assessment to resources available and arguing for an unachievable plan.

The planning for the Brown family and the problems of specialisation

The last of my themes concerns some of the negative consequences of the process of specialisation within Child Protection. In Sharon and Mary's case the separation of the process of assessment as a specialist activity resulted in a delay in coherent planning. It increased the length of time Sharon and Mary were separated, thus affecting the outcome of plans to rehabilitate. It also meant that they were involved with 4 social workers over a period of weeks. One may only imagine what this indicated to Mary, already seen to have a problem of establishing long term relationships or to Sharon whose short life had been filled with transient adult figures. It is something of a contradiction to be saying that one sign of a healthy family is its ability to 'make and sustain deep and warm relationships' while expecting that family to share its most painful problems with a number of interchangeable professionals.

Summary of evaluation and conclusion

I have considered the processes and practices of assessment, using the Orange Book, and have attempted to identify positive and negative elements of assessment both as a general activity and in this individual piece of work.

The model used in the Orange Book is comprehensive and systematic, enabling a full picture, based on factual evidence, to be built up. It offers some useful tools such as ecomap, genogram and the flow chart. However, it is largely dependent on a question and answer approach, which worked with Mary but would have been less appropriate in the case of a less forthcoming and articulate parent. Work with children is always likely to need the use of toys and games to gain access to the information needed. The individualistic bias was a problem. While structural factors influencing family functioning might be recognised, the assessment is still directed at individual abilities to cope. It does not offer a framework for looking at an empowering approach and the need for structural change. All Equal under the Act (MacDonald 1991) is more helpful in its approach. As is the new Framework (DoH et al 2000).

This particular assessment illustrates some of the problems arising from the lack of a universally agreed yardstick of 'good enough' parenting and the influence of value judgements on the interpretation of evidence. Thus in the case of the Brown family one could focus on the positive aspects of Sharon and her relationship with Mary together with the risks of long term care and hasten a return home. Another view would be to stress the problems in Mary's and Sharon's relationship and the risks of sexual abuse and therefore delay a return home. This difficulty can be compounded by the lack of research evidence (as is the case when assessing potential risk factors in the area of sexual abuse) and points up the problems and complexities in attempting to protect a child while at the same time promoting the child's wishes and long term interests.

While acknowledging a number of unresolved issues inevitable in complex human situations, I believe these should not obscure the significant benefit to child care practice of an emphasis on bringing together clear and comprehensive information. Nor are all the difficulties insurmountable. With Mary I was able to work with her not only to address her individual views and needs, but to build into the assessment plans to promote awareness of the factors in her life situation which she shared with other mothers in similar situations. Ideas to support and strengthen her sense of power and control could be developed. Value judgements can be acknowledged and taken account of and models continually evaluated in the light of new information. The Orange Book is helpful in noting that

> *The worker must remain receptive to the findings of research, and to new ideas and methods and continually evaluate what is offered both here and elsewhere. (p.5)*

In an assessment, the skill lies in using models and research findings to illuminate a problem within its social context, while always recognising that

> *human beings and families are unique and intervention must be specifically tailored to their particular needs and circumstances. (DoH, 1988, p.5)*

References

Adcock, D. & White, R. (eds) (1985) *Good Enough Parenting : a framework for assessment.* BAAF, Practice Series 12.

Baldwin, N. & Spencer, N. (1993) 'Deprivation and child abuse: implications for strategic planning in children's services.' *Children and Society,* 7, 4, 357-370.

Bebbington, A. & Miles, J. 'The Background of Children who enter Local Authority Care' *British Journal of Social Work,* 19, 5.

Bullock, R., Little M. & Millham, S. *(1993) Going Home: the return of children separated from their families.* Aldershot: Dartmouth.

Christopherson, R. J. (1988) 'Intra Cultural Variations in Perception of Child Abuse and Neglect: An examination of Public Attitudes in Gt. Britain and the Netherlands' . Paper to the VII International Congress on child Abuse & Neglect.

Children Act 1989. London: HMSO.

DoH (1986) *Inspection of the supervision of social workers in the assessment and monitoring of cases of child abuse when children, subject to a court order, have been returned home.* London: DHSS.

DoH (1988) *Protecting Children: a guide for soical workers undertaking a comprehensive assessment.* London: HMSO.

DoH (1989) *The Care of Children: Principles & Practice in Regulation and Guidance.* London: HMSO.

DoH (1991a) *Patterns and Outcomes in Child Placement.* London: HMSO.

DoH (1991b) *Working Together under the Children Act 1989.* London: HMSO.

DoH (1991c) *A Study of Inquiry Reports 1980 - 1989.* London: HMSO.

DoH (1995) *Child Protection: messages from research.* London: HMSO.

DoH/DfEE/Home Office (2000) *Framework for the Assessment of Children in Need and Their Families.* London: Stationery Office.

Finkelhor, D. (1986) *A Source Book on Child Sexual Abuse.* Beverley Hills: Sage.

Gawlinski, G., Carr, A., McDonnell, D. & Irving, N. (1988) 'Thurlow House Assessment For Families with Physically Abused Children' *Practice,* 208-220.

Higginson, S. (1990) Distorted Evidence. *Community Care* 17th May, pp.23-25.

Jones, D. Pickett, J., Oates, M. & Barbour,R. (1987) *Understanding Child Abuse.* London: Macmillan.

Macdonald, S. (1991) *All Equal under the Act?* REU London.

Macdonald, G. & Roberts, H. (1995) *What works in the early years: effective interventions for children and families in health, social welfare and child protection.* Barkingside: Barnardos.

MacLeod, M. & Saraga, E. (1988) 'Challenging the Orthodoxy: Towards a Feminist Theory & Practice'. *Feminist Review,* 28, 16-56.

Millham, S., Bullock, R. Hosie & Haak, M. (1986) *Lost in Care.* Dartington Research Group: Gower: Aldershot.

O'Hagan, K. (1989) *Working with Child Sex Abuse.* Milton Keynes: Open University Press.

Oaklander, U. (1978) *Windows to our Children.* Highland N.Y., The Gestalt Journal Press.

Parton, C. (1990) 'Gender Oppression & Child Abuse in' *Taking Child Abuse Seriously;* Violence Against Children Study Group.

Stainton Rogers, W., Hevey, P. & Ash, E. (eds) (1989) 'Taking the Child Abuse Debate Apart' in *Child Abuse & Neglect.* Open University.

Thoburn, J. (1990) *Success & Failure in Permanent Family Placement.* Aldershot: Avebury.

Waterhouse, L. & Carnie, J. (1992) 'Assessing Child Protection Risk'. *British Journal of Social Work,* 2, 47-6.

16
Assessing family strengths

Vivienne Barnes

When I asked Jane (mother) about her understanding of the Core Group Plan for Claire, she carefully stated the agreed plan for family assessment as requested by the Court. There was then a brief silence before she asked, 'What does an assessment mean? (Rushton 1992).

What does an assessment mean?

Assessments are currently the cornerstone of social work, both under Community Care legislation and in work with children and families. The detailed forms required for Comprehensive Assessments to enable, for example, an admission to a residential home, are matched by the detail of information required by social workers in carrying out risk assessments in child protection work.

The parent quoted in the above piece of research into the functioning of 'Core Group Reviews' was clear that she did not know what an 'assessment' means. But how clear are social workers about the meaning of an assessment? What is the meaning and function; and how free are assessments from value-laden judgements?

In this chapter, I shall examine some of the issues surrounding family assessment work; how assessments by social workers are influenced by values; how they are affected by issues of, for example, race, gender, class and disability. I shall also look at the relevance of predictive studies for social workers engaged in the assessment of risk and likely outcomes in family situations.

I shall illustrate some of the issues and pitfalls of assessment work with a case history of a 12 year old boy who had been physically assaulted by his mother's partner. I was involved in assessing risks and likely outcomes if he went to live with his natural father and stepmother.

Central to my analysis is the consideration of children's wishes and feelings in the assessment process; seeing the assessment as a shared task between professionals, carers and children. I shall refer to the different requirements involved in assessment for differing social work purposes - for example a fostering placement or placement with relatives. Some of the pressures which have led to changes in legislation will be considered.

Values and anti-discriminatory practice

A social worker or any other professional who has to assess the strengths of families will necessarily bring to the task her or his own personal values. These are likely to be linked to views and prejudices arising from personal experience of families as a child and as an adult. Societal influences also need to be understood, media and political images of the happy family with two perfect looking white parents and two children. This mythology underpins political propaganda about 'a return to family values'.

In reality, the family outlined above is a minority experience in modern Britain and other Western countries (Stainton Rogers 1989). Experiences in families with a lone parent are common - most usually this parent is female. The experience of discrimination, for example by black or disabled parents can seriously undermine confidence in parenting; and this discrimination can easily be perpetuated and even compounded by professional workers (Diorio, 1992, PAIN 1992).

Standard assessment guidelines such as that of Polansky quoted in a much used text 'Good Enough Parenting' (Adcock and White 1985) emphasise white middle class values with traditional gender divisions, placing the onus of care of children (and thus the onus of blame if anything goes wrong) on women.

For example, Polansky's 'Childhood level of living scale' suggests ratings based on whether:

> *Mother plans meals with courses that go together.*
> *Child has been taken fishing.*
> *There are dirty dishes and utensils in rooms other than the kitchen.*

Other ratings which take no account of cultural differences concern the setting of bedtimes, saying prayers before meals, whether there are many books in the household and the state of repair of the home. Some of these clearly show prejudice against those who attempt to provide parental care whilst living in poverty.

The Department of Health guide to assessments *Protecting Children* (DoH 1988) contains similar but less extreme discriminatory attitudes, eg:

> *The incidence of mild depressive or anxiety states in child abusing mothers is ... quite high. Many of these women have quite flat personalities, low self-esteem and explicit physical symptoms such as headaches, tiredness etc. (p.50)*

The guide does not take account of the normal experience of women's isolation, tiredness and depression as child carers, as explored for example by Frude and Goss (1980) who found that 96% of mothers reported that they had days when 'everything got on top of them', and 57% admitted to hitting their child really hard at least once. The guide takes inadequate account of the extent to which responses and behaviour of parents - often it is mothers who are the focus of attention - may be related to the social and economic circumstances in which they are trying to provide care. The new Framework (DoH et al 2000) attempts to deal with some of these problems.

Stereotypical attitudes

Cultural and other discriminatory attitudes are not only unjust and stereotyping, they can be dangerous. For example, the inquiry into the death of Tyra Henry (London Borough of Lambeth, 1987) highlighted a lack of understanding and insensitivity in assessment of the needs of Tyra's grandmother, a black African Caribbean woman who was caring for Tyra. Because of the popular stereotype of African Caribbean women as capable and resilient against all the odds, Tyra's grandmother was afforded little assistance by professional workers, with the consequence that she could not cope and let Tyra return to her mother, who in turn was unable to cope, with fatal consequences.

Sensitivity to individuals and to different ways of bringing up children is therefore, a vital element in any assessment. When social workers are attempting to carry out an assessment of a family, where they have little understanding of cultural issues, they are likely to need the assistance of workers who do understand (Ahmad, 1990).

Negative attitudes are frequently expressed by professional workers towards women in families where a child has been abused by a male partner. Women are habitually regarded by society as the natural protectors of children; and where a child is physically injured or sexually abused, women are often blamed as much as the male perpetrators, because they were unable to protect the child. Parton (1990) and Macleod and Saraga (1988) expose professional attitudes which avoid an accurate assessment of male responsibility for many acts of abuse. Women tend to bear the brunt of child protection procedural hassles, even when they are not directly blamed (Barnes 1993). It is usually women who take their children to be medically examined and who are asked to attend case conferences, women who have to allow professional workers into their homes and show willingness to cooperate with complex time-consuming protection plans.

All these possibilities need to be evaluated by a worker embarking on an assessment of family strengths and needs. Other, more apparently objective criteria also need scrutiny.

Predictive studies

All children's assessments focus on the need to consider potential risk to a child within the family. The Jasmine Beckford enquiry report (London Borough of Brent, 1985) advocated the possibility of predicting the likelihood of child abuse; and predictive elements such as step parenting and previous incidents of abuse were cited. Predictive studies aim to make family assessments an objective and exact science. Studies such as that of Greenland (1987) suggest that factors such as parental abuse of drugs or alcohol, history of suicidal attempts, criminal assaults, a step parent carer and a previous history of abuse or neglect, should be taken into account as predictors of child abuse.

Browne and Saqi in Browne Davies and Stratton (1988) report their quite sophisticated research into predictive elements. A complicated two stage screening process was operated. This was able to predict one case of child abuse out of seventeen which could have been expected from the indicators. Clearly, there is a long way to go before risk assessment becomes an exact science. The only universally quoted factor predictive of abuse appears to be evidence of previous abuse.

What are the implications for social workers in practice? Many research studies examine family weaknesses and do not consider their strengths. The following case study illustrates how an assessment can benefit from focusing on family strengths also, and involving carers and children in the process.

Case study - assessing family strengths

Martin's family history

Information for the case study came from Social Services' records dating back ten years and my own more recent involvement as social worker with the family because of Martin's alleged abuse.

Martin was the youngest of four children born to Annette. She moved from her native Belgium to England after marrying John, whom she met whilst he was working abroad. The couple had two children, Fiona and Anthony, before the marriage broke down. Annette then remarried and had a third child, Julia. Martin was the only child of her third marriage to Sam, which ended five years before the alleged abuse.

The names and some of the circumstances of the child and family have been changed to ensure confidentiality.

Neither of the older children, Fiona nor Anthony, had lived at the home for approximately five years. According to records they had both moved to foster care at around the age of fourteen because of Annette's rejection of them. Therefore the family unit, living at the family home for the past five years, had consisted of Annette, her children Julia and Martin, and sometimes Annette's current partner.

Both Martin and his sister Julia told me that they were brought up to be fairly independent. Martin said that he was unable to rely on consistency with regard to meals, bedtimes, etc, and he and Julia did a lot of the household tasks. I saw evidence of his mother's heavy drinking, and the children said that this had become more of a problem since Annette's partner, Fred, moved into the family home eighteen months previously.

Annette had been made redundant from her work which had given her a lot of personal satisfaction and self-esteem. Since that time the family had to cope with living on the bare minimum finance which Income Support affords. Annette was an assertive woman who could be loving towards her children and great fun to be with. However, possibly because of her dissatisfaction with her own life, she could switch to being hostile and cold, and Martin said he found this frightening and bewildering.

From my work with Julia and Martin, I observed that they had developed a very close relationship, possibly in part because of their shared difficulties.

Involvement of Martin's family with social services

The family had been known to the local Social Services Department for approximately ten years. Annette had used the service for financial and emotional support with her family and for day care. Social workers were involved in the 'reception into care' of Fiona and later of Anthony. There was also an allegation by Annette that Martin had been sexually abused by his older brother Anthony, before the latter left home. This allegation was denied by both boys. Other child protection issues included concerns by neighbours and acquaintances that the children were left on their own whilst Annette went out to the local pub, and that they were left with inadequate food. Upon investigation, these allegations were denied both by Annette and by her children and declared malicious by Annette.

Shortly after Fred, Annette's new partner, moved into the family home there was a violent row between Julia, her mother and Fred. Julia left and went to stay at the home of her boyfriend's parents. From that time, Martin was the only child in the household.

Alleged abuse

It was only at his mother's instigation, when she said that she herself had been assaulted by Fred, that Martin reported Fred's repeated serious assaults on him.

Martin said that his mother had ordered a taxi to tell the police but had then asked Martin to go on his own. Martin showed the police bruises to his back and legs which he said were the result of assaults by Fred. He described several recent incidents.

He said that his mother and Fred returned from drinking one night recently and he woke to the sound of breaking glass. He claimed that Fred grabbed him by the throat and hit him about the throat and body. He said that he hit his head on a chest of drawers during the assault. He claimed that he was too frightened to explain to anyone at the time how the bruises occurred. Martin described another recent incident when Fred and his mother had been drinking. Martin had run to a friend's house because Fred had lashed out at him. After he had returned the next day, Fred allegedly threatened him that he would 'leave in bits' if he ran away again. Martin's back was bruised mid-centre along the spine and he said that this was caused as he was being forced backwards against a table towards the wall. Martin said that a few days later he heard a crash in the dining room. He ran in and allegedly saw Fred with clenched fists and his mother lying on the floor. He said that Fred picked up a chair and threw it at him. It allegedly caught his ear which was sore for some hours. Martin said that Fred had told him he would be 'battered' if he told anyone.

According to Martin, his mother changed her mind after sending him to the police; and she denied any assault to herself or to Martin. He was left feeling puzzled and betrayed. Julia also, having initially supported Martin's stand with regard to Fred, changed her allegiance and supported her mother.

Despite these pressures on him, Martin decided that it would be preferable to leave home and go into foster care rather than to return and face the threats and actual violence meted out to him by Fred. There appeared little scope at this stage for work to reunite Martin with his mother as both she and her partner denied that there was any problem for Martin at home. Care proceedings were instigated by the Local Authority following the recommendations of a child protection conference.

Martin asked that his father, Sam, be contacted; and contact was established between father and son shortly thereafter. They had not seen one another for approximately five years. Sam had moved away and remarried.

It soon became apparent that Sam had a genuine desire to care for his son and a lot to offer in terms of his material and emotional well-being. An assessment was needed of this potential placement for Martin with his father.

Legal context of placement with relatives

With regard to the rehabilitation of children to parents, laws have changed with the changing emphasis on the rights of various interest groups, in part as a result of public concerns expressed through various pressure groups. The main protagonists in this field are:

1.   Parents and groups concerned with parents, and family rights.
2.   Children and those concerned with children's rights.
3.   Local Authorities and Central Government/Policies on state intervention move along a continuum of state control at one end and family control at the other.

In the Children and Young Persons' Act 1969, rehabilitation to family care is discussed mainly in terms of 'Revocation of the Care Order' and 'Home on Trial'. There is little emphasis on the Local Authority's duty to encourage parents or other relatives or friends to resume or take over the care of a child who is the subject of a Care Order. The restrictions on parents' and relatives rights are given more emphasis. The Child Care Act 1980 placed emphasis on rehabilitation from Voluntary Care. An Authority with a child in Voluntary Care, must 'endeavour to secure that the care of the child is taken over by a parent or relative or a friend where this is consistent with the child's welfare' (S.2(3)). Advice, material and financial assistance could be offered by the Local Authority (S.1(1)).

Home on Trial placements were not clearly regulated by the Children and Young Persons Act 1969 until in 1989 the Charge and Control Regulations 1988 were implemented. This followed a number of child death inquiries, and concerns that children were not adequately protected when at home, even when still subject of Care Orders. The Jasmine Beckford Inquiry 'A Child in Trust,' (1985) was particularly influential in this regard. The Charge and Control Regulations were introduced to ensure that more thorough investigation, assessment and review of children on Care Orders placed with relatives was undertaken.

Children Act 1989

Following the inquiry report on Cleveland (1987), more emphasis was placed on the rights of parents and other relatives and the part they should play in a child's life. This occurred because of the public perception that in Cleveland, children were removed from their parents without full investigation or assessment by the local authority of the potential of parents and other relatives to care for the children. In the Children Act 1989 the family is seen to include a wider network than hitherto. It is expected that there will often be someone within the network who is willing to, and capable of, caring for a child.

The Children Act 1989 brought about a potential loosening of local authority control with regard to placements with relatives, at least during the process before a Care Order is made, i.e. at the Interim Order stage. A relative or friend can apply for a Residence Order, and in theory this could be granted without any investigation of the applicant. In practice, however, courts are wary of making such a decision without an assessment of some kind. The nature of the assessment, however, depends on individual authorities, local practices and can therefore, vary enormously.

Different types of assessments

Child care assessments within Social Services are required for a number of purposes and require a variety of depth, detail and investigation. For example, assessments of prospective adopters and foster carers are among the most detailed, with lengthy prescribed formats. The local authority is accountable to society for the care provided to children by these carers, and has responsibility for choice of placement.

Potential childminders and private foster carers undergo a much less extensive assessment by the local authority. Parents are regarded as retaining their responsibility for the child care provided by these groups.

For assessments of placements with relatives such as that in my case study, there were no clear guidelines in the local authority in which I was currently working. The situation both legally and in terms of policy and practice was far from clear.

The DoH guidelines for 'Charge and Control' placements (1988) (changed to the 'Placement with Parents etc' under the Children Act 1989) stated that the aim of assessment should be 'to identify all the factors which contribute to a general picture of the carer, her family and way of life'. Under both sets of regulations, written references are required from all agencies who may be involved or have relevant information, i.e. police, probation, health, education and personal references are also required. In the local authority for which I was working, a short report was required and the placement approved at middle management level. If court proceedings were still pending or there was some legal dispute about child's residence, a statement could also be needed for court.

Assessment of Martin's situation

It may be argued that it is desirable for assessments to be undertaken by a worker who is not already directly involved in a case. A worker who is already involved may have preconceived views and wishes about the outcome of the assessment; and this can therefore, be 'professionally dangerous'(Dale et al., 1986). In Martin's case I was hopeful that the assessment would prove positive as this seemed to be the best hope for Martin's future, compared with the uncertainty of fostering or the return to the terror experienced at his mother's home. Unfortunately, resources frequently do not meet with demands in social work, and there was no worker available to do an independent assessment when this was needed. I was, therefore, careful at all stages of the process to check my perceptions with my supervisor.

My assessment in this case was based on:

1. What was known of Sam's history from Social Services' records, and from the account of his ex wife, his current wife, and himself.
2. Visits and discussions with Sam and his wife, Kathy.
3. My observations and those of the foster carers of Sam's and Kathy's interactions with Martin during contact visits.
4. Checks with, and information from, relevant agencies and referees.
5. Examination and consideration of Martin's reactions to his father and Kathy by myself in conjunction with my supervisor.
6. Consideration of the views of Martin and his proposed carers about the placement.

Assessment: Looking at strengths

Guidelines for assessing family strengths were not widely available. The DoH *Protecting Children* (1988), and a locally-developed, more 'user friendly' framework for assessments (see chapter by Over, McCarrick and Wood) were used in this case to build a positive picture of the carers, while my assessment of Martin's needs and feelings about the possible placement used Fahlberg (1981) and lifestory books and guidelines.

Relationship between Sam and Kathy

In making an assessment of Sam's relationship with his second wife, Kathy, and the couple's relationship with Martin, the DoH 'Protecting Children,' publication (1988) was a useful resource, particularly the sections 'Individual Profile of Parents, ' The Couple Relationship', 'Networks', 'Finance', and 'Physical Conditions'. Although the publication is more commonly used for risk assessments following child protection investigations, it can provide useful checklists for other assessments.

Sam's relationship with Kathy, his second wife, appeared to be settled and stable. Sam said that he gradually learned to trust her, which was difficult for him at first because of the negative experiences of his first marriage. Kathy had a large supportive family network, some of whom I met during visits. There were many leisure activities which they enjoyed together, e.g. sailing and fishing, which Martin also loved.

For Kathy, forging a new relationship with Martin from scratch, it was important that she was aware of potential shifts in the balance of her relationship with her husband if Martin came to live with them. She had two grown up children from her first marriage who had left home, but were living nearby. Her previous experience of bringing up children within her first marriage and subsequently with her second husband, gave her a useful understanding of shifts in family dynamics. Kathy said that she did not think it would be easy taking Martin into the family.

As a couple, their behaviour with Martin showed understanding and patience. For example, despite Sam's excitement at the possibility of at last being together with his son, he was able to contain his disappointment when contact had to be stopped for a month because legal objections to this continuing were thought to be in force. He was able to help Martin through this difficult time by keeping in touch by telephone and sending cards and letters.

Agency checks and references on Sam and Kathy were all positive except a previous conviction of Sam (see below).

Martin's reactions

Martin himself never wavered in his wish to be with his father and he found it hard to consider that life might not be one hundred percent perfect if he went to live there. Father and son found that they had a lot in common in their personalities and their hobbies.

Assessment - considering possible weaknesses

Clearly an assessment cannot be complete without some consideration of potential risks and weaknesses. In this case most of these appeared to be concerning events in Sam's past.

Sam's history was known to Social Services from five years previously, when he was married to Martin's mother. This history gave cause for concern in relation to many of the factors associated with abuse by Greenland (1987).

Sam had a tempestuous relationship with Martin's mother, Annette. He had on one occasion attempted suicide because of his jealousy over his wife's infidelity. He had also been convicted of Grievous Bodily Harm against her, and had been moved to a Probation Hostel. He admitted that they had indulged in very heavy drinking.

Martin's mother was awarded custody of Martin and Julia when her marriage to Sam broke down. Sam's access to them was denied by the matrimonial court. However, he continued to try to communicate with the children and to send Christmas and Birthday cards. Annette tried to stop this. She said that she felt aggrieved because her ex-husband still owed her money.

In detailed discussion with Sam himself, he was honest about the events of his first marriage, about the heavy drinking that they both indulged in and his extreme jealous rage when his wife stayed out at night and when he heard from acquaintances and from Annette herself about her other men friends. Sam was aware that there was no excuse for his violent behaviour. However, he felt that he had been young and inexperienced at that time, and thought that he had changed and matured.

Another negative indicator regarding the potential placement for Martin, according to some predictive studies, is that he would be with a step-parent. The risk of abuse by step parents is addressed by Ward in Stainton Rogers et al (1989). Ward quotes from Neustatter (1986) that step parents implicated in abuse tended to be men, and from Finkelhor (1984) that the common notion that step parents are more likely to abuse than natural parents, is not supported by research. He concludes that substitute parenting, however, is on the whole experienced as more demanding and less rewarding than natural parenting.

Since Kathy was likely to be the carer with primary responsibility for Martin, by virtue of the fact that she was female and that gender roles within the family were traditional, this was a vital area for discussion. With some encouragement, both Martin and his father were able to look critically at their expectations of Kathy. They became more willing to share the extra tasks that would be involved in Martin's move into the family.

Work with Martin: Assessment and preparation

Work with the child involved in a family placement is a vital part of the process of assessment. I undertook work with Martin prior to placement to check out his feelings, and subsequently to prepare him for a move from the foster home where he had settled very well.

Martin was a very rewarding child to work with in many ways. He was lively, enthusiastic and unusually articulate for his age. However, his verbal skills could easily deceive the worker about the level of his understanding. Information given to him needed to be checked out several times to be sure he had got it . Martin hated writing. His academic ability was well below average - at this stage it was not clear whether this might be related to disruptions and stress throughout his childhood. Our written work together was always kept simple. I often wrote down the thoughts and ideas he expressed, for example for reviews and in some of the exercises we did to help him assess his situation.

Examples of assessment work with Martin

In one work session, I used the list of feelings reproduced in Fahlberg (1981, p.25). I had to shorten the list and simplify it, as many of the words are too complicated even for a very bright 12 year old (see appendix 2).

I was hoping to help Martin express and understand some of his feelings about his mother and father, as part of the process of enabling him to participate in decisions about his own future.

Martin was asked to close his eyes and remember the last time he saw his mother, to remember where they were, what clothes he was wearing and some of the things they said. I then asked Martin to underline three of the words on the list that best described his feelings at the time. Martin underlined *puzzled, frightened, miserable*.

The occasion of seeing his mother had been a recent supervised contact visit at Social Services. We talked about each of the feelings in turn. For example, Martin explained that he was 'puzzled' still because his mother had told him to go to the police and complain about Fred's treatment of himself and her. She had even called the taxi, and Martin had thought she was coming with him at first. Now she was angry with him for having told the police. I asked Martin to think why his mother might have changed her mind. He said he thought she was frightened of not being able to get back in her house if she told on Fred. He felt hurt that this was more important to her than himself. I reminded Martin that his mother wanted him to return now. Perhaps she had hoped that the police would come back with Martin and remove Fred. Martin agreed this was possible, and felt happier with this version of events. We talked about checking this out with his mother, but had to accept this would not be possible at present since she would not say a word against Fred. Martin thought this was because she was frightened of Fred.

We talked about the other feelings Martin had identified. Discussion of his feeling 'miserable' led to talking about his mother's anger, vented at Martin because he wished to go and live with his father. Martin had not previously been fully aware of his mother's angry feelings about his father and what had caused these. Martin was able to get some idea of his mother's perspective from talking about this and to keep the 'emotional door' open for her.

Next, I asked Martin to close his eyes and remember the last time he saw his father in the same way as he had done with his mother. He underlined the feelings *excited, happy, worried*.

Martin had last seen his father at a contact visit at the foster home. At that time, his father made him 'happy' and he was 'excited' about the visits and 'worried' that something would happen to stop him seeing his Dad. His father took him for nice meals, told him stories about fishing and joked with him. Discussion of his feelings led to talking about whether it would be so good if Martin actually lived with his father and Kathy. Martin was not sure that all families had arguments. We talked about some of the other families Martin knew well, like that of his schoolfriend, David, and the foster family. Martin could see that in these families, which he felt were happy ones generally, people still fell out and shouted at one another sometimes. We also talked about the newness being exciting and how this can wear off and about Kathy's feelings when Martin and his father were so excited and happy. Martin was able to see that she might feel left out if they were not careful.

This discussion appeared to achieve its purpose of helping Martin to be more realistic about life at his father's.

In another work session, Martin and I used the idea of the child's 'Ecomap' adapted from the reproduction in Fahlberg (1981 p39), a graphic representation of one's world at the time, including houses, school, significant people, etc (see Appendix 1). I drew this out for Martin on a large sheet of paper, putting in extra details that would be appropriate to his life experience. I explained to Martin that this was a picture of his world, and that we could look at it when he had finished filling in his own personal details to see if there was anything he needed any help with at the moment.

Martin had fun filling it in and spent time colouring, especially his father's house. When he had finished we spent time talking about what he had written, much of which was self-explanatory, e.g. in 'Things I like to do' he had written 'football', 'ride my bike'. Martin had written 'Julia' under 'I worry about' and this led to a discussion about people and things Martin would miss if he moved, and ways of keeping in touch.

Martin was worried about leaving his sister Julia behind. She had recently moved back home again and Martin was afraid that she might be harmed by Fred. Martin felt he was letting her down by moving away. I asked Martin how he felt when Julia had moved out last year. He said he was pleased she was safe then, because Fred had attacked her; but said he had missed her. Martin could see from this that Julia might feel the same way about him leaving. We talked about Julia having somewhere to go if she wanted to leave (i.e. her boyfriend's parents' house) and this reassured him. We also talked about ways of keeping in touch with Julia by letter or telephone, even if initially direct contact would not be possible because of their mother's restrictions.

We considered Martin's list of friends that he had written on the Ecomap. Martin said he would really miss the boys in his neighbourhood that he grew up with. He had relied on them when things were bad at home. Again, we talked about keeping in touch with people by letter and phone; and we drew pictures of letters and phones, and lines for links with people on the Ecomap. At first Martin was not very keen on the idea of writing and needed to be persuaded that it was not like school work, and that spelling and neatness did not matter so much. Martin's father and Kathy had already promised that friends could visit if he moved there and we agreed it would be a good idea to talk to them again about this and about contact with Julia.

Martin said he would also miss his school and football team. We talked about the new school, having to make new friends there and perhaps trying to join the football team. As I was due to visit the school I promised Martin I would talk to the staff there about football at the school and let him know what was going on there.

Another important factor in Martin's preparation was the self protection work undertaken, to try to help Martin feel more confident about summoning help should he again find himself the target of abusive behaviour. Martin felt very positive about having told the police of Fred's assaults, even though this had happened at his mother's instigation and she had later denied it. However, he was worried that in a similar situation, i.e. if threatened and bullied by a powerful man, he would feel intimidated and be unable to tell anyone. I assured Martin that most children and also adults found it difficult to act against a powerful bully. Martin considered whether self defence classes would be useful to him, but agreed that against somebody nearly twice his size, fighting back might put him in further danger. Michelle Elliot's book 'Keeping Safe' (1986) was a good aid to discussion. Martin came to realise that he had done absolutely the right thing by telling adults with the power to take appropriate action, i.e. the police.

Consequently, we worked out a list of people and phone numbers which might be useful to him if and when he moved. Martin was reluctant to consider that he might need to use these at his father's home, but did agree to take this precaution. Our list included my phone number, local Social Services, Childline and the local police. We agreed that we would add to the list when Martin discovered more local people he could trust, and Martin undertook to make sure that he always had money for the phone.

Assessment conclusions

From all the assessment work undertaken it was found that the most important positive indicators about Martin's proposed placement with his father and stepmother were:

1. The commitment and enthusiasm for the placement on the part of all three parties (Sam, Kathy and Martin).
2. The apparent harmony and stability of Sam and Kathy's relationship and family life.
3. The fact that all three had made successful adaptations to changes in important relationships in the past (both Sam and Kathy had adapted to their second marriages; and Martin had adapted well to his move to a foster home).
4. Although Sam had exhibited some worrying behaviour in the past, he appeared to have matured and to have learnt from his experience.

One of the negative factors concerning the placement was the possibility that Martin might lose touch with people in his life who had been important to him, e.g. his mother and sister, and some of his friends. However, work could be undertaken to keep Martin's links with these people.

Ongoing assessment and counselling

Assessment is not a once and for all occurrence. The assessment process continued as a dialogue between myself and the family long after Martin had moved there. I had to make time to visit regularly in the early stages, despite problems of distance and pressures of other work. This was particularly important since the local Social Services Department, which had been informed prior to Martin's move, were unable for many months to undertake any monitoring work - although they were willing to respond to emergency requests by the family.

It was important for me to see Martin on his own to give him a chance to talk freely about his new life as well as to see everyone together as a family. On my visits, I also made sure to forge links with staff at Martin's school to facilitate good communication in case they were aware of problems Martin was experiencing.

Sam and Kathy were initially anxious for help on practical matters, e.g. Child Benefit transfer. They also wanted advice on Martin's bedwetting. This had been a concern before Martin's move, but stopped completely after 3 months at his father's. Martin's concerns were to do with settling in at school and finding new friends. He was feeling different and an outsider because of his accent and his newness. I engaged Martin's class teacher as an ally, as she had also recently moved there from Martin's area of the country; and she was able to offer him time and support with feeling different. Martin wanted to talk over his concerns about Julia and about his friends back home whom he was missing. Initially, Martin was the only young person at his father's home, and he found the change rather difficult to adjust to after having been in a foster home where there were lots of children of all ages. Consequently, Martin's father was pulled in as playmate and this led to a change in roles which was not always pleasing to Kathy. She found that to begin with, while Martin and his father were still in the initial excitement of the move, they tended to ally against her in a playful but irritating way. However, I helped the family talk over this difficulty and adjust their behaviour. The situation was also eased when Kathy's 21 year old son moved back home; and as Martin got to know him and they became friends, this eased the pressure on Sam and Kathy's relationship. Kathy complained of Martin's lack of routine with regard to personal cleanliness, but was able to make allowances when I explained to her about the complete lack of any such routine in his former home.

Contact

One of the most important issues throughout continued to be contact. The importance for children of contact with loved family members has been stressed in the Children Act 89. A lot of work on this issue has been done by the Family Rights Group whose publication 'Keeping Children and Families in Touch', (1986) contains useful research data and case histories. It stresses the importance of links with parents, siblings, grandparents and other family members.

Martin's contact with his family was an important issue before his move. Martin would not send his mother a Christmas card despite encouragement from myself and from his father and stepmother. I kept in touch with Martin's mother, but she did not respond to my repeated invitations to see Martin or to write to him. She appeared preoccupied and overwhelmed by her financial and domestic problems, particularly the ongoing violent behaviour of her partner, Fred. Martin himself thought he would never want to see his mother again, but agreed to keep this topic open for discussion. I also had to do some hard work with Sam and Kathy, who as Martin became more settled with them, felt that seeing his mother might upset him. We talked over the difficulty for children and their sense of loss if they cannot have contact with former loved ones.

Julia moved away from her mother's home again shortly after Martin's move to his father's, and this enabled her to express her wish for contact with Martin, which her mother had blocked. I took her to see Martin and they were extremely happy to be together and share news. They continued to write to one another and use the telephone for contact. I worked with Sam and Kathy to help them gradually to trust Julia enough to let her visit. Initially, they had been extremely worried that she might reveal their whereabouts to her mother, which would have been likely to cause a great deal of trouble for them as she was likely to harass them.

Conclusions

The assessment process outlined above illustrates some of the considerations necessary in any assessment of child placements.

It emphasises the value of building on perceived strengths as part of an ongoing process of assessment. It identifies the pitfalls of relying solely on known predictors of risk in child care, without a careful examination of the context of these and looking at other important positive factors in a family situation.

Above all, it illustrates the importance of involving those concerned, children, carers and others of significance in a child's life, in the process of assessment.

References

Adcock, M. & White, R. (1985) *Good Enough Parenting: A Framework for Assessment*. London: British Agencies for Adoption and Fostering.

Ahmad, B. (1990) *Black Perspectives in Social Work*. Birmingham: Venture Press.

Barnes, K. V. (1993) 'Information and Advice in Child Protection Investigations'. *Unpublished research, University of Warwick*.

Browne, K. & Saqi, S. (1988) 'Approaches to Screening for Child Abuse and Neglect' in Browne, Davies & Stratton (eds): *Early Prediction and Prevention of Child Abuse*. Wiley and Sons.

Child Care Act 1980 London: HMSO.

Children Act 1989 London: HMSO.

Children and Young Persons Act 1969. London: HMSO.

Charge and Control Regulations (1988) *Accommodation of Children*. DoH.

Dale, P., Davies, M., Morrison, T. & Waters, J. (1986) *Dangerous Families*. London: Routledge.

DoH (1988) *Protecting Children: a Guide for Social Workers Undertaking a Comprehensive Assessment*. London: HMSO.

DoH/DfEE/Home Office (2000) *Framework for the Assessment of Children in Need and Their Families*. London: Stationery Office.

Diorio, W. (1992) 'Parental Perceptions of the Authority of Child Welfare Caseworkers' *Journal of Contemporary Human Services*, Family Service America pp 223-235.

Elliott, M. (1986) *Keeping Safe: a Practical Guide to Talking with Children*. London: Bedford Square Press.

Fahlberg, V. (1981) *Helping children when they must move*. London: British Agencies for Adoption and Fostering.

Family Rights Group (1986) 'Promoting Links', *Keeping Children and Families in Touch*. London.

Finkelhor, D. (1984) 'Child Sexual Abuse', *New Theory and Research*. New York: Free Press.

Frude, N., & Goss, A. (1980) 'Maternal Anger and the Young Child' in Frude, N. (Ed) *Psychological Approaches to Child Abuse*. Batsford.

Greenland, C. (1987) *Preventing CAN Deaths: An International Study of Deaths Due to Child Abuse and Neglect*. London: Tavistock.

London Borough of Brent (1985) *A Child in Trust*: The report of the Inquiry into the circumstances surrounding the death of Jasmine Beckford

London Borough of Lambeth (1987) *Whose Child?: Report of the Public Inquiry into the death of Tyra Henry*.

MacLeod, M., & Saraga, E. (1988): 'Challenging the Orthodoxy: Towards a Feminist Theory and Practice. *Feminist Review*: No 28, Spring.

Neustatter, A. (1986) 'The Wicked Stepfather'. *The Guardian*, 10th June 1986.

PAIN (Parents Against Injustice) (1992): *Child Abuse Investigations: The Families' Perspective*. Stansted: PAIN

Parton, C. (1990) 'Women, Gender, Oppression and Child Abuse' in Violence Against Children

Study Group, *Taking Child Abuse Seriously*. London:Unwin Hyman.

Rushton, J. (1992) 'Core Group Reviews' *Unpublished research*, University of Warwick.

Secretary of State for Social Services (1988) *Report of the Inquiry into Child Abuse in Cleveland 1987*. London: HMSO.

Stainton Rogers, W. (1989) in Stainton Rogers, Hevey & Ash, eds *Child Abuse and Neglect* Milton Keynes: Open University

Ward, A (1989) 'Caring for Other People's Children', in Stainton Rogers, Hevey & Ash (eds) *Child Abuse and Neglect* Milton Keynes: Open University.

Appendix 1. Child's EcoMap

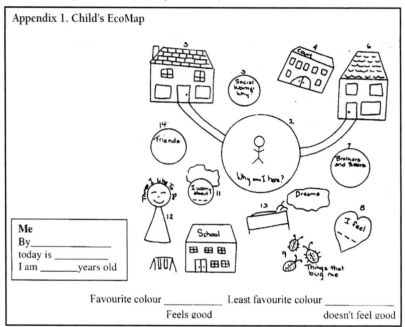

Me
By_____
today is _____
I am _____years old

Favourite colour _____ Least favourite colour _____
Feels good   doesn't feel good

Appendix 2

Abandoned	Deserted	Ignored	Resistant
Afraid	Disappointed	Lazy	Sad
Angry	Embarked	Left out	Scared
Betrayed	Excited	Lonely	Strange
Brave	Fearful	Mad	Terrible
Cheerful	Foolish	Mean	Threatened
Concerned	Fortunate	Miserable	Trapped
Condemned	Furious	Naughty	Unafraid
Confused	Happy	Out of control	Wicked
Contented	Hate	Powerful	Wonderful
Curious	Helpless	Puzzled	Worried
Delighted	Homesick	Rejected	
Depressed	Hurt	Relieved	

17
A partnership approach in working with a family

Chris McCarrick

This chapter describes work which I undertook in a family where a boy of four years had been placed on the child protection register after fingertip bruising had been noticed at his nursery. The case was allocated to me when the colleague who had been responsible for the investigation and follow up work for four months left the department. I had been involved in a home visit with him during the investigation.

Details of the family, the background to registration and a summary of the work done before I took on the case are given. Issues arising from the early work in the case - including problems of labelling, judgemental attitudes and use of jargon, are discussed. The attempts made to engage with the family following some difficulties in this early period are described. The way in which I attempted to recognise power relationships whilst working towards partnership, and to recognise the expertise of the parents and build on their strengths, is explored.

Case summary

Family			
	Mother	Janet K	33 years old
	Father	Peter K	28 years old
		Sean K	4 years old
		Adrian K	3 years 3 months old
		Ian K	1 year 9 months old

The family had recently moved from a small terraced house to a large three storeyed house. To do this they had taken on a large mortgage. Peter was in regular full time work, paid at average industrial earnings. Conditions were basic rather than comfortable.

In July Sean was referred to the Social Services Department because fingertip bruising had been noticed on his thigh. The parents gave an account of rough play by Sean and Adrian which had resulted in broken crockery. Father smacked Sean. He acknowledged what he had done with regret. All the children were taken for a medical examination, with parents' agreement. No other signs of abuse were observed. However the investigation highlighted several safety aspects of household arrangements which needed attention. Detailed explanations were given to the parents of child protection procedures, legal requirements and possible responses, as well as their rights and options at every stage.

Following a case conference, all the children's names were placed on the register. The male worker involved in the investigation was appointed as key worker. The main focus of the work in the first few months was monitoring the situation, particularly looking for any further bruising.

Work with the family

When I was allocated the case I thought it important to reassess needs and problems, to identify specific areas of work, to agree goals with parents, to aim for open and active participation. My intention was to help in a practical way in order to erase the parents' sense of 'being spied on'.

In describing the process of my work, I shall try to give an overall picture and look critically at events, judgements, action and inaction which had an effect on the family's progress.

Information available

At the time of the case conference, a number of issues of concern were noted. I had criticisms of the way some of these concerns were described, and the evidence on which they were based. My criticisms and questions follow the concerns, in brackets.

1. Yale lock on the bedroom door which the children could not reach.
2. The children were sleeping on the top floor and the parents on the ground floor at the time of the incident.
3. There were three flights of stairs and only one stairgate.
4. Previous bruises had been noted by nursery but had been dismissed as normal child play.
5. Hygiene/medical care - ie nappy rash on Ian; Sean had a middle ear infection; Adrian had an inflamed ear.
6. The management of the children was left solely to Mr K.
    [*My view was that this statement was fallacious and sexist, and contributed to labelling Janet, devaluing her as a woman, wife and mother, leading to a focus on her as the problem. Peter was in full time work, often working 6 days a week. This information was available at the time of the investigation, yet an assumption was made that Janet did nothing with the children during most days, nor when Peter was there. The fact that she had looked after them for four years without known problematic incidents went by without notice or due credit. Nor was it highlighted that the current referral had arisen because Peter hit Sean, rather than because of a concern about Janet.*]
7. Janet was on anti-depressants.
    [*In the case conference minutes there is a reference to Peter's comments that Janet has problems and gets irritable if she does not take her tablets. Janet in my observation showed a great deal of patience with the children. Far from showing irritability she*]

seemed to tolerate behaviour which others might not have done. This raised issues for me about supervision of the children, but the details of her actual behaviour were not fully explored. Janet did engage in repeated handwashing and at the stage of the investigation had raised a question about the connection between Ian's nappy rash and hygiene. She indicated that she had sought medical treatment for it, but it had not yet cleared up.

My impression from the minutes was that an image of Janet had been created, as someone who was passive, phobic, not caring for her children, where her valid statement of seeking help was seen negatively. The impression was both of criticism for seeking advice and blame because the nappy rash had not cleared. She did also refer to the fact that it was she who looked after the children during the day - but this was not picked up as evidence. Janet's 'mental state' was seen as a problem in her caring for the children and a source of pressure on Peter which could be linked to his hitting Sean. Information was available to the case conference that Jane had shown phobic behaviour through handwashing for six years, that she had taken an overdose and made other self harm attempts before her marriage. There had been no repeat of this self harming behaviour since her marriage and the birth of her children - yet this was not looked at in a positive way in the case conference reports and minutes, but identified as a risk to her children.

A letter available to conference from a psychologist referred to sexually abusive advances from a relative which Janet had resisted. No connection between this and her phobic behaviour was explored, so that the protection plan might include supportive work with Janet. Rather, it was her inadequacies which seemed to be the focus of attention.]

There were other concerns raised for me by the case conference minutes. Nursery representatives referred to Sean and Adrian as 'behind' when they started at the nursery. They had not however been seen as sufficiently delayed in milestones to be referred for further investigation. It appeared that the easy focus of toilet training provided the only rationale for this judgement. There is not a compulsory age for a child to be fully in control of bladder functioning. I am sure that all parents have their views on toilet training. Janet and Peter made it clear to me later that they had a view that parents could 'feel when children are ready for toilet training'. Yet in the conference minutes Janet was described as 'agreeing with tasks but not following through'. No concrete examples of this were given. Somehow an impression was building up of children with developmental delays, possibly exacerbated by mother's lack of attention to training, without close scrutiny of precise information based on observation or other evidence.

Nursery staff had on a number of occasions questioned bruises on the boys, which Janet had had no explanation for other than play and playfighting. She was criticised for not talking to staff, yet her view was that she felt uncomfortable because she was being watched. Staff described the boys: 'as accident prone', 'poor speech', 'slow manner', 'wary of strangers', 'not excitable when mother returns', 'don't like change'. Very little information was given about actual *incidents* which provided evidence of these concerns. No plan for working on them constructively had been identified. There was no reference to the fact that mother regularly got the children up and ready for nursery on time - no easy task for anyone with three small children.

My view was that a number of relatively minor concerns appeared to have been focused on in a judgmental way. Had the approach been different, registration might not have been seen as necessary. The situation described here illustrates vividly the problems raised in 'Messages from Research' (DoH, 1995) about where the thresholds for investigations and case conferences should be placed. An approach which emphasises shortcomings and inadequacies is likely to maintain a focus on surveillance, monitoring, protection, rather than assessment of need and plans to work in partnership to mobilise strengths and resources.

The issues raised by Shemmings (1991) about objectivity and evidence in social work records were apparent in the material I had access to. An account of the circumstances of the bruising which led to the investigation changed from 'hit' by father in case notes to a 'blow' in the conference report. In case notes about the investigation, the boys are described as clingy and withdrawn, with no discussion about the possibility that this may be an entirely normal and positive reaction to a medical and child abuse investigation by strangers.

The purpose of the protection plan was not elaborated beyond monitoring, and providing a family aide twice a week for two hours with a focus on

- monitoring the children
- behaviour management
- budget.

Situation on reassessment

When I was allocated the case, after a few weeks' gap, it emerged that other professionals - family aide, nursery staff, health visitors - were unclear as to their roles.

Peter had shared with them some anxiety that his wife was taking more than her prescribed dose of anti-depressants, and he was concerned about her ability to supervise the children. He was threatening to leave her and take the children with him.

The family aide did not feel that much progress was being made, and she was feeling stuck. She said if she tried to encourage play with the children, she would be left to play with them whilst Janet did something else. She felt that help with household tasks was not very productive either. Janet appeared to be the sole focus of the work at this stage, so I told the family aide that I would review her role when I had made a reassessment. Meanwhile, I suggested that she should ask Janet what tasks would be helpful, encouraging her to feel in control and to gain confidence.

Janet's GP had referred her for a psychiatric appointment and it was likely that a Community Psychiatric Nurse would become involved.

There was little evidence of agreed activity in relation to the family from other professionals. Sean had recently moved to nursery school and teachers were still trying to get to know him. Ian was attending nursery with his brother Adrian. Staff there were looking out for further bruising. A new key worker had just been appointed, so she and I agreed to coordinate an action plan.

In my first discussion with Peter he made it clear that there was no real question of leaving his wife, but he felt stuck for someone to turn to to resolve issues. He had no family nearby to talk to, no close friends. His wife's mother was, he thought, exacerbating the situation by supplementing Janet's tablets with her own.

My response to his worries about the medication was to advise him to speak to the GP - preferably with his wife - to ascertain safe levels. I emphasised that I wanted issues to be discussed openly, I did not want to be cast in the role of referee. He had indicated that he wanted to take control of his wife's medication. I used this to open up a discussion of his wife's rights, and my wish to work in partnership with them both. Peter said that he wanted the children's names to remain on the register in order to make Janet get help. This gave me an opportunity to explain fully the purpose of the register. I emphasised that Janet's cooperation had to be voluntary and that there were ways of working which did not need to rely on coercion. I reminded him that the children were initially subject of a case conference, and then registration, because he had smacked Sean. I explained that I saw it as my role to work with the family to help them resolve problems, meet the needs of all of them, so that registration would no longer be necessary.

I arranged a second meeting with Peter and Janet, emphasising the need for openness and my interest in hearing the views of both of them on what the problems were. It became clear in this first interview with Peter that he did not think there were financial strains on the family.

A turning point

On 5th November, when I was away from the office, the family aide brought the boys to the Social Services Office. Adrian had a bruise on his forehead and hand. The family aide was told he had fallen down some of the stairs at the weekend. The family aide took the boys to the Home Care Organiser who in turn directed her to the Senior Social Worker. He then asked the family aide to take the boys home and get Mum to take them to the GP.

When I returned to the office on 6 November I was concerned about the following issues:

a.   the boys had been brought to the office without mother's knowledge and consent;
b.   the Home Care Organiser, the Senior and then the GP had all looked at the boys;
c.   the Senior had asked the family aide to undertake a task which was clearly a social worker's task.

It was necessary to deal with these issues, not only to make sure similar incidents would not happen in future, but to ensure role definition, task distinction, openness and good practice.

I had discussions with the family aide and Home Care Organiser and explained requirements and expectations. I also discussed the situation with my line manager and the Senior Social Worker.

My meeting with the parents turned out to be very productive, fortunately, as they could with justification have been very angry.

I emphasised the voluntary nature of their co-operation, the importance of being open, critical, asking questions, so that we might all aim for agreed goals. From this first session I observed that Janet lacked confidence, though she still had plenty to say, with humour. Peter had a tendency to speak for her. In future sessions, this became a humorous point and she was able to remind him he was doing this and give him an elbow dig in the side as a reminder. It emerged that their 'family rules' were not clear. We discussed whether there was sufficient consistency in the handling of the children. They acknowledged some manipulation by the children and frustration on Peter's part. They knew they needed an agreed approach but Peter thought Janet ought to do it his way, she believed that discussion and agreement may be more fruitful. Both felt that their upbringing and present lack of friends and family contacts had left them without good role models. They felt unsure who to ask for advice. They did indicate they were keen to co-operate, take on any offers of help or suggestions - not just because of the register but also for their own benefit as a family.

They pointed out that stress was a factor. Peter recognised that he was sometimes irritable with the children when he should have been dealing with the person who aroused those emotions, for example telling Janet's mother he was annoyed with her for giving Janet tranquillisers.

Janet felt under pressure at being watched by the nursery and family aide and having to ferry the children back and forth so many times. She said this served to increase her handwashing.

I asked if they would like me to look into getting a volunteer to escort the children.

I talked about my aim of open participation, saying I would try to ensure that all professionals would be factual, to avoid the 'spying' aspect. I suggested we should aim for positive progress for the children and also aim for more appropriate ways of helping them as a family. Janet said she wished to control her phobia. She agreed I could follow up what was happening with health professionals.

Peter and Janet agreed to keep individual diaries for me for a week and do a flow chart of their lives to give me some idea of them as people as well as a family unit.

We wrote down a resume of points covered and agreed.

We had a discussion of the register and procedures which I think helped them feel more involved, reassured and increased their co-operation. They had shown me round the house, as I had not seen it since the initial investigation. There had been vast improvements not only in some of the safety aspects but also it seemed better organised and better furnished. Sleeping arrangements had been changed. I acknowledged this to them positively - which they said had not previously been done.

Praise can serve as a positive boost to self-esteem, and be a great motivator. It seemed very important, after criticisms had been made, to recognise when things had been remedied to make sure they did not think that I was looking out for more things to criticise.

The diaries and flow chart

These records were helpful to me as keyworker, giving an insight into their daily life and also their life stories. I think they are too personal to the family to give much detail from them here.

The diaries revealed a very insular family with a mundane routine. There seemed little special time for anyone as an individual or for fun as a family. Janet's treat was going to town on a Saturday afternoon with her Mum. Peter never went out. They never went out at weekends either to the park or on other outings or to relatives. When Peter was looking after the children when he got in from work - bathing them, putting them to bed - Janet was doing the cooking, washing up and getting the children's clothes ready for the next day. It was she who got all the children up every day, bathed, breakfasted and to nursery for 9 a.m. Peter was already off to work.

The flow charts revealed that although Peter was confident and intelligent he had not had a significant role model and he never felt sure if he was doing things right with the children, how to play with and enjoy his children. Janet's revealed a very painful and confused history which she later discussed in detail with me. The handwashing seemed to be associated with a sense of guilt and feeling dirty. She described the sexual abuse she had experienced, her attempts at self mutilation. It seemed likely that the abuse and the phobia were linked. I judged that Peter might be undermining Janet's confidence by speaking for her, and her self-esteem by criticising her child care, however unwittingly. I judged that further work with them might be helpful on these aspects.

Core group review, 20 November

There was a review of the case when I had had the case approximately three weeks. I was able to emphasise certain points at the review:

- there had been great improvements in the home re safety and sleeping arrangements;
- the focus had been on Janet, but not enough positive acknowledgement of her care of the children had been given, there had been insufficient involvement of Peter;
- although professionals had said the boys had progressed it was unclear what the nature of the progress was, how it had been charted or observed, and whether the parents' involvement in this had been sought.

Action plan

It was agreed that the Health Visitor would do centile charts and developmental checks, advising parents.

The family aide had done a brief observational period at evening and weekend with Peter and the children which had been discussed with the parents. With their

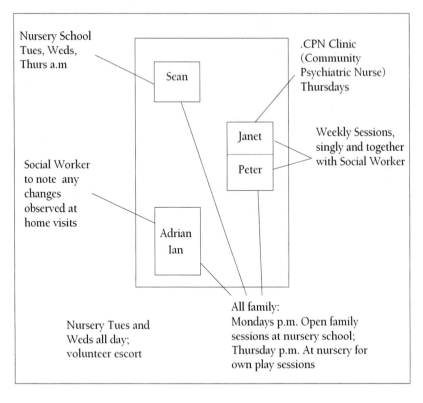

Nursery School
Tues, Weds,
Thurs a.m

.CPN Clinic
(Community
Psychiatric Nurse)
Thursdays

Sean

Janet

Peter

Weekly Sessions,
singly and together
with Social Worker

Social Worker
to note any
changes
observed at
home visits

Adrian
Ian

Nursery Tues and
Weds all day;
volunteer escort

All family:
Mondays p.m. Open family
sessions at nursery school;
Thursday p.m. At nursery for
own play sessions

agreement it was decided to end the involvement of the family aide, unless there were further issues of health and safety. Parents were aware of the concerns which had been raised and keen to accept responsibility for ensuring safety. This giving back of responsibility was viewed very positively by them.

The chart above shows agreed activities with the family.

I wrote to all the professionals and the parents following the review, arranging dates and times for internal reviews, clarifying roles and aims. My plan - agreed with parents - was to see parents individually and together, to consider issues of safety and wellbeing for the children as well as individuals' needs. I would observe changes and note progress in relation to safety aspects and handling of the children. Direct work with the children and with the whole family was planned at the nursery and the nursery school. There was emphasis on stressing Janet's positive qualities and engaging Peter more fully. The other professionals responded well to this approach. Clear information was given to Janet and Peter about what was to be observed, what expectations different professionals had in relating to the children. They were assured that they would be given feedback regularly and kept fully informed about what was happening and any concerns there might be. Setting out this approach led to Janet behaving as though a weight had been lifted from her shoulders. My evaluation was that this allowed both parents to become more relaxed, feel happier, and make progress.

In the Thursday afternoon family sessions - arranged specifically for them - the key worker offered ideas and examples of constructive play with the children, encouraging the parents to try things out. The Monday afternoon sessions at the nursery school were similar, but open to other families as well. Peter did not manage to attend all these, because of his work commitments. Peter and Janet found it useful to meet other parents in those sessions, and realise that they were not the only ones with difficulties.

I undertook two informal reviews with the parents in the next three months. The first one concentrated on play and stimulation. The second focused more on affection. We began with clarifying what we intended to do, what we hoped to achieve, and checking if there were any particular questions needing answers. Peter always came to our sessions with well prepared questions and with a folder of papers.

We explored the knock on effects of having more enjoyment with the children. Greater stability and security seemed to have followed and the parents thought there was less frustration for them all and fewer tantrums from the children. We were able to use humour to explore the dynamics between Peter and Janet, for example when Janet said she would like to go out more and Peter threw up obstacles such as: no money; too cold; no car. With prompting they were able to come up with their own examples of how to have fun cheaply and give new experiences to the children. They turned a cupboard in their front room into a toy cupboard.

In our second review, Peter took responsibility for noting important aspects of our discussion. We started our discussion with a decision to dispose of catalogues which the children cut up and played with - parents had been alerted by the nursery that there might be health hazards from them through lead and other toxic substances.

We progressed from discussion of play to consider how to work on affection. Janet and Peter agreed that they would continue their work on play. Peter normally only kissed the boys goodnight, believing from his own upbringing that open affection with boys was not the done thing. Janet had her own reasons for finding physical displays of affection difficult. However both were enthusiastic about making progress to more outward shows of affection, and about continuing to talk about their own feelings and hopes in this.

We also talked about ways in which their partnership might be more supportive. They came to an agreement that Peter would not criticise Janet in public and that Janet would take responsibility for having her say, even if Peter couldn't readily break his habit of opening his mouth first.

Both parents were extremely responsive, keen to hear suggestions and to act on them. It was a great pleasure to work with them, around a simple plan. My regret was that there had not been this clarity from the very beginning, because a number of unhelpful fears and negative experiences had to be undone. I observed that the parents' demeanour changed substantially during this short period, which in turn was reflected in the children's manner and behaviours. They were observed to be less erratic, more predictable. The speech of all of them showed marked improvement. Their demands on parents were for more constructive attention and were generally more positive in tone. They appeared to respond well to increased shows of affection and greater stimulus in play.

The parents were given regular positive feedback from me and from nursery workers. They also pointed out to us changes, such as an extra stairgate, different toys, the boys' reactions to new experiences.

Summary

My initial aims of assessing risk and needs within the family were quickly met, and particular areas to work on agreed. The practical concerns about health and safety were easily and rapidly met. The initial focus on monitoring was changed to a positive, collaborative approach. Through full involvement of the father it was possible to have open, constructive relationships and work to meet the needs of mother and father as well as the children.

* The task of the family aide, once clarified, was completed and the service withdrawn. This was a significant sign to parents of progress and offset the previous negative feelings about monitoring.
* Work with the children will continue at the nursery and nursery school, but family sessions will be time limited. A volunteer has been found to take the children to nursery.
* The case was taken off the child protection register six months after I began to work with the family. A voluntary arrangement for supportive work continued.

A number of factors were important in the positive progress made. I think that the full explanations given to parents, and the importance placed on active participation by both, enhanced their motivation and cooperation. It also ensured that professionals gave clear, succinct accounts throughout, of what they were aiming to do and their views on progress made. Delegation of tasks, with the key worker coordinating work overall, was also important. The nature of the risk was relatively low, but the family were struggling with considerable problems. Working with them to build on their strengths, following an assessment in which they played a major part, led to improved quality of life for the children and parents, as well as meeting the original expectations in child protection.

References

Dartington Social Research Unit (1995) *Messages from Research*. London : HMSO.
Shemmings, D. (1991) *Client Access to Records: user participation in Social Work*. Aldershot: Avebury.

18

'Unfit and blamed': Lessons from mothers whose children have been sexually abused

Annie Mullins

'I did feel an unfit mother, I didn't feel worthy of them anymore'

Introduction

The problem of child sexual abuse remains a disturbing and high profile issue. Press reports of events such as the West trial, the Dunblane massacre, the Detroux case in Belgium; the murders of Sophie Hooks and Daniel Handley; the constant unearthing of systematic and calculated abuse of children entrusted to the care of public authorities bring public indignation and outrage.

Currently there is much emphasis on the release of convicted sex offenders into the community and whether and how communities should be informed about and protected from them. However, there appears to be less concern with the aftermath of abuse: how children who have been abused actually cope with the damage and disruption to their lives and those of their families. It is often women, particularly mothers, who are left trying to pick up the pieces when a child discloses that they have been sexually abused. Yet there is overwhelming evidence that it is generally men who sexually abuse children. In my experience it is the *mother* to whom professionals often turn to ensure protection of the child from further 'risk' and a supportive and therapeutic environment for her child. Hence this chapter is concerned with the experience of *mothers* rather than *fathers*.

The chapter draws on my work in a social services department during investigations of child sexual abuse and child protection case conferences and experience of individual and group work. I also draw on a small-scale research project focused on feelings and issues that women faced in dealing with the aftermath of abuse.

In reviewing the literature and research about mothers whose children have been sexually abused, I will highlight work which suggests that women generally do respond positively to their children, in contrast to earlier studies where mothers were characterised as '*inadequate*' and accused of '*colluding and failing to protect their children*'.

I will give an account of group work with women whose children have been sexually abused, based on principles which give priority to children, whilst recognising and valuing women's rights and needs. This work was informed by the available research.

It assumed the need for support to enable women to come to terms with shocking and distressing information and circumstances associated with child sexual abuse.

The group work draws attention to the professional investigation process as a distressing phase, in the aftermath of hearing about the sexual abuse of their children. During the group work, it became evident that the women had insights and experiences that should inform professional practice. It therefore seemed appropriate to explore their experiences of the child protection investigation process more closely and help them to articulate them through a small-scale research study. The research included some of the women who participated in the group work, and other women who had not received any formal therapeutic intervention.

The women's narratives draw attention to a number of themes and insights relevant to a review of professional practice in child sexual abuse. Their accounts vividly illuminate their experience of trying to come to terms with the knowledge that their child had been sexually abused, and with the responses of close family, social networks and professional agencies. These responses were often unhelpful and problematic at a time of crisis, when they needed considerable support and understanding to cope with the traumatic emotional arena they had been thrust into.

Overall, what emerges from the group work and the research is the centrality of 'mother blaming' in society when children are sexually abused; the importance of professional investigations in setting the context for future interventions and the critical need for engagement of women if children are to be protected and helped. A range of practice implications need to be addressed if we are to protect children and ensure positive outcomes for their futures, particularly the continuity of relationships with their mothers and long term security within their families.

Theoretical debates on mothers of children who have been sexually abused

Harriet Dempster's (1993) and Carol Ann Hooper's (1992) reviews of the literature relating to children who have been sexually abused suggest that mothers are believing and responding supportively to their children. The studies they refer to (Myer (1984); de Jong (1988); Faller (1988); Everson et al (1989); Sirles & Loftberg (1990); Gomes-Schwartz et al (1990))contrast with earlier studies based on small clinical samples which viewed mothers as 'inadequate', responding poorly to the knowledge of their children's experience of sexual abuse. Historically, mothers were accused of colluding with abuse and failing to protect their children (Bender & Blau (1937); Sloane & Karpinski (1942); Kaufman et al (1954); Lustig et al (1966) referred to in Hooper (1992).

De Jong (1988) found that over half the mothers who were supportive to their children experienced emotional changes similar to women who have been raped. Dempster (1993) in her study suggests that mothers' responses have similarities with those of sexually abused children. Hooper (1992) suggests that a significant finding of some studies is that responses are affected by the mother's relationship with the abuser. Mothers where the abuser is a current partner are the most likely to have difficulty in offering support. Hooper argues that women who discover their children have been abused by a partner or member of the family go through a traumatised experience of loss, which highlights the relative powerlessness of mothers in the domestic and private domains of the family.

These studies offer an alternative conceptual framework for understanding and accounting for women's responses in adjusting to and accepting that their children have been sexually abused. However, my practice and research indicates that 'mother blaming' is still prevalent in the professional domain, with limited consideration of the shock, trauma, betrayal and loss that women experience when confronted with the sexual abuse of their child. As MacLeod and Saraga (1988) state:

> *A woman does not commit her life and security to a man she believes capable of molesting his own children. Psychiatrists and experts in this field cannot find any identifying features among abusers - so how are women supposed to identify an abuser before they marry them? People will very readily talk about 'colluding mothers' but we should ask ourselves if you were told, or began to suspect that your brother, husband or friend was abusing his children, would you go straight to the police? In their powerless position women are expected to be more aware, more resourceful and more courageous than the doctors, social workers etc...*

Only a small number of the women with whom I worked had approached statutory agencies - police or social services - for help. The women had chosen to approach a variety of informal networks in the first instance, including family, friends and members of their church.

Farmer & Owen's (1995) study, focusing on interventions, decision making and outcomes in child protection found 'The conduct of the investigation affected the way in which family members reacted, and to whom they turned for comfort and help'.

Their study has been helpful in revealing the power that investigations have in setting and determining future outcomes for children. The study found that mothers of sexually abused children became the focus of scrutiny and were placed centre stage in professional interventions. In defence, women sometimes formed an alliance with the alleged perpetrator, to protect themselves from the threat of agencies. When efforts were not made to strengthen the mother and child relationship children were 'sometimes unnecessarily removed from their families or even left in families with the abuser present' (Farmer & Owen 1995).

Working with mothers

In the early 90s when I began working with mothers whose children had been sexually abused, I was unclear myself as to what to think and feel and how to respond to women whose children had been sexually abused. I was conscious of ambivalent feelings and difficult questions, such as 'how could she not know her child was being sexually abused?' 'had she colluded with the abuse on some level?', 'had she herself been abused as a child?' These questions reflected issues raised at case conferences and professional meetings held to make recommendations about how best to protect children from further sexual and emotional abuse.

Women were more often than not excluded from such meetings, and were treated with suspicion, even when not seen as implicated in the abuse of their children. The work of MacLeod and Saraga (1988) was particularly helpful at this time, providing a theoretical framework to examine critically the dominant views and debates that shaped professional understandings and responses to mothers and children. It meant probing my own responses and perspective and daring to make sense, outside the 'orthodoxy', of the responses of mothers with whom I came into contact. These were mainly traumatised and agitated responses, including at times the denial of their children's sexual abuse.

It was clear that if we hoped to achieve more positive outcomes with children who had suffered sexual abuse, it was important to help and support mothers. As Hooper (1992) states:

> ...it is considerably more important to children that their mothers are enabled to support them where possible, than anything else professionals do.

Individual work with women

The professional context of my child protection work was a multi-disciplinary team, in a specialist child protection unit in an inner city area. The main focus of our work was to undertake assessments of 'risk' and to offer therapeutic work to children and their families where abuse had taken place. This had allowed me the opportunity to develop creative and innovative responses to both children and families, with the time and support to undertake more in-depth work than is usually possible in a fieldwork setting.

I had begun to give time and support to women on an individual basis. As this work progressed, common themes, issues and dilemmas became apparent: loss, betrayal and shock. It seemed a logical step to introduce some of these women to each other, on the premise that they may be able to offer support to one another. The individual work with women particularly highlighted the sense of grief, isolation, shame and stigma that the women felt, similar to their children who also felt they were the only ones experiencing this awful nightmare. The breaking down of the isolation on its own seemed a vital and clear basis for undertaking group work with women.

Issues in undertaking group work with women

Support for mothers was vital if we were to make any progress in our main aim of securing the safety and well being of the children. This posed a potential conflict of interest between mother and child, and before we could proceed, we had to make it clear that any information about a child being at risk would need to be passed on to the appropriate agencies or colleagues, to safeguard the child's interests and ensure safety.

Inevitably, this highlights the limitations and dilemmas of offering a therapeutic or supportive service to women, men and children within a statutory setting. The responsibility to report any information about child abuse undoubtedly has threatening implications for women. It can leave them suspicious and afraid, often unable to seek help. The following statements reveal the enormous fear that women had of the role of statutory services, and their fear of losing their children.

> 'I was really frightened I would lose my children, I was really frightened if I told anybody that my children would be taken away from me and I didn't know who to tell. I was frightened they would take the kids off me, so it was sort of kept quiet and we tried to handle it.'
> 'I was frightened of the police and social services being involved cos I know and I've heard they take away people's children and that they'll blame me.'

Also reflected in these statements are women's own expectations that they will be blamed and held responsible for the sexual abuse of their children. Their perceptions of social workers certainly inhibited women's confidence in seeking help and approaching professional agencies and led them to conceal the crisis they were in.

Issues of difference and discrimination

Additional complex issues arise for women subject to discrimination on the basis of 'race', disability, and sexual orientation. Black women, for example, may feel further constrained and fearful due to anticipated racism in the practice of the police and other agencies. Women may feel placed in a position of 'betraying' their partners and community if they approach statutory institutions, with the consequence of possible reprisals from within their networks. One woman reflected her ambivalent position stating:

> 'I just wanted him to stay in prison and suffer, but I was worried what might happen to him being black and all ... '

David (1985) has commented on the vulnerability of working-class women to the risk of state intervention, with notions of what makes a 'good' mother deriving from middle-class values. The position of black mothers has also been commented on in terms of the contradictory construction of motherhood. Not only is a black woman seen as 'inferior' from a racist viewpoint, she may also be viewed as the producer of more black people, and thus perceived as a threat.

Brah (1987) has argued that Asian women have been presented as 'docile and passive victims of archaic customs and practices, and of domineering Asian men'. In responding to women whose children have been sexually abused these stereotypes and assumptions may render Asian women as 'hapless victims', judged to be unable to protect their children; thus failing to address their resilience and struggle in protecting both their children and themselves in a racist society and abusive families.

Day (1992) suggests that:

> An analysis of women's experiences of family life, mediated by class and race, and the state's

relationship to the institution of the family is central to a social worker's ability to comprehend the complexity of women's lives.

The over representation of black children in care (Ahmed, Cheetham, & Small 1986, Barn 1990, Barn 1993), suggests that black women's parenting is placed under scrutiny in ways which may result in 'losing their children'.

Farmer & Owen's (1995) research stressed the high anxiety women had about losing their children and how it inhibited them from revealing difficulties of alcohol or violence in their families. Their fear of the possible consequences in a number of cases led them to minimise or conceal such problems during the investigation stage. We should not underestimate the strength of fear which parents and families have of losing their children, when we are intervening in their lives.

Managing the fears

Our way of trying to minimise the adverse consequences of these fears was to focus discussion on them in an introductory meeting and subsequently to formulate a 'written agreement' about how these issues would be approached between us and the women. We had to address the real possibility that we would be requested to feed back to case conferences and planning meetings information about their children, which meant there were limits on confidentiality.

We raised this again in the early stages of the group meetings, assuring the women that if there was a request to report back to professionals, we would do this in conjunction with them, and that there would be no surprises. On a more positive note, it also meant we could advocate for women in a supportive way at such meetings.

We further agreed to keep notes on all the group sessions to a minimum and record themes, rather than personal details. We would ensure they each had a copy of the notes. The recording also served as an evaluative tool both for workers and the women, in reflecting on their experience and progress within the group. Approaching these issues at the beginning of the group work gave the women a clear view of the context of the work and allowed them to check out and discuss any fears or reservations they had before attending the group.

Group work approach

The idea for a 'mothers' group' was simple, based on the premise that women who had similar experiences may well be better placed to support each other in a meaningful way and to offer genuine understanding and empathy. Meeting other women seemed very important, when they, like their children, believed that they were alone facing an ordeal associated with great shame, guilt and stigma.

Forming the group

With a colleague, I gained agreement to plan and set up the first group. This was to be experimental with careful review of the process and the contribution the group made in the lives of both the women and their children.

We approached the women who had been involved in individual work about their interest in forming a group, having already explored a number of issues and suggested they may benefit from meeting other women in similar circumstances. Initially, a number of the women were hesitant about meeting other women. After some discussion about their anxieties four women agreed to meet. They were very anxious and very unsure as to what to expect. The first meeting was low-key and informal. As facilitators, we felt it was important that the women took their time in divulging any information and did not feel under pressure to reveal any personal details. We had prepared the women by helping them to think of some questions they might ask the other individuals when meeting them for the first time e.g. where do you live, how many children do you have, do you work etc. We felt it was important the women did not identify themselves or each other only in terms of sexual abuse, attempting to discourage the idea that this was central to their current identity.

Role of the workers in facilitating the group work

It was decided that two members of staff who could support and complement each other should facilitate the 'mothers' group'. As a child protection social worker I was to co-facilitate the group with a colleague from an adult therapeutic, mental health, community based team. This allowed us to combine our knowledge and skills in working with women on issues of child sexual abuse from two differing perspectives. This partnership was balanced in a number of ways, including experience and ethnicity, with one black and one white woman. Black and white women were using the service so 'race' dimensions were important in the work

We agreed to work in a fairly non directive and supportive way within the group, facilitating and enabling the women to define as much of the agenda as possible, but also bringing information to the group and possibly suggesting exercises or topics to help them along.

Supervision

A supervisor was located within a psychiatric hospital social work team, who herself had previously run a structured and time limited group with women. Again time was spent in sharing our approaches, understandings about child sexual abuse, and exploring our values and our attitudes to some of the difficult and often contradictory issues involved in this area of work. This was to prove invaluable throughout the course of the group, particularly at moments when we found some of the women's accounts distressing, confusing and sometimes overwhelming, as they revealed further details about what had happened in their families.

Running the group

In time the group's existence became known and other women were referred. An important step at this time was to involve women who had started the group in leading the introductory meetings alongside a facilitator. This enabled existing members to feel more confident and active in supporting other women, and enabled potential new members to feel more reassured, less afraid. This active support and growing confidence in the group enabled women to offer each other support outside the group. On occasions they accompanied each other to court appearances and other difficult meetings.

We decided that the group work should be based on similar principles to that of our individual work:

- allowing women to tell their own account of events in their own way and time;
- providing support to deal with imminent crises;
- examining difficult and often contradictory feelings and responses to the child or the alleged abuser within a safe and non judgmental atmosphere;
- emphasising that they were not responsible or to blame for the abuse of their children;
- sharing appropriate information and material with them;
- helping to improve women's self esteem and confidence;
- promoting a self help network amongst the women;
- supporting women in responding to their children's needs and distress;
- providing practical information and support.

Open group work

An open approach was decided on, so that women could receive support, as and when they needed it, rather than having a structured and time limited group. We felt the advantages of an open group were:

- access to support when women want it;
- repeated sharing of information as new members join may lessen the power, secrecy and taboo of sexual abuse;
- members at different stages of the process could give each other encouragement and support;
- allows women control over how they use the group, both attendance and input;
- new members may prevent the group becoming stagnant.

We felt these advantages overcame the potential disadvantages of:

- new members may feel excluded from group culture;
- newer members may not know group information which is important to their understanding of another member's difficulties;
- older members may not wish repeatedly to share the same information with new members;
- possibly greater risk of breaches of confidentiality;

- group may find it hard to resolve conflicts between group members with arrival of new members and uncertain attendance.

Practical considerations

If women are to be able to take up support or services, practical considerations are vital. The location and accessibility of the group was a crucial issue. Our supervisor prompted us to think whether the group should be run in a social services establishment, as it would affect how comfortable the women would feel in attending. She had herself run a group within a Health Centre and the benefit of undertaking it in a community resource meant the women did not feel too stigmatised or self-conscious in attending. However, the issue of child care, and limited financial resources meant that we had to proceed within the social services facilities. However, the positive factor was that the child protection unit was based in a day nursery used by the local community and it was not necessarily identifiable as a child protection agency.

Childcare is inevitably an issue in a mothers' group. Because the project was based within a nursery setting, we were able to negotiate arrangements for caring for the women's children in a safe and secure environment. In addition we had a group room that was comfortable and accessible.

Transport was also a key factor in supporting the women in attending the group. When we visited women who were new to us, some of them were fearful of leaving their homes and had difficulties going out. This seemed to be a reaction to internal and external responses to the sexual abuse of their child, which was in the public domain for some of the women. Between us we collected women and returned them to their homes after the group had finished. As in many accounts of group work, this informal contact was constructive, helping the women to feel more relaxed about attending. Picking them up broke the ice and getting a lift home helped them wind down, after what may have been an intense and emotive session.

Methods to facilitate the group

Our approach to the group work was to encourage the women to set the agenda for the sessions, so they could identify the issues they wished to discuss and explore. This was important as the women had already experienced intrusion into their lives during the investigation process and we did not wish to replicate this. The women needed very little prompting to share their feelings and experiences, and the group often ran out of time. Sometimes the group would begin with a round of 'how I've been in the last two weeks' and this would identify quite specifically the issues the women needed to address and the support that was needed. What emerged from the women's sharing of experiences was that although the investigation of the abuse was over, other events such as court hearings, custody and access disputes, children's difficult behaviour, other people's responses, debt, housing difficulties, continued. The women would feel they had make some progress only to find a short time later that they were pushed back to a state of immobility and crisis by ongoing events. The women needed support over a long period of time. The women readily supported each other, at times reminding each other that they had moved on, but there were likely to be set backs.

As workers, we drew on some of the work of the former Gracewell Clinic (now Faithful Foundation) and their work with sex offenders and non-abusing parents. One of their key priorities was giving women information about how the offender had systematically constructed the context in which to abuse their child, by misinformation, construing the child as problematic, and eventually distancing the child from the mother as a source of help. Although encouraging the women to set their own agenda and develop their own understandings about their experiences, we did attempt to convey this vital information to them. In order to do this we drew on a range of materials, including videotapes of documentaries such as the Channel 4 production 'Breaking the Silence' and 'A Nightingale Roars' by Constance Nightingale.

This was very powerful for the women and provoked a number of emotional and distressed responses. The women identified with the accounts in the videotapes and were able to use them to explore their feelings and experiences. In some instances they were able to bring to the surface feelings that they had previously been unable to share or articulate for themselves, such as anger and great sadness and loss.

We also used written accounts by mothers of sexually abused children, which they were able to take away and use as a basis for discussion at future sessions. Again these accounts were immensely powerful, but being able to take them home to read and re-read, allowed a more reflective approach in subsequent group sessions, and women were able to consider their own responses to the material and how they changed over a period of time.

We used a number of exercises with the women, where women responded to a number of statements, for example:

'When I first heard about the abuse I ...'
'I did not want ...'
'The person I would have most liked to talk to was ...'
'I needed to know ...'
'The thing I would like most to say to the abuser is ...'
'Thing I would most like to say to my child is ....'

There was a range of responses to some of these prompts and exercises, with some women feeling very sad and distressed, others getting in touch with their anger about the betrayal by the men they had loved and trusted. Some women found thinking about their children's responses and pain very difficult and felt they had contributed to the distress by their own reactions to them.

Evaluation of the group work

Most women responded positively to the opportunity to give their own accounts, to say how it was for them and have the space to talk about themselves, outside the role of being a 'mother' or 'partner'. We were impressed by their ability to express the difficult and often ambivalent feelings and responses they had towards their children, partners, relatives and themselves. Their feelings ranged through anger, hostility, guilt, sadness and tenderness.

The women said they benefited in different ways from the group and from meeting each other. Their understanding of their children's and their own responses to sexual abuse developed: they were able to open up specific areas that had been difficult to address and experience a range of feelings that had been repressed. The sense of isolation and stigma was lessened by meeting other women. They began to consider their broader experiences as wives, mothers, daughters, friends, and as women in society shaped by their class, race and educational status.

Some examined their relationships with the men who had abused their children and the painful loss and betrayal this meant for them. They expressed the difficulty of facing a future without a partner, as well as the difficulty of ever trusting anyone again. Their troubles and difficulties continued long after the initial revelation of the sexual abuse of their children, in just as distressing and traumatising circumstances, when there were court and contact disputes about children.

Many of the women had their own histories of violence and abuse both in their childhood and as adults. Many of these experiences were prompted and brought into focus by the abuse of their children. Some women recovered memories of their own abuse as children. Some women had experienced extreme violence at the hands of their partners. Their accounts illuminated their qualities of resistance, determination and strength. As workers, we were very humbled by the women's experiences.

We were confronted by the complexity of child sexual abuse, how it connects with other aspects and forms of violence; the expectations within society of women as 'mothers' and 'wives'; and the inadequate and often punitive responses women experience from professional agencies and within their own communities. Our experience was potentially immobilising. However, we found that sharing and reflecting on it could release energy. This strengthened our commitment to working more sensitively and effectively in this area of work. Poignantly, perhaps, the group work with the women highlighted the complex and uncertain landscape of child abuse, a socially constructed phenomenon that will always be contested. The themes which the group work highlighted were echoed in the research study.

The following section will focus on some of the detail of the experiences of the women involved in the group work and in the study. This detail encourages critical reflection on how we may respond to women and their children more effectively, when intervening in their lives, particularly at the investigation stage.

Women's own experience of violence

There is much current attention to domestic violence and its effects on children. Almost all the women who attended the group, or were interviewed as part of the research project, recounted a range of experiences of violence experienced at the hands of their partners, who had sexually abused their children. The women's accounts are disturbing in the severity and length of time they had suffered. The women often felt powerless, fearful and trapped, as is captured in their accounts:

'... I mean I took enough beatings off him for years, I'd been physically abused by him for years and years, and I took that because he was my husband and because he was their dad and I didn't want them to be without a dad ...'

'... he was threatening to kill me and was telling me in great detail on the telephone about this petrol bomb he had got for me and how he was going to get me with it ...'

'... I suffered that night with just being mentally abused, physically abused and raped (pause) I just bled, I went through the night knowing that ... being quiet otherwise he - I was going to die'.

'... although I knew it was rape nobody else would ...'

Previous research findings have indicated a significant incidence of domestic violence by sexual offenders towards their female partners. Hooper (1992) quoting Dietz & Craft, (1980), Truesdell et al, (1986), Gordon, (1989), suggest that mothers are subjected to violence alongside their children, as opposed to men transferring control and violence from them on to the child. This is an important consideration for professionals, particularly because of the impact violence has on women's parenting and coping strategies. Graham et al (1988) suggest that a common survival strategy is to identify with the abuser's worldview. Dobash & Dobash (1992) also comment on the recurring hopes and promise of change, which together with self blame and desire to make marriages work, result in women continuing attempts to make relationships survive.

It is significant that motivation to leave these violent partners often came finally as a result of knowing about the sexual violence to their children, rather than the violence to themselves. Two women summed this up:

'... I just didn't know how to handle it ... and I tolerated all the badness from him but this I couldn't handle ... I told him I hated him and I couldn't accept what he had done ...'

'I just wanted him to go, I didn't want to see him, I didn't want him in my house or anything ...'

Like child sexual abuse, domestic violence is a complex matter. Where women are subjected to violence they may also be blamed or condemned for not protecting their children against violent men. Milner (1994) argues that allegations against fathers in child protection investigations are often redefined into allegations of neglect on the part of the mother, which not only serves to obscure men's behaviour but results in mothers becoming the primary focus for child protection investigations. O'Hagan & Dillenburger (1995) extend this view, challenging practitioners to stop avoiding men when intervening in family situations.

Women's responses to their children

A number of the women oscillated between believing and not believing their children. They could not make 'a round peg fit a square hole' and were at a loss how to come to grips with the information that their partner or close family relative, whom they had loved and trusted, could have done this to their child:

> '... it was just one vicious circle and I just didn't know who or where I was any more and I didn't recognise my kids, I felt they weren't my kids anymore, I just didn't understand them anymore, I didn't recognise them ...'

> 'I've had problems with her (child) all along_ stupid things like he's supposed to have been abusing her for five years but at that point we'd only been together three and half years and stupid things like that ...'

> '... at one stage I wanted Barry (child) taken off me, because I just had had enough, I mean I said to Paul (husband) I am going to kill him. I think I would hurt him because I felt I was batting my head up against a brick wall'.

Supporting sexually abused children is fraught with difficulties and contradictions for mothers, and it is important that we develop a more complex understanding of their responses. We drew on a 'bereavement' model, assuming women would undergo a number of processes, through denial, rage and possible acceptance of the fact that their children had been abused, rather than seeing them as 'colluding' or 'failing to protect'. Hooper (1992) quoting Remer & Elliot (1988) claims:

> The secondary victim must feel supported and understood to be able to comprehend and let in the experience of the primary victim; a difficult and sometimes threatening task.

A number of the women found it difficult to envisage a life without their partners and found it tempting to think that their children were telling lies or were blaming the wrong person. At times the knowledge of and attempts to understand what their children were alleging were almost unbearable for the women. Herman & Hirschman (1981, pg145) reflect on the dilemma faced by mothers:

> In addition to coping with the father's pressure and threats, she is compelled to shoulder the responsibility for her family alone, something she does not want to do, or feel capable of doing, as she is sacrificing whatever financial or emotional security that existed in her marriage for the sake of a daughter who has often seemed more of a rival than a child. However, hard she tries to avoid blaming her daughter, there may be times when she quite simply hates her.

The role of blame

Women blamed themselves for the sexual abuse but also were blamed by others, including their own families, children and on occasions the alleged perpetrators. It was not necessary for anyone else to tell them they were responsible for the sexual abuse of their children: they were the first to blame and condemn themselves in many instances. Women felt dirty, that they had somehow not fulfilled their partners' sexual and emotional needs, that their lives had been a waste of time, as the time spent with their partners had been based on lies and deceit. Accounts of their self-blaming were powerful and distressing to hear:

> '... as far as I was concerned it all seemed my fault and I was obviously no good to my husband, if he had got to turn to little girls, especially his own children, so I was obviously no good as

mother or as a wife ...'

'Well I feel dirty because of what happened to Katie (child) I was to blame because if I had been better in bed maybe he wouldn't have touched her and I know that's not true because if the man wants to do it they are going to regardless ...'

'... because you hear so much that it is the woman's fault and I couldn't even to this day, I can't see where it was my fault, yet still I even took that on board , that it must have been my fault'.

A number of the women indicated that they saw themselves as failing to meet their sexual partner's needs, that they were not 'getting enough'. This appears to derive from the assumptions of men's rights to sexual access in marriage or partnership. This is also reflected in public and theoretical explanations. The according of blame and responsibility is important, as it has implications for how the women perceive themselves and how they respond to their children. As Hooper (1992) suggests, the self-blame and societal apportioning of blame prevents the women from resolving the loss for themselves and potentially immobilises them, which in turn may leave their children at further risk of abuse.

The blaming of mothers by family and social networks

Many of the women first turned to their extended family and social networks for support and comfort. The responses of others to the sexual abuse of the children were mixed and often resulted in further pressure and distress for the women. One mother described her own mother's response in the following way:

'... her attitude was, 'why didn't you come and tell me and then I could have beaten her (child) and Michael (abuser) could have got away with it', and that really hurt me because I couldn't understand why she would say something like that ...'

Denial of sexual abuse played a part in the responses of extended family and social networks, not dissimilar to that of the mothers themselves:

'I told my family. My mum doesn't like to hear about it and doesn't want to know... she doesn't want to acknowledge that child abuse goes on. I don't know why'.

Many of the women experienced blame by their close family and social networks. The enormity of mother blaming in society became apparent, as the following statements reveal:

'My Kenny (husband) was, me mum was, because of splitting up their marriage, me sister was blaming me.... John (brother) was blaming me, they blamed me right from the start... so I suppose I've been blamed left, right and centre...'

'Well it was friends and relatives and the same lady who Safina (child) had spoken to (about the abuse) ... she was in charge of the church, she was having meetings at night and they were supposed to be having prayer meetings which start at 8.00pm. till 9.30pm. and she goes on to about 12 o'clock and the night was spent discussing me!'

'My family actually came round and blamed me ...They said, if I had left him there and then, I wouldn't have been with him for that to happen to Katy (child). I still do blame myself because in some ways it's true...'

These blaming and negative responses further enforced the women's sense of guilt and responsibility. They had forfeited any notion of their own needs for support or comfort. These responses involved further losses of relationships for the women and children, generating more agitation, hostility and over protectiveness at times. MacLeod & Saraga (1991) comment on these experiences as:

> '... a major assault on her identity as a woman, as a partner, as a member of a community, culture, religion, her extended family, after all as a mother these kind of things do not happen to the children of good mothers, do they? It's a contradiction in terms.'

As professionals we must not take it for granted that women and children will receive supportive and understanding responses where sexual abuse in the family has taken place. It may be that work is needed to help extended families address their own responses of disbelief, anger and betrayal. In certain circumstances, women and children may need protection from relatives or local communities. Many of the women experienced forms of harassment and violence at the hands of others, as a result of the abuse. We must not under estimate the impact the knowledge of child sexual abuse has in the public domain and the fear and difficulty it creates for women and children. They must live daily in a society that is ill informed about and ill-equipped to deal with child sexual abuse.

Isolation and stigma

Following the initial investigation, when partners often left the family home, many women were faced for the first time with having to be single mothers and cope with everything on their own, including making decisions about such things as finances. The women felt under considerable psychological and social pressure from neighbours, the local community, churches where they were members, and the schools that their children attended. It was unclear at times who did and who did not know about the sexual abuse. One mother used to run out to hang her washing up and run back in so her neighbour did not have a chance to speak to her.

The isolation, fear and loss of control in many aspects of their lives which mothers experienced were enormous. The pressures and difficulties took the shape of external, as well as internal torments. Women needed very practical as well as emotional responses to support them in their crisis. Finances were of particular importance, for some partners had been the main wage earner and they found themselves catapulted into poverty, suddenly having to deal with benefit and housing agencies, being assessed, completing application forms, dealing with the bank, employers, and the legal system. Alongside this, they had on some occasions to reveal the reason for the new-found circumstances.

Women's responses to social workers

Women at the early stages of finding out felt under enormous pressure from professionals to prove they had not known about the abuse and that they would 'protect their children'. One mother was very angry towards the field social worker, who made her position clear that she 'believed the child'. The mother felt the social worker was therefore against her husband, wanting to believe the 'worst of him', and that ultimately social services wanted to split up their family. The women were very explicit in their descriptions of how social workers responded to them at this crucial time:

> *'Yeah I was upset and thought why have they left me here. I felt they had just dumped me in a room and left me to get on with it. I felt at that time that there should be somebody there supportive to lean on. I mean Katie (child) was OK, she was walking around picking up leaflets ...'*
>
> *'... the first thing they asked me was why I had waited, why had I waited to tell someone and I told them I wasn't sure what to do, I was in a bit of state ... I found it difficult talking to complete strangers ... But it was the weekend so it was who ever they'd got ...'*

MacLeod and Saraga (1991) emphasise that the way the bad news is delivered to women is crucial in setting the pace and atmosphere for following interventions, and ultimately in protecting children. They further stress the importance of appreciating that the child and the perpetrator have known what has been going on for some time and it is the mother who may be hearing the news for the first time. This highlights the question of how and when professionals should convey to mothers that they believe whole heartedly their children's allegations of sexual abuse. Women have been living with their children, believing that they know their children better than anyone else. Yet here is a social worker telling the worst possible news, that a partner, or close family relative, has been sexually abusing their child, with a sense of certainty. Perhaps a more tentative or at least sensitive approach is needed in trying to support women in coming to terms with this devastating news.

As one of the mothers stated:

> *'... and another thing, I don't like social workers coming and telling me about what to do with my child ... I know my child better than they do - they just don't appreciate it'.*

This may go some way to avoid distancing the mother or encouraging her into a potential alliance with the alleged abuser, particularly when she feels her family is under threat from the statutory agencies, with whom she may have had no previous direct contact. It is worth bearing in mind that the alleged offenders have an investment in women feeling threatened by external agencies. They may use this to promote fear and anxiety.

Conclusion

The consequences of child sexual abuse on all our lives are complex. Abuse can be devastating to those experiencing such violence. The womens' accounts in this chapter reflect the difficulties they had to deal with over a lengthy period of time, often long after professionals left their lives. Violence in families takes many forms, whereby emotional, physical and sexual abuse may be intertwined, part of a continuum of control, often in the hands of men. Undertaking the group work with the women allowed us the opportunity to hear and understand in more depth the pain, the emotional roller coaster that many women and children endure, in their fight for survival and attempts to hold on to splinters of their lives.

We learned a great deal from the women, and as workers had to face questioning and reappraisal of former beliefs and approaches to families. Innovative approaches often mean taking a risk, asking the very people who are suffering what they need, and what will help them. It means taking the risk of learning to work in a more open, self-scrutinising way, which potentially opens the door to criticism and self doubt. One of the most powerful lessons for us as workers is that there is no certainty in this area of work, nothing can be taken as a given. We need to listen to the lived experience of women and children who have suffered sexual abuse and its consequences if we are to form alliances with women to protect children and promote their rights.

References

Ahmed, S. (1986) Cheetham & Small J. (eds) 'Social work with black children and their families'. London: Batsford.

Barn, R. (1990) 'Black Children in Local Authority Care: Admission Patterns', *New Community* 16(2) pp 229-46

Barn, R. (1993) *Black Children in the Public Care System*. London: BAAF/Batsford.

Bender, L. & Blau, A. (1937), 'The reaction of children to sexual relationships with adults', *American Journal of Orthopsychiatry*, 7: 500-18

Brah, A. (1987) 'Women of South Asian origin in Britain: issues and concerns', *South Asian Research 7,1.*

David, M. (1985) 'Motherhood and social policy: a matter of education'. *Critical Social Policy 12.*

Day, L. (1985) 'Women & oppression: race, class and gender', in Langan, M. & Day, L. (ed) *Women Oppression and Social Work*. London: Routledge.

de Jong, A.R. (1988), 'Maternal responses to the sexual abuse of their children', *Paediatrics*, 81. 1: 14-21.

Dempster, H.L. (1991), 'The Aftermath of Child Sexual Abuse: Women's Perspectives' *in Child Abuse & Child Abusers: Protection and Prevention*. L. Waterhouse (ed) Research Highlights Social Work 24. London & Philadelphia: Jessica Kingsley Publishers.

Dietz, C.A., Craft, J.L. (1980), ' Family dynamics of incest: a new perspective'. *Social Casework* December: 602-9.

Dobash, R. & Dobash, R. (1992), *Women, Violence and Social Change*. London: Routledge.

Everson et al (1989), 'Maternal support following disclosure of incest'. *American Journal of Orthopsychiatry.*

Faller, (1988), 'Why Sexual Abuse? An Exploration of the Inter Generational Hypothesis'. *Child Abuse & Neglect* 13: 342-9

Farmer, E. & Owen, M. (1995), *Child Protection Practice. Private Risks and Public Remedies.* London: HMSO.

Gomes-Schwartz B., Horrowitz, J.M. & Cardarelli, A.P. (1990), *Child Sexual Abuse: The Initial Effects.* London: Sage.

Gordon, L. (1988), 'The Politics of Child Sexual Abuse'. *Feminist Review,* 28.

Gordon, L. (1989), *'Heroes of Their Own Lives: Politics and History of Family Violence,* London: Virago.

Graham, D.L. R., Rawlings, E. & Rimini, N. (1988), 'Survivors of Terror. Battered Women, Hostages, and the Stockholm Syndrome', in Yllo, K. & Bogard, M. (eds), *Feminist Perspectives of Wife Abuse.* London: Sage.

Herman, J. L. & Hirschman, L. (1981), *Father-Daughter Incest,* Cambridge: Mass Harvard University Press.

Hooper, C-A. (1992), *Mothers Surviving Child Sexual Abuse.* London & New York: Tavistock/ Routledge.

Kaufman, I., Peck, A.L., Tagiuri, C.I. (1954) ' The family constellation and overt incestuous relations between father and daughter'. *American Journal of Orthopsychiatry* 24: 266-78.

Lustig, N., Dresser, J.W., Spellman, S.W. & Murray, T.B. (1966) 'Incest, a family group survival pattern'. *Archives of General Psychiatry* 14: 31-40.

MacLeod, M. (1996), Talking with children about child abuse. *ChildLine's first ten years.* London: ChildLine.

MacLeod, M. & Saraga, E. (1988),'Challenging the Orthodoxy: towards a feminist theory and practice'. *Feminist Review,* 28: 16-55.

MacLeod, M . & Saraga, E. (1991), Clearing a path through the undergrowth: a feminist reading of recent literature on child sexual abuse'. In P. Carter et al (eds), *Social Work & Social Welfare Year Book 3.* Milton Keynes: Open University Press.

Milner, J (1994), 'A disappearing act: The differing career paths of fathers and mothers in child protection investigations'. *Critical Social Policy* No. 38.

Myer, M. (1984), 'New Look at Mothers of Incest Victims'. *Journal of Social Work and Human Sexuality,* 3. 47-56.

O'Hagan, K. & Dillenburger, K. (1995), *The Abuse of Women Within Child Care Work.* Buckingham: Open University Press.

Remer, R. & Elliot, J.E. (1988), 'Management of secondary victims of sexual assault'. *International Journal of Psychiatry* 9, 4: 373-87.

Sirles & Loftberg (1990), 'Factors associated with choice in intra family child sexual abuse cases'. *Child Abuse & Neglect.* 14: 165-70.

Sloane, P. & Karpinski, E. (1942), 'Effects of incest on the participants'. *American Journal of Orthopsychiatry* 12: 666-73

Truesdell, D.J., McNeil, J.S. & Deschner, J.P. (1986), 'Incidence of wife abuse in incestuous families', *Social Work,* March-April: 138-40.

19
From victim to survivor :
The groupwork support of sexually abused boys

Andrew Durham

Introduction

This chapter discusses a groupwork project which was set up to support a group of boys who were victims of organised sexual abuse. They were abused during their attendance of Computer Clubs set up by two men named Harry and Gordon. The boys had to wait for almost two years following their disclosure before giving their evidence in court.

I was employed by the local Social Services Department as a specialist 'direct work' social worker. My role was to provide supportive intervention for these boys.

The incompatibility of the evidence demands of the legal process and the therapeutic recovery needs of the boys is highlighted. The Memorandum of Good Practice (HMSO 1992) has tried to address this issue with the introduction of guidelines for the production of video taped evidence. However, because this is based only on partial implementation of Pigot's (1989) proposals, children are still required to attend court trials for cross-examination. The chapter will try to show that in spite of problems in the system for investigating and prosecuting in cases of sexual offences which hinder supportive and child centred practice, it is possible to identify and execute certain areas of supportive and therapeutic intervention before a trial, without contaminating evidence.

Issues relating to the sexual abuse of boys are discussed - these include: a) Under reporting; b) Victims committing sexual offences; c) Organised Abuse. This is followed by a detailed practice example of groupwork support. The experience of the boys involved is consistent with the issues raised in the literature.

The chapter is critical of the need to compromise therapeutic programmes for the sake of preserving evidence and emphasises the need for social workers to maintain the principle that the welfare of the child is paramount when children are involved with legal processes.

Children, evidence and therapeutic intervention

The incompatibility of the evidential demands of the legal system and the needs of children in child abuse cases has been well documented in the literature (Spencer and Flin 1990, Davies 1992, Aldridge and Freshwater 1993.) It is agreed that children's attendance at such trials is at least stressful, if not traumatic. In cases of child sexual abuse, where a child may be in need of therapeutic assistance, the experience at trials may be particularly traumatic. In such cases, any pre-trial discussion of any matters relating directly to the evidence of the alleged abuse is likely to prove difficult if the reliability and spontaneity of the evidence is to be preserved. The child is required not to discuss the evidence, but to keep it freshly in mind for repetition at the trial. The child has to wait until after the trial before being able to talk through the abuse and receive therapeutic intervention.

This problem has not been resolved by the introduction of The Memorandum of Good Practice following the Pigot Committee, as it is still necessary for a child to appear live in court for cross - examination, after his or her evidence in chief has been admitted in the form of a video recording. This has been only a partial implementation of Pigot's proposal. He had suggested a second video recording of the child's cross - examination in Chambers soon after the first video interview. This would have solved the problem of therapeutic work being delayed by slow moving legal processes.

The current system has the therapeutic needs of abused children and the evidence requirements for a successful prosecution balanced on the opposite ends of a fulcrum. The task is to maintain that balance throughout a very difficult waiting period. If the decision has been made for a child to go to court, then the balance is already moving towards evidence. The task then becomes a damage-limitation exercise, as inevitably, at least in the interim, the child will suffer stress as a result of such a decision.

When the child attends court, Spencer and Flin state:

> *In summary, the major stress factors for child witnesses attending trials appear to be associated with; (a) the long delays waiting for the trial; (b) lack of legal knowledge resulting in misunderstanding and fear of the unknown; (c) repeated pre-trial interviews; (d) re-scheduling of trials; (e) delays and the lack of adequate waiting facilities and information in courts; (f) unsuitable design of court rooms; (g) confronting the accused; (h) insensitive interviewing techniques used in cross - examination; (i) inadequate protection of the child during cross - examination; (j) lack of social support for the child giving evidence.* (Spencer and Flin 1990 Page 297)

These issues have major implications for the nature and content of a pre-trial support programme and in planning sensitive well managed support on the day of the trial. The immediate therapeutic needs of the child must be considered, as well as longer term therapeutic needs.

Factors relating to the sexual abuse of boys

(a) Under - reporting

From the review of research by Watkins and Bentovim (1992) and other works (Peake 1989/90), it would appear that there is a considerable under-reporting of the incidence of sexual abuse of boys. The reasons for this may include: fears and misunderstandings about gay sexuality; responding to stress through externalised behaviour; the culture of male self reliance; feeling responsible for the abuse. These factors combine to influence ideas and beliefs about masculinity and male sexual behaviour. There are also arguments that there may not be an adequate response to allegations, because of: lack of supervision; blaming the boy; denial by professionals and the power of the paedophile lobby.

   Other factors which may be involved include loyalty to the offender, and pleasure in or enjoyment of aspects of the abuse.

   The fact that within society homosexuality is persecuted and that within this social context there are widespread fears, confusion and taboos about sexual identity may also discourage openness about the subject. It is important that these and other possible factors in under-reporting should be considered when designing assistance and recovery programmes.

(b) Victims committing sexual offences

   Ryan (1989) argues that victims of sexual abuse experience many dysfunctional outcomes, emotional, developmental, behavioural, in communication, helplessness, fears, depression and somatic complaints. She also refers to sexual abuse as learned behaviour where victims recreate their own experiences of abuse. 'Traumatic sexualisation' is referred to as developmentally shaping inappropriate sexual behaviour. It refers to the fact that long-term victims of abuse have been exposed to the distorted rationale of the offender, and warns that victims may find identification with the aggressor more comfortable than the identity of victim. 'This article hypothesises that experience in the treatment of sexual offenders may have important implications for how we treat identified victims of child sexual abuse, in order to prevent the development of sexual offending'. (Ryan 1989 p.326).

   In addition, Furniss describes the path of victim to victimiser as a circular and self-reinforcing process. 'The sexualisation of anxiety and frustration in the context of increasingly estranged or hostile relationships towards girls and women, leads to the danger for sexually abused boys to become sexual abusers themselves'. (Furniss 1989 p.59).

   The experience of abuse itself may entail a mixture of emotional betrayal and distrust and the meeting of a child's need for attention and nurturance, generally creating a great deal of confusion for the victim. The abuse may cause physical pain, but may also cause pleasure and sexual arousal. This confusion can also lead on to an eroding of the victim's self-esteem. The isolation enables guilt and powerlessness to grow. Ryan refers to this being translated into: '..fantasies of retaliation in order to regain control'. (Ryan 1989 p.327). Identification with the aggressor may become a means of mastering helplessness.

It must be remembered that sexuality and sexual development also takes place in a wider social context. The majority of perpetrators of sexual offences are male, but not all have been abused. The predominance of a culture which relates masculinity to control, power and self-reliance will have had a significant impact on male adolescents. This may be particularly influential on those who have low self-esteem and a lack of confidence, creating feelings of inadequacy and a lack of control or dominance. If cultural and social pressure dictates a need to be otherwise, then inevitably conflicts and problems arise.

These social factors strengthen the fears of sexually victimised boys, as does the idea that abuse victims become abusers. There will inevitably be an inaccuracy in the statistics relating to this, as there is an under-reporting of male abuse. However, given that some adult sexual offenders were victimised as children, this is sufficient for a sexually victimised boy to experience a great amount of anxiety and fear about his future. This is a complicated area which justifies much further discussion and debate. It is important to take account of fears of becoming an abuser when designing support programmes for sexually abused males.

(c) Organised abuse

The H.M.S.O. Working Together Under the Children Act 1989 states: 'For the purposes of this Guide, organised abuse is a generic term which covers abuse which may involve a number of abusers, a number of abused children and young people and often encompass different forms of abuse. It involves, to a greater or lesser extent, an element of organisation'. (H.M.S.O. 1991 p.38).

It goes on to describe organised abuse as including small paedophile or pornographic rings with most members knowing one another; as well as large networks of individual groups or families in which not all participants will be known to each other. Peake in discussing the Paedophile Lobby states: 'An unknown proportion of those promoting adult child sexual contacts are intelligent, with positions of responsibility, and often they are part of considerable networks of like-minded people'. (Peake 1990 p.14).

Practice example: groupwork support of sexually abused boys*

Summary of events

The boys served by this project lived in a small town on the outskirts of a Northern England City. They had attended computer clubs which had been set up locally by a man named Harry*, who was a Computer Studies Lecturer and another man named Gordon, who was a Legal Clerk. These men were known to each other. Harry's club was

---

* All names and locations are fictitious.

for boys aged under eleven, Gordon's club was for boys aged eleven and over. Some of the boys had attended both clubs; boys moving from one club to the next was an established process. The club evenings involved computer activities, games and trips out. Occasionally there were residential overnight trips during school holidays and at weekends.

After concerns had been raised relating to the continued presence of boys at Gordon's house, and other concerns relating to the behaviour of one of the boys, a joint Social Services and Police investigation was set up - over thirty boys were interviewed. There were clear statements from eleven of the boys relating to acts of sexual abuse which had been committed against them by Harry or Gordon, or both, over periods ranging from two or three months, to periods of four years. Most of the boys were loyal to Harry and Gordon. It later became clear that some of this loyalty was borne out of fear, particularly in relation to Harry. However in part loyalty was an attribute of a genuine friendship, particularly in relation to the boys who attended Gordon's club. This made the investigation both confusing and difficult.

Because of the legal system, the complexities of the case and *possibly* the professional status, knowledge and skill of the offenders, the process of prosecution lasted for almost two years. During this period there were several 'warnings' for court appearances, some of which involved the boys attending court sessions which resulted in adjournments. These repeated delays caused the boys a great deal of anxiety and stress.

Both men were convicted on a number of counts of sexual abuse. They were given short prison sentences.

Setting up the Support Groups

When the Crown Prosecution Service had made the decision to proceed with a trial, a multi-agency meeting with representatives from Police, Social Services and Education was set up. At this meeting the setting up of a Support Group was proposed by myself and Social Services colleagues. Following this it was necessary to negotiate with the Crown Prosecution Service and the Prosecution Barristers about how it would be possible to run a support group without influencing or causing problems with evidence. It was also necessary to advise them that this practice would be in accordance with the Child Welfare recommendations of the Working Together Document. A close liaison with the Crown Prosecution Service was set up and maintained by myself throughout the pre - trial phase. The Defence lawyers were made aware of the group and were given a basic outline of the group programme. There were no specific challenges about the support groups in court, although the accusation of collaboration was an aspect of the defence case.

It was recognised that there needed to be a speedy acknowledgement of the difficulties the boys had experienced so far, and that they needed a support system for the future, which would reduce their anxieties and break down their isolation. There was also an emphasis on giving the boys a choice about appearing in court.

I was introduced to each family by a member of the initial investigation team. After I had given each boy an initial support interview which gave him and his parents an opportunity to raise questions, further interviews were arranged for the boys, at their request, in groups of two or three. This was necessary, in order further to break down fears and anxieties, before entering into a full group. The boys chose particular friends from the proposed group with whom they felt they would like to discuss the idea of a support group. This suited the pace of events, as the Social Services Department were still in the process of identifying co-workers for the groups. The following two support groups were set up: Group One for six boys aged fourteen - John, Richard, Mick, Paul, Keith and George; Group Two for five boys aged ten to thirteen - David, Peter, Mike, Micky and Dylan. The members of Group One were an established peer group, all members living on the same estate. Group Two members were only acquainted through occasional Computer Club sessions and some residential trips. The Groups were led by myself as the support coordinator and two female co-workers, one for each Group, in order to provide a mixed gender group leadership.

During these initial stages, it was clear that all the boys were experiencing a considerable amount of stress and anxiety, and had felt forgotten since their disclosure interviews, which had taken place several months previously. It was unfortunate the investigation had taken so long and that it had not been possible to get the support groups set up at the beginning. Some families experienced conflicts of opinion between parents and children about attending court, or over guilt and anxiety about the boys not being able to tell their parents about the abuse. Some parents felt guilty, especially as some had developed friendships with one of the offenders, Gordon. He had gone to great lengths to ensure the confidence of some parents. Two years previously, there had been allegations about Harry's Club and parents had turned to Gordon and received reassurance from him that the matter had been dealt with without police involvement. At this stage Harry's Club had been closed down, supposedly due to the intervention of Gordon. Harry continued his contact with the younger boys through his provision of residential trips. The prospect of Gordon being an abuser himself was, at the beginning of this investigation, beyond the realms of belief some parents.

Following the introductory stages, the boys welcomed the prospect of attending a Support Group, especially in view of their not attending any group activity since the closure of the Computer Clubs. The boys also welcomed the proposal that attendance at a Support Group was a decision independent of attending court and giving evidence, and that the decision about court could be made by them during the process of attending the Support Group sessions. This was particularly important for Richard who was initially reluctant to attend a group and was struggling with his loyalty to Gordon. The situation was similar for George, whose parents initially wanted him to have nothing further to do with the process. Eventually his parents allowed him to make the choice - he had strong wishes to attend the Group. Most of the families expressed concern about the boys. Some were suffering from disturbed sleeping patterns, they were often moody and appeared unsettled. As soon as the boys began to feel that they were being involved in a process of exercising choices and were not being seen simply as court witnesses, then their commitment to the process developed, and their anxieties began to reduce. For practical reasons, Group One was set up two months ahead of Group Two, which was set up by a similar process of individual interviews, sub-group sessions, then commencement of full group sessions. Each Group met on a weekly basis for the first four months. Sessions then alternated between weekly and fortnightly as circumstances dictated.

Group programme

A. Pre-Court Programme

1. Identifying Support and Building Self-Esteem

Developing mutual support, presentation of plans for the Group Programme, discussion and choices. Activity based sessions to enhance self-esteem and to develop a group identity through cohesive group processes. The activity based sessions were generally alternated with work based sessions, so as to support the coverage of a difficult and distressing programme.

2. Going to Court

Giving out basic information about the court and the nature of the adversarial process. Visits to local courts, role plays, discussions. Emphasising the importance of telling the truth. Identifying personal strengths. Stress reducing techniques.

3. Sexuality and Sex Education

Identifying pre and post court areas to be worked on, i.e., not discussing the abuse before the trial. The boys were asked to approach myself in the event of any distress which they felt could not be addressed within the group sessions. Basic sex education programme. Used 'Man's World' board game to facilitate discussions about sexuality, sexual orientation, gender roles, sexism etc.

4. Protection Issues

Checking out knowledge of good touching, bad touching. Being able to say 'No' to inappropriate contact. Being able to identify safe adults to tell. Ensuring a continuation of understanding and support from families.

The pre-court phase of the programme was characterised by the need to balance evidence requirements and welfare/protection issues. The boys were asked not to discuss aspects of the abuse with each other.

During the court trials, one for each offender, the group leaders attended and supported the boys throughout. Prior negotiations were made with the court for the provision of suitable waiting facilities.

B. Post - Court programme

1. Discussing the court experience

Explaining the outcome of the trial. Acknowledging everybody's contribution, sharing feelings.

2. Secrecy

Looking at the role of secrecy in sexual abuse, as a means of maintaining silence.

Looking at the advantages of breaking down such secrecy and sharing feelings, anxieties and events.

3. Abusers

The characteristics of abusers and their behaviour. How an abuser can present different faces to different people. Discussing abusive processes, targeting, grooming, maintaining silence. How the abusers set up sexually oriented games. Feelings about the abuser now. Identifying abusers in the future.

4. The abuse

Open discussion by each person of the abuse they suffered. Allowing group members to compare and corroborate their experiences. Challenging denial within the group. Discussion of feelings about the abuse and a sharing of difficulties as a result of the abuse. Highlighting the safety of the group and the advantages of talking about experiences and fears.

5. Further issues of sexuality and sex education

Looking at the nature of sexual assaults on children, comparing them to the group members' own experiences. Ensuring protection in the future. Identifying and addressing sexualised behaviour and sexual messages. Discussing issues around masturbation, sexual fantasies and memories of the abuse. Discussion of tension relief and the possible sexualisation of non-sexual problems. Relationship attitudes, sexism, gender roles and stereotypes.

6. Fears arising from the abuse

Fears around enjoying some aspects of the abuse and concerns around gay sexuality. Loyalty to the abuser and mixed feelings. Fears of becoming an abuser. Emphasising issues of sexuality as a developmental process not being fixed by experiences. The importance of talking through difficulties and solving problems as opposed to hiding them and building up fears. Emphasising the harm of sexual abuse and the need for help and guidance in recovery.

7. Sources of future help

Family, friends (each other), availability of local resources. Contacting Group Leaders if necessary in the future and/or other members of the Social Services Department.

8. Evaluation

Questionnaires, discussion, comparison of early group material to more recently completed work. Focusing on feelings and the extent of recovery and the ability of Group members to protect themselves and be protected in the future.

Groupwork methods

The sessions were structured so as to allow members of the Groups to bring their weekly news or any immediate problems which they wished to discuss, before embarking on programme material. A Pool Table was available as a popular means of providing group members time out from stresses and strain. Art work was also used in the form of graffiti sheets. Large sheets of paper, sometimes blank, sometimes headed with comments related to the day's programme were left out with coloured felt pens. This provided a good vehicle for the expression of feelings and comments, sometimes anonymous, sometimes signed, generally in the form of cartoon drawings with comments alongside. Brainstorms, both individual and group, listing of issues, initially without comment from other group members. Role plays were also used when appropriate, especially in relation to court and in relation to demonstrating saying 'No', with the younger Group. The 'Mans World' board game was used as a vehicle for discussing sexuality issues.

During the two year period, Group One was taken on two residential trips. On both occasions these were organised to respond to delays and adjournments, and were geared towards enhancing self-esteem and alleviating stress created by the length of the process. Some Group One members had to attend both trials. The trips were requested by the boys. It was acknowledged with the boys by myself and the co - worker that they may have concerns about the fact that they had been on trips with the offenders. Differences between previous group experiences and the support group were constantly highlighted, most notably the presence of clear and firm boundaries of acceptable behaviour and a constant sharing of information with parents. Additionally the groups were always co - worked, they were clearly recorded and were discussed regularly in supervision.

Group process

Group one	Trial	Group two	Trial
John	Harry and Gordon	Peter	Harry
Paul	Gordon	David	Harry
George	Harry and Gordon	Mike	Harry
Richard	Harry and Gordon	Micky	Harry
Keith	Gordon	Dylan	Harry
Mick	Harry and Gordon		

The main difference between the older Group One (14 - 16 year olds) and Group Two (10 - 13 year olds), was that Group One was a well established peer group which met frequently outside the group sessions. With the exception of one young person, all the members of Group One lived on the same Estate, within five minutes walk from each other. The six members of Group One had attended both Harry and Gordon's Computer Clubs as a group over a four year period. By contrast, some of the members of Group Two had only met other members on one holiday trip which they had attended. For some of the younger members, there was only one trip attended, and no attendance of Computer Club sessions. Two members of the Group had spent time with Harry on an individual basis.

For both Groups, the pre-group interviews, the individual sessions and the small pre-group sessions facilitated a smooth development of trust and peer group support. For some members of Group One, loyalty to Gordon created an initial reluctance to get involved. It was also acknowledged that group members may be fearful of entering into another group experience, after the experiences they had suffered. In the event, the converse was true. Attendance with friends (peers) created confidence and security and immediately enabled group members to fell less isolated. After one or two small group sessions centred around low key discussions and games of pool, all members were eager for the group sessions to commence. For some of the boys, these sessions represented the beginning of feeling supported and believed. One or two boys had been unable to discuss the abusive incidents with their parents and had been very isolated. Fears were looming large, there had also been very little discussion amongst peers. The tendency had been to play down and forget the incidents. This was mirrored by the delay in the professional response, after interviews. Although the boys, at the time of being interviewed, had been told that the case may go to court and they would receive support, the reality was several months delay.

Members of Group One had suffered much more lengthy and entrenched experiences of abuse than members of Group Two. They had been initially involved with Harry and then under the guise of problems being sorted out, entered into an even more extensive abusive experience with Gordon. Two of the boys, Richard and George, had spent large parts of their leisure time with Gordon over a two year period. They had the view that they themselves had been responsible for their relationship with Gordon becoming abusive. In the early pre-court stages of the Group, they had been told on several occasions that they were not to blame. This did not solve their problem of feeling guilty altogether, but as their view of the abuse became more distanced, their feelings of guilt lessened. After the court hearing it was possible to discuss the long term process of how they became involved in an abusive situation.

The facts of the abusive experiences had been identified as an area not open for discussion until after the court hearing. It was acknowledged that all parties were aware of the facts and of the difficulties of not being able to discuss them. It was as if the facts had been locked into a visible bubble for all to see, but not touch. Having established this, it was then possible to look at all the other therapeutic needs, not directly relating to the facts, and devise the ways and means to address them.

Raising self-esteem, empowerment, ensuring an age appropriate level of understanding of sex and sexuality, and ensuring that all the boys within both Groups had discussed protection issues, became the focus of the pre-court group meetings, alongside ensuring that all boys were adequately prepared for the court appearance itself.

Once the boys had been given the knowledge concerning court hearings, both in the form of written materials and role plays (not related to child abuse cases), and had visited one or two courts, they began to be less fearful of the prospect of appearing in court, with the exception of three of the younger boys. For these three boys, Peter, Micky and Dylan, final re-assurance came when it was established that they would be giving their evidence through a live video link.

Use of art and graffiti

As stated, the boys in Group One were very ambivalent about giving evidence against Gordon. Richard and George particularly suffered a great deal of anguish and confusion before they could come to terms with giving evidence against a person who had been a friend. The early Group sessions were characterised by expressions of this anxiety and confusion. There would be considerable mood swings within the space of the two to three hours of the Group evening. During the early sessions, both Groups chose to express some of their feelings by taking advantage of the opportunity to draw images and graffiti in colour on the large sheets of paper provided. Often several group members would contribute their efforts together on one sheet of paper, forming a collage of thoughts and feelings. Group members would also sit and doodle whilst discussions were taking place. This process was a good aid to concentration, but also a means of breaking down the intensity of some of the discussions. We tried to ensure that group members were still involved in discussions whether or not they were drawing at the same time. Often the doodling would be directly relevant to the issues being discussed.

The resulting drawings for both Groups served to indicate the level of confusion and anxiety the boys were experiencing. For Group Two the drawings often featured monster-type images. These monsters would soon be scribbled out. The drawings also featured court scenes copied from information leaflets. Again the defendant would be represented by monster-type drawings or drawings with genitals detailed and then scribbled out. Such drawings were handled by the group workers in a low key manner, so as not to draw any attention to possible evidence implications. Often the drawings would be collected in without comment, as part of the routine clearing up. On some occasions comments were invited from either the Group Leaders or other group members. Not all drawings related to the court case, there were drawings of each other, of cars, patterns etc.

For Group One, the drawings portrayed images of a greater level of disturbance and confusion. They were generally sexual drawings, depicting phalluses with comments and sexual expressions alongside. The expression of anxiety was very evident in these drawings and would sometimes shock the boys after they had drawn them. After the trial, the earlier drawings were looked at again. The boys had forgotten some of the drawings and were surprised by them. George commented that he never thought things had been that bad. There were many of these drawings, often densely filling every corner of a Flip Chart sheet. These images in themselves suggested very high levels of confusion and anxiety.

Behaviour and group dynamics

The levels of confusion and anxiety were also confirmed by the behaviour of the boys in general. Two of the boys in Group Two would often appear to express their anxieties against each other. Within the group there were two identifiable sub-groups, Peter and Micky being one, David, Mike and Dylan being the other. Eventually Micky gained acceptance into the other sub-group, leaving Peter as the group scapegoat. This situation had to be continuously managed. Most of the conflict took place between David and Peter. David was generally anxious about both the abusive experience and the court delays. This situation was compounded by the fact that he had not found himself able to discuss his abusive experiences at home. Peter would often appear to set himself up to bear the brunt of David's anxiety. Both boys and the rest of the group were responsive to the group leaders intervening and working out solutions and compromises for all parties concerned in the conflicts as they arose. An example of such a situation was when Peter had turned round in temper to David and said that he was lucky because at least he lived with his father, the fact being well known in the group that Peter was very unhappy about living separately from his father. An equally angry response from David drew attention to the fact that his situation was similar with his mother. In response to this outburst the whole group engaged itself in a supportive and empathic discussion about the difficulty of having separated parents. Peter's parents reported a history of similar patterns of peer group conflict at school and stated that the group had helped Peter find better ways of responding to bullying and being isolated, and that he was becoming more able to discuss these problems at home. Group One also had its scapegoat in Mick, this took the form of humorous baiting and never resulted in the violence suffered occasionally by Peter. Unlike Group One, the boys in Group Two never united to commit acts of group mischief.

Group One would often get together and engage in acts of mischief and vandalism. This often followed court adjournments when they felt that there would never be an end to the process , and that the abusers would remain unpunished. Sometimes food and biscuits would be thrown around the room, other times holes were kicked and punched into partition walls, plants would be broken and pulled up. More humorously, on one occasion the entire group entered a small room, undetected, whilst the Group Leaders were packing away equipment, and emptied the polystyrene contents of approximately ten bean bags, only to be discovered when they were literally up to their necks in the evidence of their misdemeanour. The remainder of the session and longer, was taken up by the group collecting the debris into dustbin bags.

There were some internal conflicts in Group One. John was sometimes aggressive and was often unable to back down from challenges from the other group members. On one occasion he had a nasty confrontation with Paul which required rapid intervention and separation. Both boys were very upset and were able to see the futility of their actions. Also on occasions, Keith would be bad tempered and take this out on other group members.

After court

When the boys were finally able to discuss and compare each other's feelings, they were able to acknowledge openly the pleasurable aspects of the abusive experiences and talk through their understanding of what had happened with the Group Leaders. This included discussions relating to the grooming process and how the boys were tricked into cooperation. They were looking back at the age of sixteen on events which had occurred from the age of eight to thirteen. They had the benefit of hindsight and well developed peer support. They were no longer isolated with unique fears they dare not mention.

The concerns of the boys in Group Two after giving evidence in court were more related to the aftermath of the court process and the possibility of reprisals from the abuser after release from custody. There was no guilt expressed about having spoken against the abuser, although the boys were aware that it was their evidence which had resulted in his being locked up. At different stages most of the boys from both groups expressed some degree of concern about the suffering of a prison sentence.

During the post-court phase there were discussions relating to possible long term effects of having been abused. One of the issues which caused concern was the fact that the abuser was male, and whether or not this implied homosexuality on the part of the boys. This was more of an issue for the older boys in Group One, although there were some questions raised in Group Two. There were also some comments about abused children becoming abusers. Whilst no individual expressed any great fears about this, one boy stated that he could see the potential for this to happen if a victim of sexual abuse did not receive help. This led onto a consideration of the fact that the boys had been set up by Gordon to abuse each other. It was acknowledged that this had made it more difficult for the boys to report their abuse. When they did report the abuse, the boys stated that it was embarrassing and that they were worried about what they had done. Their understanding of this increased when they received the full details of the prosecution summary, which identified the deliberate manipulation by Gordon in attracting the boys to his house. The same was true of the manner in which Harry had manipulated Richard and George to go to his house. The similarity of the manipulation by both abusers had caused Richard and George to feel responsible for what had happened. With the benefits of the full facts, alongside discussion, they were able to recognise the abusive processes which led to the betrayal of their trust and friendship; how their involvement with the abuse had enabled the abusers to maintain a sustained period of secrecy and deception of parents. Gordon had established friendships with some parents. One parent to this day finds it difficult to believe that Gordon committed the acts of abuse for which he was sentenced. The link between the two abusers through the computer clubs made it even more difficult for the boys to break the secrecy of their abuse and compounded their feelings of responsibility and blame. It also served to prevent the first attempt to communicate the abuse from being reported to the police.

There had been a feeling amongst the group members and Group Leaders that Keith had never fully been able to acknowledge his experiences and that this was causing him problems. Richard, George and Paul were keen to help Keith with his denial as they had been present when he was abused. Some of the boys in this group were anxious about the fact that they had in their eyes cooperated with and experienced pleasure in the abuse and had confusion and misunderstandings about their developing sexuality and sexual orientation, and concerns about homosexuality. These issues only came fully into the open in the post court phase. Some areas had previously been discussed in a general way during the earlier sessions on sexuality and general sex education, where oppressive attitudes to sexuality and sexism had been explored. By the time of the post-court phase, anxieties were generally lessened, partly because the court stage had finished and partly because they had grown in confidence and self-esteem during the lengthy waiting period.

Over time the boys were able to contrast their abusive experiences to their experiences in the Support Group - the fact that it was possible to form positive relationships with adults, particularly male adults, without an accompaniment of abuse. On occasions the boys would make an open comparison between events in the Support Group and events in their former computer club. As time progressed the level of trust in the groups reached a point where the boys were able to look back and see how they were cajoled and tricked into abusive situations. The support group process attempted to help the boys in being able to identify the qualities of relationships they might value in the future. Through discussion and comment on their interactions with each other they were helped to develop respect for each other and people which would counteract using power and coercion in future relationships. The particular importance of this within sexual relationships was emphasised.

Outcome and evaluation

Throughout the unexpectedly long lives of both Groups, the Group Leaders observed increased levels of confidence and self-esteem. This was borne out by comments from the young people to the effect that they felt better and had valued being a member of their Support Group. Topics which had been the subject of personal fears and secret anxieties were finally discussed openly. Some boys showed a greater level of initiative and independence, and became more able to take part in discussions and make decisions about group events and topics. There were comments on the evaluation forms about the value of being listened to and having the opportunity to take time to discuss feelings and have questions answered. The attendance rate for both groups was close to one hundred per cent. The art work towards the end of the group was much more related to hobbies and interests, and showed much more humour, there were no longer any sexual comments or sexually explicit drawings of the abuse. Most of the tensions and conflicts between group members had subsided.

The fact that the boys had to wait for almost two years before giving their evidence meant their having to hold on to deeper anxieties of the abusive experiences for an intolerably long time. This was a clear example of the incompatibility of the demands of the legal system and the therapeutic needs of victims of sexual abuse. Several of the boys openly stated that they felt that their enjoyment of the Support Group had to some extent compensated for this. At times, however, their actual experiences and responses spoke against this. Furthermore, these comments were made after the court process had concluded and was a sharp contrast to the anxieties expressed in response to news of further adjournments. Throughout the lives of the Groups, anxieties were expressed individually by all eleven group members, relating specifically to the trial delays. They had to cope with the knowledge that a stressful event was still to occur at some undefined point in the future, and the fact that this was preventing a full therapeutic discussion of personal experiences and feelings relating to the abuse. The boys' enjoyment of the Support Group sessions was a compensatory feature. The extended running length had enabled a rebuilding of self-esteem. This was in spite of the system and its delays.

If it had been known at the outset that the delay would be two years long, then the process would have been considered to be contrary to the welfare of the boys and it is likely that a decision would have been made to cover the topics of the post-court programme much sooner. Such a decision would have damaged the prospect of a successful court outcome to the extent that the case may have been dropped. Many child sexual abuse investigations fail to reach the court system for reasons relating to the weakness or lack of evidence. This case could have been one such example.

The pre-court phase had addressed issues relating to the context in which the abuse had occurred, when covering general sex education. Most notably issues were discussed relating to developing masculinity in a society which emphasises dominance and self-reliance as an expression of masculinity and generally supports the expression of homophobia. Such issues have the potential to exacerbate and deepen the anxiety of an abused male. We took pains to talk about such issues supportively but without any direct reference to sexual abuse, with the knowledge that it was likely to be the case that privately held anxieties were being addressed. When, during the post-court phase, these issues were fully addressed in the context of the sexual abuse, it was clear from some of the comments and reactions of the boys that they had listened carefully to and benefited from the earlier discussions. They demonstrated understanding and made reference to the earlier sessions and were able to enter into the discussions with a degree of ease.

Inevitably, a Group programme of this length and nature will have an impact on its Leaders. This impact will possibly differ between genders. A male worker has to face comparisons with the abuser and needs to identify boundaries and highlight the absence of sexual abuse. A female worker has to face possible stereotyping and sexist attitudes and can feel isolated in an all male group. These factors dictate the need for close communication between workers and a well-worked out and agreed consistent response to situations which may arise. All the workers discussed ways of demonstrating non - oppressive, respectful relationships, in their behaviour with each other and with the boys. These factors also highlight the need for the Leaders to provide mutual support, and to receive joint and individual supervision on a regular basis. Unfortunately the supervision occurred more on an individual basis than on a joint basis. The mutual support and cooperation between the group workers to some extent compensated and replaced this. In view of the unexpected length of the groups, each group worker required and benefited from the sustained support of colleagues from their respective Teams.

Conclusions

The incompatibility between the therapeutic needs of sexually abused children and the demands of the legal system to preserve evidence, was vividly demonstrated by the experience of the boys in the Groups. Throughout the process there were clear expressions of anxiety from all of the boys in relation to the delays in the court process.

This fact highlights the need for social workers involved in this area of work strongly and consistently to advocate and negotiate for the needs of children who are caught up with the legal system in this manner to be given priority.

The experience of the boys in this project supports the view expressed in the literature that Groupwork is an appropriate and desirable response to male child sexual abuse, particularly in relation to organised abuse involving several children. The proposals for such work are likely to require strong negotiation for acceptance by members of the legal system, and detailed plans which justify how the work will give priority to the children without jeopardising the reliability of evidence.

The project has shown that it is possible to carry out certain areas of work which could be described as therapeutic, before a court trial, without interfering with evidence. Most notably areas of work which address issues relating to the context of sexual abuse, which have potential to exacerbate and deepen the level of anxiety of an abused child. The split of a therapeutic programme into pre-court and post-court phases was helpful to all parties, particularly the boys who were able to see that difficult areas of work which they may be worried about, are on the agenda for discussion at a later stage.

It is emphasised that such a split is a compromise and not a solution. The solution requires an adjustment of the legal system to enable a child's role in that system to be concluded at a very early stage, so as to free the child to receive a full therapeutic programme.

The Group Programme could be adapted for shorter time periods and for individual cases.

The project has demonstrated that some of the problems identified in the literature in relation to male child sexual abuse were experienced by the boys in the Groups. Most notably: anxieties relating to legal processes; guilt, feelings of being responsible; confusion over sexuality; fears relating to other people's reactions; difficulties in discussing matters with parents; anger at the abuser; feelings of betrayal; distortion of trust; damaged family relationships; fears of becoming an abuser, or at least acknowledgement that the possibility of becoming an abuser requires discussion; fears relating to homosexuality; confusion over the pleasurable and enjoyable aspects of the abuse; damaged or low self-esteem; expressions of anxiety through behaviour; being embroiled in a web of secrecy and being prevented from feeling able to communicate the facts of the abuse because of the status of the abuser; feeling isolated by shame and secrecy. The project demonstrated that it was possible to address these issues through Groupwork.

It was not possible at the outset to predict the extent of the delay. Had a prediction been possible, then it is likely that all parties concerned would have seriously questioned the validity of a court appearance. However, circumstances as they were, caused an incremental extension of the pre-trial waiting period beyond anybody's expectation or imagination.

The extension of the Group process as a result of the delays had a compensatory spin off in therapeutic terms, although direct therapeutic work relating to the abuse itself did not take place until after the court appearance. The workers and boys believed that a degree of therapeutic healing took place through the positive Group experiences and activities , in the form of increased self-esteem and empowerment through knowledge and confidence building. There was visible relief after a positive outcome at the eventual court appearance, where responsibility was finally placed where it belonged, on the offenders.

It is hoped that the boys involved with the project will continue to recover and re-adjust to life without court cases, secrets and fears, and will continue to develop along the path of transition from victim to survivor.

References

Aldridge, J. & Freshwater, K. (1993) 'The Preparation of Child Witnesses', *Journal of Child Law*, 5, 1

Bolton F., Morris L. and MacEachron A. (1989) *Males at Risk . The Other Side of Child Sexual Abuse*

Davies, G.(1992) 'Protecting the Child Witness in the Court Room', *Child Abuse Review*, 1, 33-41

Finkelhor D. and Associates (1986) *A Sourcebook on Child Sexual Abuse.* Sage

Furniss,T. (1990) 'Groupwork Therapy for Boys' (pp.49 - 61) in *Working with Sexually Abused Boys*. Edited by Hollows and Armstrong TAGOSAC 1990

Furniss, T.(1991) *The Multi-Professional Handbook of Child Sexual Abuse. Integrated Management, Therapy and Legal Intervention.* Routledge 1991

H.M.S.O. (1991) *Working Together Under the Children Act 1989*

H.M.S.O.(1992) *The Memorandum of Good Practice*

Peake A. (1990) 'Under-Reporting the Sexual Abuse of Boys' (pp.3 -19) in *Working With Sexually Abused Boys*. Edited by Hollows and Armstrong TAGOSAC 1990

Peake A. (1990) *Working with Sexually Abused Children, A Resource Pack For Professionals.* The Childrens Society 1990

Pigot T. (1989) *Report of the Advisory Group on Video Evidence.* London Home Office

Porter E. (1986) *Treating The Young Male Victim of Sexual Assault : Issues and Intervention Strategies.* Safer Society Press 1986.

Ryan G. (1989) 'Victim to Victimiser - Rethinking Victim Treatment', *Journal of Interpersonal Violence*, 4, 3, pp.325-341

Spencer, J.R. & Flin R. (1990) *The Evidence of Children, The Law and the Psychology.* Blackstone Press Ltd

Watkins, B. and Bentovim, A. (1992) 'The Sexual Abuse of Male Children and Adolescents : A Review of Current Research', *Journal of Child Psychology and Psychiatry*, 33, 1, pp.197 - 248. 1992

20
Private fostering of Nigerian children: A community based approach to child protection and welfare

Alban Unsworth

The community social work team in which I worked as a Senior Social Worker experienced a sudden explosion of concern about the extent of private fostering arrangements for Nigerian children and the conditions of these children, within a local authority housing estate. This concern provided a strong motivation for me to undertake a further period of study in child protection, to ensure that we could respond sensitively and as effectively as possible to these emerging problems.

Although the problem came to our attention before new guidelines on private fostering had come into force following the Children Act, I hope that the account of how we worked to protect the interests of the children involved will be of interest still. It illustrates the complexity of trying to go beyond a case by case approach, where an individual social worker does her or his best to meet the needs of an individual child, to an attempt to improve services generally, developing protection and support. The complexity of such attempts, the understanding needed of links between social and cultural factors, policy, legislation and practice, the breadth and depth of work involved are relevant to all social work situations. This account may be of particular interest to those preparing work under the Post Qualifying and Advanced Award framework of CCETSW.

The chapter will give an account of the limited literature we were able to draw on in understanding the history, origins and extent of the use of private foster care of West African children in the UK. It will describe the responses of one community social work team to problems associated with private fostering and our attempts to protect a group of Nigerian children in our area.

Background

The council estate which became the focus of our concern has a population of approximately 8000, on the edge of a small town in the Midlands. It is an area of high social need.

There had been a small number of private foster placements in the area for a number of years, mainly confined to a small group of families, generally offering a reasonable standard of care to both white and black children. Placements of white children were usually short term. The few black children in placements were from Nigeria and generally remained in the families until student parents had completed their education in Britain, when they returned to Nigeria.

Around 1989 the situation appeared to change dramatically. During the next two years there was a substantial increase in the number of placements coming to the attention of the team. The children were entirely of Nigerian origin, mainly from the Yoruba people. Most of the children had been placed through an informal network of contacts between people living on the estate and Nigerian families in the London area. The contacts had been initiated through local residents responding to advertisements in *Nursery World* magazine.

Two people were the main brokers, receiving children and then finding other families to foster the children. As far as we were aware initially, they received no financial benefit from their brokerage.

As soon as we became aware of this activity - we had by now discovered at least 40 Nigerian children living on the estate - we thought it essential to try to inform ourselves of the circumstances of the children and of what knowledge and initiatives there might be nationally which could guide us.

Relevant literature

There was very limited literature available. Below I summarise some of the writing we were able to draw on. Most of what we could find was concerned with the private fostering of West African children, whose parents were thought to be students (Craven 1968; Holman 1973). In Holman's study 60% of private fostering arrangements were for West African children. He found that 35% of children were placed following an advertisement in local papers or national magazines. He indicated that in almost all respects private foster care was less satisfactory than local authority care.

In 1975 the Commonwealth Students' Children's Society had organised an international seminar on 'The African Foster Child in Britain'. The seminar recognised unmet child care needs and recommended attempts to find alternatives to private fostering and to improve supervision of placements. A need for education on the issues involved - for students, social workers and foster parents - was identified.

Studies in the 1970s and 1980s (Ibru 1977; Goody and Muir 1982) paid considerable attention to parents' educational activities and the extensive use made of private fostering and daily minding.

Ellis (1982) had drawn attention to the influence of socio-cultural factors on the child care arrangements made by students.

The DHSS (1982) undertook a study of private fostering in nine social services departments. The study found that most of the children in private foster care were West African. The reasons for placement and for the lengthy periods of placement were difficult to discover. Little information was forthcoming about the arrangements for their long-term care. The study revealed disorganised departmental records, with no reliable administrative system to collect basic information.

All these studies pointed to major problems in the arrangements and standards in private foster care. The Save the Children Fund responded to these concerns about West African children in private foster care by establishing the African Family Advisory Service. Laurie Joshua, Senior Project Worker with the Advisory Service, argued that a reassessment of the situation was needed. He was helpful in drawing attention to the inaccuracy of describing West African children in private foster care as though this involved equally all nine nations from Senegal to Cameroon. The studies had in fact revealed that the vast majority of placements were of Nigerian children.

Prior to the 1950s relatively few West Africans travelled to the UK, although a small number have been doing so since the late nineteenth century. During the 1950s there was an enormous increase in the numbers of West Africans, particularly Nigerians, coming to the UK, the majority for further education. Most were men and came alone. Many suffered from isolation and racial discrimination during their stay. In 1955, in an attempt to remedy these problems the Colonial Office suggested that married men coming to the UK to study should be advised to bring their wives and children.

The ensuing difficulties in obtaining adequate child care arrangements were not anticipated by the British Government or the families themselves. It would appear that the British Government envisaged that the wives would care for the children. According to Ellis: 'In West African culture it is traditional for women to be financially independent of their husbands.' Consequently on coming to Britain, wives as well as husbands were keen to make the most of educational, training and employment opportunities. The financial difficulties experienced by married students receiving often inadequate student grants had also not been anticipated.

For many of these students it was natural for them to place their children with foster carers. Fostering is, according to Ellis, a traditional welfare mechanism in West Africa. Children frequently live away from their parents, for a wide range of reasons. Stapleton (1975) stated that 'Almost every child born in West Africa is a wanted child ... children are regarded as the greatest blessing and barrenness the greatest curse, to such an extent that a barren woman is frequently despised and distrusted'. Men are respected for and their status enhanced by the number of children they have. Families place a lot of pressure on couples to have large families. Stapleton states that in West Africa there is a real sense in which 'all children are everybody's children, or at least very much the concern of the community as a whole, and it is not only the parents who are involved in the way a child grows up.' The socialising process is carried out by the whole community.

The fact that these children are so wanted does not mean that the parents would always expect to maintain a close contact and be responsible for their upbringing. The extended family is of great importance and children will frequently be brought up by members of the extended family. Children may live with a relative for a wide variety of reasons. A child may be 'given' to a childless relative, or sent to live with a relative in an area where the educational opportunities are better. They may go and live with an elderly relative who needs support. Discipline in children is seen as important, and children may be sent to live with an older relative or teacher in order to learn discipline.

There is a wide range of reasons why a child may be brought up by relatives. Giving one's child to the care of a relative is not seen as fostering, and is not thought of in the same way as in Britain. A study in the mid 1970s in Ibadan, Nigeria, showed that one third of all adult Yoruba, whether single or married, had at least one child in their care who was not their own. Because it is a normal pattern in many parts of West Africa for a child to be brought up by alternative carers, many African families see no problem in seeking foster parents when they are in Britain. 'They do not see this as a family breakdown but as an adaptation of their traditional patterns to meet the needs of their new way of life.' (Stapleton, 1975)

This view of child rearing contrasts sharply with traditional British views. Vivian Biggs in her address to the 1975 International Seminar 'The African Child in Great Britain' noted

> *The English foster mother is usually very conscious of the one-to-one relationship between mother and child, which she believes to be the foundation of good child care. .... The African mother on the other hand sees fostering as the temporary care of her child by a substitute mother. She is unable to believe, initially at any rate, that there could be any confusion about who is the mother of the child. From this stand point, and believing (often wrongly) that the child is very adaptable, African parents in London frequently advertise for foster homes in the Nursery World, newsagents windows, or local papers in and around London.*

In Holman's (1973) study over 35% of the children in the sample had been placed via an advertisement in a newspaper or magazine. The first advertisement in *Nursery World* which can positively be identified as having been placed by non-British parents appeared in the magazine in 1955, and was placed by a Nigerian.

An analysis of *Nursery World* adverts by the African Advisory Service revealed that between 1956 and 1960 a total of 640 Nigerian children were advertised for placement; between 1966 and 1970 the number had risen to about 6,700; but between 1971 and 1975 the number fell to just over 3,000.

The large increase in numbers between 1966 and 1970, led to the British Council issuing a warning to male students that they should leave their wives and children behind in Nigeria when they came to study in the UK. There was a dramatic drop in numbers over the next five years.

More recent figures of the number of Nigerian children advertised in *Nursery World* were: 1979-1983: 2,500; 1984-1988: 3,331. The figures for the period 1984-1988 when broken down reveal the following: 1984 (469), 1985 (497), 1986 (614), 1987 (819), 1988 (902), an increase of 92% during the 4 years (Joshua 1989). These figures take no account of the large numbers of children who may have been placed through informal networks.

In February 1990 *Nursery World* decided to suspend any further publication of advertisements from parents for private fostering following a television programme which highlighted the magazine's role in the growth of private fostering. The publisher considered that as a result of media attention, the wider public had become aware of the adverts and people with suspect motives may seek out children via the publication. However the publisher regretted that this action was necessary, as he felt that the adverts went some way towards preventing children being placed through underground networks.

Although information is far from complete, most suggests that the majority of West African children privately fostered are Nigerian. Since the early 1960s Nigeria has been amongst the three countries sending the largest number of students to the UK. However in the period 1984-1988, which saw the largest rise in private placements, the number of Nigerian students coming to the UK fell substantially (British Council Statistics of Overseas students; 1986/1987 British Council, London 1988).

The African Family Advisory Service carried out a review of the child care cases referred to them by local authorities in the period 1986-1988. In the period reviewed AFAS received a total of 205 referrals from local authorities involving Nigerian and Ghanaian children, who had been received into statutory care. Due to the lack of such basic information as the children's identities, or addresses for the parents, AFAS were unable to act in 85 of these cases. Of the remaining 120 cases, 92 children were Nigerian, 17 were Ghanaian, and one child was from the Republic of Benin.

From the 92 referrals made involving Nigerian children, the AFAS were able to make the following observations:

1. 79 of the children were born in Nigeria and had arrived in the UK within the five years prior to their reception into care.
2. 87 of the 92 children were privately fostered, and both parents were resident in Nigeria at the time they were received into care.
3. 5 of the children had one parent in the UK at the time they were received into care. For most, the mother's right to remain in the UK had lapsed.
4. In 33 of the 92 Nigerian cases the court or local authority made the decision to reunite the children with their families in Nigeria. In 22 cases the court or local authority decided that the children should remain in the UK. 37 cases were awaiting decision.

Two distinct features were identified in the situations of the 87 Nigerian children privately fostered. In 66% of the cases the children's parents were permanent residents of Nigeria, who had visited the UK with their children on a short stay visa, and returned to Nigeria without their children. In 33% of the cases, one or both of the children's parents were at some point in time believed to have been students in the UK prior to returning to Nigeria without their children.

Although the review carried out by AFAS is skewed, to the extent that the study population consists only of those cases referred to the AFAS by local authorities, it nevertheless provides further support to the view that the description 'West African children' and 'West African student parents' is misleading. The majority of the children in private foster placements in the UK are Nigerian, and very few nationals of other West African states use private fostering in the UK. A significant number of Nigerian parents who place their children in private foster care are not students, although some parents may have been students in the UK prior to returning to Nigeria without their children. The use of private foster care seems to have changed since the 1950s and 1960s when it was mainly used by students.

Fostering in local areas

This national trend was very much reflected in experiences of private fostering in our local area. The children placed were almost entirely Nigerian, mainly from the Yoruba people. The majority of the parents of the children placed were not studying or working in Britain. In most cases we discovered that the parents had returned to Nigeria between the date of placement and the date at which we became aware of the placement. A few of the children had been born in Britain, but in the main the children had entered the country with their parents on short-term, visitor visas.

It was not possible to discover accurate current figures for the number of children placed in private foster care. The Department of Health produces annual statistics of placements which have been notified to the local authorities who in turn notify the Department. However it is acknowledged that not all local authorities keep records or notify the DoH. Many private foster parents do not register with the local authority. According to the Department of Health figures, a total of 2,873 children are known to have been placed in private foster homes in 1988. They are however only snapshot figures on a given day and do not necessarily reflect the numbers of children who pass through private foster placements in any year.

The cases referred to the AFAS are those in which the local authority are aware of the placements and have intervened for one reason or another to remove the children. However AFAS contend that some local authorities avoid interventions in these placements in the belief that these are 'private' arrangements between a child's parent and the foster parents.

The Midlands council estate which was our concern was just one area where informal private fostering networks existed. There were 400 Nigerian children privately fostered in an area of Hampshire, and similar smaller clusters in Lincolnshire, Devon, East Sussex, Hertfordshire, Kent, Dorset, Wiltshire, and Leicestershire.

The sharp decline in the number of Nigerian students coming to Britain, and the increases in the number of children advertised for private fostering was occurring at a time when the Nigerian economy was suffering a massive slump. The African Advisory Service quoted a World Bank report (1988) which showed 37% fall in the country's Gross National Product from $72 billions to $39 billions in 1987 and a corresponding fall in Gross National Product per capita from $700 to $360.

The slump in the Nigerian Economy was in part attributable to the sharp drop in World oil prices. Oil is a significant export earner for Nigeria, and the previous high oil earnings served to fuel a rapidly expanding economy and a high level of investment in the social infrastructure e.g. education, medical services (Joshua 1990). The economic crisis in Nigeria continues, along with major political upheaval.

Motivation of parents

Economic pressures may explain in part the motivation of parents placing their children in private foster care in the UK. It has been suggested that some Nigerian women have travelled to Britain in pregnancy with the specific purpose of using the comparatively good medical facilities. Some children may then have been left in this country, whilst the mother returned to Nigeria, to benefit in the first few years of life from these medical facilities. These early years are the years when a child is most at risk especially in a country with inadequate medical facilities. Our experience in the Midlands was that most children were placed as babies or very young children and generally returned to their parents between the ages of two and three. The natural parents appeared to trust British families to provide good standards of care. Ironically some may have been placing their children in areas of high social deprivation in families where the care offered was below that found in local authority approved homes.

Nigeria is a former British colony with a long standing close relationship with the UK and many of the institutions are modelled on the British system, English remains the official and common language. It has been suggested that some Nigerian parents see it is an advantage for their children to gain a veneer of Anglicisation, and derive some status for themselves by having their children privately fostered in the UK. However, without substantive research, suggestions about possible motives remain largely speculative.

The fact that Nigerian parents were able to enter the UK with their children and at a later date leave without their children was due to a long recognised loophole in immigration controls. The AFAS researched entry patterns and found that most of the children entered the country on six month visitors' visas. Visitors were not entered on the Home Office computer and there were no exit controls on them. If questioned about the whereabouts of the children, parents were able to say that the children had already left the country (Joshua 1990).

Legal background

The main legislation guiding private fostering prior to the implementation of the 1989 Children Act was the Foster Children Act of 1980. Whilst it identified the duty of the local authority to 'ensure the well-being ... and visit foster children' regulations about such visiting were never issued. Nor was the provision in the Act that the Secretary of State should make regulations requiring *parents* to notify the local authority when placing a child with foster parents activated. *Foster parents* were required to notify the local authority of their intention to foster a child - except in an emergency.

The local authority had power under the 1980 Act to impose requirements on foster parents about the number, age and sex of foster children and to specify accommodation and equipment that must be provided for them. Foster parents had a right of appeal.

A great deal was left to the discretion of local authorities. The Act did not however give them a mandate to approach private foster placements in the same way as they assessed and approved foster parents they would use for children in their own care.

The Act gave powers to regulate and prohibit, rather than approve. To use their powers they would need to gather evidence about particular persons or premises for submission to the Juvenile Court. The 1988 Boarding Out Regulations did not apply to privately fostered children.

The legal position allowed local authorities to adopt a minimalist approach to private foster care. Atkinson & Horner (1990) argued that local authorities interpreted 'private' in a way which gave priority to the parents' right to choose the type of family and upbringing which they wished for their child. They referred to a study in one local authority which showed that social workers did not apply the same standards to privately arranged foster placements as to those they were assessing for local authority use. They suggested that issues of attachment and re-attachment were not given much attention. Children fostered privately had often been placed at a very young age in homes where they remained for considerable periods with people ill- equipped to keep connections with the birth family alive , ensure a strong sense of cultural identity or prepare the child for return home.

During the passage of the 1989 Children Act, AFAS, local authorities, and a number of other child care agencies and pressure groups had submitted amendments intended to address some of these issues. However they had been unable to persuade the Select Committee to include the main body of the private fostering section: the requirement for pre-placement enquiries and the duty to consider the child's racial origin, religion and cultural background. Assurance was given however (Hansard 23.10.1989) that regulations would address these issues.

The 1989 Act requires birth parents to notify the local authority if they intend to arrange private fostering. It limits to three the number of children foster carers may foster. Private foster carers with more than three children are subject to regulations under a separate section under children's homes.

The duties of local authorities in the Act are broadly similar to previous legislation but with the intention that duties would be strengthened in the accompanying regulations.

The Act refers to the need for regulations in three areas:

1. The circumstances in which local authorities should visit private foster children and how local authorities should carry out their functions in respect of these children.
2. Detailed requirements regarding the notification to a local authority of a proposal to foster a child privately.
3. The circumstances in which a person is disqualified from privately fostering a child without the consent of the local authority.

As part of the work arising from the concerns of our team, AFAS invited me to become a member of their Practice Development Group, to look at the practice implications of public policy and legislation. In particular the group studied the Children Act:

1. To advise on the regulations for private fostering.
2. To draw up guidelines and a code of practice, to accompany the regulations.
3. To promote the code of practice and raise awareness.

The group had the opportunity to meet with Social Services Inspectors to examine and comment upon draft guidelines and regulations.

This national involvement was seen by the team as central to improving conditions for children in the future as well as relevant to ensuring that practice within our own local authority would improve.

Local responses and strategy

We were first alerted to a potential problem when local Health Visitors let us know that a few Nigerian children had recently been brought to the clinic by their private foster carers, and that they had also come across other Nigerian children during their routine visits to families on the estate. A small number of the private foster carers subsequently presented themselves at one of our offices and informed us of their placements.

At this stage the team did not realise the full extent of private fostering on the estate, but realised that there were a number of private foster carers who had not visited the office. With the assistance of local Health Visitors we compiled a list of carers known to have placements who had not come to the office. We wrote to these foster carers inviting them to visit the office. The majority did not respond.

Our team at this time was experiencing a severe staffing crisis - with six vacant social worker posts. Given the staffing situation it was felt that little more could be done to address the problem until the staffing situation had improved.

We arranged for the local evening paper to carry a press release drawing attention to the need for anyone privately fostering to notify the Social Services Department. The press release was also carried in the local 'Freebie' newspaper delivered to every home in the area, and a similar article was published in the community newspaper for the estate where we had learned the fostering was common. As soon as the staffing position improved sufficiently the team began actively to pursue those private foster carers who had failed to make contact with the office. It was only at this stage that we gradually became aware of the full extent of the network of private foster carers that had developed in the area.

Considerable social work time was expended in locating private foster carers and making contact with fostered children. Often we were seeking people who did not wish to be located. Often particular children had to be tracked through a succession of previous placements.

In addressing the issues of private fostering of Nigerians the team found itself entering an area of work and expertise never previously encountered by any team members.

The area itself is overwhelmingly white and working class. All the social workers within the team were white. None of us had substantial experience of working with client groups from minority ethnic groups. Few members of the team had any previous experience of private fostering. We needed to establish a clear and agreed value base to underpin our approach to the task. Our knowledge and understanding of the history and background to the private fostering of Nigerian children in Britain was minimal. It was with the agreement of the team that I was given the opportunity to study some of the relevant literature and make contact with groups who could advise us. Considerable discussion took place within the team, both informally and formally through team meetings, to arrive at a shared and agreed value base. The team were well aware of the inherent difficulties and problems surrounding the trans-racial placement of children. We believed strongly that all placements should seek to meet the needs arising from the child's cultural, linguistic, and religious background, and that wherever possible children should be placed within families of the same cultural background. In these terms alone therefore we found the practice of placing Nigerian children in white families with no Nigerian connections unacceptable.

We should have liked to be in a position where we were legally empowered to end this practice. Given that we were not currently in that position, we felt a strong obligation to ensure that the children were not placed in premises or with persons with whom they were either at risk or standards of care were unacceptably low. We were clear that should we find such circumstances, we would seek prohibition. In placements where prohibition was not felt to be appropriate we would seek to raise standards of care, and work towards raising carers' awareness of the importance of promoting and maintaining the child's links with their parents and with their cultural background.

We soon discovered that we had to work within an inadequate framework of legislation and departmental procedures in respect of private fostering. Difficulties were compounded by the team's lack of familiarity with the legislation, a lack of familiarity shared by our legal advisors. The procedures and accompanying forms primarily concerned themselves with notification and registration, but were unhelpful in terms of the mechanics of prohibition, disqualification, requirement notices, and private foster placement reviews.

With our legal section, with consultation from AFAS, we devised a procedure and accompanying set of forms to enable the team to issue notices of prohibition, disqualification, and notices of requirements, and designed an explanatory leaflet.

We arranged a series of individual initial visits, where we asked the private foster carers to sign a form indicating that the provisions of the Act had been explained to them and that they had received a leaflet explaining to them the general outlines of the regulations. This was an important document as it could subsequently be used in a court of law as admissible evidence. Many of the private foster carers had failed to notify the health authorities of their placements, and we therefore asked that they complete a standard letter we had devised to the Senior Nursing Officer. None of the carers we visited had written consent from the natural parents to obtain medical treatment for the children. In those cases where the foster carers were still in contact with the natural parents we asked them to ensure that the natural parents gave their written consent.

We had received no prior notification for any of the placements visited. As we only had power to 'regulate or prohibit', a decision was made with the team manager about the number and ages of children the private foster carers should be allowed to foster; what accommodation, equipment, materials, should be provided by the foster parents; and in what circumstances prohibition of premises or persons was required.

It was important at this point to distinguish between 'disqualification' and 'prohibition'. Some people are disqualified from undertaking private fostering, for example families where children have previously been removed by the local authority on child protection grounds. The local authority can also prohibit premises or persons believed to be unsuitable, although the Act gives no guidance as to 'unsuitability'.

We required the removal of a number of children where private foster carers were 'disqualified' because children were residing in households from which children had previously been removed, or where a Schedule One offender was in the household, or there were clearly unsatisfactory home conditions. Ten placements were ended by disqualification and prohibition.

A major issue confronted by the team was how to manage the removal of children from disqualified and prohibited placements. Clearly if a placement is to be prohibited suitable alternative carers must be identified for the child. The department did not have a number of culturally appropriate placements available. Like other local authorities before us we found that we had to strike a balance between our responsibilities to safeguard the welfare of the children against the right of the natural parents to choose a placement for their child.

In consultation with AFAS and our legal section we decided only to remove to local authority care those children who were felt to be at immediate risk. We made contact with the natural parents and informed them that the placement had been prohibited and requested that they make alternative arrangements for the care of their children within a specific period of time. It was made clear that if the child was not removed from the placement we would seek the child's removal to care through the Juvenile court.

Nine children were removed by their natural parents. We asked the natural parents to contact the office before they removed their children, but only one of the parents did so. The rest collected their children directly from the private foster carers and returned with the children to addresses in London. We passed this information on to the local authorities in London, with a request that follow up visits be undertaken. We received no feedback from the 'home' local authorities. We had no guarantees that the children were collected by their parent. The children may well have been placed in another private placement elsewhere in the country. We found our powerlessness to *ensure* the welfare of the children extremely worrying. It made us determined to pursue ways of preventing such unsatisfactory situations in the future.

One child entered our care. The Children's Services Team were unable to offer us a culturally appropriate placement within our area and had no existing agreement with other local authorities to seek appropriate placements. We had to obtain the agreement of the Divisional Director with responsibility for child care to approach other authorities and to fund an outside placement. The child was eventually placed with African/ Caribbean foster parents in a neighbouring city.

In most of the placements visited it was felt necessary to issue requirement notices. The requirement notices were time limited and social workers returned to the private foster placements to ensure that their requirements had been complied with. It was made clear that failure to comply could result in prohibition of the placement and/or criminal prosecution. In only one case was it felt necessary to initiate a criminal prosecution.

In a number of cases where the household was clearly overcrowded we limited the numbers of children the carers could accommodate. We insisted that all children should have their own cot or bed. We required all homes to provide basic safety equipment, fireguards, stair guards, etc. and required that all children should have adequate play space and equipment. Our overall objective was to raise standards within private foster homes.

Initially we met some resistance from carers to our involvement, however as foster carers came to realise that we intended to continue visits on a regular basis, carers began to comply with our requirements.

We were also engaged in increasing the awareness of the foster carers about the needs and difficulties of the children, as well as ensuring networks locally knew about our expectations. We made it clear that we wished them to use us as a source of advice and assistance in meeting the needs of the children placed with them. Some foster parents were already experiencing difficulties in meeting primary health care needs, particularly hair and skin care. It was not uncommon to come across children who had developed eczema and brittle hair. Jointly with local health visitors we were able to give advice about the dietary and hair and skin care needs of the children placed with them.

There was little understanding amongst carers of the major issues of cross cultural placement of children. We were only at the beginning stage of working to improve this situation. It was a very painful and difficult situation - one where we felt that we could generally do little more than prevent major physical harm. We felt trapped in a system which was quite inadequate to promote the well-being of the children.

We were able to locate the two key informal 'brokers' on the estate. One of the brokers clearly viewed private fostering as a money making exercise, and persistently defied all requirement notices and the eventual prohibition notice placed upon her. Her own fostering activities were eventually brought to an end by criminal prosecution. The second broker established a good working relationship with social workers. She was horrified to discover that a number of children she had introduced to the area had subsequently passed through a number of placements and in some cases had ended up in entirely unacceptable placements. She became very active in encouraging carers to inform us of their placements, and frequently sought children out on our behalf. She decided to end her own private fostering when her current placement came to an end. She worked actively to discourage families on the estate from becoming engaged in these activities.

We continued to visit private placements on the estate, adopting the boarding out regulations as our guidelines for frequency of visiting etc. All placements were visited at least every twelve weeks, and a formal review form completed. New placements or subsequent placements within the same family were visited immediately we were notified.

The number of placements reduced dramatically. Many carers stated that they did not wish to take further placements. There were a number of reasons behind this sharp decline. We ended a number of placements through prohibition, and this together with local knowledge that the team intended actively to 'regulate' private fostering discouraged many potential carers. Private foster carers had experienced difficulties in receiving agreed regular payments, and had become concerned when parents failed to visit as regularly as agreed. We also became aware that natural parents and informal brokers in London had been discouraged from seeking placements on learning of our proactive approach. This led us to put continuing effort into encouraging a national, collaborative approach.

I visited the Nigerian High Commission and discussed our experiences with a senior welfare officer. I was particularly concerned that we had been unsuccessful in following up through the London borough local authorities, those children whose placements had been prohibited. It was agreed that High Commission staff would visit the addresses we had been given, both in London and in Nigeria. He also agreed to arrange for contact to be made with the parents of children in continuing placements. His view was that the practice of private fostering should be actively discouraged by the Nigerian authorities.

When the team first became involved in visiting private foster placements in the area, we had little knowledge of the history and background to the private fostering of Nigerian children in the UK. Initially we had naively assumed that the children were likely to be the children of Nigerian parents who were working or studying in the UK. We were bewildered to discover that in many cases the parents had returned to Nigeria, or that the children had been brought to the UK in order to be privately fostered. It appeared to us that some children had been effectively abandoned by their parents.

We were fortunate in being able to make early contact with the African Family Advisory Service who were able to supply us with a great deal of background information to the history of private fostering in the UK, as well as providing us with invaluable practical advice and consultancy. Through AFAS we were also able to make contact with other local authorities and share and contrast our experiences. The relationship with AFAS continued after the main local work had been done, through my involvement in the practice development group.

Ensuring the spread of information

We felt it was important to share our experience as widely as possible, so arranged a number of training and staff awareness sessions for colleagues from other teams. The sessions were intended for workers who were directly involved or likely to become involved in the registration and supervision of private foster placements of Nigerian children. Several placements had come to light in the catchment areas of adjoining community teams. We suspected that some of these placements were due to our pro-active approach: 'squeezing out' placements into adjoining areas.

We used TV films and videos to give background information about Nigeria's economic and political problems. A member of the Nigerian High Commission gave a presentation about the cultural diversity of Nigeria and the sociocultural background to the private fostering of Nigerian children in the UK. A Nigerian broadcaster and journalist spoke about her own traumatic experiences as a Nigerian child fostered in the UK and the continuing difficulties she faced as an adult.

We were able to show a video of a programme about a fostering network similar to the one we had been working with as an introduction to an account of our local work. We discussed the strategy we had developed and the impact of the new legislation.

We looked at primary health care needs of African and Caribbean children and considered signs and symptoms of abuse and neglect. We were helped in this by a West Indian foster parent from a neighbouring city. She gave a practical demonstration and talk about dietary, skin and hair care needs. These sessions were much appreciated by social workers, though on their own could only be seen as a minimal response to a nation-wide problem.

We continued to try to improve the general understanding of private fostering and trans-racial placements through a variety of means - supporting local and national radio programmes, journal articles and through the national AFAS working party. We made a contribution to working parties in our own department concerned with private fostering and the needs of children from minority groups. The department substantially increased attention and priority given to private fostering.

Whilst we felt that we had some measure of success in improving the situation locally, we remained concerned that local authorities nation-wide needed to develop a collaborative strategy, working with Nigerian and other black groups and agencies. However committed we might be as a team, we were very limited in our understanding of Nigerian cultures and felt that we were only able to achieve the most basic level of protection for some children.

This work represented a beginning - we continued to try to improve our service through work with foster carers and others to raise their awareness of and commitment to issues of loss, attachment, identity. For all of us it was a major learning experience, which we hope helped to focus public and professional attention on a long neglected subject.

References

African Family Advisory Service: (1989) 'Private Fostering and West African Children.', 'Briefing Notes and Amendments relating to Private Fostering.', 'The African Family in Britain', 'Facts about Nigeria'

Atkinson, C., & Horner, A. 'Private Fostering - Legislation and Practice'. *Adoption and Fostering* Vol. 14, No 3. 1990

BBC Television: The World About Us series, 'Nigeria, Squandering of Riches'

British Council: *Overseas Students in Britain: A handbook for those concerned with the welfare of the overseas student*

Colonial Office (1955): *Colonial Students in Britain: A report by Political & Economic Planning Section.* London

Commission for Racial Equality. 'Fostering Black Children.'

Commonwealth Students' Children Society (1975) Report of a Seminar on 'The African Child in Great Britain'

Community Care (1991) 'Nigerians meet SSD's over Fostering' *Community Care* 31st January 1991

Craven, A. (1968) 'West Africans in London'. London, Institutional Race Relations

Department of Health and Social Security (1982) 'Study of Private Fostering' London: North Region

Ellis, J. (1982) 'Differing Conceptions of a Child's Needs: Some Implications for Social work with West African Children and Parents.' in *West African Families in Britain: A Meeting of 2 Cultures.* London: RKP

Goody, E., Muir, C. (1982) 'Parenthood and Social Reproduction.' London: Cambridge University Press

Holman, R. (1973) 'Trading in children: a study of private fostering.' London, Boston: Routledge and Kegan Paul

Ibru, C. (1977) 'Nigerian Parents and their Children' MPhil thesis North London Polytechnic

Jarvis, I (1989) 'Cashing in on the Hopes of Black Children.' *Social Work Today* 2nd February 1989

Joshua, L. (1989) 'Babies caught up in Drug Trade.' *Community Care* 6th July 1989

Leeds University: slides and taped commentary, 'Signs and Symptoms of Abuse and Neglect in Non-Caucasian children'

Nigerian Department of Information: 'A Brief History of Nigeria', 'Nigeria at a Glance', 'Perspectives of Nigerian Culture'

Ogden, Joy. (1991) 'Culture Shocks' *Social Work Today* 21st February 1991

Race Equality Unit. Black Children and Private Fostering Working Group. London: REU/NISW.

Regulations and Guidance: Section Nine Private Fostering, Children's Act 1969. London: HMSO

Race Equality Unit. (1993) *Black children and private fostering. London: NISW*

Save the Children (1997) *Private Fostering.* London

Sone, K. 'A Private Practice' *Community Care* 21st May 1989

Stapleton, P. (1975) 'Child Rearing in West Africa.' BASW

The World Bank: 1988 Data Atlas

TV programme: Facing South Series, 'A Private Arrangement'

Warwickshire County Council. *Social Services Department: Report of Working party on 1989 Children Act and Private Fostering.*

21
Promoting effective family support and child protection for Asian children

Sandeep Atkar, Norma Baldwin, Rajinder Ghataora, Vyomesh Thanki

Introduction

This chapter will share experiences from a project set up in partnership between NSPCC and the University of Warwick to explore family support and child protection needs of Asian communities and encourage the provision of services sensitive to these needs. The wider context of the project, its aims, issues involved in setting it up and some of its findings will be described. The importance of interdisciplinary and holistic approaches to child protection and family support will be discussed.

The project aims to explore with children, young people, parents and local workers:

- the strengths of families and groups within Asian communities;
- successes, difficulties and stresses in bringing up children;
- support needs of parents and children;
- the effect of problems such as housing, money, unemployment, relationships, racism;
- priorities in protecting children;
- views and definitions of abuse;
- what services are needed to prevent and respond to harm;
- how to influence the development of family support and child protection services;
- how to facilitate and encourage supportive networks in the areas of the project.

The project began in 1993, with funding and support from the Barrow Cadbury Trust, NSPCC, Birmingham, Coventry, Sandwell and Warwickshire Social Services Departments and the University of Warwick. It was jointly managed by NSPCC and the University of Warwick.

Sandeep Atkar and Rajinder Ghataora were the development workers. Their tasks were to gather information from Asian communities in two Midland local authorities; to share this information within the communities and to consider in detail with professional groups in education, health and social work services the implications for future child protection and family support services.

Work included:

- extensive liaison and consultation with local groups, agencies and networks;

- focus groups, individual questionnaires, interviews;
- consultancy and support in child protection cases;
- wide dissemination of findings and detailed discussion of the policy and practice implications with agencies involved.

There was enormous interest in the project from a variety of groups. They expressed a strong sense of urgency about problems of child protection and family support amongst Asian communities and concern at the lack of an overview of needs and resources which might help in addressing them. A review of relevant literature revealed only limited and fragmented knowledge available about the extent of child abuse and responses to it.

The lack of concrete information coupled with the enthusiasm and commitment of those we worked with led to some tensions. We were anxious to disseminate our findings on a continuous basis, and were invited to give presentations about the project to numerous local groups, to groups of social work students and at regional and national conferences. Whilst these presentations and our liaison work contributed to general debate and consciousness about child protection issues within Asian communities, the scarcity of hard information led to pressures to generalise from our pilot work before that was appropriate. However we were very much encouraged by the readiness to consider the issues we and others were raising.

We hope that this account will do justice to the complexity of what we found, whilst also providing some straightforward pointers to improving support for Asian groups and families and preventing harm to children.

Many of the issues raised are relevant to current discussions of support for *all families*, but within this broader picture the particular experiences and needs of Asian families are central.

Context

There is a growing recognition that children from minority communities have not been well served in child protection. The lack of equity in how social work agencies respond to black children in need of care or protection highlights the continuing significance of 'race' (Barn et al 1997). Government departments have not collected data regarding race and child protection and, according to Corby (1993, p.69) 'few studies check their samples for ethnicity'. In Gambe et al's (1992, p.75) view 'most of the existing literature ignores the fact that we live in a multi-ethnic or a multi-racial society', and little concern is shown with the issue of protection of black children from abuse.

In 1978 the Commission for Racial Equality/Association of Directors of Social Work working group concluded that the response of Social Services Departments (SSDs) to 'multi-racial communities has been patchy, piecemeal and lacking in strategy'. Ten years later Roys (1988) argued that this conclusion was still valid. All the available evidence indicated that black people were under-represented in the supportive aspects of social services and over-represented in those aspects that involve 'overt social control and institutionalisation'. Black people's experiences are so negative that a service is sought only in the most desperate circumstances (Roys, 1988, p.210). In 1989 the Commission for Racial Equality survey showed that SSDs had failed to meet their duties under s71 and s20 of the Race Relations Act 1976 - the requirements to tackle discrimination and promote equality of opportunity in employment and in the provision of services (CRE, 1989).

Not only do black people face overt racism, but according to Roys (1988) they also suffer from 'liberal overcompensation' (see also Channer and Parton, 1990). Confusion and guilt over the issue of race may lead social workers to suspend their normal professional judgments - in the case of Jasmine Beckford such an approach was associated with a tragic outcome. At the other extreme, Gambe et al (1992 p.78) referring to Ahmad's (1989) observations, point out that practitioners may be engaging in a punitive or coercive approach where they 'do not hesitate to remove black children from families considered unsuitable or whose child care practices are perceived to be sub-standard'. Barn (1993, p.108) found in her research that some social workers adopted a rescue mentality, were highly zealous and could over-react, rather than intervene with an open mind.

Barn (1990 p.229) argues that although over the last few decades much has been written on children in public care, 'scant attention has been given to the situation of black children'. None of the nine DHSS funded studies included in the 1985 report entitled 'Social Work Decisions in Child Care', focused on the 'race' dimension. In her own research, Barn found that while more black children were referred because of family relationships, marital difficulties, financial reasons, marital problems as a result of discrimination in housing and employment, and mother's mental health, greater proportions of white children were referred as a result of children's difficult (or delinquent) behaviour and child protection concerns. Her findings clearly demonstrated that not only did social workers fail to hear the voice of black children, but practitioners' negative attitudes, racial stereotyping and pathologising actively worked to the detriment of black families. Her more recent work shows that while there may have been progress in some areas, many problems continue (Barn et al 1997).

Given the accounts of inequity in responses to minority communities, it is unfortunate that 'race' has become such a contentious issue, leading some commentators to complain about the 'new orthodoxy' of anti-racism. Phillips (1993) complained that CCETSW's pronouncements on 'race' amounted to nothing but 'diktats' , Pinker (1993) referred to the emphasis given to anti-racism as 'a lethal kind of looniness'. In response to these concerns, Harwin (1993) stressed the need for social work to concentrate on 'outcomes' of interventions for all sections of society. However, Waterhouse (1993, p.9-10) noted that we know 'little about the position of children from diverse ethnic origins and how they fare in the decision making process'. In addition, what we lack in Britain is specificity on the 'micro' aspects of protecting children: referral patterns, impact of assessment and investigation, child rearing practices and priorities, the provision of family support services or therapeutic intervention (see Gough, 1993, p.275-284). Whilst findings reported in Messages from Research (DoH, 1995) provide useful evidence to back up arguments about the need for services which concentrate on assessing needs holistically, which pay more attention to support and prevention, they do not offer the necessary levels of detail to fill in the gaps. As the present situation remains one in which the bulk of social work help is being limited to children in need of protection, the low level of referrals in relation to significant harm of children from some minority groups needs careful exploration.

Effective, preventive and supportive measures may obviate the need for formal, controlling interventions and go some way towards improving black people's experience of contact with social services. Sensitive and appropriate child protection services where harm has been demonstrated also remain a priority, however.

Equity and diversity

Child protection work, according to Stone (1990, p. 76), 'takes place in a society which is class based and in which women and racial minorities are generally disadvantaged'. SSDs and voluntary organisations reflect these social and structural inequalities. Apart from acknowledging the existence of institutionalised discrimination, one of the major difficulties in trying to achieve equity in service delivery for children from diverse backgrounds is the lack of data that would help to map an accurate picture of the extent of unmet child protection needs across different minority ethnic communities. This reflects the general reluctance to engage with the diverse ethnicity of people in Britain from Asian, African, Caribbean, Greek/Cypriot, Turkish, Chinese, Romany and Arab descent, as well as those from white indigenous and white European backgrounds.

The NSPCC figures on trends in child abuse appear to show an over-representation of ethnic minorities among the parents of children on child protection registers (see Creighton, 1992, p.28). However, the NSPCC advises that these trends be treated with caution as strictly comparable figures for black families with dependent children were not available from census data when the research was carried out. NSPCC figures were collected from a sample of areas which included a high proportion of urban areas and proportions of minority groups may have been higher than the national average. Creighton suggests that, assuming minority ethnic families have a greater number of children per family unit - in comparison with white families - it could be that minority group children are in fact under-represented on child protection registers. Our preliminary investigations in Midlands' local authorities showed this to be the case. The under representation could be interpreted as a reflection of minority children enjoying better levels of protection, family support and surveillance within their communities. Alternatively, it could indicate a failure on the part of the agencies involved in child protection work to have sufficient contact with black and other minority children, to enable them to respond sensitively to potential harm and to make appropriate referrals (Ahmad, 1989).

The Department of Health (DoH, 1993) agreed to collect data supplied by SSDs on the ethnic origin of children looked after and those accommodated in secure units. DoH's concerns have centred on the concentration of ethnic minorities in the juvenile justice system and local authority accommodation. Within the broad category of 'ethnic minorities', African-Caribbean children, and in particular children of mixed heritage, continue to be over-represented, whereas South Asian children (those from India, Pakistan and Bangladesh) remain under-represented. What is still lacking is a clear understanding of trends in referrals for children from diverse communities and their support and protection needs. An emphasis of this chapter is that hard statistical information needs to be backed up with detailed understandings of the priorities, experiences, needs and lifestyles of minority groups.

Under the framework of Children Acts there is a clear expectation for social workers to give due regard to issues of race and ethnicity. SSDs and Social Work Departments have had the opportunity to develop an information base recording details of ethnic origin on referrals and child protection registration. Combining this knowledge with census data relating to ethnic background at the local ward level offers the ideal opportunity to make sense of how black and white children are faring in the child protection system (see Creighton, 1992, p.28).

The Hifazat Surukhia project was set up to try to increase understanding of the child protection needs of Indian, Pakistani and Bangladeshi children and their families. The development workers hoped to learn more about the context of 'harm' in South Asian communities and the implications of this for SSDs, police, health, and education services as well as voluntary organisations. The study aimed to address the support needs of Asian communities, taking account of the material circumstances in which they bring up their children. An essential emphasis was on the need to recognise diversity within groups.

Our hope was that our study, alongside nationally available data on all children, black and white, could make a contribution to understanding and promoting the conditions in which children thrive. There is a need to go beyond a focus on 'race' as an exclusive category, to consider how it interacts with other economic, social and cultural factors. Such an approach has the potential to illuminate the specific needs of children from many groups, including those of mixed heritage. A close examination of the context of child rearing and parental practices of socialisation and discipline in diverse communities can increase understanding of ways parents cope under stress and hardship and in conditions of poor housing, harassment and hostility (Creighton 1992; Amin & Oppenheim 1993; Graham 1993). Such an approach is in line with the Children Acts' (England, Wales and Scotland) emphasis on developing supportive and preventive services and providing for children in need.

Key ethical issues

The project raised some serious ethical considerations. The prospect of a set of powerful, mainly white organisations conducting research in Asian communities raised the question: on whose terms would the study be carried out? Suspicion will inevitably surround such organisations. To engage in such work may be seen as colonising, or paternalistic. To fail to engage in such work is to collude with present inadequacies in the services available to black children and families.

An initial concern centred on the appropriateness of seeking access to children and families who may have had to deal with child protection problems. On what grounds is it ethically justifiable to inquire into the private and confidential aspects of family life? The justification for our chosen method of fieldwork activity was based on commitment to try to make the research endeavours relevant and beneficial to local communities.

Through close involvement with statutory and voluntary agencies and with local Asian groups, we hoped that the study would lead to improvements in the quality of social work practice and service delivery. Barn (1993) found that when she asked agencies to collaborate in providing information, they were keen on the study as long as it was looking at black families, but instituted bureaucratic barriers when they realised the focus was actually on examining social work decision-making. In contrast, agencies involved in our study had identified the need for improvements in their family support and child protection services for Asian groups, they were closely involved in identifying key questions and in discussing findings and issues raised. We tried to devise working methods which tied development work to the research process at every stage.

Another key issue was the extent to which children and families could feel involved in the way the study was designed and directed. Would local communities share the level of importance attached to the subject matter by the researchers, appreciate the aims and objectives of the project, and be willing to co-operate? Child protection is an area of research that needs to be handled particularly sensitively (see Gough, 1993, p.280). Gaining access to and the co-operation of children, young people and their families whilst guaranteeing anonymity, is exceptionally difficult. Would the publication of the findings stigmatise local people, leaving them experiencing further discrimination? How could we ensure, for example, that the communities were not seen as citizens with 'special' problems and guard against child rearing in Asian communities being seen as a model of cultural pathology? Such concerns focus on how information collected is interpreted, and what meaning and emphasis is attached to the findings.

The problematisation of ethnic communities means that reference is sometimes made to culture as if it were deficient and therefore responsible for creating problems. Asian people can thus be treated as victims of 'deficits' that exist in their communities, perpetuating stereotypes, myths and distorted images of minority ethnic groups. Finally, an analysis that focuses on 'minorities' rather than on their material circumstances could be considered inherently flawed. A fuller understanding of the situation of minority communities requires an analysis not only of their internal dynamics, but also the wider social context, such as levels of employment, quality of education, housing, health and social welfare services, as well as the impact of living in urban or rural areas. These were some of the issues which concerned us in setting up our consultation with South Asian groups.

The research used a multidirectional approach (Ahmad, 1989) aiming to capture a picture of the needs, development and views of children and their parents or carers, hoping to take some account of changing dynamics of parental responsibility, of the influence children have on their parents and the impact of westernisation on minority communities.

The emphasis was on working alongside local communities and negotiating with them the terms of engagement. The priority was to give children and their families an opportunity to articulate their own needs and their views on the most sensitive ways in which instances of 'harm' may be investigated and appropriate forms of support provided. In turn, the statutory and voluntary agencies aimed to improve their understanding of the child protection needs of Asian communities, and take positive action which would be of discernible benefit to children and families.

Project leaflets gave information about agencies who could offer help in a range of circumstances, but emphasised that the responsibility for child protection cases remained with the statutory authorities, not the project workers. There were however many dilemmas in developing relationships with participants.

Language, culture, power and partnership

The complexity of working across cultures and languages is illustrated by our attempts to find appropriate words in the predominant Asian languages, to articulate definitions and concepts of harm, abuse and protection. As Punjabi and Urdu were the main languages for the project areas, after substantial discussion the words *Hifazat* and *Surukhia* were chosen as the name for the project, words conveying protection, keeping safe, in these languages. They have connotations of caring and support, rather than a hard legalistic sense. This was important in enabling the project to avoid a eurocentric and purely professional stand-point, and to make a positive attempt to obtain the views of parents, young people and others.

We were able to give attention to strengths and supports within families and communities without denying the possibility that abuse occurs and without seeing cultural differences as negative. Whilst attempting to respect and draw out differences we attempted not to treat cultural practices as either static or monolithic. Numerous assumptions and stereotypes exist about Asian communities originating from the Indian sub continent, even though

- There are 3 major religions and numerous others with substantial followings.
- There are at least 5 different languages (and many dialects).
- There are different castes and groupings.
- The identification with 'home' is different eg Punjab, Bangladesh, Gujerat, Pakistan, etc.
- There are different generations and therefore different experiences and attitudes.
- There are differences in education, socio-economic position and different family values and patterns.

The last point needs particular emphasis, as every family has its own unique kinship pattern, its own views on acceptable and normal family life, its own dynamics and ground rules.

The project workers were often asked 'Is this normal or unusual for an Asian family?' The workers did not see themselves as 'cultural experts' and believed that only the particular family could be seen as expert on its own cultural norms, values, dynamics and practices.

We tried to acknowledge that there are issues about whose standards are used to judge culture and whose standards are used to define child abuse. No culture condones child abuse, even though there may be very different views about what constitutes abuse (Baldwin et al (1990). In discussion about the aims and objectives of the project we tried to differentiate between the definitions and perceptions of abuse which different families and groups may have and the common understandings and definitions of abuse which are represented within current boundaries of British law, without claiming that these are consistent and scientifically validated.

We acknowledged and explored changing trends in family life and attitudes and in child rearing practices within and between communities. The Children Act 1989 and accompanying guidance is the first legislation to recognise explicitly the holistic needs of children, valuing social as well as personal needs, recognising the importance of material, spiritual and emotional well being.

The Children Act stresses the need to work in partnership with children, parents and community groups. This was a priority in the project. In making contact with professional and voluntary groups, in talking to women, school children, mixed groups and professionals we paid attention to:

- building networks of support which recognise the strengths and expertise within communities, validate their work, respect their priorities.
- values and process, recognising that they are as important as the content of research or development work.

Principles of community development informed our attempts to develop partnerships with local people in the action research. The time scale for building up trust and genuine collaboration is necessarily long and involves substantial preparatory work, getting to know the geography, culture, resources, working with local networks. This seemed especially important when working with minority groups who might have many reasons to suspect the good intentions of welfare agencies, who might feel powerless and oppressed.

The work of the project

Preparation

We gathered substantial demographic information about the areas, about the resources available and particularly about groups and organisations who would be able to offer support and information to the Asian groups and individuals we would be working with. 'Contact' lists of individuals and agencies who could help minority groups, who had language skills, who had access to resources, were included in the leaflets about the project. These were widely distributed. They were available in the majority of Asian languages. We also negotiated clear agreements with NSPCC and the local authorities about how child protection concerns would be handled, and what supports could be provided for any individuals or families approaching us with difficulties.

Before starting pilot work with a women's group, girls' group and boys' group, we discussed how to take account of the different cultural understandings, language and symbols relevant to child protection and abuse. We explored a range of understandings, meanings, expectations in relation to:

- children's needs
- discipline

- harm to children
- teaching about sexuality
- sexual abuse
- confidentiality
- consultation/partnership

For example, confidentiality - in English - has many different meanings, depending on who is using the concept. A researcher, a doctor, a child protection worker, might have very different understandings. Different again would be the meaning for a mother or a child. When such a concept is translated into another language, account has to be taken of the range of meanings it may have, how it relates to cultural priorities and expectations. Ideas of respect, authority, responsibility, were discussed in trying to come to some common understanding of confidentiality both in relation to the research and in relation to child protection. There was not one word which could define confidentiality. Groups would have to consider ideas about keeping secret anything they had heard about each other; leaving the information behind when they left the group. The project's strict code on confidentiality - our responsibility to keep information anonymous and confidential except in circumstances where a child might be harmed - would have to be explained, considered in the light of different views about children's needs, rights, development.

To achieve partnership we had to be ready to go at the pace of those we were working with, to allow them to redefine concepts and priorities, to take seriously their views about keeping children safe. This meant taking account of their social circumstances, practicalities relating to health, childcare, mobility, the daily realities of prejudice and racism. Changing cultural patterns, priorities, had to be acknowledged across boundaries of class, culture and language. The workers had to consider the relevance of their own professional concerns to the lives of the participants.

We negotiated with a wide variety of groups - voluntary, statutory, religious - as well as individuals, the practicalities of what partnership meant. As issues of gender are crucial in family support and child protection it was agreed that the female researchers would focus on forging links with young people and with mothers. Our intention to work separately with men was difficult to achieve within our limited resources. However both workers had opportunities to gain information about views and priorities of men and some supplementary work was done for us by a male worker with an all male group.

The workers' *roles as research and development workers*- encouraging partnership and participation in the research, ensuring that legal expectations and definitions of abuse and significant harm were understood and the consequences of abuse recognised - were fraught with tension, conflict. Inevitably some of the insights which arise from such complex work will be partial or conflicting. We had to be comfortable about trying to document a changing, multi-faceted picture.

The pilot phase

Some details of the pilot phase illustrate the level of attention which we felt was needed to the *process* of the project. This approach was used throughout the project.

Work was done with three groups of women and young people in one area, discussing knowledge and understandings of abuse, exploring issues to which we needed to be sensitive.

The groups were drawn from two neighbourhoods where about a quarter of the residents belong to a minority ethnic group. In both, 45% of the 0-4 year old population (borough average 15%) comes from minority ethnic groups and 55% of 5-9 year olds (borough average 19.3%).

The first group, run in collaboration with a Rape Crisis Centre, was drawn from an established Asian Womens' Craft Group at a family centre. Attendance was on an 'open door' basis so that the number of women who attended every week varied.

Two other groups were drawn from a local school, a group of girls and a group of boys, each with five participants - aged about 13 years. Rajinder worked alone with these groups.

Access

Access to all three groups was very carefully negotiated. In the case of the young people, workers in the education department were approached, then relevant individuals at the school, before the participants themselves were identified and they and their parents asked to give consent to being involved. As the project's success depended on the establishment of good working relationships with children and young people, it was essential that their rights were observed and their concerns, needs and wishes properly documented. At the same time, we acknowledged the need to ensure that parental responsibility was respected and due recognition given to the particular sense in which Asian communities - like others - may not easily differentiate between children's rights and the rights of the family. Family pride and family honour may be important factors that shape the degree of freedom a project may have in developing partnerships within a local community.

Structure of the pilot work

The nature of work with the groups was varied - to reflect different expectations, interests and experiences of mothers and of young people. This variation characterised the work with subsequent groups.

'Open' attendance policy of the women's group meant that there was some fluctuation in attendance. Our expectations were too 'professionalised' at first and our 'structured' methods of group work too formal: we had to renegotiate types and levels of discussion to match the environment.

Because it was difficult to obtain information systematically in this way, it was decided to supplement our information through the use of a structured interview at the last session, to take further some of the views expressed.

In the 2 pilot groups in the schools, discussion was supplemented through information from a quiz used as an ice breaker at the beginning and a questionnaire at the end.

In all groups there were conflicting attitudes and opinions. The possibility that people of all kinds can hold contradictory views at the same time, as individuals and as groups, was amply demonstrated. It remained a striking feature of the information which we collected throughout the project.

Discussion points

In all pilot groups discussion began with questions about what was considered abuse. The boys began with a view of abuse related to parents' treatment of children, for example *'when parents hit a child'*. Their focus was largely on punishment. In the boys' group there was a view that girls were more at risk than boys. The discussion implied a view of their own role as protectors.

For girls the discussion moved to a more serious level of abuse - rape, beating up and sexual harassment. They also discussed racial harassment as physical abuse.

Discussion with the women's group began with an emphasis on extreme physical maltreatment of children, and an example was given of a young child who had been murdered. This discussion of extreme events may have been an attempt to distance themselves from the discussion, reflecting discomfort and disbelief that these were the sort of things one would want to talk about. However there was an acceptance that abuse happens frequently, and that it was something which affected them as individuals.

The embarrassment and shock which most groups feel in confronting the unpalatable reality of sexual abuse was apparent in this early group. It had to be handled with sympathy, sensitivity and humour. One woman's response, roughly translated as 'you're going to talk about dirty things' was helpful in breaking the ice, making it possible to go into greater depth and sharing.

In the girls' and women's groups there were discussions of the definition of abuse, the boundaries between physical, sexual, emotional abuse and the effects they had. In all groups throughout the project complex issues of gender were highlighted.

Access groups

Care had been taken to ensure that we had access to a wide range of agencies and groups, with individuals who could speak minority languages, so as to be able to refer people on when needs and problems were identified. Some of the individuals who helped with the pilot phase became active members of an access group which continued to support the project and feed back the implications to their agencies and groups.

In this early phase a wide range of contacts was made and an 'access group' established in both areas - groups of local professionals who would act as a support network and facilitate contacts. They helped a great deal with the focus and methods of the action research and the dissemination. They were central to our attempt to lessen misinterpretation and misrepresentation at every level of the research process. Other research had shown that if practitioners are involved and consulted throughout the research process, they are more likely to be committed to and act on its findings (Caesar et al 1994).

Continuing work

The work undertaken in the pilot phase was used as the basis for planning questionnaires, interviews and focus groups in both local authorities. In both areas there was continuing consultation with agencies and voluntary groups, and arrangements to support anyone who showed distress or identified problems during the course of the project.

We had enormous difficulty in our time scale for translations of leaflets and later questionnaires. We had to go through many drafts, consultations and changes of translations in order to achieve satisfactory outcomes. The leaflets and questionnaires were widely distributed in 5 languages. However, most of the questionnaires which were returned were in English: few chose to use those in community languages.

Some of the findings, from interviews and focus group discussions involving a wide range of individuals, including parents, professionals, community leaders and young people, are summarised below. The final project reports (Atkar et al 1997 and Atkar 1997) give a more comprehensive account.

Issues in bringing up children: strengths and difficulties

In discussing strengths within Asian communities as well as difficulties they faced in bringing up children, participants emphasised culture, religion and community influences, family patterns and relationships; financial and material pressures; gender and sexuality; living in a racist society.

Many of their concerns would be echoed across all communities in Britain, others related very clearly to their experience of minority status, in a society where racism was for them an everyday experience.

What shapes child rearing practice?

As in any culture, high ideals were expressed about child rearing and how parents and children should relate:

'Children are respected in our culture.'
'The relationship between you, parents, brothers, sisters and everyone else in the family is important. There's a moral code about how you treat and are treated by others.'
'You learn about child rearing from parents - the way you've been brought up by friends, relatives.'

Culture, religion, community

'I'm proud of my culture, it's unique. If children don't have it, they don't have any heritage.'
'You need your own language, reading and writing, who you are and your identity.'

Many respondents identified wider Asian culture and community influences as significantly helping to shape their child rearing attitudes and practices. Respect for family and elders was a defining value stressed by many.

The centrality of religion to child rearing was emphasised by a wide range of respondents, both young people and adults. Some of them were specific in locating this view in a particular religious faith and its teachings.

However, in ways which mirror experience across all British communities, a wide plurality of both religious beliefs and practices emerged from the research.

In many of the responses, it was difficult to differentiate between *cultural* and *religious* influences.

Within this plurality, many respondents, including some for whom religion was personally important, emphasised the need for children to have choices. Some who started from an explicitly child centred viewpoint wanted a more distanced relationship to cultural and religious expectations.

Many participating in the research spoke about the conflicting demands for parents and children, of living with two sets of cultural expectations: 'a cultural clash - every parent's dilemma.'

For many responding, in all age groups, some defence of Asian culture and traditions was important. Responses could be multi-faceted and recognise complexities and dilemmas in the current situation.

> We can understand why Asian parents come down so hard. They are scared - want to protect the culture, traditions. But they often make things worse with young people with their reactions... Parents do need to understand kids more - that doesn't mean becoming western.

The close relationship between generation, gender and cultural conflicts was acknowledged by many respondents, who emphasised that all cultures are changing and tensions are common.

The strengths of the extended family

Across the age groups and in focus group discussions and individual interviews, most respondents identified positively with the extended family. It was seen as having a number of material and practical duties and advantages:

> 'The extended family provides childminding, ...financial support.'
> 'Families provide childminding - so children will stay off the streets. This is not such a prominent problem in Asian families in this area... Working parents find solutions so that children aren't left alone.'

The extended family could be seen as the source of some significant material values and educational aspirations, some of which were particularly highlighted when comparisons were made with white families.

It was also widely recognised that Asian extended families could provide 'emotional support', 'a strong bond', with 'all the children being treated the same.' They also ensured an 'awareness about children's health' and offered in-built help, including care when people were ill.

Such values and experiences were seen as helping to create a child-centredness which offered considerable social and emotional benefits.

'When I married the children benefited from a supportive extended family. There is a richness in the family relationships.'

'We did things together as a family, visiting places, having picnics. When we had all grown up we still did family things together.'

'Our culture is so strong, positive - even though young people don't think of it that way... It is one where children are a precious part of it - respected - cared for.'

Considerable confidence in what their own communities were achieving was expressed and a number of criticisms were made of white families' child rearing practices.

Some of the specific positions taken up inevitably contradicted each other, again illustrating that the Asian community, like any other, is having a vigorous dialogue on such issues. Indeed, in this context, debates on freedom reappeared from time to time, often interwoven with individualism versus family or community values and on regimented versus liberal approaches to bringing up children.

Many of the limitations and tensions identified within Asian families seemed indistinguishable from those which might be found in families in any culture - for example 'fighting between children' and 'the effects of favoritism - of one child getting more love and affection.'

Traditional family patterns could exert considerable pressures:

'If the boy is brought up in the UK and you get someone (a wife) from Bangladesh, adjustment is hard, there are two different mentalities.'

'These days it's hard to accept that... you should be dominated by the extended family.'

Again as in most communities, conflicts were often seen to play themselves out particularly over courtship and marriage.

One interviewee vividly illustrated that conflicts within a marriage could be sparked by social divisions other than race or religion - and in the process advocated the need for some radical shifts of attitude and practice:

'I don't believe in caste because of power... their views are dominant in society... I am not a Jat, my husband is. If his mother had a choice she would prefer someone in her own caste. She still makes comments to indicate for example: 'You have as much sense as a shoe-maker'. Religious temple leaders have the power to change this'.

Financial and material pressures

Many stresses identified were associated with poverty and living in run down areas. Extended families could be a great support in hard times, but could also bring pressures, if they expected help to come to them. Housing problems, unemployment, long working hours were often identified as sources of stress.

The local environment is crap. It is not suitable for youngsters round here. It's a council area... There's loads of crime around here, break-ins, violence, mostly unmarried mothers, tramps *hanging around, bad music. There's no respect for what's right and wrong. Many parents just ignore what their children are doing. Children are out of control - there's no consideration... The parents don't discipline their children... It's unhygienic - it needs to be made cleaner... It's not a good area to bring up kids - too much influence of sex and drugs. It's a rough area...*

Gender and sexuality

Some respondents identified stereotypical views in the wider community, people believing that Asian families did not value girls. Many did however see the role and power of young women within extended families as a problematic area:

'Girls are not seen as individuals - but as daughter, sister, wife, married or unmarried.'
'Boys reinforce cultural pressures on girls.'

For many respondents, women, and especially young women, were seen as constrained, sometimes severely disadvantaged - though again in ways which are similar in other cultures and communities.

'I have nieces who get asked to clear the table... Boys are allowed to run wild. Girls should be treated equally... It depends on upbringing.'
'Our parents are too protective of us, there are different expectations for girls about being allowed to go out.'

The 'set' roles and divisions of labour between husband and wife and father and mother could be seen, especially by women, as creating tensions:

'My husband says: 'You have to keep a woman in control'... My husband's attitudes towards boys is very sexist - he allows them at the youth club.'

These gender attitudes and practices within families were by no means monolithic. Some emerging differences of view between parents could be a source of tension in their own right.

'Homosexuality - that's repressed in the community and so are sexual experiences.'
'Subjects around sex are kept very hidden. It's a subject not spoken of... It's a taboo subject.'

However, patterns were seen to be changing.

Violence against women and children

The possibility of family pressures and gender roles being associated with domestic violence was acknowledged by some respondents. Sometimes the references were indirect, personally distanced or implying it belonged to the past.

However, personal experience (some of it first-hand) was acknowledged:

'(Her) husband was an alcoholic and beat her up badly.'
'My son saw domestic violence - linked with emotional abuse.'
'One girl aged 17 - they got her married - there was no father. There was lots of violence a few

days later. Her mother said: 'Go back, your place is with him.' She needed support. Two or three times she came back.'

Some accounts acknowledged the traumatic effects on children caught up in family violence.

'When parents fight children get left out and are alone. The children feel ill, disgusted, sad and want to be out of the house.'

'It has an emotional effect. The child can't understand and blame themselves, they keep the anger within them, can't express what's happening, feel guilty... Most take the mother's side, so the relationship with the father deteriorates...'

'The child was traumatised, the worst environment a child can grow up in. My nephew looked scared when his father was fighting. Something can happen which affects them for the rest of life... How the child views other people, is violent, aggressive and he can't trust them.'

Living in a racist society

The endemic and institutionalised nature of racism in British society was constantly highlighted:

'When a man beats up a black person and the black man hits back the black person gets arrested.'

Racism was part of everyday experience, severely affecting individual and family experience.

'In Muslim culture you ... must wear a scarf on your hair. Some English say: 'You've got nits, that's why you wear a scarf'. Others say: 'Your clothes aren't ironed, you smell and you don't have a bath.'

'Racists shout: 'Paki kingdom' at school'

'You face racism every day. We are abused over and over again. Abused at work, at school.'

'On the bus if Asian people talk loudly, they really get commented on but if it's Polish no-one says anything and accepts it because they are white...'

'Racism exists in school. They don't respect our culture. The headteacher treats Asian kids differently.'

Such everyday immersion in a racist environment was seen as capable of producing an internalized awareness of racism from a very early age:

'Children are intuitive. My 6 year old will tell me which white children like Asian kids and which don't - children know.'

'In Britain there's a decreased chance of success. A child of two will know, once he's in the nursery it will be visible. Out of the house everything is white.'

Even where no violence was involved, racism often resulted in exclusion and alienation:

'There's a lack of confidence in children as we know we are discriminated against wherever we go - employment, schools, colleges, We are always second class... Preference is given to their own first.'

Sometimes there seemed to be 'loop back' effects into families and communities, adding an extra set of sensitivities about their own personal behaviour and cultural patterns:

> *'What are English people going to think of us? Whites are looking for reasons to get at us.'*
> *'Children say 'Mum, don't wear Indian clothes.''*
> *'My son is ashamed of me because I don't speak English'*

Defining and understanding abuse

There was a very wide range of views about what behaviour counted as abuse:

> *'Abuse is hitting children, smacking, emotional abuse, family problems, parents can't afford things... There is no point in just focusing on one thing but there is a need as abuse starts from a need.'*
> *'...Danger/cruelty;... physical/mental abuse;... harm; torture - mental - when parental relationships break down;... bullying... calling names; emotional blackmail. Sexual - not just intercourse. Financial - not getting enough or excessive pocket money. Excessive hitting/ smacking...'*

One respondent, when suggesting that 'there are very few incidents of child abuse up to the age of 8-9 - only neglect' seemed to be placing neglect outside a definition of abuse. Others simply expressed uncertainties or acknowledged unresolved questions:

> *'Emotionally it's hard to know if a child is abused.'*
> *'Class, income, religion suggest issues present themselves differently. Affluent Sikhs will have the same issues as poor Muslims but just articulate them differently.'*

Abuse in a cultural context

One of the adult focus groups openly explored some of the complexities of the issues involved in relation to actual child-rearing situations:

> *'..if a child is wearing a dirty dress it becomes neglect but... the child may be fed twice a day with a hot meal... Parents may think: 'Well, they're going to get the dress dirty again so it can be washed the next day. They think the money they will spend on that, they will pay for the food with.'*
> *'Parents won't just open a tin but will make a good meal. If there's five or six kids, they'll think we'll wash the clothes tomorrow.'*
> *'Neglect' particularly was seen as open to such cultural confusion.*
> *'Neglect issues -not knowing how to act or saying 'this is how we do it back home'. When they (parents) are in this society, the goal posts have changed.'*

A number of adults questioned whether neglect was generally well handled through the child protection system. A suggestion was made that parents needed to be given breaks - with community support - rather than be interviewed by outside agencies if there were worries about neglect. It was felt this would also have a positive effect on children through positive role models and being with other children from their own cultural background. This emphasis on preventive approaches and supportive help in assessing need echoes some of the points made in Messages from Research (DoH 1995).

The women emphasised a sense of being able to be supportive and involved - seeing neglect as something they could do something about, involve themselves with families having difficulties, if opportunities could be encouraged. The experience of the Henley Project (chapter 22) also suggests that a wide pool of women who will offer support is readily accessible, with support and encouragement.

Another issue given substantial attention was the needs of parents who have mental health problems. Experiences of a number of women involved suggest that the child protection systems did not work for them in a supportive way. For one woman, her experience of having had children put on the child protection register was so traumatic (even though they were by this time de-registered) she was unable to recount any of the episode without constant tears.

'There is conflict about how many of the issues are 'child protection'... The assessment procedures are being used to presume guilt unless proved otherwise... whose value base is the norm - what is acceptable or not? There is cultural confusion and stereotyping of families.'
'It's cultural that Asians are more disciplinarian than whites - but it's an individual thing. I don't think Asians hit children more than whites.'
'Abuse is not being recognised - there are different concepts of discipline in communities as well as stereotyping about different types of abuse - e.g. a belief that some cultures encourage chastisement.'

These differing cultural definitions of physical punishment and where the line between it and physical abuse should be drawn were sometimes seen as creating considerable strain between Asian families and the services they encountered. The problems of both under and over reactions of professionals were identified and experiences of stereotypical reactions were common.

The strengths and support within Asian communities and extended families, outlined in the earlier sections, supported the commonly expressed views that a number of community safeguards were present in Asian communities, which served to protect children and support families, making abuse and neglect quite rare.

Sexual abuse

An exchange between two women in one of the focus groups vividly illustrated some dilemmas in defining sexual abuse, both in general terms but also very specifically in relation to culture and especially language:

First woman: *Parents seem to be becoming stricter by each generation - because with more information they have to make more rules. I sometimes worry that my husband hugs my daughter - my mother complains that you shouldn't do this and she will say: 'You should not touch a young girl' - a very young girl who is reaching adolescence or has reached puberty.*

When you hear about abuse happening you know that elders' sayings do have some truth in them.

Second woman: *The word 'sher-na' is ambiguous. It can mean 'to touch', literally; or to touch playfully - to tease or touch in a more sexual way. It may not always be obvious in which way a child could be talking and therefore it is vital to really listen and understand what a child says to you.*

This questioning, probing concern was common in the discussions about defining abuse. Women were very ready to acknowledge the difficulties and complexity of the subject.

As in most communities, sexual abuse was the most difficult and uncomfortable issue to discuss. Finding appropriate language was a real difficulty. All groups acknowledged the existence of sexual abuse. Its hidden nature was recognised. Girls gave some examples of the unwillingness of their families, and friends, to deal with harassment and abuse, or even to talk about it. They also gave examples of being blamed for being abused.

'I had a friend and her brother-in-law tried something on her and she told someone - it all came out - she got the blame and she didn't do anything.'

There was greater reluctance to acknowledge sexual abuse as a significant community problem in the men's group than in the women's and girl's groups.

Community pressures were acknowledged by many groups and individuals. A young woman was raped by eight men - from a different Asian community:

'Who was she going to tell? She went out with one of them... Communities are all so tightly knit so it is very difficult to disclose sexual abuse.'
'Fear of being ostracised by the community might stop me reporting abuse.'

Some respondents had particular concerns about abuse relating to children with disabilities - though this was not seen as an issue necessarily of more concern than in other communities.

The complexity of intervening in sexual abuse, its wide ranging effects, was acknowledged particularly by girls and women. The role of religion and religious and community leaders was seen as central to making progress, breaking down taboos and secrecy. The general view was that there was still far too little discussion of such matters within Asian communities.

Home alone

Parents and professionals showed considerable ambivalence about labelling leaving a child at home alone as abuse. While acknowledging potential risks, they struggled to clarify if and when it was acceptable to leave children on their own. Not surprisingly age and maturity emerged as key criteria for deciding this.

'It wouldn't be abuse if the child was left for half an hour. But you'd have to think: 'What would the child get up to'.'

Racial abuse and bullying

Bullying outside the home was seen as widespread. It emerged as a main focus of the research.

'Bullying... affects all children severely. In the past it was not taken seriously and then the child feels powerless.'

A connection between such bullying and abuse was widely assumed during the focus group discussions. Ultimately such bullying could lead to great personal tragedy:

'Children commit suicide.'
'People do kill themselves because of bullying'.

Outside the home, and especially at school, family solidarity could apparently be a vital defence against bullying - though it was not always offered.

'You need older brothers and sisters in... school to stick up for you. On your own you've really had it.'
'There is family pressure to stop children reporting bullying. The severity of the bullying depends on whether parents will react.'

Mostly it was assumed that the statutory services had a responsibility to combat such bullying. One youth focus group which provided examples of racial harassment and bullying suggested that what was required in their school was a committee where children could go in confidence.

Another believed that:

'Our school will try to stop it by showing it will not be tolerated. Its policy is to kick out offenders.'

Another youth focus group highlighted the complexity of the issues:

'Bullying in school exists - our school will acknowledge it... The school tries to listen to parents. Unfortunately there has been a backlash against Asian kids from white kids and families when the school has come out against racism.'

Who might people go to with concerns about abuse

All groups were asked who were the most likely people they would turn to if they had concerns about themselves or others. Discussion with young people consistently highlighted the importance of family networks. Girls were less likely to say they would consult parents than were boys. Girls more often emphasised cousins, sisters, aunts.

Groups frequently mentioned teachers as an important source of information, contact, support. Another much needed practical support identified by the young people was for schools to have counsellors - both male and female - 'People you can go to talk to about anything.'

ChildLine was mentioned as particularly appropriate in situations where it would be easier to talk to a stranger.

Girls were more likely to be aware of risks of harm as well as of incidents of actual harm, and were more likely to talk to someone about it.

Informal networks of support were vital for women in dealing with actual or potential abuse.

Some women did have a wider awareness of agencies to go to, such as SSDs and family centres. However groups had been recruited through a range of professional and voluntary sector groups, so levels of awareness were likely to be higher than average.

Particular difficulties were highlighted where local authorities had never consulted with community groups until a major case was under investigation: this made it very unlikely that official agencies would be seen as accessible or helpful.

There was particular emphasis amongst the men who were interviewed on the importance of handling difficulties within their own communities and networks.

Confidentiality and sensitivity to culture, social and family circumstances were emphasised as key attributes of services respondents might be willing to use.

Community strengths

There were many divergent views within the groups we consulted and enormously varied experience. A strong message which came from the consultation about the context of bringing up children, was that Asian communities saw themselves as:

- Strong, vibrant, energetic, creative;
- Supporting, trusting and sharing;
- Questioning, disagreeing, changing.

Many expressed pride in maintaining positive environments for their children in an environment which was often:

- Stressful, hostile;
- Racist and personally and culturally destructive;
- Economically and socially disadvantageous.

This was the context which they wanted researchers and service providers to understand, in its complexity and contradictions. This was the context to which we tried to relate our more detailed consultations about views on family support and child protection needs.

Conclusions: Implications for services

A wide range of people supported the project through these groups, and continue the work, trying to take account of the views expressed.

The sensitivity of the subject matter we worked with, the fears surrounding it and the complex power relationships between children and adults, communities and community leaders, women and men, between minority families and professionals, meant that the work was slow and painstaking and findings were multi-layered.

Asian groups' perceptions were that their generally *collective* approach to social and family responsibilities and their traditional closeness to and respect for children provided safeguards which many believed were absent from some white groups. Nevertheless dangers of relying on these safeguards were identified. Community members gave examples of isolated families, bearing many burdens, single mothers struggling without support to recover from domestic violence and provide a safe home for their children.

There were also illustrations from professionals and community members of workers holding back from responding to concerns because of fears of racism. There were no clear cut answers to our original questions about whether under representation of Asian groups in child protection related to community strengths or to fears of referral. Rather there was confirmation of the complex and contradictory dynamics identified by Ahmad (1989).

Young people particularly emphasised the need for education of communities, to encourage disclosure, support victims, insist that responsibility lies with the offender and prevent girls being blamed for being abused.

Young people and adults believed that there was still an urgent need for commitment from agencies to consultation and partnership with communities, in a continuing dialogue.

There was strong emphasis on the need for agencies to develop family and other support services which would be influenced by the communities, and child protection services which would be sensitive and culturally aware.

There were many echoes of findings from other studies, about gaps in provision and the importance of ensuring access for minority communities to personal social services responsive to their needs (Barn, 1993; SSI, 1992 (a) & (b) and 1993; Barn et al 1997).

We should like to highlight some of the implications for policy and practice, in promoting effective family support and protection for Asian children.

The need for widespread information

- about what is seen as significant harm and abuse of children;
- about the responsibilities, rights and duties of parents;
- about the duties, responsibilities and powers of different agencies in relation to children;
- about the action which will follow any reported concern and the procedures under which it will be undertaken.

Such information needs to be readily accessible to children and young people, parents and other adults, in written and other forms, in minority community languages.

Community leaders can play a key role in opening up debates, in spreading information, in encouraging openness of communication within community groups and in families - as a protective strategy.

These suggestions are only likely to be effective if undertaken routinely with local communities, rather than as a response to contentious cases, when anger and defensiveness will be common.

Availability of support

Family and community support services need to be based on genuine understandings of priorities, strengths, resources and conflicts within communities, drawing on detailed consultation and involvement. Agencies in statutory and voluntary sectors need to commit themselves to partnership with each other and with local people to develop services which match the needs of minority and majority groups. Respondents suggested the need for a much more open relationship between service providers and local groups, where social and family pressures could be addressed.

What is needed

- welfare agencies which recognise the multiple pressures within communities and base their strategic plans for family and children's services on this wide contextual understanding;
- agencies who can offer support and who have workers speaking minority community languages, publicising their services widely, in schools and other places accessible to young people, as well as places frequented by adults;
- advice sessions, easily accessible, sensitive to cultural needs, and support for self help groups appropriate to different cultural experience and expectations;
- adequate childcare facilities, including safe play areas for children, more playgroup activities; more after school/leisure activities;
- encouragement to religious centres to play a role - particularly important in getting key men into the discussion, opening up the role of men;
- more community based workers; speaking appropriate languages;
- readily available support for parents under pressure and stress, to enable them to give time to their children;
- clear anti bullying strategies in school; serious commitment to deal with racism, sexism, bullying;
- support based on a recognition that there may be confusion, fear and defensiveness; individuals generally are able to hold conflicting views at the same time, and professionals need to develop the confidence to work constructively with such views;
- recognition that only a minority of abuse may be brought to the attention of statutory agencies; most children and young people are likely to talk of abuse only to close family members and friends, sometimes to teachers;
- the helpful role which teachers and other professionals can play should lead ACPCs to consider the need for confidential *advice sessions* where young people and adults - who have been abused or know of others who have - may talk about options available; counselling services need development.

Bullying, racial and sexual harassment and abuse

Attention needs to spread beyond abuse by parents and carers. The significant harm which can be caused through bullying, racial and sexual harassment and abuse needs more widespread recognition, as does the harm resulting from disadvantages of many kinds. These may be the most prevalent forms of abuse, damaging large numbers of children and young people.

Anti-racist and culturally sensitive practice

There is a need to stress, in good practice guidelines and in training, that anti-racist and culturally sensitive practice cannot be achieved if black workers are seen as 'cultural experts'. Families and individuals are the only experts on their own situation, family and cultural norms and dynamics. It is through *partnership approaches which probe people's own priorities and views* that differences can be acknowledged, stereotyping avoided and sensitive, anti-oppressive work achieved. A community development approach to providing equal opportunities for all groups, to achieve safety and well-being within their families, neighbourhoods and within wider society is needed, alongside sensitive and individually focused services.

The two development workers of the Hifazat Surukhia project are now employed with support from the NSPCC and one of the local authorities originally involved, to implement some of these recommendations. Their work includes a project to provide independent advice to families where there may be child protection concerns, information and advice to community groups, work within communities to increase knowledge and awareness of child protection issues. They are involved in training and development work with other agencies and professionals and with supportive volunteers to increase understanding of the experiences of minority groups.

References

Ahmad, B. (1989) 'Child care and ethnic minorities' in B Kahan (ed), *Child Care Research, Policy and Practice*. London: Hodder and Stoughton.

Ahmad, B. (1989) 'Protecting Black Children from Abuse'. *Social Work Today* 8th June.

Amin, K. with Oppenheim, C. (1993) *Poverty in Black and White*. London: CPAG.

Atkar, S. (1997) *The Surukhia Project: Child Protection Conferences, Core Group Reviews, Strategy and Planning Meetings*. Report to Coventry Social Services Department. Coventry NSPCC.

Atkar, S., Ghataora, R., Baldwin, N., & Thanki, V (1997) *Hifazat Surukhia: Keeping Safe*. NSPCC & Universities of Dundee & Warwick.

Baldwin, N., Seale, A. and Johansen ,P. (1990) *Race in Child Protection. A code of practice*. London: REU.

Barn, R. (1990) 'Black Children in Local Authority Care: Admission Patterns' *New Community*

16(2) pp 229-247.

Barn, R. (1993) *Black Children in the Public Care System*. London: BAAF/Batsford.

Barn, R., Sinclair, R., & Ferdinand, D. (1997) *Acting on Principle: an examination of race and ethnicity in social services provision for children and families*. London: BAAF.

Caesar, G., Parchment, M. and Berridge, D. (1994) *Black Perspectives on Services for Children in Need*. London: National Children's Bureau and Barnardo's.

Channer, Y. and Parton, N. (1990) 'Racism, cultural relativism and child protection' in Violence Against Children Study Group, *Taking Child Abuse Seriously*. London: Unwin Hyman.

Commission for Racial Equality (1989) *Racial Equality in Social Services Departments: a survey of equal opportunity policies*. London: CRE.

Commission for Racial Equality/Association of Directors of Social Services (1978) *Multi racial Britain: The Social Services Response*. London: CRE/ADSS

Corby, B. (1993) *Child Abuse*. Milton Keynes: Open University.

Creighton, S. (1992) *Child Abuse Trends in England and Wales 1988 - 1990*. London: NSPCC.

DHSS 1985 *Social Work Decisions in Child Care: Recent research findings and their implications*. London: HMSO.

DoH (1993) *Children Act News* Issue No 8. London: VOLCUF.

DoH (1995) *Child Protection: Messages from Research*. London: HMSO.

Gambe, D., Gomes, J., Kapur, V., Rangel, M. and Stubbs, P. (1992) *Improving Practice with Children and Families. A Training Manual*. Leeds: CCETSW.

Gibbons, J. (1992) (ed) *The Children Act 1989 and Family Support: Principles into Practice*. London: HMSO.

Gough, D. (1993) *Child Abuse Interventions. A Review of the Research Literature*. London: HMSO.

Graham, H. (1993) *Hardship and Health in Women's Lives*. London: Harvester Wheatsheaf.

Harwin, J. (1993) 'No safe havens for dogma pedlars' *Times Higher Education Supplement* 1st October.

Phillips, M. (1993) 'Oppressive Urge to Stop Oppression' *The Observer* 1st August.

Pinker, R. (1993) 'A lethal kind of looniness' *Times Higher Education Supplement* 10th September.

Roys, P. (1988) 'Social Services' in Bhat, A., Carr-Hill, R. & Ohri, S. (eds) *Britain's black population: a new perspective*. 2nd Edition. Aldershot: Gower.

SSI (1992a) *Concern for Quality, 1st Annual Report of the Chief Inspector, Social Services Inspectorate 1991/92*. London: HMSO.

SSI (1992b) *Inspecting for Quality, Evaluating Performance in Child Protection* London: HMSO.

SSI (1993) *Raising the Standard, 2nd Annual Report of the Chief Inspector, Social Services Inspectorate 1992/93* London: HMSO.

Stone, M. (1990) *Child Protection Work: A Guide to Professional Practice* London: Venture Press.

Waterhouse, L. (ed) (1993) *Child Abuse and Child Abusers: Protection and Prevention* London: Jessica Kingsley.

22
Family support strategies:
The Henley Project

Norma Baldwin and Lyn Carruthers

Resources for child care and protection were increasingly directed towards investigation of child abuse towards the end of the 1980s and beginning of the 1990s. Crisis work with individual families came to dominate services. More general provision of supportive services was being cut. In the Henley Ward of Coventry - an area with many disadvantages - a group of social workers, staff in education, health care professionals and researchers came together to seek ways of keeping alive practical commitment to family and neighbourhood support. The Henley Project was set up as part of this commitment. The project set out to document local people's views of what was needed to support families in bringing up their children in health and safety and to develop a neighbourhood strategy to take account of their views.

This chapter describes the characteristics of the neighbourhood, the Project's work in partnership with local residents and professionals and some of the activities and initiatives associated with it. A detailed account of the project is written up in 'Developing Neighbourhood Support and Child Protection Strategies: the Henley Safe Children Project' (Baldwin and Carruthers 1998).

Perspectives and principles underlying the project

The known links between disadvantage and high child protection referrals, childhood accidents, major health problems, crime, poor school attainments, family problems, (Tuck, chapter 4 in this volume, Acheson 1998, HM Treasury 1999) were a major source of concern. Workers were committed to finding ways of taking account of them in planning at the local level. We knew from other research and evaluations of projects some of the characteristics of successful early years and family support initiatives (Garbarino1980, Schorr 1988, Chamberlin 1988, Gibbons 1990; Blackburn 1991 & 1992; Gibbons 1992).

Successful projects

- offered a broad spectrum of services, from flexible and informal, through to intensive;

- were family and community oriented;
- recognised that needs were interconnected and untidy, crossing bureaucratic boundaries;
- were supported by the participative commitment of groups and organisations serving the locality.

Ready access to a range of supportive services, where parents themselves had involvement and control and where agencies worked in partnership, was important.

We tried to take full account of these characteristics in setting up the Henley Project, basing our work on principles of partnership and community development.

Characteristics of the Henley Ward

The ward is on the edge of the industrial city of Coventry (population about 360,00). It has a number of public housing estates, accommodating 35.5% of households, as well as more affluent areas of private housing. Housing is mainly low rise. Although there are many areas of open space, at the time of the project there were no parks or supervised play spaces in the area.

Parents described a variable picture of life in the neighbourhood. Many had experiences of close support from neighbours, community involvement, networks of common interest and strong local attachments. Yet they were bringing up their children in an environment of disadvantage and stress. The project's activities were concentrated in the districts of the ward which had been identified as in the most disadvantaged 10% of all enumeration districts in the Midlands region at the 1991 census.

Neighbourhood disadvantages

- high unemployment; more than 40% of adults economically inactive;
- in the most disadvantaged areas of the ward, over 40% of the population aged under 18;
- high proportion of low birthweight babies;
- for children under 5, the highest rate of accidents for the city;
- high proportion of children on the child protection register;
- highest rate of emergency hospital admissions for the city;
- highest crime rates for the city (including burglary and sexual assault);
- highest number of children in the care of the local authority.

The work of the project

Following extensive preparatory discussions with groups of local residents, advice and support centres, welfare professionals and politicians, a detailed consultation was planned. The intention was to allow the concerns of local parents to drive the action and research and development work.

Over 270 parents, mainly white, mainly mothers, were involved in giving information though focus and discussion groups, in personal interviews and written accounts. Minority ethnic groups in the area - a very small proportion of the population - were initially reluctant to discuss concerns with white dominated agencies. Additional work was undertaken with city-wide organisations supporting black groups, to discover their views and experience. The views of a further 66 parents were gathered in this way. A student attached to the project engaged in some detailed discussions with parents who were themselves disabled, or had children with impairments, to supplement our understanding of child care issues for them. Local workers and managers of services were also involved, individually and through focus groups.

Some of the main themes arising from these discussions were concerns about the social atmosphere and physical environment, dissatisfaction with local access to resources and supportive services for families and children and the need for parents to show continuing resourcefulness in the face of stress overload.

The social atmosphere and physical environment

Parents valued the spaciousness of the area and living near the countryside, with green fields and a canal. They said shopping and transport were good but both were expensive.

Many valued the helpful, positive community spirit which they experienced:

'People are very helpful and help one another and they stick together; the neighbours are friendly.'
'Close community - good friends have stayed close friends.'

Yet alongside this was a perception of a more negative and destructive atmosphere. A recurring theme throughout the project was the interconnection of personal difficulties and the social environment. Parents were afraid to let children into public spaces because of crime, drug dealing, bullying, dangerous rubbish and high risks of traffic accidents.

'We are worried about other children our children are going to mix with: bad language; encouraged into vandalism, thieving, fighting!'
'There are lots of young children on the street at inappropriate times of day and evening.'
'Sometimes I think I'm abnormal for not letting my daughter play out in the area; being involved with the project has made me feel better about this; it has made me understand that I have good reasons to watch them carefully.'

Fear and intimidation were common experiences. Examples were given of residents reporting car thefts, burglaries and vandalism, being attacked, having their houses broken into, being subjected to threats, and other intimidation.

In a workshop organised with the local Community Safety Mediation Project, some women - all of whom had children - talked about their experiences. They expressed feelings of anger, frustration, isolation and imprisonment. They said they often experienced of fear for themselves and for their children's safety.

This workshop took place shortly before an upsurge of street troubles involving stolen cars, damage to property, fighting and assaults on police. Residents were incensed that media attention at that time was on the young people who caused the disturbances rather than on the experience of residents trying to cope with daily life and the demands of bringing up children. They did not feel that the full complexity of the situation was being publicly acknowledged.

Discussions with minority ethnic groups and with families of children with disabilities revealed additional dangers which they faced from harassment, bullying and attacks:

'It's not safe for children in their own backyard, neighbours have shouted racist abuse at children through the fence as well as poking sticks through the fence into her face.'
'My son who is thirteen and deaf, is bullied frequently and has his hearing aids pulled from his ears and is taunted because of his speech difficulties.'

Parents identified many worries and problems in the physical environment and the design of maisonettes and housing, which made bringing up children difficult and stressful. They described extensive damp, poor maintenance, dangerous balconies, inaccessibility for prams, unenclosed play spaces, few suitable buildings for children's activities, litter.

Local people had many positive suggestions for change, which they fed into the increasing number of meetings, discussions, planning consultations which were being set up across agencies. Work of the Henley Project was proceeding in parallel with other developments in Community Education, a new Family Centre and a new local authority Area Management Team - there was close cooperation in planning for the area. Residents' suggestions included:

- neighbourhood watch initiatives;
- improved security arrangements - including a communication system between neighbours;
- better communication between police and residents - not just when crime is reported;
- more feedback about action taken against offenders;
- major area clean up;
- improvements to safety, supervision and general provision of children's play facilities;
- traffic calming and street safety measures;
- assertiveness training;
- a community development approach to racism and other neighbourhood problems, rather than individualised approaches;
- a neighbourhood strategy.

Resources and support services

Local people identified a number of positive resources in the area, which they felt were important to the quality of their lives and to the opportunities for children. These included a new Family Project with a purpose built centre for community activity, and a Community Education Outreach Project. They valued an advice centre for benefits, and other information giving initiatives – on local services, debt, education and training. They thought the area was fortunate in the accessibility of local schools and nurseries and opportunities to join in mothers' and toddlers' groups and behaviour management courses. An increasing number of education and training schemes were available, but financial and child care problems could hinder access.

There were mixed views about the adequacy of health and welfare services overall. Some of the parents consulted had experiences of substantial support from health, education and social work services. Others expressed the views:

'There was nothing for me when I needed it!'
'All agencies need to examine the way they are viewed by the public.'
'I have a letter saying that my doctor will strike me off his list because I have called an emergency doctor out.'
'The children have had illness, sickness, diarrhoea, linked to where they live and play, as well as animals. The doctor has advised me to change doctors because they had had to give too much time and medicine to my family.'

A small group of local mothers who discussed health problems thought that the high number of visits from their area to the casualty department of the hospital and the high number of emergency admissions were in part because of doctors' attitudes: an unwillingness to take women's and children's complaints seriously. Minority groups said better information was needed locally about some of their particular health needs - such as sickle cell anaemia.

Women took initiatives in exploring health needs, visiting a Women's Health Centre, setting up discussions and presentations at the Family Centre.

Parents identified numerous supports and services which needed to be readily available to enhance their and their children's lives and ensure their health and safety. They wanted improvements in school and holiday care for children, sitting in and respite services, help to get children to and from out-of-school activities, help with transport for appointments and family outings, activities for older children. They particularly wanted to have access to counselling services for parents and for children, and to be able to rely on readily accessible help and support when children's behaviour is difficult or family problems are pressing.

Resourcefulness in the face of stress overload

Many of the parents who discussed needs in the neighbourhood gave details of long term stress associated with bringing up children in this disadvantaged area. For many families living on low incomes, resourcefulness was essential to daily and weekly survival. They had to look out for second-hand clothing and furniture, help each other with child care and cheap but stimulating activities for children. When they were going through additional personal difficulties, the accumulation of stress could bring them to the end of their tether and their coping strategies might begin to crumble.

One family - a married couple with three children under five - described their situation when they were expecting a fourth child. The mother had to be rushed to hospital prematurely. They had no support from extended family. The father, who was unemployed, had dilemmas about how to maintain routines for the children, visit his wife and make preparations for the expected baby. Travel to take one of the children to the nursery, to do the shopping, to claim benefits, was a major problem. He tried to get help from Social Services, in part because of worry about the danger that his wife might suffer again from post-natal depression, but they were not able to offer help at the time he felt it was needed. A local church group gave some help after the baby was born.

He said that he felt distraught, with great uncertainty about how long the situation was going to go on. He was worried about his wife and baby surviving; he felt exhausted; his feelings were building up, he was not eating properly. He was lonely and worried, with no-one to talk to. He experienced great frustration about asking for help and not getting it.

> 'What kept me going was love of my wife and children and efforts to keep to a routine. If the situation had gone on any longer I don't know what would have happened.'

Help and support families need

He felt he needed support during the day, someone to take care of the children occasionally for a couple of hours while he did some jobs, such as shopping. He particularly wanted answers to questions which were worrying him: for example the hospital and health centre had different weights for the baby and he did not know which one was right. He associated this muddle with the need for the baby to go back into hospital, soon after coming home.

He would have liked more time on his own when visiting his wife at the hospital, so would have welcomed some opportunity for the children to be cared for at the hospital during some visits. He felt let down by Social Services, who had said they would help but failed to send any one.

The mother described how worried, tired, exhausted she felt at this time. The baby had feeding problems, an allergy to formula milk and an eye infection. They were awaiting rehousing because of overcrowding. She felt that neighbours expected too much of them - they were often seen as coping because they were not complaining, when sometimes they were near desperation. She as well as her husband was very disappointed at the lack of help from neighbours and Social Services. They both described how all their commitment to each other and major reserves of resourcefulness were needed to keep going and to prevent their relationship crumbling.

Another account of long term difficulties was given by a mother talking about caring for a child with a condition which had resulted in epilepsy and memory loss (described as Sturge Weber). She had difficulty in convincing professionals of the need for diagnosis and intervention:

> 'The whole problem is that you are not listened to; the only person who knows a child is the parents, because they live with them 24 hours a day.'

She felt she often met the view that she was being 'a neurotic mother'. She spent many years trying to be included in assessment and planning, trying to access resources and support. She believed that they only succeeded in getting any resources for their daughter or achieving change - such as a move to a school appropriate for her needs - because they fought for everything.

Parents commonly related that it was very difficult to get professionals to listen to and take seriously their own definitions of their needs, or to engage holistically with their personal and social situations. They often experienced fragmented responses, sometimes judgmental views. Although for a minority there had been creative, imaginative and committed help from individual workers, the overall impression given was that the formal systems of help and support had major inadequacies. Families felt they did not get access to help at crucial times, when practical and emotional stresses were bringing them to the end of their resources.

There was a strong consensus that gaining benefit from these systems for their children was dependent on the determination and resourcefulness of parents; or occasionally on luck.

Linking experiences with research findings

Parents who worked with us - they were most usually mothers - wanted to be involved in defining and assessing their own needs, rather than dependent on professionals' assessments, or the rationing priorities of an agency. Parents' views about the risks which may follow if they are not able to get help when they are experiencing major problems is reflected in research findings that parents whose children go on child protection registers have often unsuccessfully sought help in the twelve months prior to registration (Dalgaard 1991, DoH 1991). The Social Services team had very high referral rates for child abuse investigations and found it very difficult to provide informal family support. They worked closely with the Henley Project, however, to review neighbourhood needs and develop strategies of family support for the area.

For some families, informal systems of support were non existent or unreliable. Yet for others, informal support provided a lifeline, or made a major difference to their quality of life. One mother who became seriously ill with Multiple Sclerosis had regular substantial help from a friend in caring for her child. This carried on for several months, until support services could be negotiated through health and social services.

Some group members who lived near to each other had reciprocal arrangements for looking after or keeping an eye on each other's children, helping each other organise time to take on outside commitments. When there was trouble on the streets it was helpful to know that there were people nearby watching out for them - particularly as telephone wires were sometimes deliberately cut before trouble started.

Garbarino & Sherman (1980) documented increased risks of harm to children in areas where it was difficult to access informal networks of support. Gibbons (1990) described how helpful parents found it to have ready access to a range of supportive services in a neighbourhood. Many studies have demonstrated the importance of informal supports and the increased risks of harm where these are not available (Schorr 1988; Melton & Barry 1994; Garbarino 1995; McDonald et al 1997).

The mothers who worked with the Henley Project had a very sharp analysis of the difficulties they faced in the area and of what was needed to support them and their children. Their energy, commitment and resourcefulness were impressive, as was their understanding of the linkage between personal difficulties and wider social issues. A number of them were active both within the Henley Project and with the Family Project in developing a wide range of self-help initiatives, such as Drop In sessions, crèche facilities, support for parents who might be isolated.

Parents' priorities

> 'Other people look at you and think you deserve to be in this situation, that it's your fault and that you are happy living as you are and that you don't want to improve your life and the lives of your children. We feel we are caught in a trap that we can't get out of, though you do learn to survive. But you don't want just to survive, we have standards too, we want a nice home, to be able to live amongst friendly, respectable neighbours, have a clean tidy estate instead of looking out on piles of rubbish and litter.'

Parents involved with the project commonly expressed a determination to provide the best possible opportunities for their children. They were concerned about the physical and social safety of the area - wanting greater protection from cars, rubbish, dogs, other people's unsafe behaviour, reflected in theft, assaults, vandalism, drug dealing, harassment.

The two most often mentioned resources which parents wanted to see developed in the area were safe, supervised play space and affordable and accessible child care.

The need for community planning was continually stressed. Key action points which the consultation emphasised were:

Family support
- *practical*: child care - daily, evenings, respite; emergency sitting services; user friendly clinics, surgeries, shops etc; safe play areas; accessible transport;
- *social and emotional*: local social networking; counselling for parents and children, accessible when they say they need it; behaviour management and preparation for parenthood classes;

Social environment
- *attention to*: safe constructive play and activities for all ages; crime, drug abuse, violence, bullying, racism, sexism, prejudice; 'macho' destructive street cultures; negative, alienated behaviour of young people; intimidation of children with

disabilities; aggressive assertion of power by white people; male attitudes to power and sexuality.

Partnership, participation, opportunities
- needs-led flexible services;
- recognition of expertise of local people, power to identify needs and control resources, using local skills and networks;
- links to training and job opportunities; anti-poverty strategies; anti-oppressive policies and practices.

Processes of work

The partnership principles of the 1989 Children Act were central to the work of the Henley Project. We were particularly concerned to explore and develop the implications of Section 17, which sets out the duty of local authorities to safeguard and promote the welfare of children in their area who are in need. The project's value base, promoting the rights and well-being of all children and redressing disadvantage and inequalities, demanded close collaboration with a wide range of agencies, groups, parents and young people. It drew on traditional community development models, assuming that partnership approaches were most likely to ensure effective use of expertise, skill, resources and commitment (Henderson 1995; Cannan and Warren 1997; Sinclair et al 1997). We tried to give as much attention to the way we worked as to the content of the material we collected and the issues we explored.

Inclusion of minority groups

We had to take specific steps to try to remove barriers to access to the project for parents from minority ethnic communities, and for parents and children with disabilities. It had quickly become clear that black families were reluctant to join in group or individual discussions about their experience. We had substantial discussions with city-wide black groups about this and with their support set about raising additional funds to employ black workers to involve local black and other minority residents. The city-wide organisations remained involved in this work. Similarly, because of difficulties of gaining access to families where a child or parent was disabled, we set up a focused project where a student developed links across a wider area, to ensure a reasonable representation of views.

Differences had to be acknowledged and respected, with networks being built up with a wide range of agencies and through widespread publicity, to gain the trust and involvement of black groups and parents and children with disabilities. The New Links Project, set up as a result of the Henley Project, continues this work. The Hifazat Surukhia Project described in chapter 21 also built on this work.

We also had to encourage local people who felt powerless because of social disadvantage, or because they had previous experience of being consulted about the area but saw no positive outcomes from this, to give us the benefit of their experience. We were at pains to give them continuous feedback about what use was being made of the information they gave and to demonstrate that their efforts were having an impact.

Long timescales

The approach was slow and painstaking, building up networks locally, leafleting, consulting, providing advice sessions on matters of concern - such as child care, children's safety, health - sharing information about local resources. We worked with a wide range of residents' groups, community, education and employment training groups, and encouraged local residents to help us through their own networks. We saw it as essential to provide suitable premises for meetings, practical help with child care, stimulating crèche and play facilities for children, in preparation for working with parents and throughout the project.

There had been substantial discussions before the project started with a number of voluntary and statutory agencies and the beginnings of a multi-agency steering group had been formed. We took another six months in discussions with a wide range of local groups and individuals before we felt that we had adequate representation of parents and local workers on the steering group. This group then played a major role in securing and maintaining the involvement of local people, in advising on the use of information gathered, disseminating the materials widely and in influencing local plans. It worked closely with professionals in education, health, social services and probation.

Gender issues

The vast majority of workers, local people and others associated with the project were women. Issues of men's responsibility for and involvement in child care featured frequently in discussion yet in spite of considerable efforts our structure and practice continued to reflect a common expectation that child care and child protection work are women's responsibility. Our limited resources were focused on *parents'* views of what was needed to ensure the safety and well-being of children, but it was very largely *mothers* who became and remained involved - a common experience in child care work and in community development.

We see it as a weakness that our working methods could be seen to reinforce women's responsibilities in child care, in an area where many single mothers already shoulder enormous burdens. Media coverage during the project, of the views of government and other groups, about the threat posed to social order by single mothers, caused much debate. There was a consensus that these views were punitive and unrealistic, as many single mothers led a struggle to maintain standards of decency and a safe caring community. Their role in preventing further deterioration in disadvantaged neighbourhoods was seen by themselves and local workers as crucial.

Many of the issues identified by parents related to problems with 'macho' behaviour and culture of young people. Proportions of offenders taken to court in the area were overwhelmingly higher amongst males: their behaviour presented major problems. The level of male domestic violence and its implication for child protection was also a concern. A number of young women, however, were also associated with a hostile destructive culture.

With hindsight, we would have preferred to challenge the 'women only' approach more substantially in our structure and working methods, had resources been available. The involvement of fathers in discussions of child care needs, roles of males in caring, would repay focused work in its own right. We were dissatisfied with what we were able to achieve in this within the timescale of the project. Those groups continuing the work in the area still grapple with these issues.

Participation in decision making

Considerable success was achieved in improving participation by local residents and carers in consultations and decisions about service provision in the area. Consultations with children were not well developed, but were increasing. Their views, along with those of parents, were taken account of in planning a local community park.

Local people become increasingly active in a wide range of developments - Under 8s Review, Area Management Team subgroups, Community Parks policy, discussions on safety. They attended numerous meetings and studied many lengthy documents. During the course of the project it became commonplace for local people to have a substantial involvement in planning and policy development. The funding of a local park and play facilities was one of the major successes for local people. They were fully involved in the detailed planning. They were also successful in getting a large number of traffic calming measures introduced in the area. A detailed neighbourhood strategy was developed involving many local residents' groups, statutory and voluntary agencies.

Child care

Timescales, expectations and styles of agencies and professional workers are very different from those of parents with young children. A great deal of careful negotiation, as well as help with practicalities, was needed to develop realistic patterns of involvement and partnership. The Henley project worker made it a priority to involve herself with city wide groups campaigning for improved child care facilities and realistic support for parents. At the same time the project tried to model good practice, by providing high quality child care to enable local mothers to attend meetings, consultations and disseminations of the project's findings. Crêches, childminding arrangements with neighbours, transport and sitting in services were all provided. A great deal of the development worker's time was spent in organising child care appropriate to the *individual* needs of parents. This was appreciated by parents as a major support in enabling them to participate fully. It released major resources of skill, time and commitment.

Towards a partnership culture - local experience and views

Many local people said at the start of the project that they were cynical and disillusioned after more than 20 years of consultation which had resulted in some short term gains but few radical improvements.

> *'What is the point of one more survey?'*
> *'There are no results - visible or otherwise. They say they are representative of the area, but only a few people are involved.'*
> *'Decisions get made then changed without further consultation.'*
> *'Parents are getting the blame for society and the community breakdown as individual units but parenting skills are not valued and parents are not supported or encouraged for doing a good job. Children's futures are everybody's responsibility.'*

Local residents feared that making themselves available for research and consultation could make them vulnerable, particularly on questions of family support and child protection. Slow, painstaking work setting up meetings, networking, feeding back detailed information to all groups about what we were writing up, what we were doing with the material, offering them advice and support sessions and other services which they had identified as necessary, did gradually build trust with many individuals and groups. A focus on working with them to identify strengths and success in bringing up children, as well as to describe difficulties, seemed to be welcome. We tried not to focus on abuse, but on the positive subject of bringing up children in health and safety.

We went to great lengths to ensure that materials developed during the project were 'owned' and influenced by participants. This sometimes meant that we were not able to use significant material because we did not believe we had full consent, or we saw ethical problems in using it, for example where highly personal information had been shared when someone was distressed. There were times when child protection concerns had to be followed up - we were generally able to do this *alongside* the parents and workers involved, with full consent - but we do not feel it appropriate to give full details in this public account.

A number of reports and summaries were prepared and public presentations given, with active involvement of local people, as well as the numerous activities and working groups set up.

There were numerous difficulties and tensions but the level of engagement, trust and openness meant that it was generally possible to maintain constructive relationships. The experience for many local people, over the course of the project, of being engaged *regularly* in working groups, consultation and planning groups, of practical needs being taken account of, of being given full feedback about the stage plans had reached or of unforeseen obstacles, made a great deal of difference to the level of commitment and willingness to be involved.

> *'The community have benefited and will benefit from the skills, confidence, expertise, experience and information gathered that we have built up during the Henley Safe Children Project.'*
> *'Gave us a chance to talk about things we believe in and that are very important, to the right people, not just to each other.'*
> *'Things can change. We can influence things - it is possible - although maybe slowly.'*

'It has made agencies aware of parents' expectations.'

'For once had a group that's done something.'

'It's important to have created a document that can be used in the future for reference, because it's got parents' views in it. These can be compared with future reports. It's got real life situations in it.'

The slow and painstaking work of the project with other local initiatives was seen by those involved as making a major contribution to a changing culture of partnerships between agencies and local people. The emphasis on full partnership and involvement of local people in planning, evaluating and resourcing initiatives required a long term commitment and culture change on the part of workers, managers and elected representatives. The whole council needed to be oriented towards customers and the community (Gaster 1994).

Outcomes and future priorities

There was enormous activity amongst local groups during the period of the project, supported by statutory and voluntary agencies, covering health, housing, crime, environment, child care and many other aspects of daily life. One of the outcomes of all this activity was an agreed neighbourhood strategy, crossing health, local authority and voluntary sector boundaries.

One of the benefits of having an agreed plan was that groups could be ready to develop new projects which were known to be needed and link these to existing work, as soon as resources were available rather than see resources wasted through overlap or fragmentation. It also meant that funding applications would have a clear rationale.

The work of the Henley Project alongside other local groups was successful in re-emphasising the key role of child care provision and family support services in areas of disadvantage. The relentless practicalities, the stresses of caring for children on low incomes in an area of high unemployment, poor amenities, dangerous streets, were kept in sharp focus. The combination of vivid accounts from parents and detailed statistics about the disadvantages and harmful experiences they faced was a powerful influence locally and in wider debates about the need to refocus from crisis, individually oriented services, to preventive and supportive activities.

Progress was made on many fronts: child care; crêches for those attending meetings, working groups, training activities; a continuing subgroup tries to ensure that issues for black families are given attention; parenting skills; education; training schemes; young people's advice and information; family support; the community park and play area, play activities and family outings; community safety; involvement in planning health provision.

Those most closely involved in the Henley Project set up a befriending project, the New Links Project, aiming to support parents and children in the area. The NSPCC agreed to fund it as part of the local plan. The project tries to address needs identified by local parents. Volunteers are trained to support local parents with young children, particularly those most likely to be isolated.

The needs of black families and of households where a parent or child has a disability are given sensitive and careful attention. Funding is available to meet language and communication needs. Members of the local African Caribbean and Asian communities are represented on the Steering Group and as volunteers.

Current core activity includes:

- running a weekly parent/carers group - 'The Together Group', as well as a bilingual Parents' and Children's Group (Hindi, Urdu, Punjabi, English);
- running 'Handling Children's Behaviour' courses;
- providing a minimum of 52 crèches a year;
- providing holiday events/activities throughout the year;
- providing a one-to-one weekly home visiting service to parents/carers and their children, through trained local volunteers;
- providing opportunities for local people who wish to become Project volunteers through training and supervision;
- providing training in child protection procedures; on domestic violence; working in partnership with parents, locally, city-wide and further afield;
- working with a group of local parents/carers to manage the Project;
- keeping up the profile of preventive work and of the interconnected needs of parents/carers and their children, through appropriate fora and networks;
- developing appropriate child care provision for children with special needs.

Local parents have continued to be involved in training social work students and social workers on a regular basis, for three local educational institutions. Students and social workers continue to value the opportunity to hear about working in partnership on child protection and prevention from the parents' perspective.

The New Links Project continues the involvement begun by the Henley Project in the local Area Coordination Team, Family Support Group, Domestic Violence groups, Under 8s work, the Early Years and Anti Poverty Fora.

Although the issue of prevention is more commonly acknowledged than previously, there are still difficulties both locally and city-wide about definitions of family support. Discussions take place in a context of cuts in the very services which need to be part of a strategic approach to prevention.

This emphasises the importance of continuing attention to process and to the need for analysis and overviews to inform planning and implementation. The difficulties of achieving integration, coordination and coherence in the face of pressures for targeted (and therefore fragmented) services persist. Family support work is clearly part of both child protection and preventive work. However, discussions of this work are split between the local Area Child Protection Committee (ACPC), where family support is discussed in relation to child protection, and the local Anti-Poverty Forum - Family Support Working Group, where family support is discussed in the context of child welfare and safety and is more readily seen as prevention. All those involved in these separate aspects need to be keenly aware of the connections in their work.

The debate about the 'balance' between child protection and family support assumes that these are two competing, or even incompatible, activities and that, in principle, services and social work activity can be refocused from child protection into family support. In fact the relationship between the two is very complex. There are many ways in which these activities may interact and, depending on the specific case, the relationship between the two can change over time. We believe that the refocusing debate should acknowledge these complexities and that simply changing definitions or reallocating resources will be inappropriate and perhaps a dangerous response to the real opportunities that the debate has provided. (NSPCC 1996, p.16).

Mothers involved in the Henley Project had a clear analysis of the connection between their private difficulties and public policies. That analysis needs to inform all aspects of policy, strategic planning and day to day practice.

We have the same fears as professionals for our children - we also have the same expectations for them as everyone else does. We have found that people do care about children but we need support to carry on caring. We want to help professionals to help us. Children need to be loved and cared for by their families and the community they live in. They need to be told that they are important and the people they share the community with are important as well. We all have a responsibility to make children safe.

References

Acheson, Sir D. (chair) (1998) *Independent Inquiry into Inequalities in Health Report.* TSO.

Baldwin, N. & Carruthers, L. (1993) *Henley Safe Children Project Summary and Final Report.* NSPCC/University of Warwick.

Baldwin, N. & Carruthers, L. (1998) *Developing Neighbourhood Support and Child Protection Strategies.* Aldershot: Ashgate.

Blackburn, C. (1991) *Poverty and Health: Working with Families.* Milton Keynes: Open University Press.

Blackburn, C. (1992) *Improving Health and Welfare Work with Families in Poverty.* Buckingham: Open University Press.

Cannan, C. & Warren, C. (1997) *Social action with children and families. A community development approach to child and family welfare.* London: Routledge.

Chamberlin, R. (ed) (1988) *Beyond Individual Risk Assessment: Community Wide Approaches to Promoting the Health and Development of Families and Children,* The National Centre for Education in Maternal and Child Health, Washington DC.

Dalgaard, L. (1991) 'From Signals to Action: Preventing Child Abuse.' Leicester: BAPSCAN National Congress.

Department of Health (1991) *Child Abuse: a study of inquiry reports 1980 - 1989.* London: HMSO.

Garbarino, J. & Sherman, S. (1980) 'High -risk neighbourhoods and high-risk families: the human ecology of child maltreatment'. *Child Development* 55, pp. 188-98.

Garbarino, J. (1995) *Raising Children in a Socially Toxic Environment.* San Francisco: Jossey Bass.

Gaster, L. (1994) *Evaluation of the Wood End/Bell Green Area Management Initiative,* School for Advanced Urban Studies, Bristol University.

Gibbons, J. (1990) *Family Support and Prevention: Studies in local areas.* London: NISW. HMSO.

Gibbons, J. (ed) (1992) *The Children Act 1989 and Family Support: Principles into Practice.* London: HMSO.

Henderson, P. (ed) (1995) *Children and Communities.* London: Pluto Press in association with Community Development Foundation.

Henley Safe Children Project Summary Report (1993) NSPCC/University of Warwick.

HM Treasury (1999) *Tackling Poverty and Extending Opportunities.* No.4 in the Modernisation of Britain's Tax and Benefit System Series. London: HMT.

McDonald, L., Billingham, S., Conrad, T., Morgan, N. & Payton, E. (1997) 'Families and Schools Together (FAST): Integrating Community Development with Clinical Strategies' in *Families in Society: The Journal of Contemporary Human Services,* March/April 1997.

Melton, G.B. & Barry, F.D. (eds) (1994) *Protecting Children from Abuse and Neglect: Foundations for a new National Strategy.* New York: The Guilford Press.

NSPCC (1996) *Messages from the NSPCC: A Contribution to the Refocusing Debate,* London: NSPCC.

Schorr, L. (1988) *Within Our Reach: Breaking the Cycle of Disadvantage.* New York: Anchor Doubleday.

Sinclair, R., Hearn, B. & Pugh, G. (1997) *Preventive Work with Families.* London: National Children's Bureau.

Biographical Notes

Sandeep Atkar was a development worker for the Hifazat Surukhia Project, exploring child protection and family support needs of South Asian Groups. She is now a development worker and volunteer coordinator for NSPCC in Coventry.

Norma Baldwin was involved in post qualifying studies and research and development work at Warwick University before moving to the University of Dundee, where she is Professor of Child Care and Protection.

Vivienne Barnes is currently a Senior Lecturer in Social Work at Coventry University. Prior to this she was directly involved in child care and child protection practice, as a social worker and as a team manager.

Lyn Carruthers was the development worker for the Henley Safe Children Project and the NSPCC New Links Project in Coventry. She is now a freelance trainer and development worker.

Christine Harrison was a Senior Social Worker before becoming a lecturer at Warwick University, where she is involved in teaching and research in child care.

Tricia David is Director of the Centre for Educational Research at Canterbury Christ Church University College and Professor of Education. She is the author of Child Protection and Early Years Teachers: Coping with Child Abuse (Open University Press 1993). The majority of her published work focuses on the position of young children in society.

Andrew Durham has been involved in therapeutic work with children and young people since 1983. He currently leads a specialist child abuse project in Warwickshire.

Rajinder Ghataora was a development worker for the Hifazat Surukhia Project, exploring child protection and family support needs of South Asian groups. She is now a development worker with NSPCC in Sandwell.

Jacqui Halson taught sociology and women's studies at the University of Kent at Canterbury. She is currently working at home as a full time mother of twins.

Brian Kearney was a solicitor in private practice in Glasgow for 14 years before being appointed to the bench in 1974. He is now senior Sheriff in Glasgow and an Honorary Lecturer in the Department of Social Work, University of Dundee. He is the author of Children's Hearings and the Sheriff Court. He advised the government on the drafting of the Children (Scotland) Act 1995.

Margaret Kennedy is a consultant and trainer in Disability and Child Protection, with 'Let's Balance the Scales for Disabled Children' in London.

Chris McCarrick has been working in the field of childcare for twenty-seven years in residential and fieldwork settings. She is currently a full-time Guardian ad Litem on the Coventry and Warwickshire Panel.

Judith Masson is Professor of Law at Warwick University and also teaches at Leicester University Child Protection Studies Centre. With support from the NSPCC she conducted research on children's representation and is currently studying police involvement in child protection.

Mary MacLeod was formerly Director of Research and Information for ChildLine. She is now Chief Executive of the National Family and Parenting Institute.

Michaela Mkandla developed and manages an NCH Action for Children 'Contact Point' project, which supervises public law contact for a local authority. She was formerly an assistant co-ordinator in child protection for a local authority.

Annie Mullins was a senior social worker in Birmingham then teaching fellow at Warwick University before moving to a policy development post with NCH Action for Children.

Adrian Over worked as a residential and field social worker with children and their families for ten years before moving to his current post as Team Leader of a residential family centre.

Janet Rushton has managed a range of services for children and families. She is currently Operations Manager, Fieldwork Services, for Northamptonshire.

Alexandra Seale was Principal Officer Equal Opportunities with Kirklees Metropolitan Council until 1996. She has been Associate Editor of the Journal of *Social Work Education*. She is presently an independent consultant, working on Social Work practice, education and organisational development and equality.

Nick Spencer is Professor of Child Health at the University of Warwick and Consultant Community Paediatrician in Coventry. His post in the University is based in the Department of Social Policy and Social Work as well as the School of Postgraduate Medical Education.

Vyomesh Thanki was a senior social worker then a lecturer at Warwick University before returning to social work management.

Sara Tibbs has worked in a variety of charities and academic settings. Until recently she was managing a youth counselling organisation. She is now Research Officer for a Barnardo's Project 'Parenting Matters' in Northern Ireland.

Vic Tuck is a Staff Development Officer with Solihull Social Services Department where he is responsible for child protection training. He has researched links between social deprivation and harm to children.

Alban Unsworth was formerly a Senior Social Work Practitioner in a Children and Families Team with Warwickshire Social Services Department. He continues to work for the authority in the Emergency Duty Team as a Senior Social Worker. In his spare time he is a Magician.

Pam Wood worked with children and families for eighteen years in a number of settings as both a practitioner and manager before becoming a manager in Local Authority Adult Services.